Getting Started with Oracle Event Processing 11*g*

Create and develop real-world scenario Oracle CEP applications

Alexandre Alves

Robin J. Smith

Lloyd Williams

BIRMINGHAM - MUMBAI

Getting Started with Oracle Event Processing 11*g*

First published: March 2013

Production Reference: 1150313

Published by Packt Publishing Ltd.
Livery Place
35 Livery Street
Birmingham B3 2PB, UK.

ISBN 978-1-84968-454-5

`www.packtpub.com`

Cover Image by Artie Ng (`artherng@yahoo.com.au`)

Credits

Authors
Alexandre Alves
Robin J. Smith
Lloyd Williams

Reviewers
Jeffrey A. Myers, Ph.D.
Ahmet Fuat Sungur
Prakash Jeya Prakash

Acquisition Editor
Grant Mizen

Lead Technical Editor
Dayan Hyames

Technical Editors
Vrinda Amberkar
Dominic Pereira

Project Coordinator
Leena Purkait

Proofreader
Samantha Lyon

Indexer
Hemangini Bari

Graphics
Sheetal Aute
Valentina D'Silva
Aditi Gajjar

Production Coordinators
Nitesh Thakur
Prachali Bhiwandkar

Cover Work
Nitesh Thakur
Prachali Bhiwandkar

About the Authors

Alexandre Alves has over 12 years of experience in software development working for large companies, such as IBM and Oracle. He has worked with network management, CORBA, JEE, web services, OSGi, BPEL, CEP, and middleware technologies in general. He is the co-author of the WS-BPEL 2.0 specification, co-author of BPEL for Java specification, author of the *OSGi in Depth* book, and a steering committee member of the Event Processing Technical Society (EPTS).

I would like to thank my family for giving me the support I needed to continue my work regardless of all other problems that life throws at you. I would like to thank my sons, Gabriel and Lucas, for providing for the fun-filled book-writing breaks, and understanding when I was in the book-writing, no-breaks (as they saw it) mode. I would like to especially thank Juliana, my wife-to-be, for her unyielding support, her caring, and especially for her lifelong understanding. For you, all is worth. Words put into a book are everlasting, so is our love.

Finally, I would like to thank my excellent co-authors and colleagues at Oracle for giving me the material and the experience I needed for writing this book.

Robin J. Smith, as a Product Management/Strategy Director at Oracle Corporation, is responsible for the Event Driven Architecture and Complex Event Processing technologies, focused on the evolution and delivery of the award winning and innovative Oracle Event Processing product, a corner-stone technology of the Oracle Event Driven Architecture strategy. Previously at BEA Systems, he successfully delivered the BEA WebLogic Event Server, the industry's first and only EDA CEP Java Application Server based on an exposed customized OSGi™ framework. At Sun Microsystems, as a software Product Line Manager for 8 years, he focused on the product management and marketing for the core SOA technologies, Netscape Process Manager and the award-winning Sun Java™ Studio Enterprise, a visual development and infrastructure environment focused on SOA, UML design tools and Java application profiling techniques. Over his career, Robin has worked in all of the major computing domains acquiring expertise as an architect for a leading Universal Content Management System and designed, engineered and implemented unique performance and systems management software for the Java Platform, AS/400, and VM Operating systems that have been used worldwide.

My deepest thanks to Phil Wilmshurst, who after a chat in the Bowlers Arms in Margate recommended me for my first computing job, starting a career at a young age which has now taken me around the world and to my computing successes in Silicon Valley, California. To Mike Leamer, who as a friend and manager motivated me to learn more and guided me to excel in my programming efforts in London. To the team at VM Software Inc., who gave me my "Famous for Fifteen Minutes" time when they purchased my unique VMMonitor product and finally, my family that inspires me to leap out of bed each morning and enjoy my continuing computing days of adventure, at my office in Redwood Shores, just south of the beautiful San Francisco.

Lloyd Williams has over 17 years of experience in the software development and IT industry. Lloyd graduated from Memorial University of Newfoundland in 1995 with a Bachelor of Commerce (Honors) specializing in Management Information Systems and Operations Management. He then moved to California to start consulting in the telecommunications industry. Since then, he has worked with numerous Fortune 500 companies around the globe in every industry. Lloyd's experience ranges from large telecommunications and automotive projects working with global systems integrators to leading the development of small event-driven RFID solutions at a small start-up.

He is currently an outbound product manager working for Oracle within the Business Integration team of the Oracle Fusion Middleware product family. He works with customers around the globe developing solutions that integrate Oracle Event Processing with SOA and BPM solutions.

I would like to thank my friends and family for their support, patience and help in producing this book as well as during many late nights and weekends working on many software development projects. I would like to thank my managers throughout the years who have provided me with opportunities to learn new skills and take on challenging tasks, as well as many clients and colleagues whom have provided invaluable opportunities for me to expand my knowledge and shape my career.

About the Reviewers

Jeffrey Myers holds a Ph.D. in Physics from the University of Michigan, where he studied energy transfer mechanisms in proteins and developed new experimental techniques in ultrafast optics. He has over 10 years of experience in experimental design, algorithm development, and data analysis. In his professional career, he has utilized relational databases and complex event processing to provide innovative analytic solutions. Dr. Myers currently works as an engineer with Northrop Grumman. His technical interests include pattern recognition, machine learning, sensors, and Big Data analytics.

Ahmet Fuat Sungur has 6 years of experience in working with Oracle products. Since 2008 he has been working in Telecommunication Industry. In his professional career, data processing technologies are his favorite subjects. He participated in several business intelligence-oriented applications, which was developed by using Java and Oracle technologies. Software architecture, distributed processing, Big Data and NoSQL databases are his other main interests. He has attended many national and international technical congresses as a speaker.

He is currently working for Turkcell, which is the biggest telecommunication company in Turkey, third in Europe. Also he holds a degree in computer engineering.

Prakash Jeya Prakash is an Oracle Certified SOA Expert and SOASchools certified SOA professional.

He started his career as a Java developer with TechMahindra and after a couple of years his career shift towards SOA started. Since then he has been working on the Oracle middleware stack. From 2008 to 2010, he worked as Tech Lead for BSS productized solution development at Nokia Siemens Networks, Bangalore, India. In July, 2010, he moved to UK and started his own company as a freelancer SOA consultant. Since October, 2011, he has been working as a Lead SOA consultant at Logica, UK.

www.PacktPub.com

Support files, eBooks, discount offers and more

You might want to visit www.PacktPub.com for support files and downloads related to your book.

Did you know that Packt offers eBook versions of every book published, with PDF and ePub files available? You can upgrade to the eBook version at www.PacktPub.com and as a print book customer, you are entitled to a discount on the eBook copy. Get in touch with us at service@packtpub.com for more details.

At www.PacktPub.com, you can also read a collection of free technical articles, sign up for a range of free newsletters and receive exclusive discounts and offers on Packt books and eBooks.

http://PacktLib.PacktPub.com

Do you need instant solutions to your IT questions? PacktLib is Packt's online digital book library. Here, you can access, read and search across Packt's entire library of books.

Why Subscribe?

- Fully searchable across every book published by Packt
- Copy and paste, print and bookmark content
- On demand and accessible via web browser

Free Access for Packt account holders

If you have an account with Packt at www.PacktPub.com, you can use this to access PacktLib today and view nine entirely free books. Simply use your login credentials for immediate access.

Instant Updates on New Packt Books

Get notified! Find out when new books are published by following @PacktEnterprise on Twitter, or the *Packt Enterprise* Facebook page.

Table of Contents

Preface 1
Chapter 1: An Overview of Complex Event Processing 7
What is event processing? 7
Relating this to a business in computing terms 9
Use case: A solution for customer problems 12
Key elements of event stream processing 16
An event 17
An event stream 17
An event type 18
Event Processing Network 19
Event processing languages and extensibility 21
Processor event node methodologies 23
Processor extensibility 26
Event processor "Intelligence Injection" 27
Holistic Event-Driven and Service Orientated Architectures 28
Predicting an event 29
Summary 30
Chapter 2: An Overview of Oracle Event Processing 31
Understanding the heritage of Oracle Event Processing 31
The Java Event-Driven Server, the bits and bytes of the architecture 33
The adopted event language 38
CQL concepts 38
The philosophy and fundamentals of developing 41
Creating an Oracle Event Processing application 43
Some hints and tips 54
Controlling from the command line 55
Watching things happen and changing what happens 58
Summary 64

Chapter 3: Adapting Events for OEP **65**
Creating and converting events **65**
Event type system **65**
Platform adapters **68**
The JMS adapter 68
The CSV adapter 70
HTTP pub-sub adapter 72
Configuring your own custom adapter **78**
Leveraging OSGi services to create an adapter 82
Packaging custom adapters 83
Summary **88**
Chapter 4: Assembling and Configuring OEP Applications **89**
Implementing the component model **90**
Exploring the EPN extensions **90**
Defining a simple Spring bean 90
Creating the event type repository 91
Setting up the adapters 91
Configuring channels 92
Implementing event-beans 93
Enabling the power of CQL processors 94
Defining a database table 94
Using caching 94
Understanding the application configuration **96**
Adapter configuration 96
Channel configuration 97
Cache configuration 98
Defining resources in the server configuration **99**
Extending the component type infrastructure **105**
Summary **106**
Chapter 5: Coding with CQL **107**
Introducing CQL **107**
Understanding CQL fundamentals **108**
Establishing your sources and destinations 109
Processing models 110
The structure and semantics of event processing **111**
Restricting streams with Windows 112
Tuple-based windows 116
Partitioned windows 119
Output 120
Controlling output with slides 126

The unbounded window 128
The constant value range window 129
The NOW window and the Last Event window 130
SQL as a foundation **130**
Joins 131
External sources 136
Aggregations 136
Ordering 137
Views 139
Set operations 140
Typing and expressions **142**
Timing models **144**
Summary **146**
Chapter 6: Managing and Monitoring Applications **147**
Configuring the logging service **147**
Provisioning applications **151**
Changing application configuration **155**
Managing server-wide configuration **159**
Controlling concurrency with work managers 159
Accessing contextual data with data sources 160
Browsing metadata with the event type repository 164
Monitoring progress **165**
Summary **170**
Chapter 7: Using Tables and Caches for Contextual Data **171**
Setting up JDBC data sources **172**
Enriching events using a database table **173**
Setting up caching systems **174**
Enriching events using a cache **176**
Using caches as event sources and sinks **177**
Implementing an event bean to access a cache **179**
Monitoring Coherence in the Visualizer **183**
Summary **183**
Chapter 8: Pattern Matching with CQL **185**
Extending CQL with OEP cartridges **185**
Blending CQL and Java **186**
Class loading in CQL 189
Handling ambiguities between Java and CQL 192
Using the JavaBeans conventions in CQL 193
Processing XML with CQL **194**
Handling XML document sources 197

Pattern matching **199**
Partitioning events for matching 202
Patterns as regular expressions 203
Controlling the number of matches 204
Working with correlation groups 207
Expiring patterns 211
Summary **213**
Chapter 9: Implementing Performance Scaling, Concurrency, and High Availability for Oracle Event Processing **215**
Scalability versus high availability **216**
Understanding performance and ways to influence **217**
Scaling Oracle Event Processing **219**
The threading model 219
Optimizing threading in channels 220
The EventPartitioner example **223**
Using concurrency with processors **224**
Partitioned versus pipelined parallelism 227
Improving performance with batching 228
General event processing, network performance tuning, and memory sizing observations 229
High availability in Oracle Event Processing **230**
Failure scenarios 232
A sample HA Event Processing application **233**
High availability quality of services **234**
Simple failover 234
Simple failover with buffering 236
Lightweight queue trimming 236
Precise recovery with JMS 239
The HA application **240**
ActiveMQ server 241
The JMS Message Client 241
Running the HA solution sample 244
Studying the Visualizer tooling for HA implementation 247
Summary **248**
Chapter 10: Introducing Spatial: A Telemetric Use Case **249**
Introduction to Oracle Spatial with Oracle Event Processing **249**
Basic geospatial concepts and use cases **251**
Geo-streaming 251
Geo-fencing 253
Bus tracking movement event patterns 256

The Oracle Spatial Data Cartridge **258**
Oracle geospatial features **260**
Tracking vehicles with an Oracle Event Processing application **261**
Key application elements 261
Bus tracking EPN 262
BusSpatialProcessor 264
Bus tracking visual user interface 268
How to run this bus tracking sample application 269
Summary **270**
Chapter 11: Extending CQL with Spatial and JDBC **271**
Creating geometries **271**
Determining if geometries relate to each other **275**
Configuring the spatial context **281**
Retrieving external tables using SQL **283**
Summary **288**
Chapter 12: Looking Ahead: The Future of Oracle Event Processing **289**
Possible technology strategic directions **289**
Evolving developer environments **291**
Service-oriented Architecture integration **292**
Event intelligence on the computing edge with Sensor integration **293**
Event container platform manipulation profiles 298
The Embedded profile 298
Fast Data for Big Data **299**
Fast data sample 302
Looking around the corner with predictive analytics **305**
More on analytics 305
A Predicting Use Case 306
Understanding the "Fuzzy" results 307
Extending insurance solutions and JDBC data cartridge summary 308
Advancing performance with embedded hardware **310**
The growing event processing standards **311**
Summary **312**
Index **313**

Preface

Events are everywhere. Events can have either positive or negative impacts on our lives and affect important business decisions. These events can impact a company's success, failure, and profitability.

Getting Started with Oracle Event Processing 11g will allow you to be benefited from the skills and years of experience from the original pioneers who were the driving force behind this immensely flexible, complete, and award-winning Event Stream Processing technology. It provides all of the information needed to rapidly deliver and understand Event Driven Architecture (EDA) applications.

After an introduction to the benefits and uses of Event Stream Processing, this book uses tutorials and practical examples to teach you how to create valuable and rewarding event-driven foundational applications. This book will provide a unique perspective on product creation, evolution, and a solid understanding of how to effectively use the product.

What this book covers

Chapter 1, An Overview of Complex Event Processing, provides an overview of the event processing technology, including the event processing language, the event processing network, and event-driven architectures.

Chapter 2, An Overview of Oracle Event Processing, provides an overview of the Oracle Event Processing, including the Eclipse-based design time, the management console, and other tools.

Chapter 3, Adapting Events for OEP, describes how to adapt external events into an OEP event, and how to convert back OEP events into external events through the use of the adapter SDK.

Chapter 4, Assembling and Configuring OEP Applications, describes how to assemble an event processing network together as an OEP application and how to configure its components.

Chapter 5, Coding with CQL, describes Oracle's event processing language, called CQL, and how it can be used to filter events, correlate events, aggregate events, and perform several other event processing tasks.

Chapter 6, Managing and Monitoring Applications, teaches you to perform management and monitoring tasks, such as deploying OEP applications, configuring work-managers, and using the logging service.

Chapter 7, Using Tables and Caches for Contextual Data, explains how to use data residing in tables and caches as contextual data when processing events.

Chapter 8, Pattern Matching with CQL, teaches you to pattern match events using CQL, a very powerful feature that can be used to find missing events, and other complex patterns.

Chapter 9, Implementing Performance Scaling, Concurrency, and High Availability for Oracle Event Processing, explores several mechanisms to improve performance of OEP applications and how to set up a OEP cluster supporting high availability.

Chapter 10, Introducing Spatial: A Telemetric Use Case, walks you through a real-world event processing case study, which makes extensive use of spatial features and telemetric.

Chapter 11, Extending CQL with Spatial and JDBC, teaches you to make use of geometry types in CQL using the Spatial cartridge, and how to invoke arbitrary SQL using the JDBC cartridge.

Chapter 12, Looking Ahead: The Future of Oracle Event Processing, takes a candid look at the future of event processing, including emerging topics such as event processing in Big Data, machine-to-machine architectures, and event intelligence.

What you need for this book

To make full use of this book, you need to install Oracle Event Processing 11*g*, which is available at Oracle Technology Network website, `http://www.oracle.com/technetwork/middleware/complex-event-processing/overview/index.html`. Select the 11*g* version, as this book is targeted toward this particular version.

Some examples make use of the Oracle Database 11*g* Release 2, which likewise can be found at `http://www.oracle.com/technetwork/database/enterprise-edition/overview/index.html`.

Who this book is for

This book is aimed for both developers as well as architects that need to learn about event processing, stream processing, and the event-driven architecture. Having some background knowledge of Java and SQL will help, but is not a must.

Conventions

In this book, you will find a number of styles of text that distinguish between different kinds of information. Here are some examples of these styles, and an explanation of their meaning.

Code words in text are shown as follows: "By using this method, you can define event types as a Java bean, `java.util.Map`, or tuple."

A block of code is set as follows:

```
<event-type-repository>
    <event-type name="Customer">
        <property name="name" type="char"/>
        <property name="address" type="Address"/>
    </event-type>
    <event-type name="Address">
        <class-name>postal.Address</class-name>
    </event-type>
<event-type-repository>
```

Any command-line input or output is written as follows:

```
com.bea.wlevs.adapters.jms;version="11.1.1.7_0",
com.bea.wlevs.adapters.jms.api;version="11.1.1.7_0",
```

New terms and **important words** are shown in bold. Words that you see on the screen, in menus or dialog boxes for example, appear in the text like this: "From within the **EPN Editor** screen, right-click and select **New** and then **Adapter**".

Warnings or important notes appear in a box like this.

Tips and tricks appear like this.

Reader feedback

Feedback from our readers is always welcome. Let us know what you think about this book—what you liked or may have disliked. Reader feedback is important for us to develop titles that you really get the most out of.

To send us general feedback, simply send an e-mail to `feedback@packtpub.com`, and mention the book title via the subject of your message.

If there is a topic that you have expertise in and you are interested in either writing or contributing to a book, see our author guide on `www.packtpub.com/authors`.

Customer support

Now that you are the proud owner of a Packt book, we have a number of things to help you to get the most from your purchase.

Downloading the example code

You can download the example code files for all Packt books you have purchased from your account at `http://www.PacktPub.com`. If you purchased this book elsewhere, you can visit `http://www.PacktPub.com/support` and register to have the files e-mailed directly to you.

Errata

Although we have taken every care to ensure the accuracy of our content, mistakes do happen. If you find a mistake in one of our books—maybe a mistake in the text or the code—we would be grateful if you would report this to us. By doing so, you can save other readers from frustration and help us improve subsequent versions of this book. If you find any errata, please report them by visiting `http://www.packtpub.com/support`, selecting your book, clicking on the **errata submission form** link, and entering the details of your errata. Once your errata are verified, your submission will be accepted and the errata will be uploaded on our website, or added to any list of existing errata, under the Errata section of that title. Any existing errata can be viewed by selecting your title from `http://www.packtpub.com/support`.

Piracy

Piracy of copyright material on the Internet is an ongoing problem across all media. At Packt, we take the protection of our copyright and licenses very seriously. If you come across any illegal copies of our works, in any form, on the Internet, please provide us with the location address or website name immediately so that we can pursue a remedy.

Please contact us at `copyright@packtpub.com` with a link to the suspected pirated material.

We appreciate your help in protecting our authors, and our ability to bring you valuable content.

Questions

You can contact us at `questions@packtpub.com` if you are having a problem with any aspect of the book, and we will do our best to address it.

1
An Overview of Complex Event Processing

In this chapter, you will be introduced to the basic concepts of **Complex Event Processing** (**CEP**), its impact today on businesses across all industries, and the key artifacts that together constitute an **Event-Driven Solution Platform**. Some of the topics we will cover are as follows:

- What is event processing
- Relating this to a business in computing terms
- Use case: A solution for customer problems
- Key elements of event stream processing
- Event processing languages and extensibility
- Holistic event-driven and service-orientated architectures
- Predicting an event

What is event processing?

In the world around us, every second of every minute of every hour, the human brain is bombarded with a limitless number of things that happen either at the same time or sequentially, or in a totally and seemingly erratic way that may not make sense immediately but as more of these things happen, we can start to understand their relevance and importance.

For example, we hear cheering in the distance, we see balloons flying in the air, music starts to play, police cars and trucks appear pulling brightly covered trailers with puppets and people waving on them, followed by ambulances, and today's date is July 4th. Individually, these events could mean anything, but together? It's probably an Independence Day Carnival Parade!

Our brain can easily determine this fact in the blink of an eye" and while not overly simple to define in computing terms, we could describe a "Parade Event Pattern" as follows:

> One (or more) police cars + followed/preceded by, or adjacent to + one (or more) carnival trucks + followed/preceded by, or adjacent to + one (or more waving people) + followed/preceded by, or adjacent to + one (or more emergency vehicles) + where music can be heard + and today's date is 4th July

Your brain is not restricted to sending information and just waiting until there is a response, or forced into following a series of fixed steps to get something done. As with this example, it is able to take the events happening now, their relevance to additional external factors such as today's anniversary date and understand a "parade" event pattern.

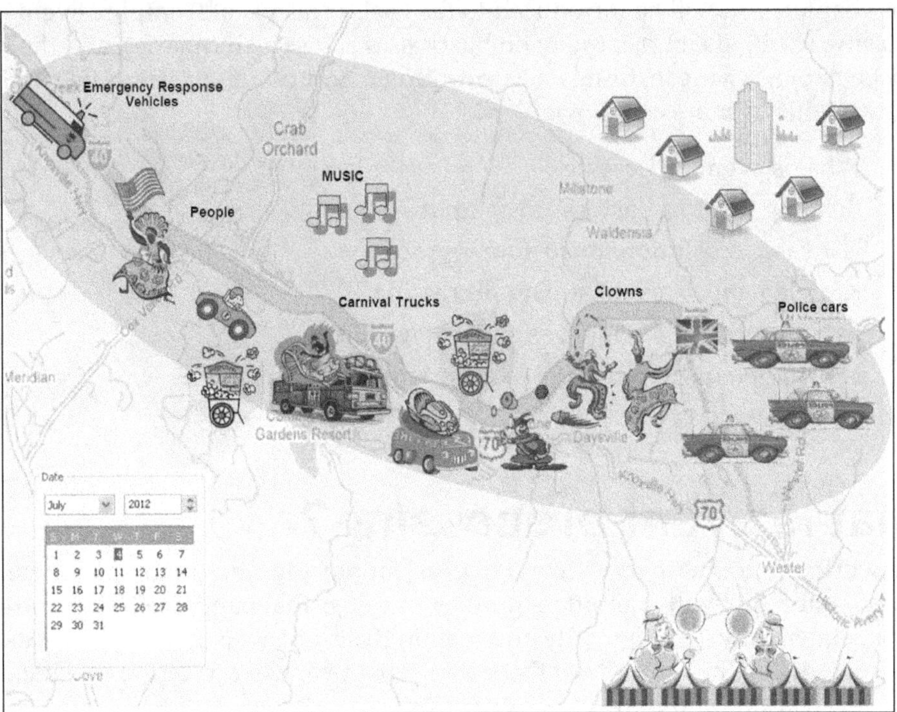

So as you learn more about Complex Event Processing, we focus on how this technology can take continuously flowing, never-ending information, from a potentially unlimited number of different places, and immediately understand how it relates to things happening right now and in the very near future, commonly known as **Real-Time Situation Awareness**.

Relating this to a business in computing terms

The problem now in the world of computers is the proliferation of data. Information arrives from many different systems, in vast quantities, at different times, at different speeds, some of importance now to certain other systems, people or processes, and some stored for later recovery and determination. Why the proliferation now?

There are many issues involved, but here are just a few major ones:

- The cost of computer power and sophisticated environmental sensor devices has become less expensive
- Networking capacities increase and become more intelligent
- The many different functional computing silos (finance systems, manufacturing systems, sales systems, and so on) are broken down, rewritten, enabling processes that can span more and more business demands
- New computer solution demands expand beyond the enterprise to include partners, customers so more and more data sources and other inputs are brought online
- Computing technology architectures such as **Service Orientated Architecture** (**SOA**) becomes increasingly successful, resulting in an ever more elaborate ecosystem of re-usable services
- A **Big Data** explosion, a term now used widely for information that arrives in high volumes, with extreme velocity, and in a wide variety of mostly unstructured formats emanating from social media sites, cell phones, and many other sources
- A growing demand from businesses that expect their Information Technology (IT) teams to respond to market situations much more effectively in real time

As we evolve and the complexity of these systems "pour" more and more huge volumes of information at computer applications, we are reaching a "tipping point" where traditional point-to-point or request-reply-based solutions of the world break down and become unmaintainable and not extendable.

A company business can be influenced instantaneously from things (events) that can happen, not only in the "cozy" understandable world within its own environment but also from activities (events) from beyond, such as from "the Internet of things"—real-time sensor device that can measure and report on a multitude of situations, including "the impending danger from a sudden rise in temperature in a food storage facility" or "the global positioning system location of a shipping container which is having an unauthorized opening with movement detection sensed from within".

Immediate impact to a company's business can also come appear "out of nowhere" emanating from a change in global business conditions indicated from the ever-expanding social media outlets, for example, Twitter, instant messaging, and so on. Millions of people at the same time can all comment on the poor condition of a new product, highlighting an immediate need to change a product design. This will inevitably affect profits and will probably significantly affect the value of the business. So companies are now inevitably being manipulated by a wide range of both understood and misunderstood events.

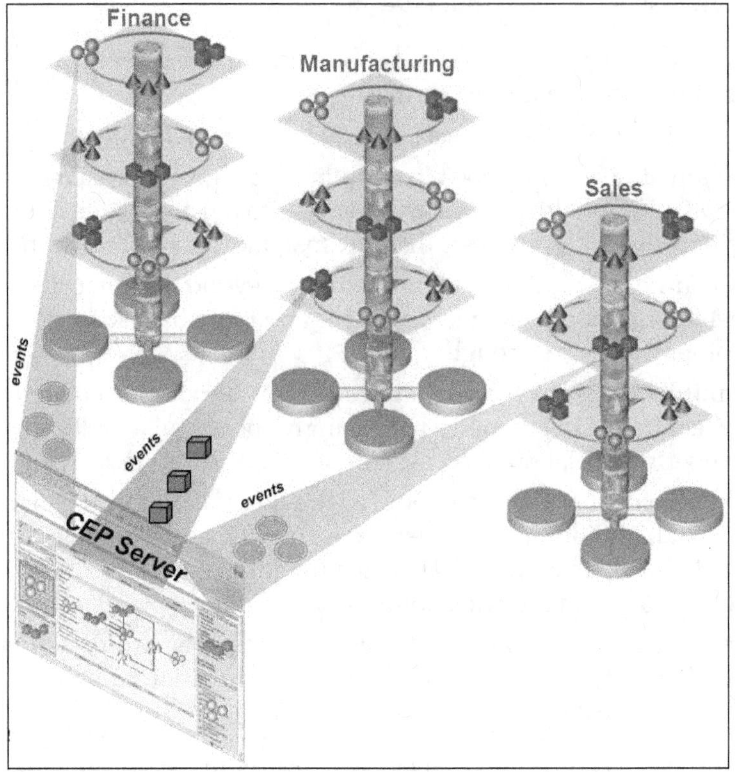

In the past, probably going back over 15 years ago, business applications have had to conform to the methodologies, structure, and interfaces from the then available computing technologies (such as databases) where information must be inserted and statically placed. Only after this can users then analyze and respond. Traditional JEE Application Servers were generally implemented, expecting a client application to send an initial request and will then only process that request through, in most cases a significant amount of logic code, before it can respond back to the client. While these technologies enable, and will continue to provide benefit in more batch-orientated, less real-time approaches, newer lower latency and faster in-memory middleware products are now available.

Event-Driven (Architecture) based systems are intrinsically smarter, or better "equipped" to handle these types of situations, processing an entire business infrastructure as events that can be immediately interpreted and handled, spanning across the many departmental "silos" such as finance, manufacturing, and sales. These types of systems are also context aware and execute when they detect changes in the environment or business world, rather than occurring on a predefined (nightly) schedule or requiring someone to initiate an execution.

As the problems associated with Big Data grow substantially over the coming years in terms of the capture, management, and the ability to process the information within a tolerable amount of time, Event-Driven technologies (specifically Complex Event Processing) can provide **Fast Data** capabilities to apply a greater level of "intelligence" and decisioning to the originating data streams much closer to the "point of occurrence".

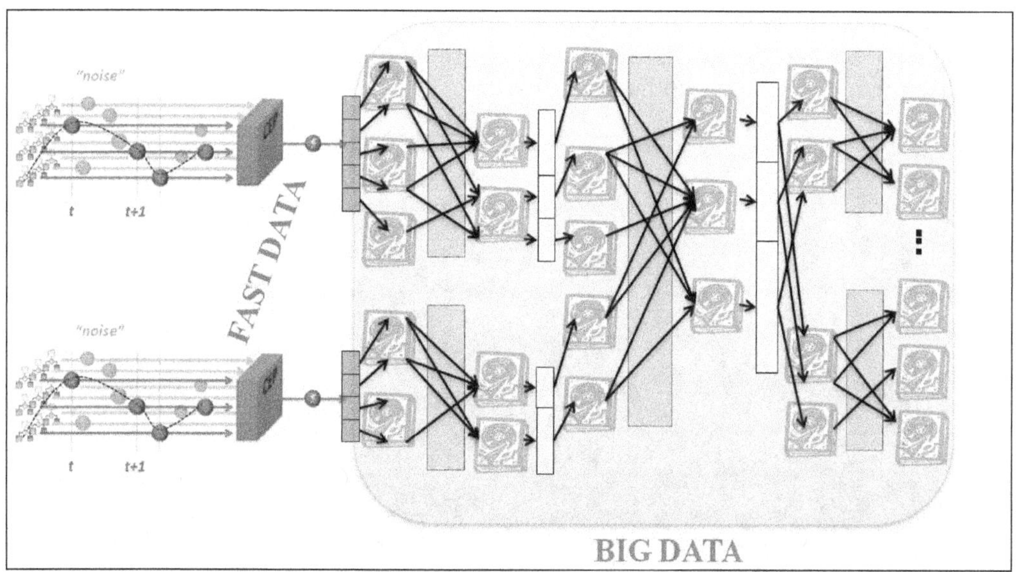

So the benefits of an Event-Driven technology approach is to turn that proliferation of data into real-time knowledge by firstly representing events (things that happen from anywhere) in standard ways, providing an ability to factor out events, route events, filter events, aggregate events, and correlate events intelligently, so that in most cases fragmented events can be evolved into holistic, solid, understandable business events, enabling the business to better view, control, and adapt to situations relatively instantaneously.

Use case: A solution for customer problems

So how are Complex Event Processing Platforms used now to solve business problems? Certainly over the past few years, this technology is being used across most, if not all, of the different types of industries.

The financial services capital markets companies are using this technology for real-time algorithmic trading and real-time risk management types of solutions. As the stock markets stream their endless financial instrument data with values which can instantly fluctuate, there is an ever growing need to effectively handle this huge volume of information, understand its impact and potential risk, and then react as quickly as possible. The better the capability to evaluate and predict the consequences of the information, and the quicker the ability to respond to the results of this analysis, the more successful the business and the more money that can be made with less exposure to business risks and threats. This type of real-time trading information can be usually visualized using **heat maps** and **scatter charts**.

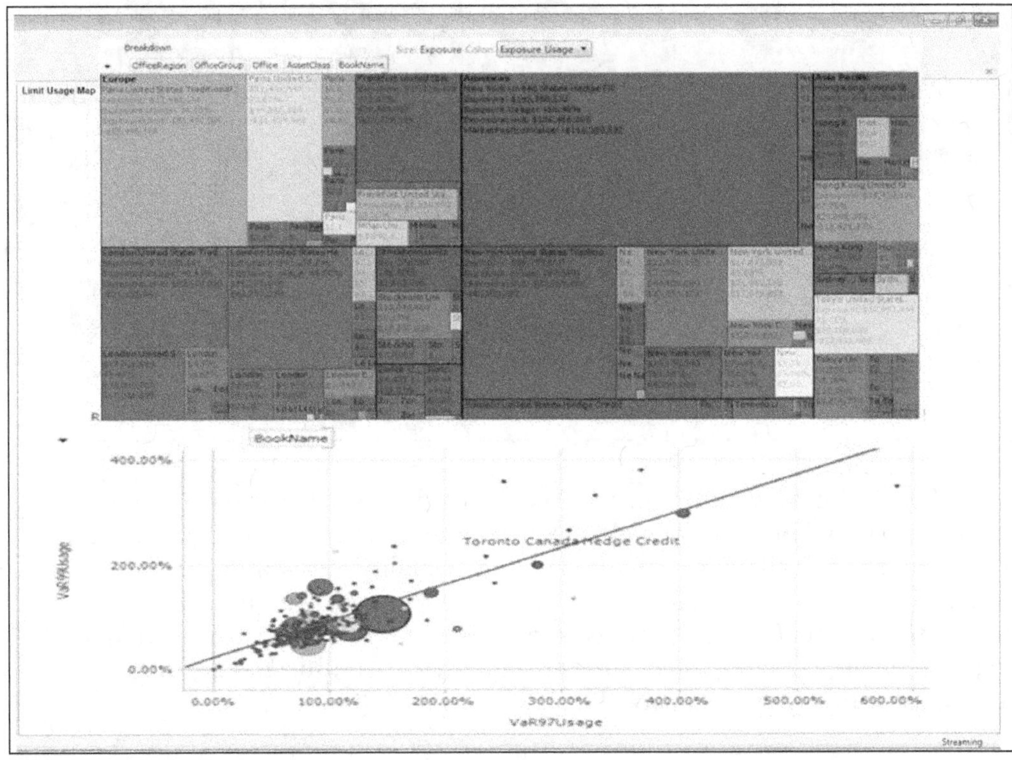

In the Electricity industry, customers are using the Complex Event Processing (CEP) platform for many new types of applications, which include Smart Meter, Smart Grid, and outage detection monitoring solutions. Sophisticated **Demand Response** (**DR**) solutions bring together system operators and the power generation companies, who contract with energy management and monitoring companies to provide energy usage load reduction services on demand. These technology companies that are using CEP-based applications contract with commercial and industrial businesses that are large consumers of energy, whom agree to curtail energy usage on demand. Streaming event devices are installed at client locations to measure energy usage and, in some cases, proactively control the load using continuous energy demand and usage data at minute or, even second, intervals. The generated profit revenue received from system operators is then passed back to the clients, relative to the number of associated load reduction dispatches.

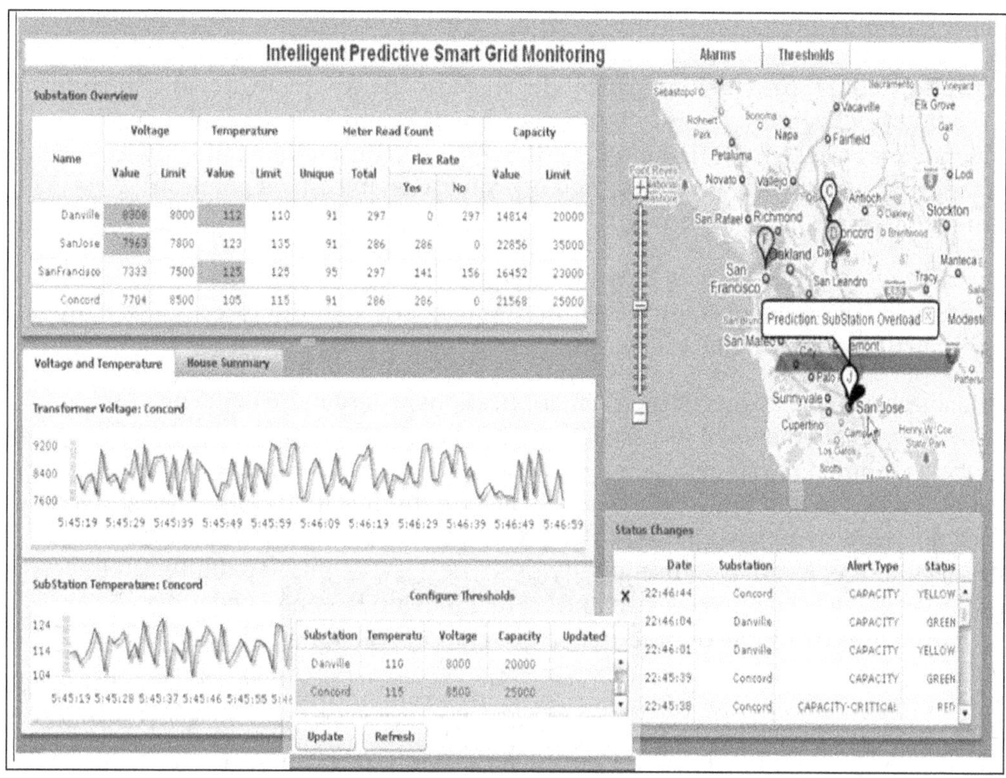

Handling real-time events has a long history in the telecommunications industry, such as those generated by the various devices on the network, events from mobile phones, or perhaps streaming **Call Detail Record** (**CDR**) events indicating the time of calls made and whether some of these calls failed. Complex Event Processing platforms provide the technology for many new applications and solutions in this domain. As in other industries, Event-Driven platforms have a broad base of possible implementations. Some businesses have created powerful network management and monitoring solutions, which can detect hardware failure-related events continuing over certain time periods, or situations where equipment has not been issuing events for some time and in these circumstances alert messages are distributed and escalated.

In the context of an enterprise-level mobile telecommunication IT infrastructure, there are many different applications coming from many different suppliers. When the overall performance is not immediately meeting expectations, it's not easy to identify which component is the offending issue in the supply chain. Therefore these next-generation management and monitoring applications (based on Complex Event Processing) provide the capabilities to show the complete, holistic "picture", providing full visibility to the situation of a business through flexibility and fully integrated features, enabling agility for the infrastructure to react quickly to changing scenarios, and providing full operability enabled by a solution designed to meet business needs.

A very powerful capability of Complex Event Processing platforms which is being leveraged in the Transportation, Telecommunications, and Public Sector domain is real-time integrated spatial analysis.

A business can use this technology in applications where there is the need to monitor the movements of its assets and resources. Using, for example, GPS (global positioning systems) the movement patterns of someone, or something can be tracked in real time as it passes through boundary points (such as security checkpoints in an airport) to identify its route and, to some extent, predict where this person or object may subsequently move next. Also, this capability can be used to analyze a current position and its relationship to geofenced areas. A geofenced area being the definition of a geographical shape (polygon) defined or declared by a series of spatial coordinates.

When a resource gets near, inside, or enters and exits the geofenced area, various actions can be immediately performed, such as a warning message of an imminent exposure to a dangerous natural disaster, or offering a big discount on a second coffee at the person's current location or soon to be, position, based on his or her current movement pattern.

First Responder emergency services solutions can use integrated spatial technologies to not only monitor a fire or hundreds of simultaneous fires, but also dynamically track the movement on the fire, affected by weather conditions (wind) or igniting hazardous materials. These types of systems can evaluate immediately the relevance, importance, and applicability of all of the related assets (fire engines, police vehicles, and so on) close to these areas. For example, if a fireman does not move in certain number of seconds when close to a fire, this could indicate a serious life threatening situation.

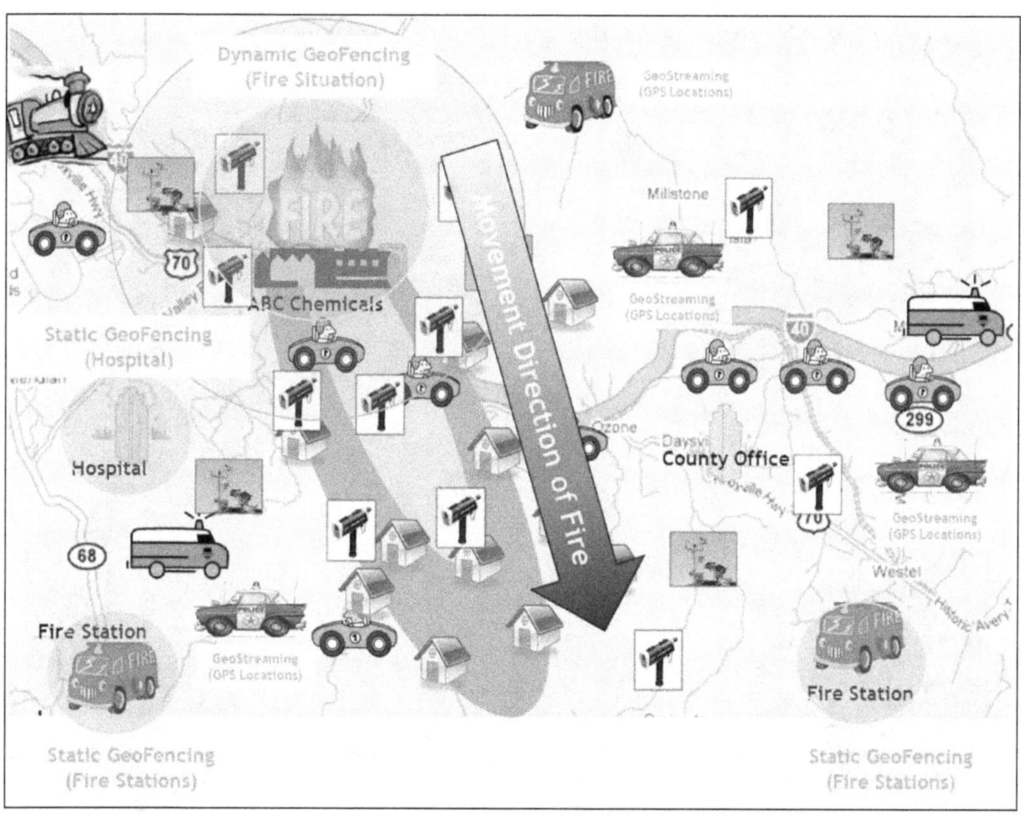

There are many other types of business solution implementations using Complex Event Processing platforms that range from online retail monitoring systems, real-time data center infrastructure management, fleet vehicle transportation monitoring, traffic flow monitoring with variable toll charging and speed control, oil fields and rig monitoring/automation, and a host of real-time sensing device opportunities, where these devices can monitor the environment inside shipping containers, or air pollution situations. The scope and different type of applications that can now benefit from using Complex Event Processing technologies are evolving just as quickly as the world is changing, with a growing need to predict and pre-empt and in, some cases, prevent situations from even happening.

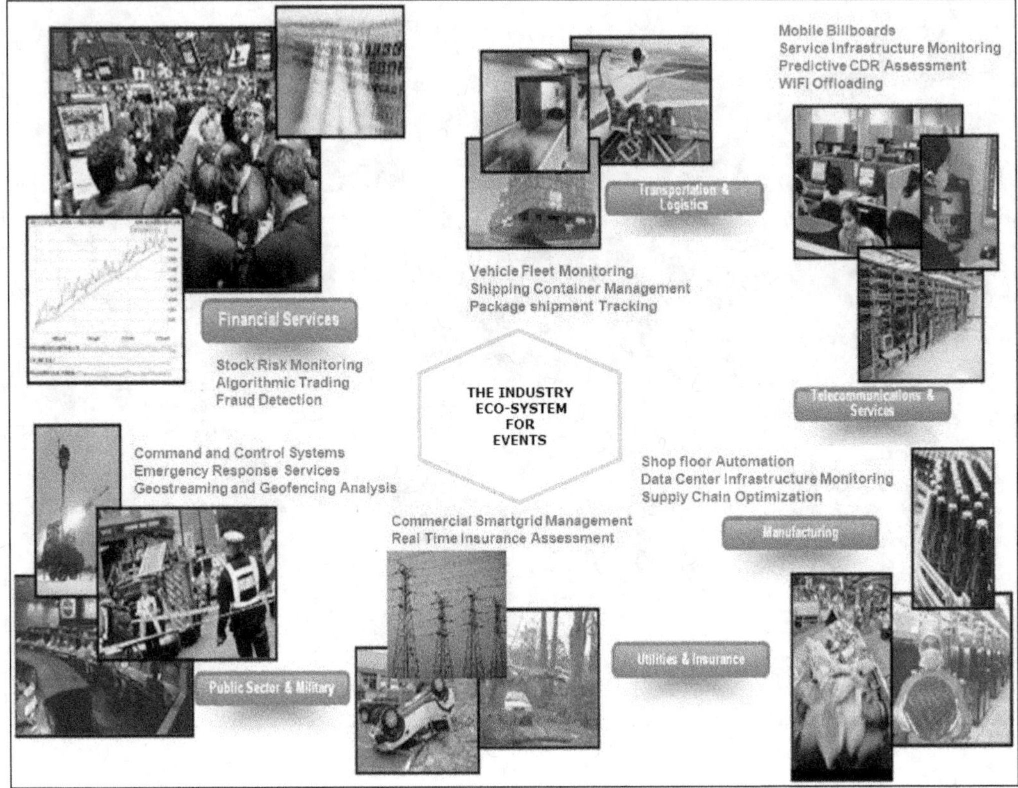

Key elements of event stream processing

During the next few sections we will explore some of the basic principles and concepts commonly used in the creation of event-driven applications. These are the major "building blocks" for any solution that handles streaming event data.

An event

What is an event and how is it defined? Many people and technical societies define an event in many different ways, but in the context of this book, an event is an object that has a change in its state immediately, or over a period of time.

For example, let's take an everyday object, a house front door.

The door's "properties" is that it is made of wood, it has hinges, perhaps separate wooden panels, screws to keep it together, a handle or knob, and it has a color, blue. When the door opens, then it has changed its "state" and effectively an event has happened.

The door can have many event states: open, closed, opening, closing, and so on. It can even have a "non-event" state, for example, if somebody turns the door handle or knob, but the door does not open in 10 seconds, then this could be a situation when although the door should have opened it didn't in a certain time period, so this is an event that did not happen, but probably should have happened, based on the fact that the door handle did turn.

Anticipation or expecting some event to happen in a certain period of time is something that your brain can easily process but in computing terms it is something that is, on most occasions, difficult to program.

An event stream

Generated by hardware sensor devices, distributed anywhere from the "Internet of things", computer applications, database triggers, or generated from any of hundreds of different sources, events arrive for processing in an event stream or streams. Event streams can have events that are continuously flowing at high volumes or arrive in sporadic intervals, but the events never end and are always time ordered, just like in the real world.

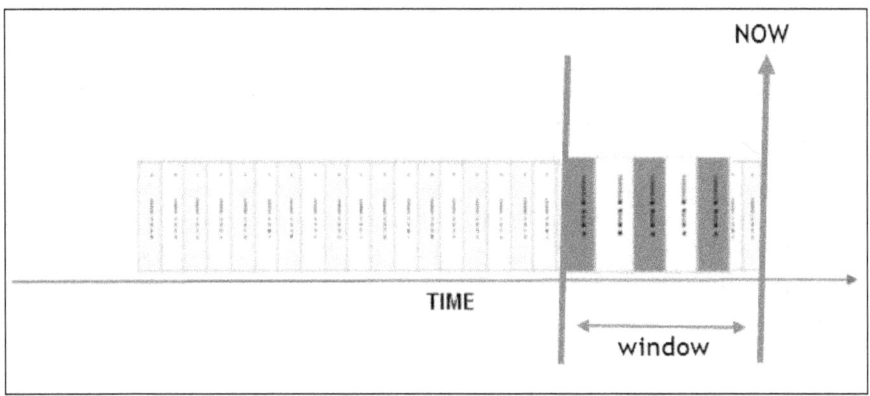

A market data feed in the financial services world, the GPS signals from your mobile telecommunications device and business events from a **Service Orientated Architecture Application** (**SOA**) are all examples of event streams.

In general terms, event streams can be simple, streaming, or high volume.

Traditional computing systems based on database or **Java Enterprise Edition** (**JEE**) infrastructures are not designed to effectively handle this type of continuously flowing event data, as the reading and writing demands to disk, or "send/reply" implementation paradigms involve increased and detrimental processing latencies or delays. So there is a need to evolve a new approach to handing these requirements and with an event-driven infrastructure it can "impose" itself "over" the event streams in memory using a defined window of time or number of events count.

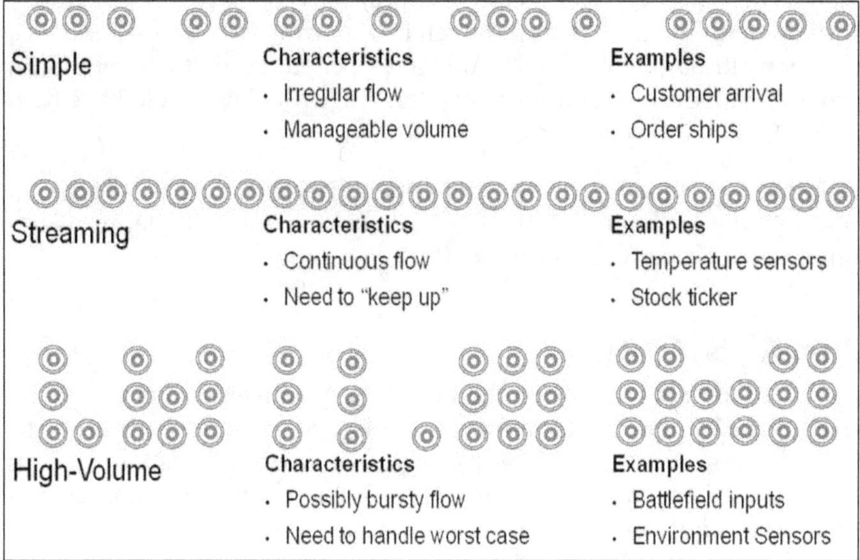

An event type

The event types that flow "along" the event stream defines the properties associated with the event. Event type definitions can range in their levels of complexity, but in most applications can be declaratively defined with a simple notation.

Using the door event example discussed earlier in this chapter, a house event stream that is continuously monitoring things that are related to all doors in a building could have a specific door event type defined with a collection of property names and their associated values.

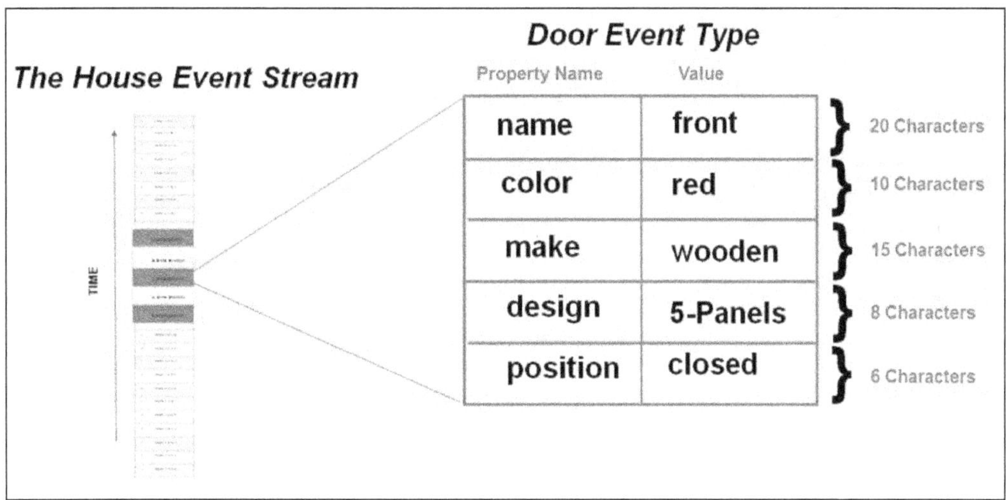

Event Processing Network

So now we have an event, probably thousands or millions of them that need to be effectively handled and processed. As these events continuously flow they need to be identified, have a response very quickly and are often "transported" only in memory, so using a database is not a recommended design option.

For this purpose, many Complex Event Processing platforms provide the **Event Processing Network** (**EPN**) (otherwise known as a **Directed Flow Graph**).

Provided as the best approach for handling streaming event data, the EPN can be generally designed and modeled using various tooling offerings. The EPN is designed as a loosely-coupled collection of event nodes, each performing a unique action on the events as they pass through the network. Each event node subscribes to one or many other event nodes with the state (conditions/properties) held in the event definition itself.

This application model design approach provides the ability for extreme event processing in low latencies with a simple way of extending and/or changing the event handing as real-time situations happen. It also facilitates a mechanism (foreign stages) to enable new event nodes to be introduced into the solution either dynamically or statically during the actual deployment life cycle of the executing application.

A well-structured EPN will probably perform beyond expectations and set the foundation for easy extensibility, integration, and solution maintenance.

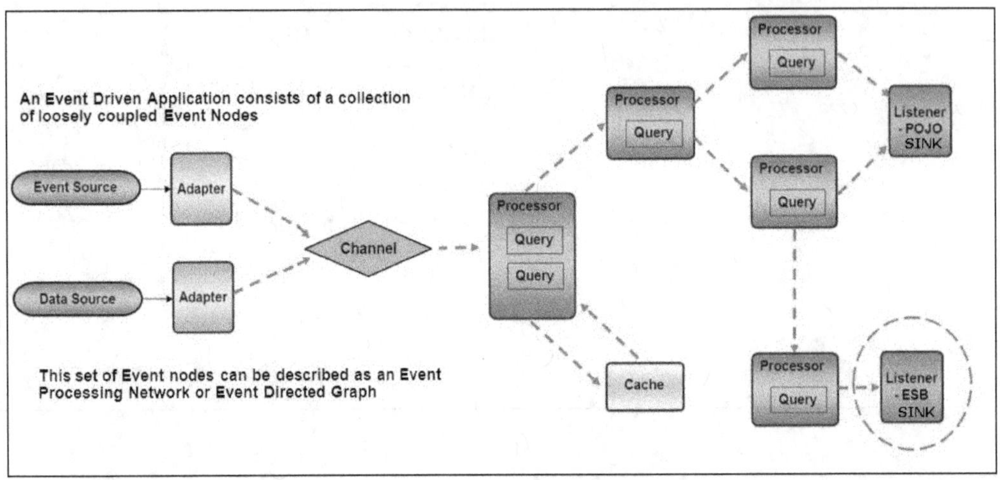

While many kinds of event nodes are evolving, most can be one or more of the following types:

- **Event adapters** provide the connectivity to event sources and sinks, and are relatively simple code implementations that normalize the incoming or outgoing data stream and convert this into event types that are processed downstream or upstream in the EPN. For example, an inbound event adapter can provide the connection to a TCP/IP socket and an outbound event adapter can provide an interface to a visual user interface.

- **Event channels** are the conduits that effectively handle the routing of events, these event nodes not only play an important role in ensuring that the various events are analyzed efficiently, but they also can have properties that can powerfully effect the performance of the application, such as controlling the amount of memory used for the events and the number of processing threads.

- **Event cache** and event POJO Bean nodes provide the in-memory persistence of long-term reference data and the solution-specific business logic written as a "Plain Old Java Object". These event nodes ensure that information needed for long periods of time can be managed, interrogated, and safely held in computing memory, and that any type of additional processing logic can be implemented. POJOs can sometimes act as event sources or event sinks. An example of using Event POJO Beans would be to include and enhance old legacy code, which has been mature and stable for a long period of time in other coded solutions, and would continue to provide additional value in the new Event Processing Network. One caveat when using this type of "old" code is to clearly understand the additional "cost", in terms of memory usage and processing load that will be incurred and how this will impact the overall performance of the new solution and this should be considered during the design phase.

- **Event processors** are the meta-containers for the powerful event analysis needed for any type of solution. There can be one or many event processor nodes in an application and they store the event processing language, which can be rules or queries that statically executes continuously on the flow of arriving events. The event processors are the core engine service of a Complex Event Processing solution, and the capabilities of such engines in most cases, dictate how successful the technology will be in delivering the desired business solution.

Event processing languages and extensibility

In most Complex Event Processing platform technologies, the **Processor Event Node**, or a similarly-defined construct (event engine), will execute the language of choice for the analysis of the events in an event stream.

For example, a car rental company might use the following business rule:

```
Driver Age Rule
Determine if driver is old enough to rent.

IF
  Rental_application.driver age  <  21

THEN
  modify Rental_application ( status : "DECLINED" )
```

Offerings in the industry currently include; State-oriented, Inference rule, Script-orientated, and Agent-orientated SQL-idioms. Some people are familiar with the business rules approach and so decide to use the traditional "what-if-then" kind of analysis. Most others decide to leverage their SQL database skills and extend that knowledge to encompass the handling of streaming data in a way that is familiar to how they interact with data that is stored and processed in a database.

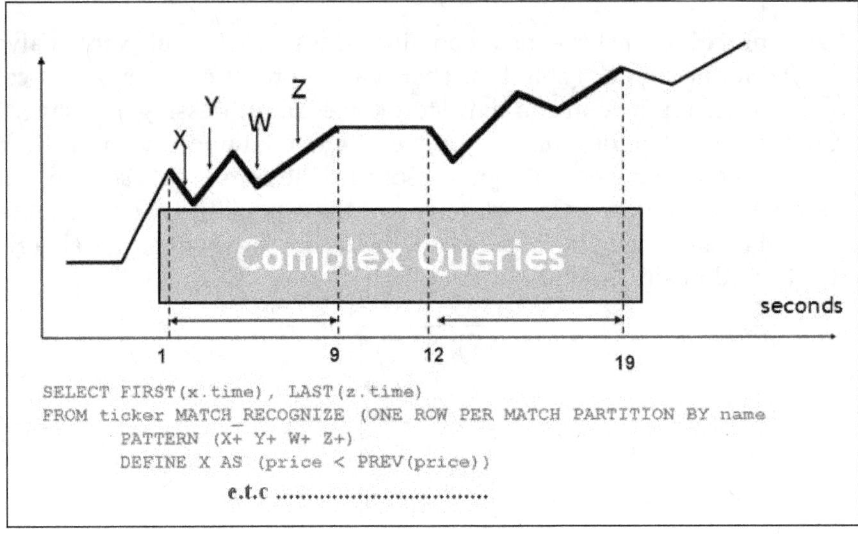

The benefits of a SQL-based event continuous query language extends the rigor of the relational model to event stream processing that can result in a more robust implementation with broader application.

These types of CEP language implementations can incorporate the well-known SQL '99 plus standards and relatively easily introduce the language extensions for the temporal and event count windowing requirements. For many, using this type of event handling approach provides now, and for the future, a single consistent language that can be used for all database and middleware application analysis processing.

Processor event node methodologies

The processor event node provides the direct analysis on the events and uses a number of various techniques.

Event filtering is applicable when thousands or even millions of events flow into an application and there is a need to ensure a time effective handling of the more important information. This can involve either removing or sending the events of no concern to another channel or path, where it can be handled separately. In this way only the events that indicate a relevance to the current application requirement are passed for further "heavy lifting" complex analysis. By using this capability the event load is more evenly spread through the application, making it far more efficient.

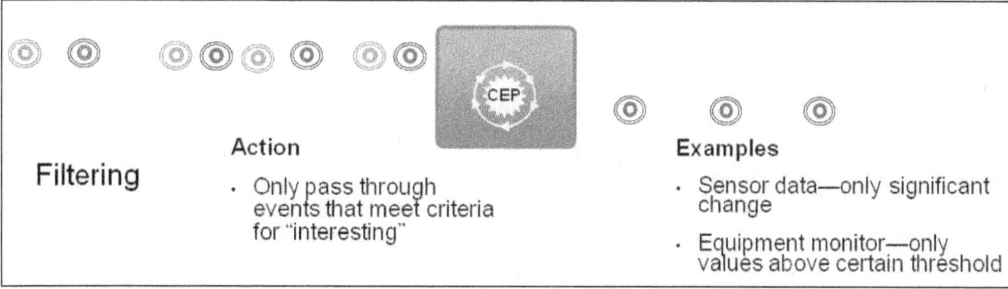

Event correlation and aggregation is generally employed after any event filtering has been performed and is a methodology to understand the relationship between different events and then join or merge these events together. For example, when thousands of events from a temperature sensor arrive providing individual values for each room in microseconds, one approach is to determine which rooms are of interest, then identify the sensors only in these rooms and finally calculate the maximum, minimum, and average temperatures over a one minute time period.

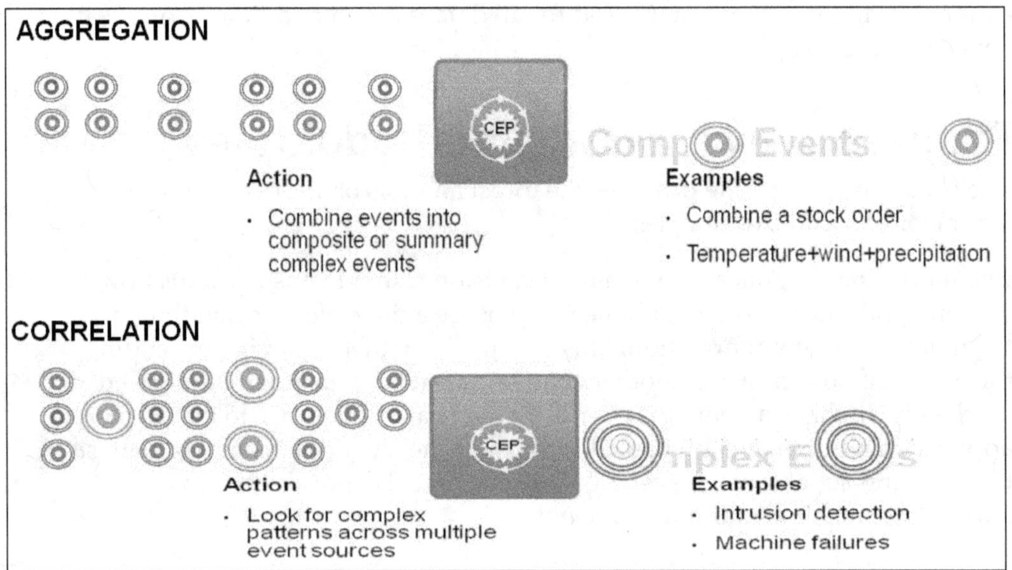

Event pattern matching enables the identification of a certain distinct occurrence in either a specific time window, that is, the last five minutes, or in the last number of events. For example, this can be an event pattern where one can identify an "order" event, followed by a "completed packaging" event, followed by a "truck loaded" event, followed by a "arrived at customer house" event, all for a specific item, in three hours. This could trigger a SMS message to the customer stating "your order has arrived". Event patterns can be without limit but are generally dependent on the semantics of the specific industry. They can incorporate "not events", where you can define an event pattern that expects event A, followed by event B, but not a C event, followed by a D event.

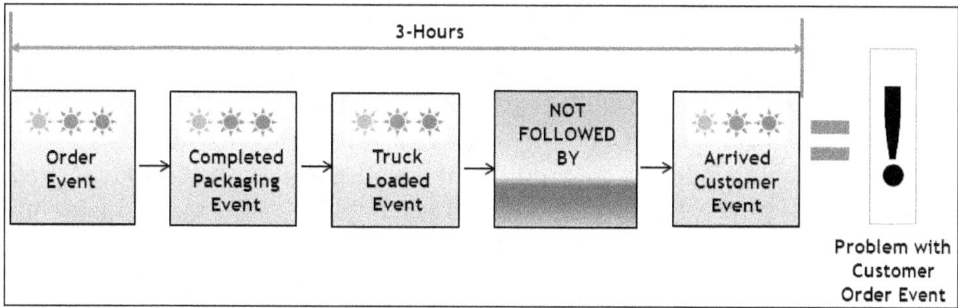

A **synthetic** or **business** event often represents the dynamic construction of an event from a collection of events or elements of events (fragmented events). In many cases, an event may arrive that has little meaning alone but when joined with contextual or reference data, it has significant meaning. Let's take again, for example, the temperature sensor in a room. This sensor may send an event that provides an ID of 005 and a value of 60. Now if we had previously saved information that indicates and ID of 005 refers to a sensor on the tenth floor of a building at San Pedro Square, in the kitchen, attached to the ceiling at the right corner, then by joining this information with the current sensor temperature value of 60 degrees Fahrenheit, we now have a much more concrete (business) event that can be passed to another piece of business logic or system for action.

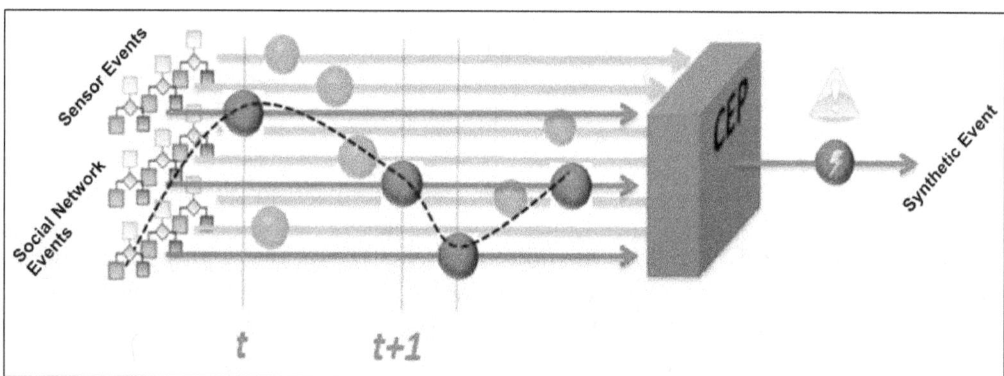

Processor extensibility

With the implementation flexibility offered by the Event Processing Network, it is important not to restrict the event processor with a limiting language implementation which does not support specialized language extensions. These extensions are driven by the changing analysis demands from the advances in the various related technologies of the future, but are also focused on enabling additional industry and domain-specific capabilities that are required by specific users.

Some event processor implementations provide the ability for easy extensibility using a capability called **data cartridges**.

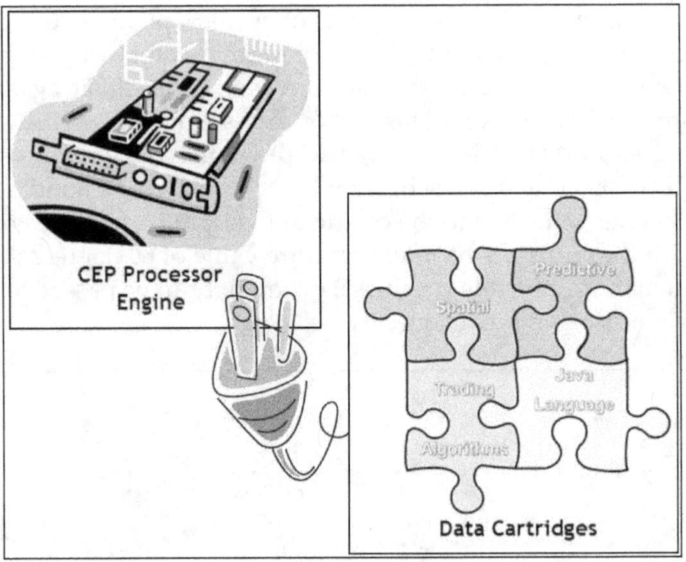

A data cartridge concept provides the notion of directly adding or plugging in new functionality to a Complex Event Processing system, so that event analysis can be added for any type of circumstance.

It would typically define a set of new object types and their behavior, and/or provide implementations for various extensibility interfaces. The purpose of data cartridges is to enable users to capture business logic and processes associated with specialized or domain-specific data in user-defined data types. It constitutes one or more of the following components: user-defined data types, implementation for these types, new operators and aggregate functions, and implementation of certain extensibility interfaces.

An example of data cartridge extensibility is to integrate specialized spatial or Java language analysis directly as part of the CEP engine service.

Event processor "Intelligence Injection"

Another topic to briefly cover in this section is the ability for event processors to be dynamically updated or changed with the rules or queries "on the fly" while the application continues to execute.

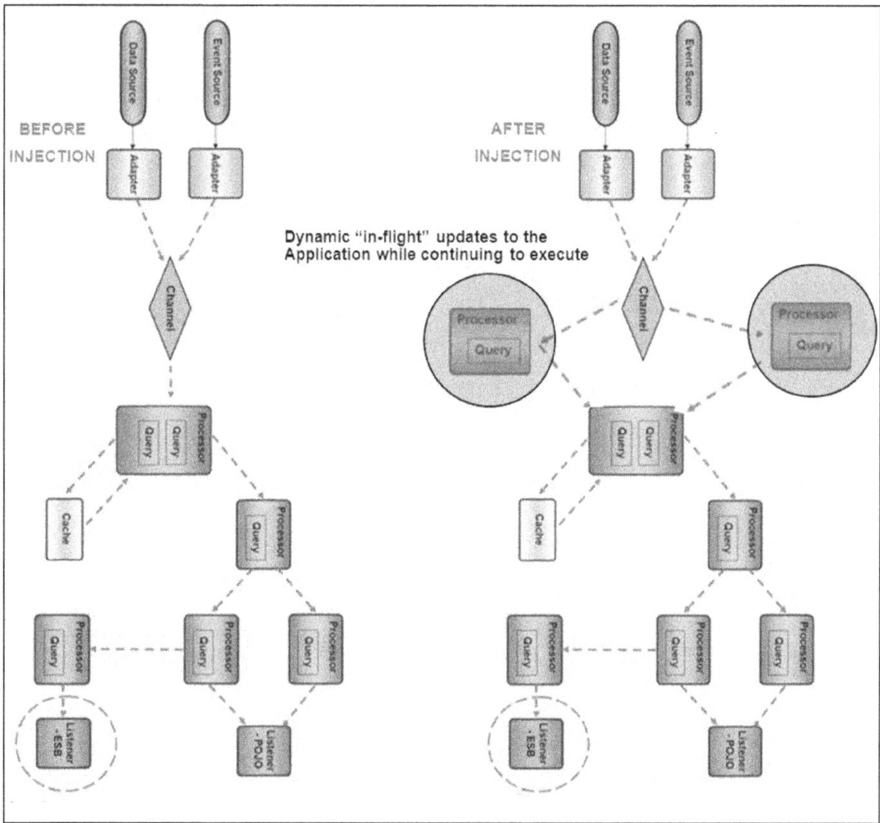

When events change in real life, your brain does not need to "reboot" in order to reassess the situation, it simply continues with the additional "event pattern" information to make a more informed decision. It may be implemented in different ways depending on the Complex Event Processing platform but most now, can provide this capability, and as these types of implementations evolve in the future, Event-driven systems potentially will have a self-awareness, self-learning, and a self-determination allowing them to adapt far more effectively to the changing dynamics of the world that surrounds us.

Holistic Event-Driven and Service Orientated Architectures

So as you can now understand, a Service Orientated Architecture design approach (send-reply paradigm) for many real-time, event-driven applications is perhaps not a good choice, and Complex Event Processing platforms have evolved over the years to address that growing need. However, in many ways an Event Driven Architecture (EDA) compliments a Service Orientated Architecture (SOA) and in many comprehensive industry solutions, these two implementation design patterns work together to solve overall requirements.

We call the combination of architectures as **Event Driven SOA (ED-SOA)**.

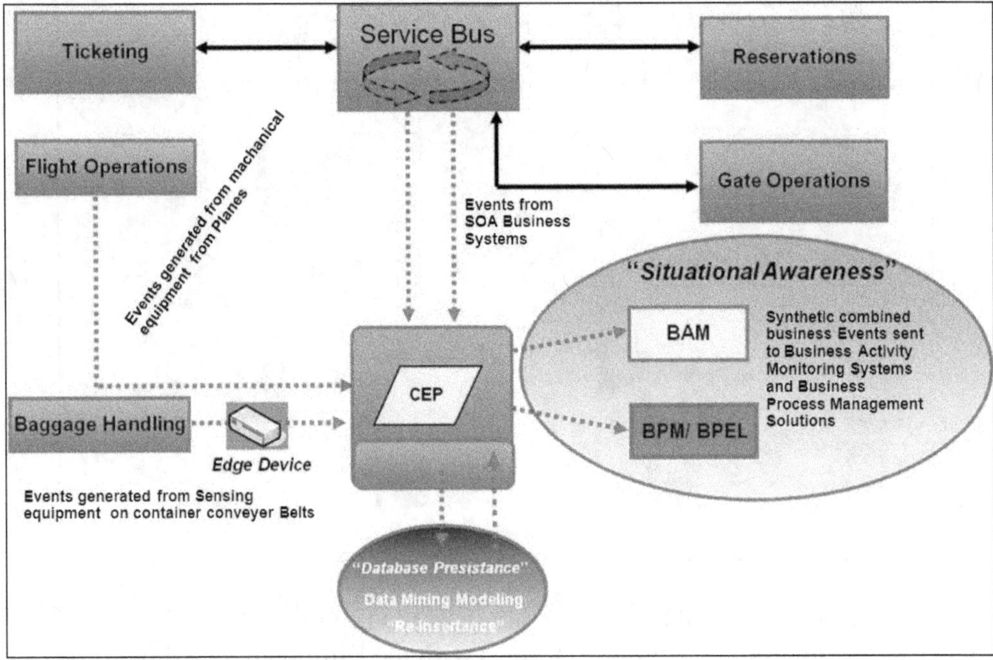

Imagine the requirement for an airport to provide a complete system that will immediately identify missing luggage from a flight and in addition, the monitoring of passenger movements in real time to provide additional VIP services (such as a fast-path access through security checks).

The Complex Event Processing platform could be utilized to process the events from sensor devices that are reading the bag locations, using an event pattern that identifies immediately when bag A has passed by sensor 5, and sensor 6, but has not passed by sensor 7 within two minutes, with this event pattern applied to every bag on every conveyer belt in every part of the airport. At the same time, perhaps from movement events using Bluetooth technology, every "opted in" passenger location event (normally longitude/latitude data) is also sent to the Complex Event Processing platform, which has an event pattern, continuously analyzing each individual passengers position in the airport against general known transit times to his or her required gate.

This system could also get immediate events from each plane which, in addition to being able to transport people around the world, are also really big event "devices" that send information such as a "pushing back from the gate" event or "wheels up and departed" event. This valuable information could assist in the real time determination on whether the plane has in fact not left the gate yet even though the fixed departure time has been passed.

As all of this real-time activity is taking place, and the results are visualized on a SOA Business Activity Monitor technology or SOA Business Processes are initiated, other relevant SOA applications such as Ticketing and Reservations leveraging a traditional SOA Service Bus could also be included in the architecture as they can provide information about the "importance" of the passenger based on his or her class of service and which gate should be associated with each passenger.

While Complex Event Processing can be used as a standalone platform, particularly where extreme high event throughput is needed together with immediate or very low processing latencies, many complete solutions now need the combination of both implementation design pattern technologies.

Predicting an event

The capability to look around the corner and predict what might happen next based on what is happening now is an extension to the event pattern matching over time or event windows used in ED-SOA solutions.

An example is when Complex Event Processing is used to monitor real-time CDRs (Call Detail Records) streaming in a telecommunications network and identifies subscriber calls that are dropping in a short period of time. Once the event-driven system has determined that a problem is happening now for a specific subscriber number, the next step is to "look back" over past persisted data, which could be large, and evaluate whether this person is more or less likely to change his or her telephone company.

The analysis of the potentially vast amount of historical data creating models that use a collection of algorithms to predict behavior is generally handled by other technologies such as data mining or real-time decisions. However, Complex Event Processing platforms can leverage these models and then use them in real time.

The value in this use case would be that the person experiencing the dropped calls could immediately get a call from customer support or a SMS text message that could automatically offer an incentive to stay with his current supplier.

Summary

Complex Event Processing Platforms are now evolving from the early adoption phase and becoming much more mainstream for many companies. There are a fair few choices on the type of event-driven platform you can invest your time in to evaluate, and deploy your next generation event-driven solutions.

In the next chapter, we will delve into the main components of the Oracle Event Processing Solution Platform, such as the EDA Java Application Container that has been optimized for performance and scalability. We focus on the evolution of the technology and its unique modular approach enabling this technology to be used in a wide variety of event-driven implementations.

More importantly, we will get you involved with the Oracle product directly, by stepping you through the process of creating an application and publishing (deploying) on your own installed version of the system, and we also show you the capabilities provided in a rich Internet application, how to monitor, and manage the system.

As you progress through the chapter, you will build up a solid foundation of knowledge that will be needed in the remaining sections of this book, and hopefully inspire you to become experts in Oracle Event Processing.

2
An Overview of Oracle Event Processing

In this chapter, we will cover the general history behind the creation of the Oracle Event Processing product, its modular service bundle architecture, and how to use the provided tooling to develop, monitor, and manage the platform. Some of the topics we will cover are as follows:

- Understanding the heritage of Oracle Event Processing
- The Java Event-Driven Server architecture
- The adopted event language
- The philosophy and fundamentals of developing
- Controlling from the command line
- Watching things happen and changing what happens

Understanding the heritage of Oracle Event Processing

Before we delve into the inner workings of the technology, let us start with a little nostalgia of how it all began.

"Welcome to the **Time and Event Driven** (**TED**) team.". This is what you heard when you were selected to join a new engineering project back in early 2007 at BEA Systems Inc. The evolution of the Oracle Event Processing, Real-time Event Stream Processing Application, and Integration Platform began with a collection of top innovative engineers, individually selected because in the past they had worked their magic to create several of the major components for the industry-leading and award-winning WebLogic Server product.

With a dynamic, constantly motivating team director and a "wise old" software product manager who had been in the industry for 30 years but never tired of exploring new ideas and concepts, the group evolved to deliver this next generation "breakthrough" technology that would lead the company into new domains and allow it to embrace new customers in a way never before possible.

The team affectionately called the product, Elvis. Why? Well, it was planned to be eventually called, the **WebLogic Event Server**, and using a few of the letters we came up with that code name, and on the first general availability release, we proudly declared and printed nice coffee cups with the words "Elvis has left the building".

To get the attention and funding for such an elaborate new product, the TED team met and interviewed several potential customers in New York and London, focusing on the financial services industry, and particularly a select target audience called **Capital Markets**, otherwise known as the **Financial Front Office**. When it came to providing a new event-driven platform, the logical place for us to start was with people that already understood the need for the complex analysis of stock trading data, with one person telling us on more than one occasion that if this technology could save one millisecond of processing time a year, it was worth one hundred million dollars to them. We never figured out how they ever came to that conclusion, but I can tell you that nothing inspires computer company executives more, and encourages high profile attention and project development spending, than having that kind of statement heard from customers.

So after several "man years" of effort, this built "from the ground up" technology was released with its first release on July 16, 2007 from the company, BEA Systems. The core foundational platform was ready for customer adoption with some basic developer tooling to get them started.

In the following year, 2008, from within the Oracle organization, the team expanded with a new strategic goal to combine, integrate, and release, what was believed as two best of breed technologies, the first, the WebLogic Event Server, and the second was a Complex Event Processing "engine", evolved after many years of research by the Oracle engineering team, as one of the most complete and powerful in-memory extensible event analytics technologies available.

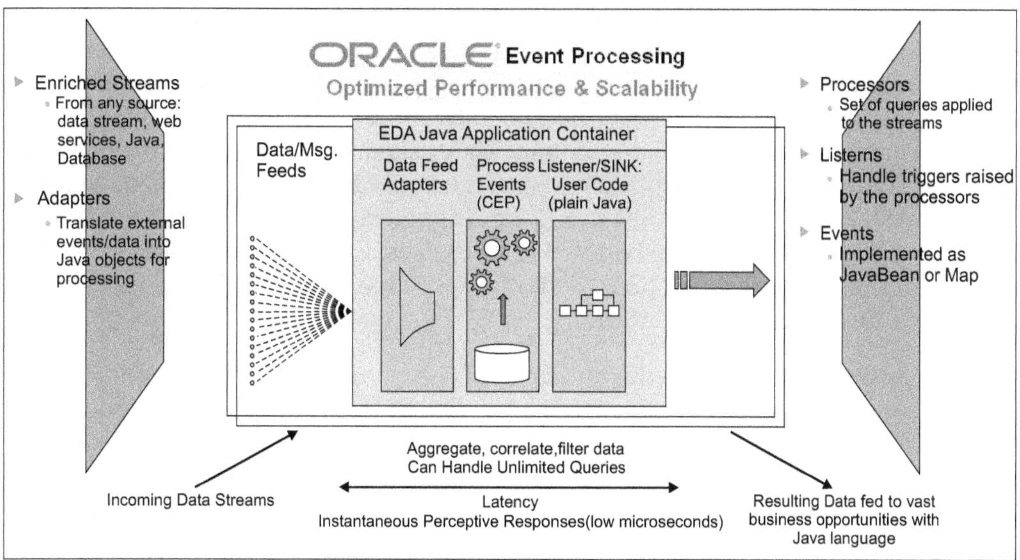

On July 1, 2009, these two technologies came together to create the first release of the Oracle Event Processing Solution 11*g*R1. Over the years since, the product has matured as a rock solid, dependable, highly available industry leading solution, now used by customers across all different kinds of industries.

The Java Event-Driven Server, the bits and bytes of the architecture

The initial design goal that came from the financial services customers was to create a new lightweight software computing platform that could efficiently process events at speed, fifty-thousand, one hundred-thousand, even one million a second, and beyond, without compromising on the ability to provide the real-time analysis needed. This analysis being the ability to identify complex event patterns in the streams of data coming from their market data feeds, such as a "W" stock trading pattern, all processed with the results, in perceptively instantaneous response times, in reality less than one millisecond and over time in the low microseconds.

Downloading the example code

You can download the example code files for all Packt books you have purchased from your account at `http://www.PacktPub.com`. If you purchased this book elsewhere, you can visit `http://www.PacktPub.com/support` and register to have the files e-mailed directly to you.

As the "art of the possible" was realized for the baseline design goals, the customers' requirements grew to encompass the need for this lightweight computing platform to be completely Java language based. This was due to the fact that in those days, and even today, C/C++ developers are generally more costly and these types of solutions are hard to modify and maintain. They asked for a Java Event Server, while similar to a traditional JEE Application Server, it could be used for the management of the complete life cycle of these unique, new applications, but did not have all the processing overhead needed to handle **Web Services, Enterprise Java Beans** (**EJBs**), **Java Connector Architecture** (**JCA**), and other JEE capabilities, which are not needed directly for an event-driven platform.

With the Java platform approach, one dreaded issue arose, that being its data garbage collection (GC) pauses, generally handled automatically and efficiently by the Java Virtual Machine, but a major bottleneck in high-performance, low-latency applications. This was resolved with work conducted by a team of Java Virtual Machine specialists, who made available a new deterministic implementation that would allow for the configuration to efficiently manage the amount memory recovery within the confines of an allowable latency period.

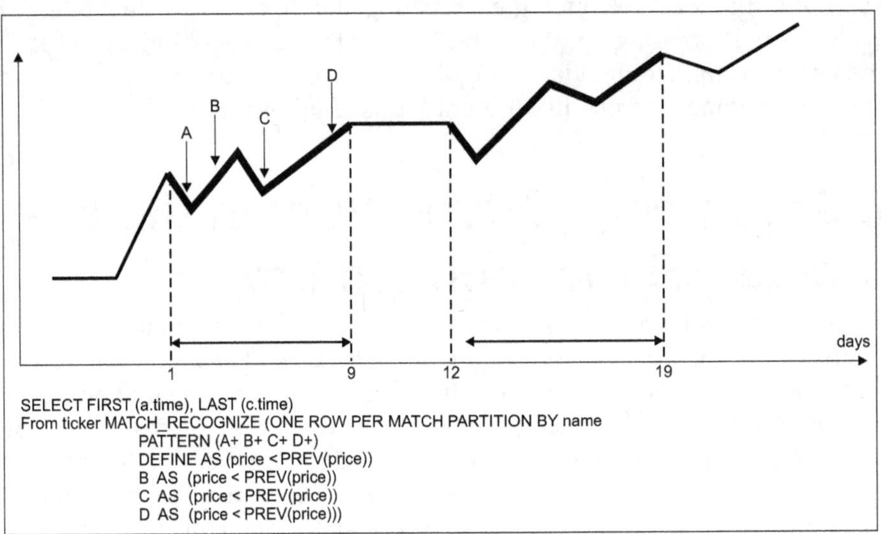
D
B
C
A
days
1
9
12
19
SELECT FIRST (a.time), LAST (c.time)
From ticker MATCH_RECOGNIZE (ONE ROW PER MATCH PARTITION BY name
PATTERN (A+ B+ C+ D+)
DEFINE AS (price < PREV(price))
B AS (price < PREV(price))
C AS (price < PREV(price))
D AS (price < PREV(price)))

The other major requirement was for this solution platform to completely support the Event Driven Architecture (EDA) Event Processing Network application model, in reality the most efficient methodology for processing continuous streaming event data.

This was achieved by leveraging the Spring programming framework, which enables each event node to be connected or "wired" together. This type of implementation would eventually provide the capability for users to dynamically manipulate the processing logic of the application during execution time, and simplify the visualization representation for developers, by facilitating a canvass/palette approach in the evolving development and deployment environments.

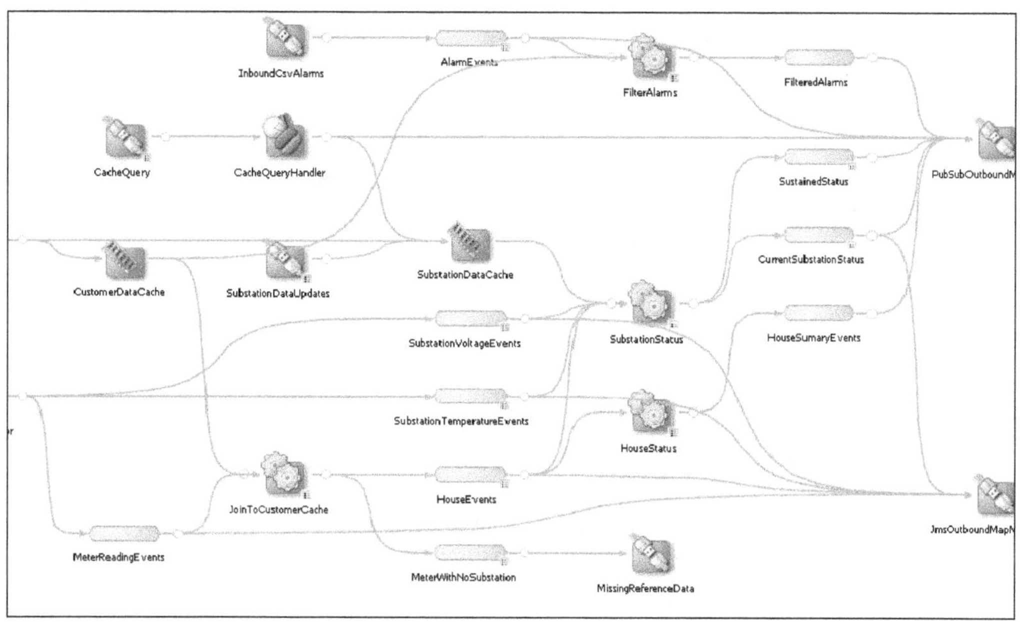

The lightweight Java container would need the capability to be deployed and executed across every facet or tier of a business, even on the sensor/device edge of the infrastructure so the amount of disk space and memory used had to be relatively small. In addition, it should provide the ability to dynamically add or remove event-related components (services/bundles) depending on the particular business/solution requirement.

To address these requirements, the architectural team selected the use of OSGi™ so that each eventing component was modularized in such a way that each could be packaged together to form a functionally-rich Java Event Server.

OSGi is best suited for this type of platform implementation as the **Open Services Gateway initiative** framework is a module system and service platform for the Java programming language that implements a complete and dynamic component model. Applications or components, which are in the form of deployment bundles, can be remotely installed, started, stopped, updated, and uninstalled without requiring the server to be restarted.

```
MANIFEST.MF

Manifest-Version: 1.0
Bundle-ManifestVersion: 2
Bundle-Name: %project.name
Bundle-SymbolicName: spatiallab
Bundle-Version: 1.0.0
Bundle-Localization: bundle
Bundle-Vendor: %project.vendor
Bundle-RequiredExecutionEnvironment: JavaSE-1.6
Bundle-ClassPath: .
Import-Package: com.bea.wlevs.configuration;version="11.1.1",
 com.bea.wlevs.ede;version="11.1.1",
 com.bea.wlevs.ede.api;version="11.1.1",
 com.bea.wlevs.ede.impl;version="11.1.1",
 com.bea.wlevs.ede.spi;version="11.1.1",
 com.bea.wlevs.management.spi;version="11.1.1",
 com.bea.wlevs.spring;version="11.1.1",
 com.bea.wlevs.spring.support;version="11.1.1",
 com.bea.wlevs.util;version="11.1.1",
 com.oracle.cep.cartridge.spatial;version="11.1.1.4_0",
 org.apache.commons.logging;version="1.1.0",
 org.springframework.beans;version="2.5.6",
 org.springframework.beans.factory;version="2.5.6",
 org.springframework.beans.factory.config;version="2.5.6",
 org.springframework.core.annotation;version="2.5.6",
 org.springframework.osgi.context;version="1.2.0",
 org.springframework.osgi.extensions.annotation;version="1.2.0",
 org.springframework.osgi.service;version="1.2.0",
 org.springframework.util;version="2.5.6"
```

Bundles are JAR files that contain resources and classes for providing a set of functionality, and they contain an OSGi manifest (as shown in the preceding screenshot) describing the bundle and its dependencies. Bundles use the JAR file manifest format composed of name-value pairs.

The foundational services needed (or the **Core Engine** as it was called) was gathered from the already industry grade, mature capabilities evolved over many years for the WebLogic Server (JEE) Container. This modularity, enabled by the OSGi Dynamic Module System, eventually included over 230 modules, all providing a variety of common services with some also from open source, such as Equinox (OSGi Backplane), Jetty, Tomcat, Spring.

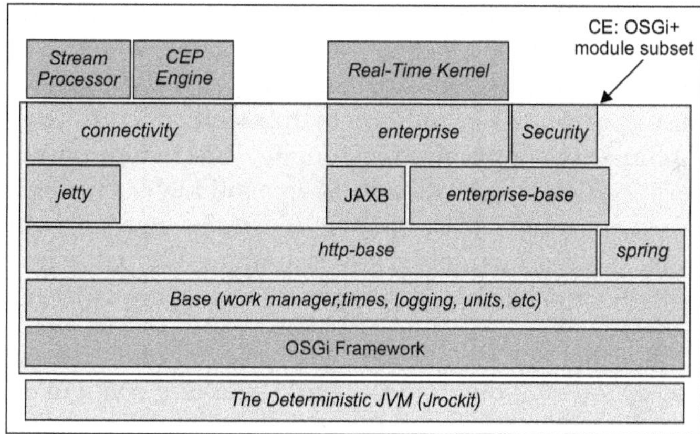

With this base functionality now in place, a series of new services (OSGi bundles) were written and packaged together to support the new requirements for customer's event-driven applications. These included Stream Management, Event Repository, a HTTP publish and subscribe engine, Coherence, and the powerful Complex Event Processor service.

One bundle of interest is the functionality provided by the **JMX API** framework, which facilitates the dynamic programmatic modification and monitoring of the entire Java container itself. Later we will describe how this framework is used by the **Visualizer Monitoring and Management** tooling.

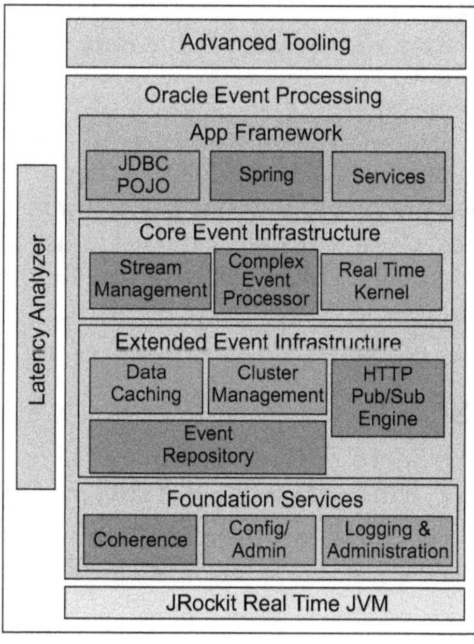

As a standards-based Java Container (Event Server), customers can use any standards-compliant Java Virtual Machine, but in situations where extreme high performance and low latencies is demanded, the provided JRockit JVM can be used with its determinism capabilities in addition to the wealth of additional tooling to interrogate and optimize the applications executing. JVM determinism is an important requirement for event-driven applications that demand low latency response times because this capability ensures the use of an optimized Java garbage collection (GC) algorithm that, in most cases, guarantees it will complete GC pause times within a certain period. With the JRockit JVM, this can be a time as low as 10 milliseconds.

For now it will suffice that you are aware of the basic foundational architecture and modular design, however over the following chapters you will encounter the functionality provided by these and the many other services included in the Oracle Event Processing Platform.

The adopted event language

Let's now turn our attention to the abstracted event language used by the Oracle Event Processing Platform, which must provide the wealth of analysis on the streaming event data. Each event processor node in an event-driven application will contain one or more query statements.

Introducing the **Continuous Query Language** (CQL), based on †Stanford University research, and encompasses the SQL-99 standards with specific additions which extends the rigor of the relational model to event stream processing, resulting in a more robust implementation with broader in-memory application.

This language approach was adopted in part so that most customers who are already familiar with database SQL could easily extend their knowledge into the world of streaming event data only needing to learn the addition semantics for temporal and event-driven querying. With one key factor being that the queries are executing in-memory on an event stream in-memory rather than a database table on disk. This language is explained in greater detail at `http://ilpubs.stanford.edu:8090/758/1/2003-67.pdf`.

CQL concepts

CQL provides the formal model for describing time, streams, and relations and enables the construction of "windows" over event streams, bounded by time or count (which is also extensible via an API), and includes event partitioning based on values and the ability to process events incrementally or in batches.

CQL defines a "working set" of events upon which you would apply queries such as filtering, aggregation, and the correlation of events. It also adds pattern matching, supporting track-and-trace scenarios (for example, detecting missing events) with **Data Cartridge Domain Specific Extensibility** involving specialized technologies, such as real-time geographical spatial analysis, as shown in the following screenshot:

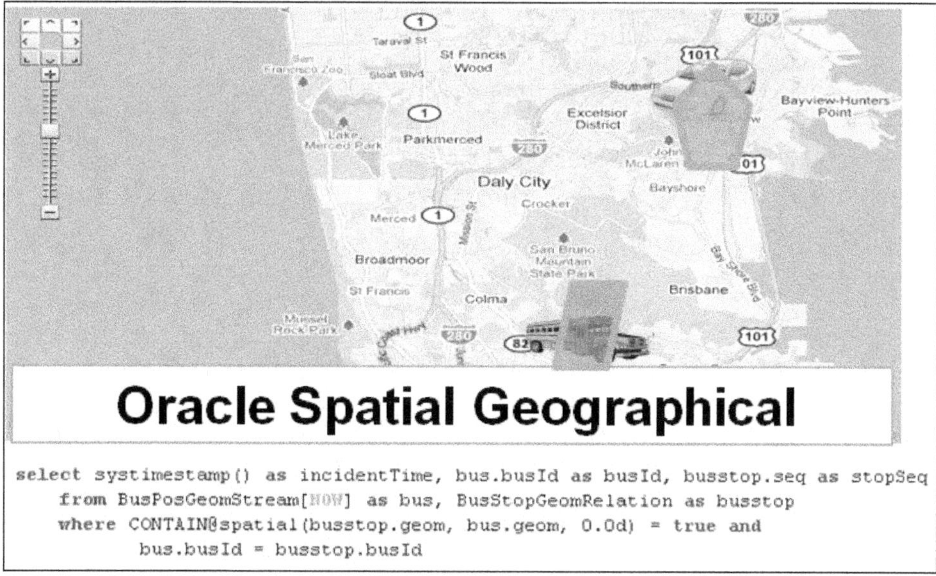

St Francis Wood
Excelsior District
Bayview-Hunters Point
Parkmerced
Daly City
Broadmoor
Colma
Brisbane
Oracle Spatial Geographical
select systimestamp() as incidentTime, bus.busId as busId, busstop.seq as stopSeq
from BusPosGeomStream[NOW] as bus, BusStopGeomRelation as busstop
where CONTAIN@spatial(busstop.geom, bus.geom, 0.0d) = true and
bus.busId = busstop.busId

Later chapters describe the Continuous Query Language in detail, but to get a taste for the completeness and power of the language, following are some examples with a general description of its purpose, which are commonly used and re-used by various companies:

```
<query active="true" id="FilterBySymbolQuery">
<![CDATA[
                    SELECT *
                    FROM InboundStockTickChannel [now]
                    WHERE symbol = "Oracle"
                    ]]>
</query>
```

Purpose: Identify a specific value in the event data and will only pass events that contain that value, effectively a filter for the stream.

```
<view id="JoinToCustomerCacheView">
    <![CDATA[
        RSTREAM(
        SELECT
            meter.date,
            meter.house AS name,
            meter.kwh,
            customer.address,
            customer.normkwh,
            customer.smartrate,
            customer.substation
        FROM
            MeterReadingEvents [NOW] AS meter,
            CustomerDataCache AS customer
        WHERE
            meter.house  = customer.name (+)
        )
    ]]>
</view>
```

Purpose: Create a synthetic event, which includes both streaming event data with reference data that was been previously persisted in the in-memory data grid.

```
<view id="SubstationSummaryView">
    <![CDATA[
        ISTREAM (
        SELECT
            houseEvents.substation,
            MAX(date) AS maxDate,
            COUNT(*) AS eventCount,
            COUNT(DISTINCT name) AS distinctSourceCount,
            COUNT(isSmartRate) AS smartRateCount,
            COUNT(isNotSmartRate) AS nonSmartRateCount,
            AVG(houseEvents.percentnormkwh) AS averagepercentnorm,
            SUM(houseEvents.kwh) AS totalkwh
        FROM
            ExpandSmartMeterView [RANGE 1 SECONDS SLIDE 500 MILLISECONDS] AS houseEvents
        GROUP BY houseEvents.substation
        )
    ]]>
</view>
```

Purpose: Calculates aggregate values over a sliding one-second window with output every half second.

```
<query active="true" id="DetectMissingEvent">
    <![CDATA[
            SELECT
                "Event has not occurred in 5 seconds" AS detail,
                "ALERT ALERT" AS alertType,
                EventMiss.tStamp AS tStamp
            FROM RelayChannel  MATCH_RECOGNIZE (

                MEASURES A.ELEMENT_TIME AS tStamp include timer events
                PATTERN( A B ) DURATION 5 seconds
                DEFINE
                    A AS A.psi > 0,
                    B AS B.psi > 0
            ) AS EventMiss
                ]]>
</query>
```

Purpose: The `MEASURES` clause gives a name to the value in the events timestamp so it can be used in the `SELECT` statement. The `PATTERN` clause defines that you are looking for an `A` event followed by the `B` event (These are defined in the `DEFINE` clause). The `DURATION` clause defines the period between events.

The philosophy and fundamentals of developing

Now that the basics have been covered in terms of the event-driven Java Container and the Continuous Query Language (CQL), let us introduce you to developing Oracle Event Processing applications. We feel the best way to understand this technology is to use it, and so we intentionally made the product relatively easy to install and get started quickly.

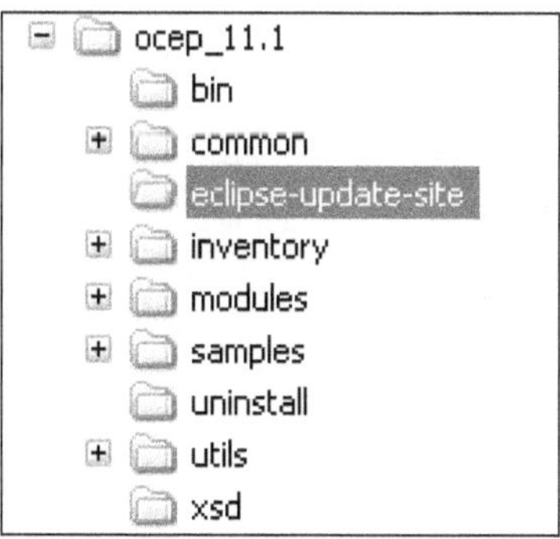

We provided a single installer media kit for each of the major platforms and when executed, with just a few basic responses Oracle Event Processing can be ready for use.

Currently available as the Integrated development environment platform is Eclipse, so in the filesystem the installer provides a plugin which should be installed into Eclipse.

This is well documented in the Oracle Event Processing documentation, so we will not dwell too much on the process, but the folder called `eclipse-update-site` (which is shown in the preceding screenshot) contains the software that you must install in your Eclipse IDE.

The Oracle Event Processing development environment is targeted at Java developers who understand the basics of Java application development techniques. All of the artifacts created during the event-driven application development process can be inspected and modified directly, so there is no "hidden black box" approach.

The main goals for this development approach is to provide first-class tooling for development of Oracle Event Processing applications, while at the same time retaining the power and flexibility of the Oracle Event Processing programming model, allowing for higher-level editing at the same time.

As the Oracle Event Processing tooling evolves, you can expect much more visual editing capabilities, which allow the developers to easily create Event Processing Network (EPN) nodes on the available canvass, join the nodes together and re-use common node implementations, such as Event Adapter Nodes for connectivity to various protocols and Event Query patterns in the processor nodes.

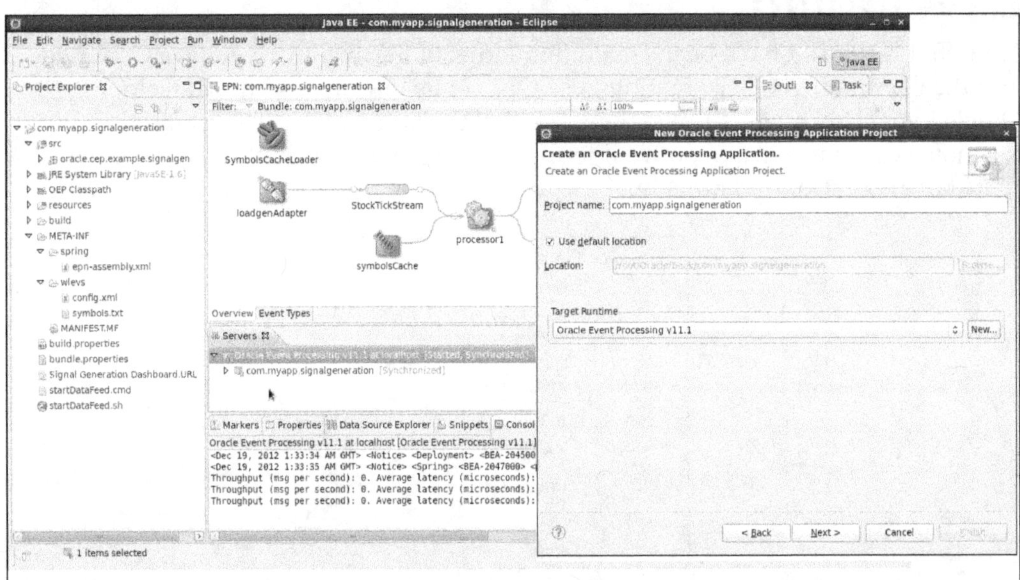

For those familiar with these types of development environments, not only can the application be created and debugged, but also the Oracle Event Processing server can be completely provisioned, started, stopped, and your application bundles published (deployed) and removed (undeployed) as desired.

Creating an Oracle Event Processing application

Now we will step you through building your first Oracle Event Processing application. By following this methodology, your installation of the product will be significantly validated so that any further efforts in building more sophisticated event-driven applications should go relatively smoothly.

The functionality of this sample application is again well described in the Oracle Event Processing documentation, however in summary the signal generation application receives simulated market data using the integrated load generation testing tooling and verifies if the price of a security has fluctuated by more than a certain percentage (initially two percent). The application also detects if there is a trend occurring by keeping track of successive stock prices for a particular symbol. If more than three successive prices fluctuate more than two percent, this is considered a trend.

Firstly ensure that you have successfully installed the Oracle Event Processing plugin into your Eclipse environment you will be able to confirm the status by selecting the **Help** menu and the **About Eclipse** Options.

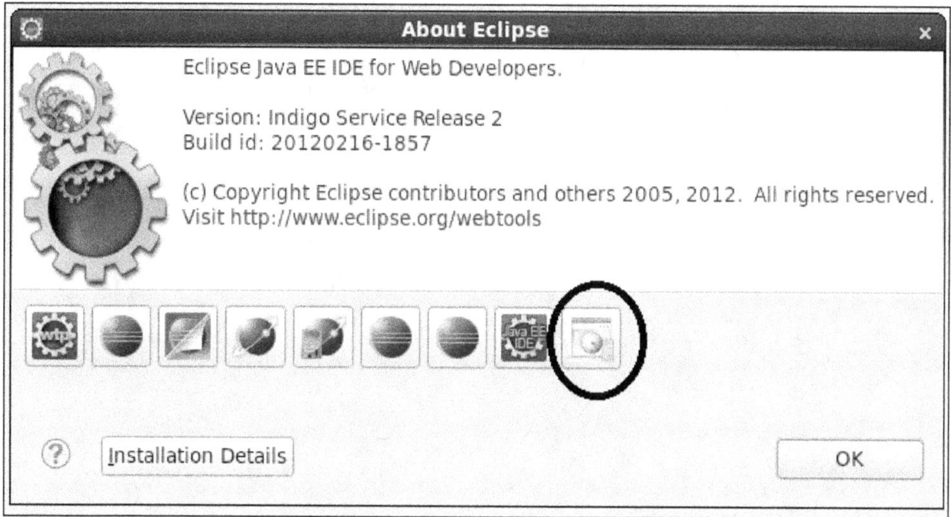

We will now start to create the sample application in the development environment. Using the menu options, select **New** and then **Other**. This will direct you to a context menu showing the Oracle Event Processing options available:

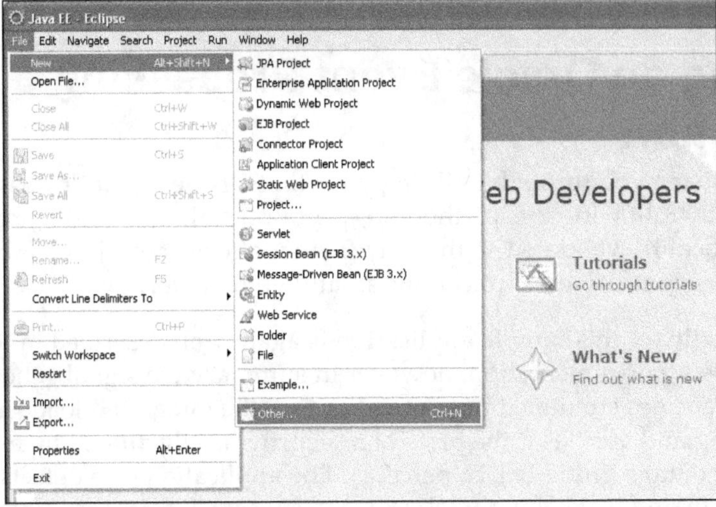

While there are currently three Oracle Event Processing-related options available, select the **Oracle Event Processing Application Project** menu option, which will invoke the integrated wizard for creating a new event-driven application from scratch or leverage one of the available sample template applications:

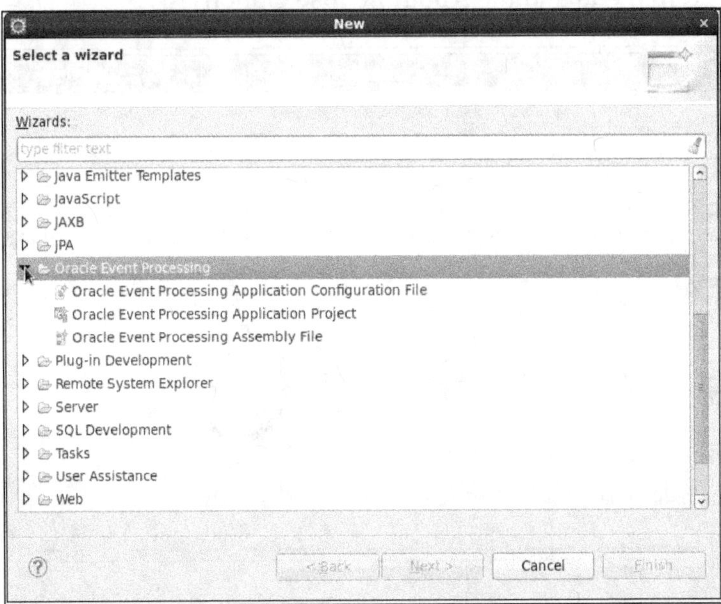

As we step through the creation wizard, we are generating the required project, Java, and metadata code for our financial services signal generation sample application.

The next step of the wizard is to request a name for the project.

Once you have specified the name (you can use the same name as shown in the following screenshot), for the first time only, you will need to specify the target runtime for the Oracle Event Processing Server:

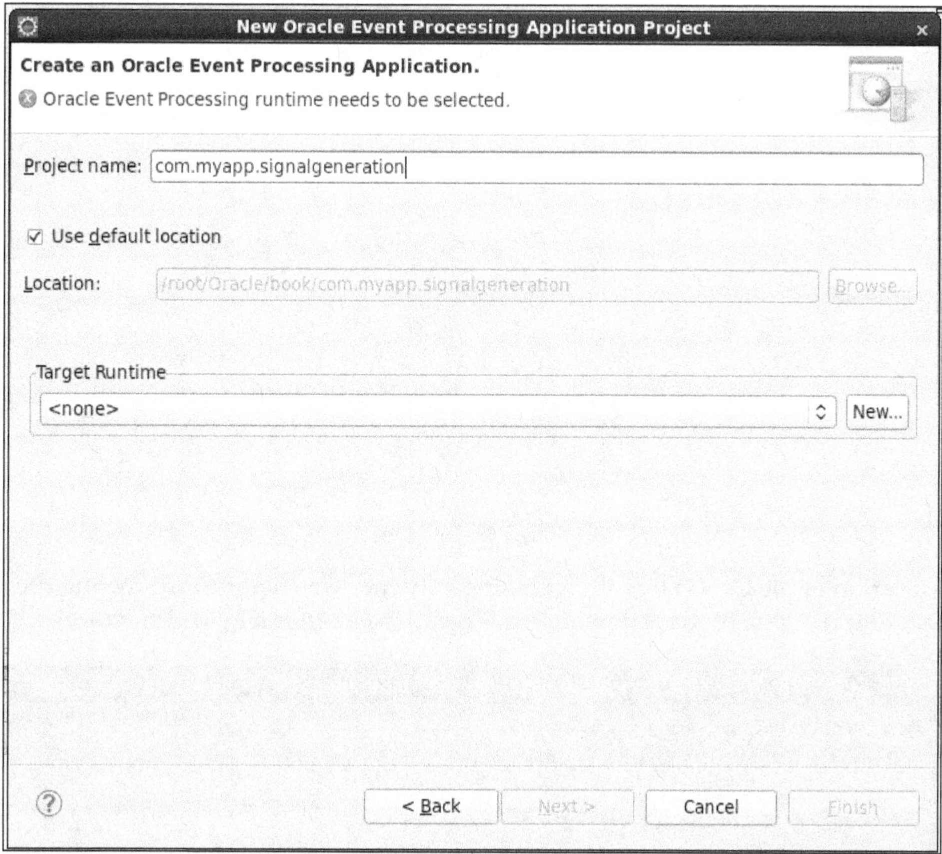

This is the location of the Oracle Event Processing software that you specified during the installation process. Select the **New** button and proceed.

As shown in the following screenshot, select the **Oracle Event Processing v11.1 Server** runtime and create a new local server by selecting the option box on the wizard panel:

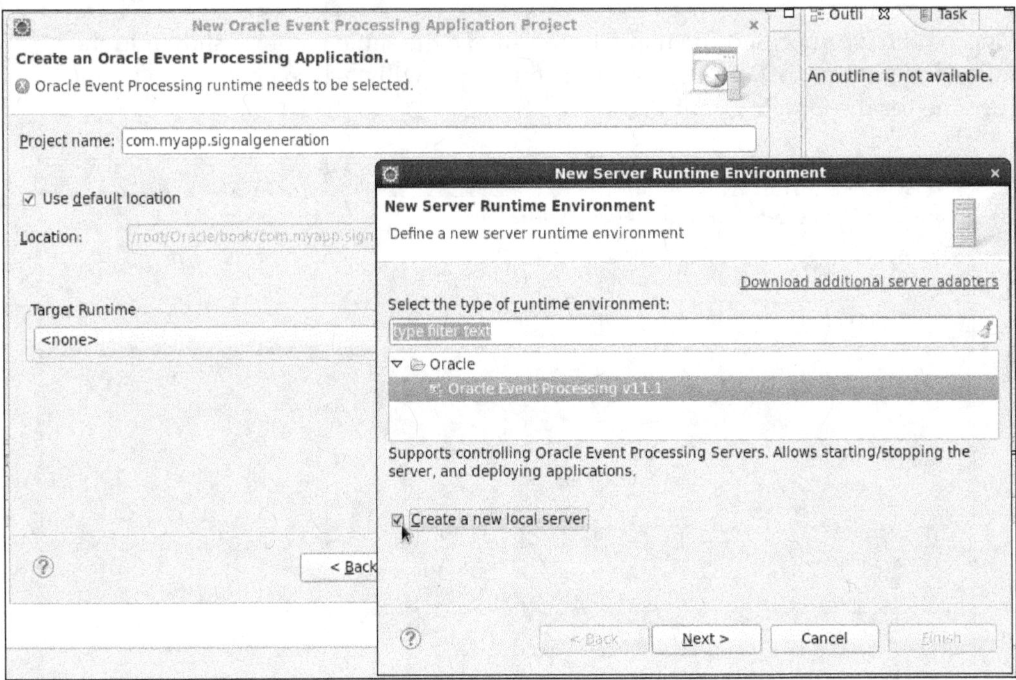

The location of the Oracle Event Processing software was determined during the installation process. In the following example, it is **/root/Oracle/Middleware**:

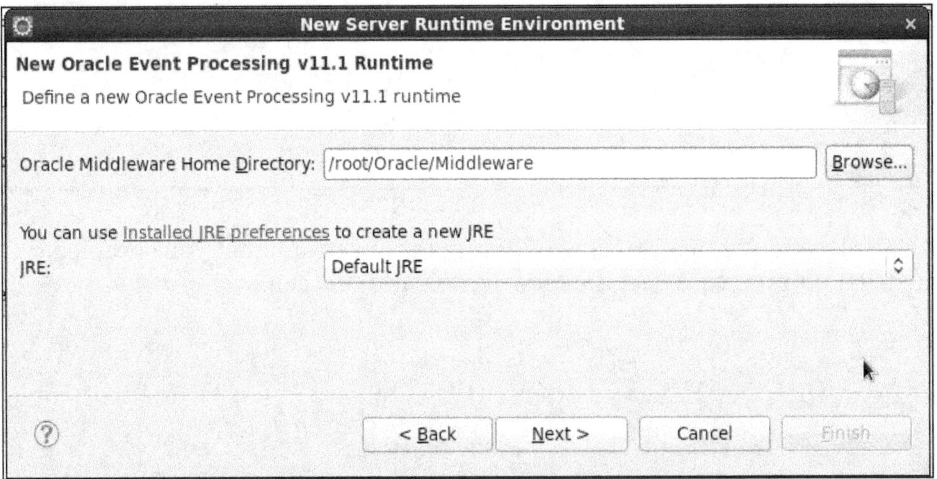

Generally, selecting the default JRE (Java Runtime Environment) is adequate for a base installation.

At this point, the **Finish** button can be selected, although it is best practice to select the **Next** button, leave the next default to local server and then on the final wizard selection panel review and validate the information so that your entries carry no errors and point to the correct Oracle Event Processing server instance:

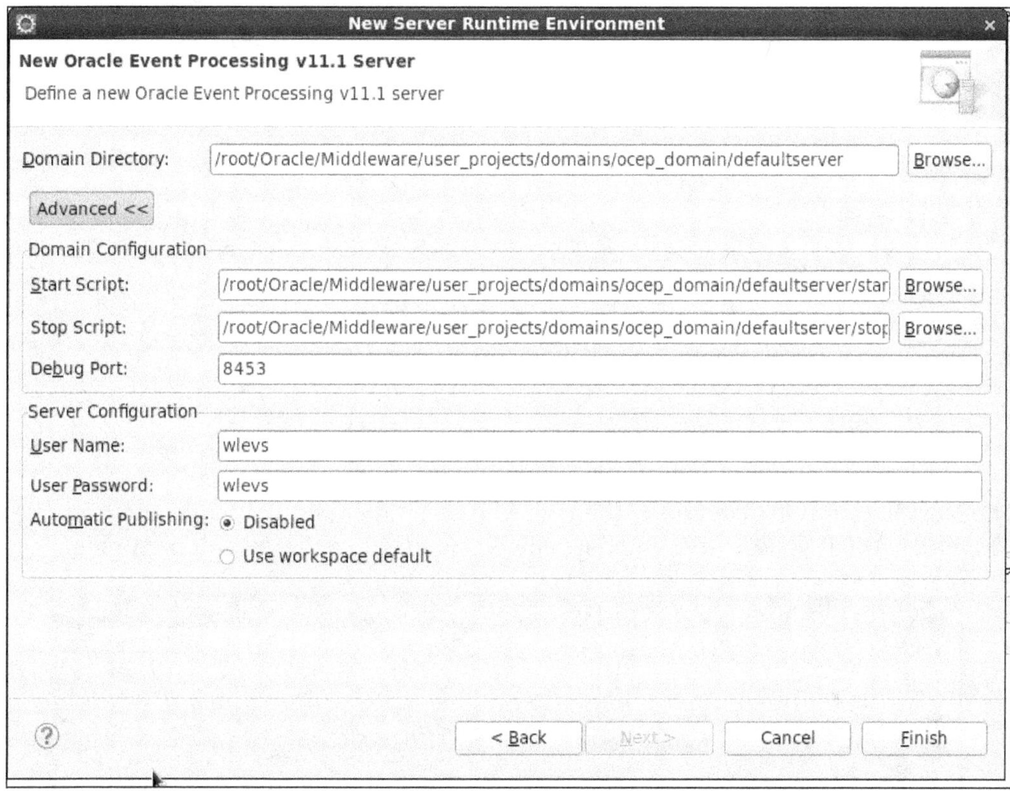

As the server wizard returns to the application creation wizard, you will now observe the new Oracle Event Processing target runtime that has been defined and ready for use.

Whenever you develop applications with this Eclipse plugin, what you have specified here is the location where the application will be deployed (published) for execution.

While a configurable option, it is usually good practice to leave the default location for the resultant project artifacts:

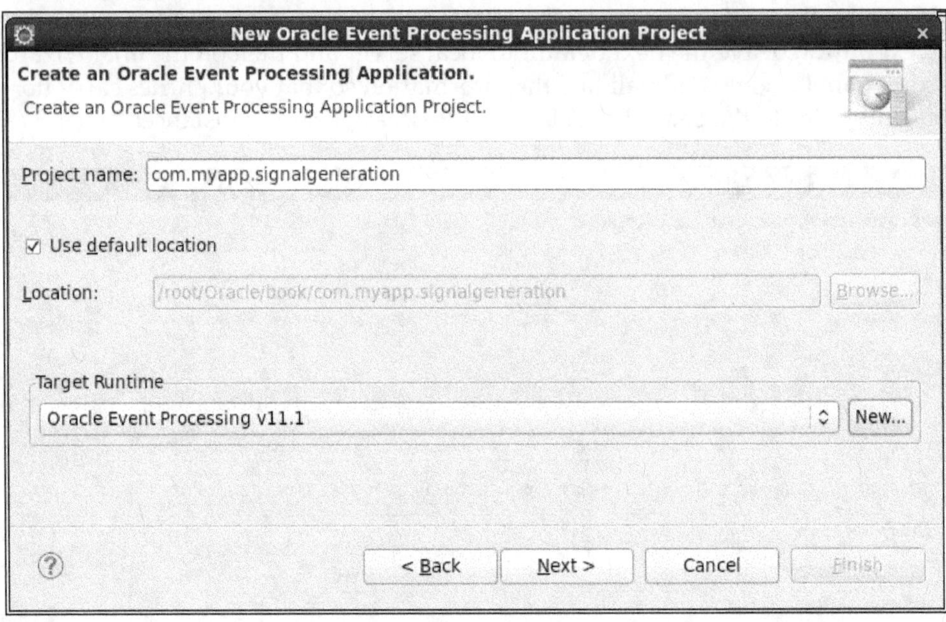

The **Next** button will take you to the wizard panel indicating the application bundle properties. What you have already specified can be left as the default parameters:

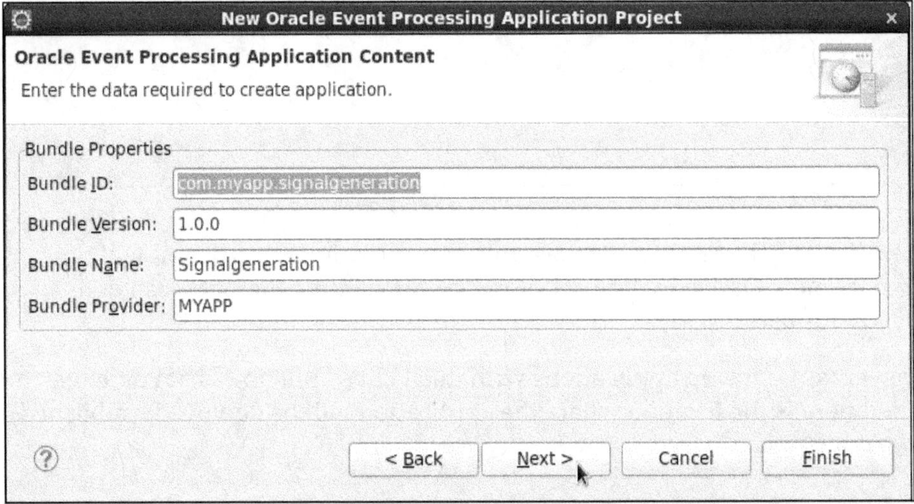

On the next panel of the wizard, you should select the **Create an Oracle Event Processing Application using an application template** checkbox. This will highlight the available sample applications that can be dynamically created. Here you will select the **Signal Generation** application and press the **Finish** button:

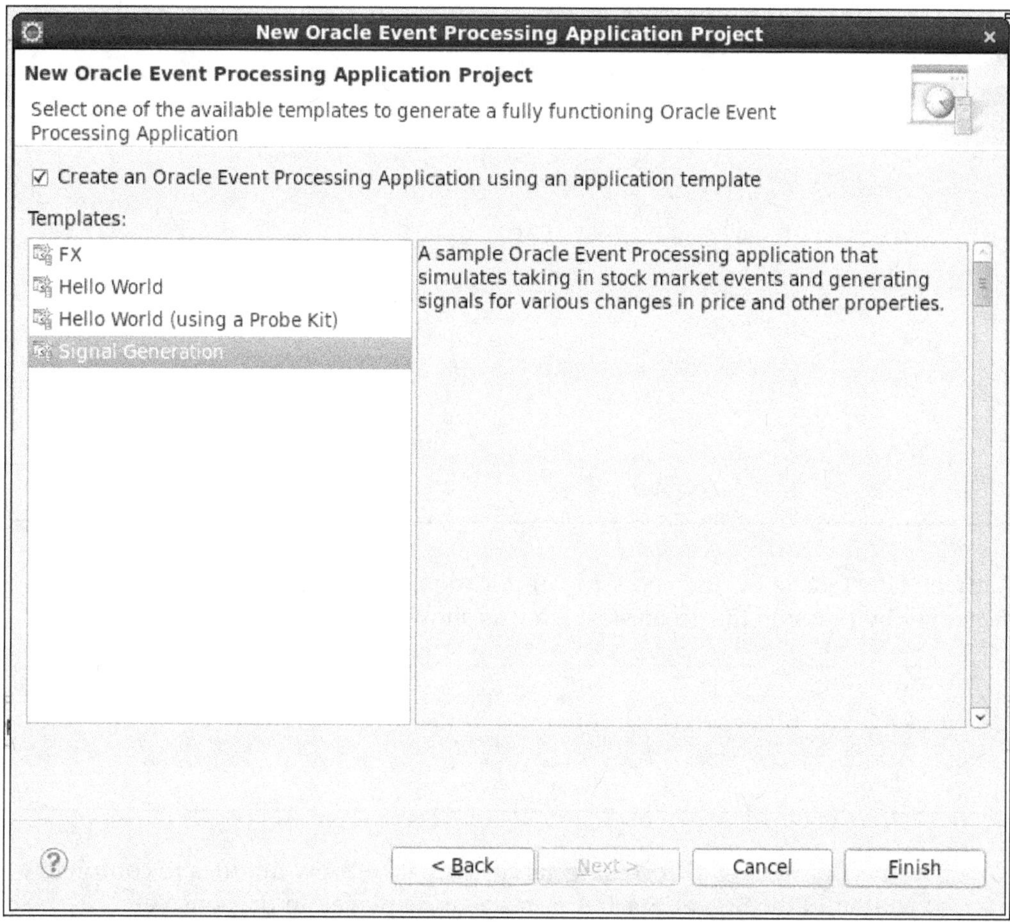

The Oracle Event Processing application creation wizard will now automatically create all of the project artifacts that are needed for this sample application, and visually represent the new application Event Processing Network (EPN).

Now let's execute this sample application:

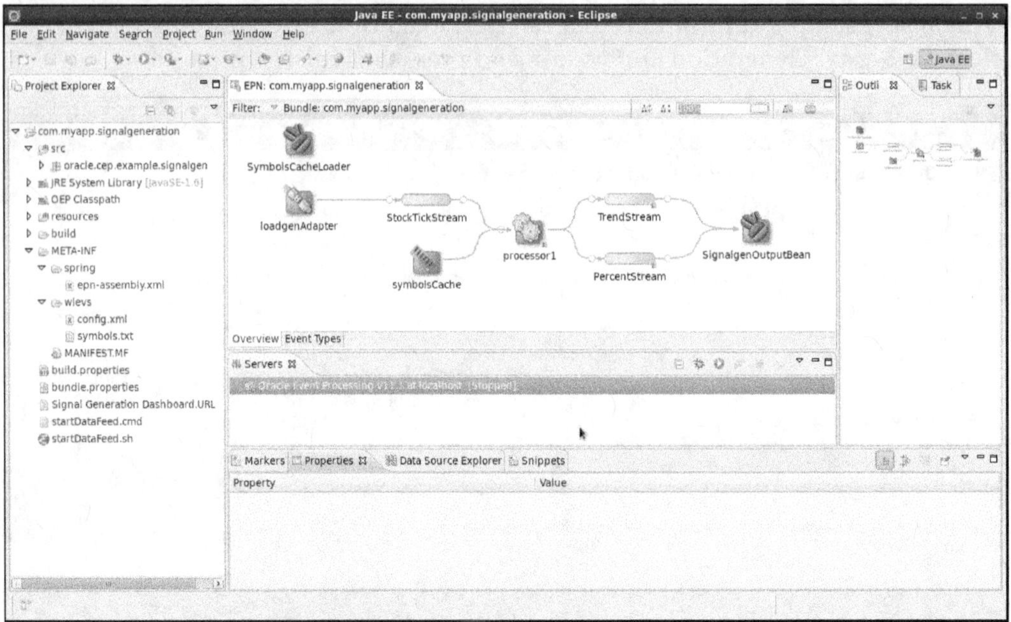

With the new Oracle Event Processing application created, the next step is to start the server by pressing the green start icon, as shown here:

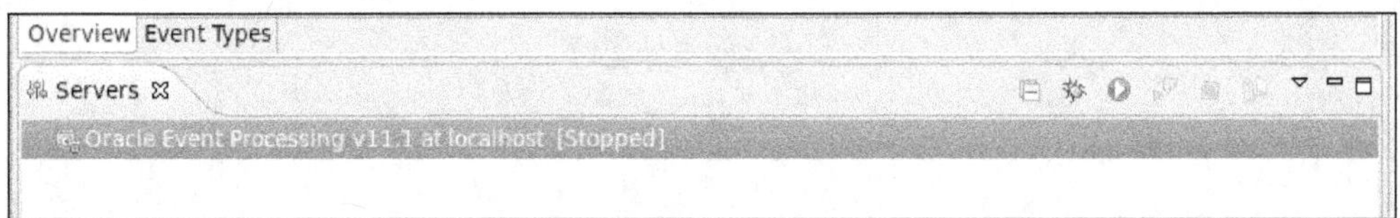

Note that the Oracle Event Processing server may take a few minutes to completely start, so wait until the **Server Started** message is displayed in the console.

At this point you can now publish (deploy) the Signal Generation sample application by right-clicking on **Oracle Event Processing v11.1 at localhost**, select the application and use the **Add and Remove** button to place onto the server:

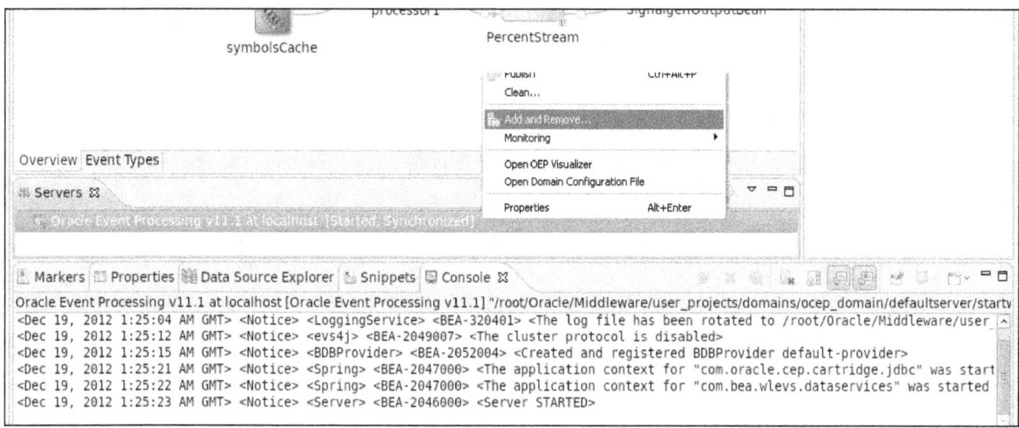

The configured selection box will show all of the selected Oracle Event Processing applications that will be published to the server, once the **Finish** button is pressed:

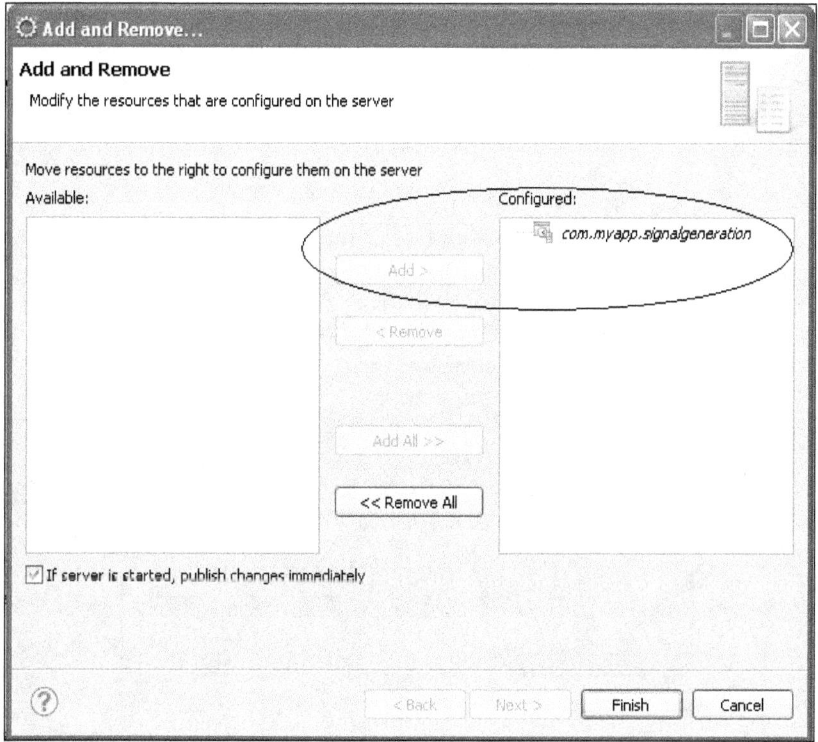

Now that the application is configured for publishing (deployment), press the **Finish** button to execute the application on the server.

After the application is successfully published to the Oracle Event Processing server, informational messages will instantly begin to appear in the console window indicating that the application is executing but as yet, does not have any stock symbol events to process, as shown in the following screenshot:

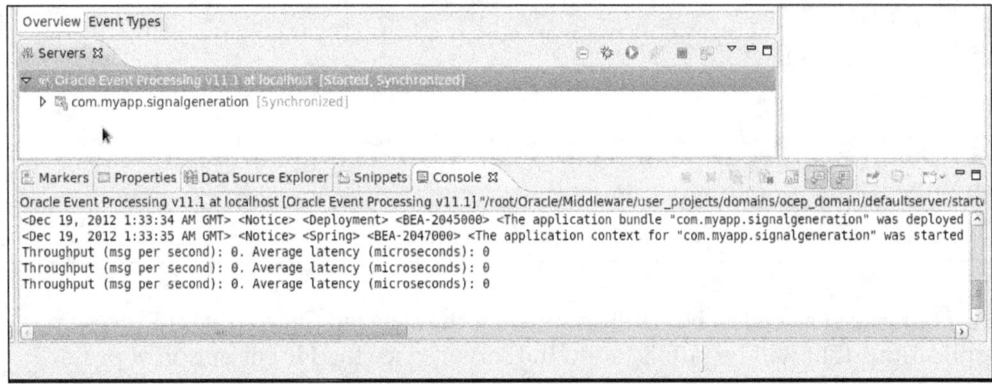

To make the execution of this sample easy to implement, during the application creation process some additional files where added to the project. The first is the `Signal Generation Dashboard URL` file, by double-clicking on this project element, a basic visual user interface will be initiated that will show the stock symbol event information:

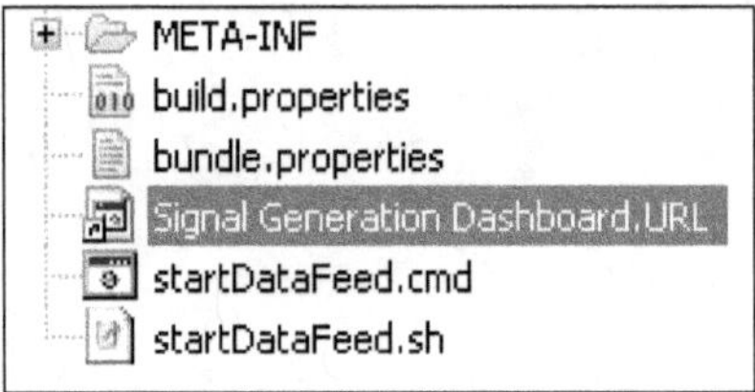

Press the **Start** button to prepare the user interface to receive the output from your Oracle Event Processing Network application:

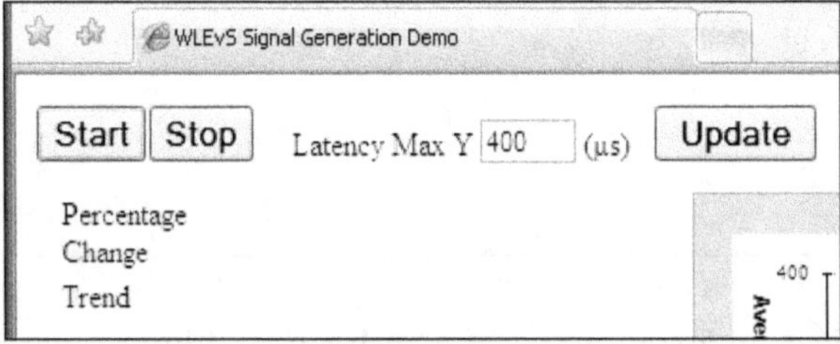

To start the simulation of stock symbol event data streaming to your adapter in the EPN, a file was added to your project called `startDataFeed`, depending on your operating system platform, double-click this project element to begin the activity:

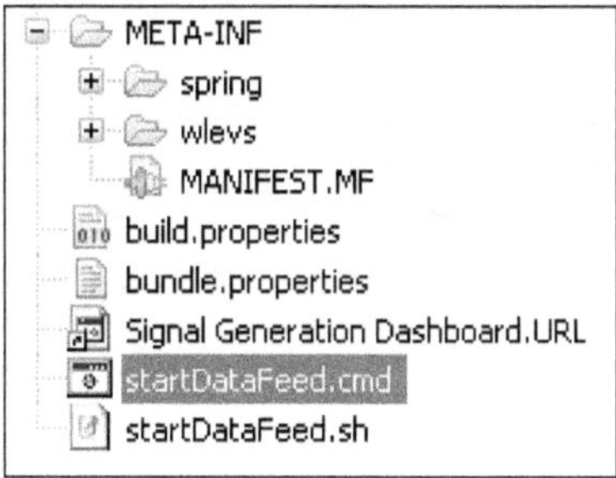

You may need to select the **Update** button to force a display refresh.

As the Oracle Event Processing application executes, you will see the results shown on the visual dashboard:

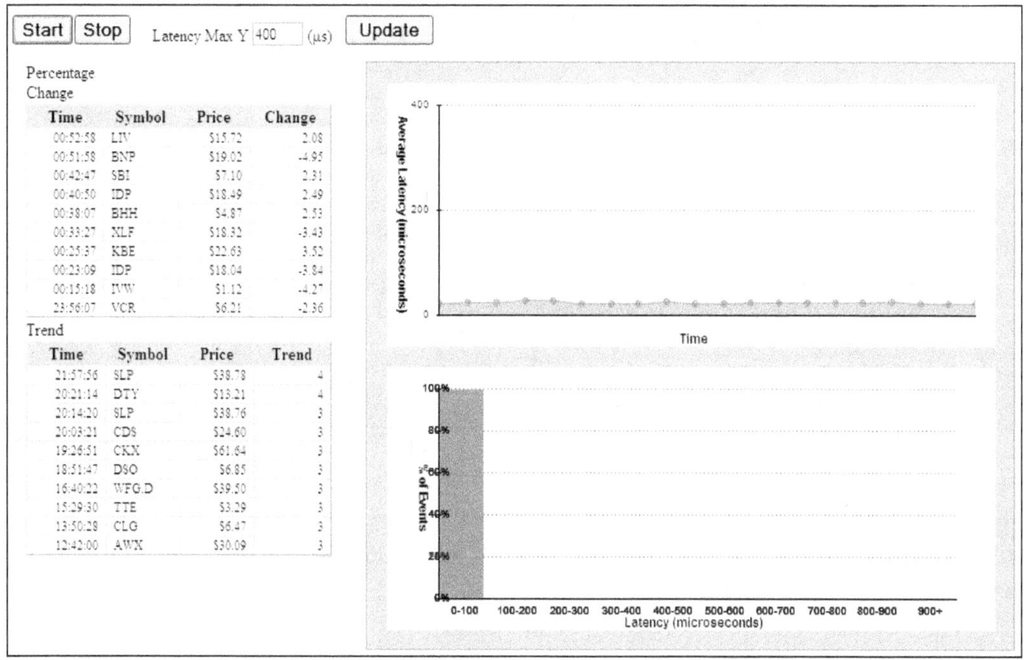

Congratulations, you have successfully entered the world of Oracle Event Processing application development!

Some hints and tips

As you will now start to use the development environment, it will be useful to remember a few developer-focused features that have been introduced over time to make applications easier to develop.

This is not an extensive list as the Eclipse environment also provided many features for rapid application development, but we do touch upon some key areas:

- Creation and manipulation of the EPN on the canvas
- Available keyword prompting
- Event type repository review and updating

The first concept is using the IDE to dynamically create EPN nodes using the right mouse click anywhere on the canvas window, and then selecting the event node from the available drop-down context window. Once the relevant event node appears, you can select its preceding event source node and then drag a line to connect to this new node by selecting and holding down the left mouse button. All of the Java and metadata code needed is automatically created for you:

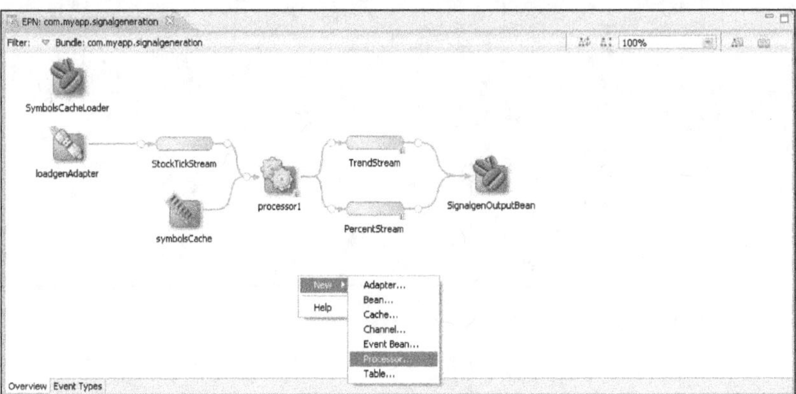

The next ease-of-use feature is to use the *Ctrl* + **Space bar** together both in generated assembly files and the CQL processor nodes. Where applicable, this request will invoke the currently available keywords in a drop-down selection box, as shown here:

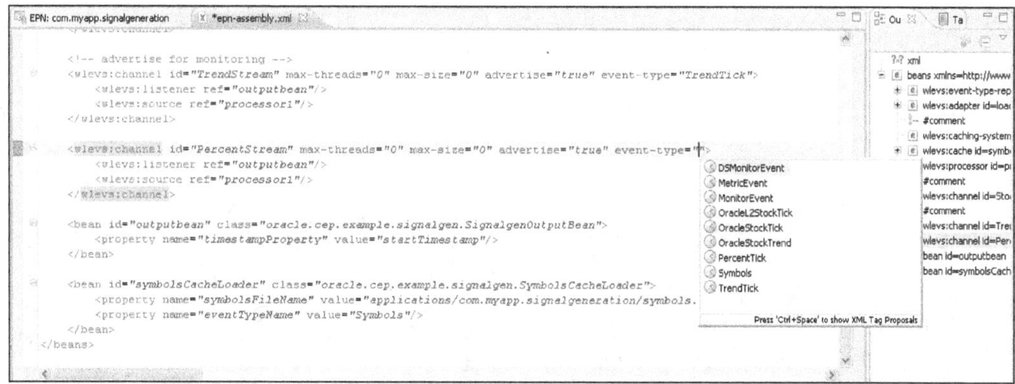

The final concept to be introduced is the visualization of the available event types for the application. By using the **Event Types** tab at the bottom of the EPN viewer window, a display window becomes available to not only review the event properties, but also to create and remove event types:

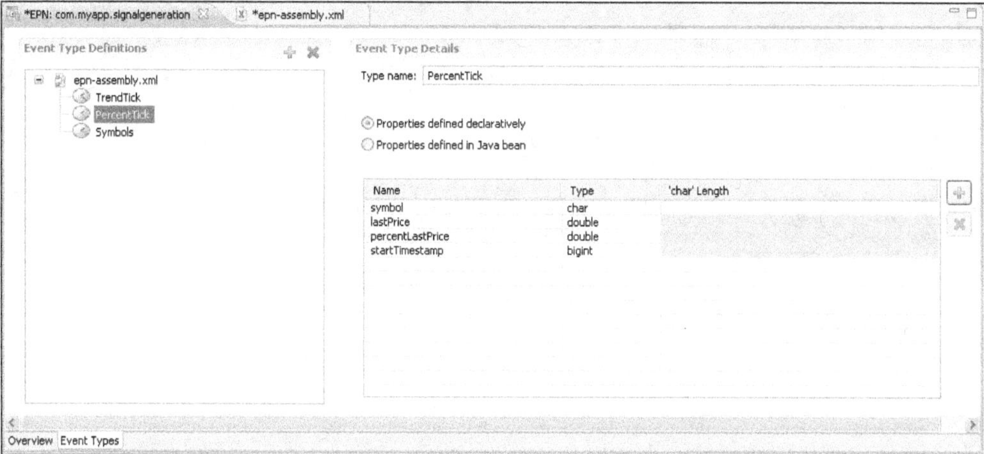

Controlling from the command line

Before we investigate the visual monitoring and management tooling capabilities of the Oracle Event Processing Platform, it is worth pausing here to also highlight some of the available interactions possible with the server from the command line. There are many situations when an IT department or developer would like to control the Oracle Event Processing server environment remotely or from within their own scripts.

As one would expect with a comprehensive event-driven Java platform, a wide and varied collection of commands are available.

Let's begin with the basics and use the Oracle command line to start and then stop the Oracle Event Processing Server:

In the lower panel of the preceding screenshot, the following command was executed:

```
startwlevs.cmd
```

This command initiated the Oracle Event Processing Server. Once this had successfully completed and the `<Server STARTED>` message was shown, the following command was executed:

```
java -jar wlevsadmin.jar -username wlevs -password wlevs SHUTDOWN
```

Using this command will gracefully shutdown the server.

Now we can be a little more adventurous and publish (deploy) and then remove (undeploy) the sample signal generation application that we created in the previous section; refer to the following screenshots:

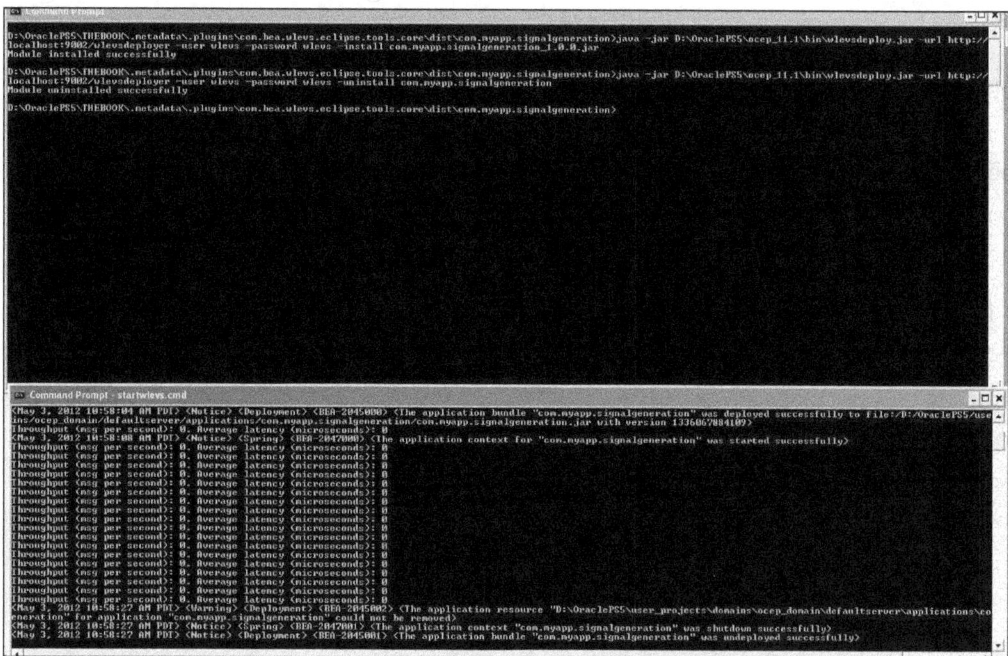

In the folder that has the created application bundle JAR file (in this case our new `signalgeneration` application), use the following command to publish it to the Oracle Event Processing Server:

```
java -jar D:\OraclePS5\ocep_11.1\bin\wlevsdeploy.jar -url http://
localhost:9002/wlevsdeployer -user wlevs -password wlevs -install com.
myapp.signalgeneration_1.0.0.jar
```

It should be noted that the `deployments.xml` file that resides in the `domain/defaultserver` folder contains the applications that are currently deployed for this server.

To remove this application from the Oracle Event Processing Server, use the following command:

```
java -jar D:\OraclePS5\ocep_11.1\bin\wlevsdeploy.jar -url http://
localhost:9002/wlevsdeployer -user wlevs -password wlevs -uninstall com.
myapp. signalgeneration
```

In this section, we have only touched on a few of the commands that are available with the Oracle Event Processing Platform, but the examples here will provide you with the basic understanding to initially evaluate the capabilities and then explore what else is possible.

Watching things happen and changing what happens

As Oracle Event Processing applications are published and executed on the server, it is important to be able to monitor and manage its deployment aspects. In the same way as an Admin Console is provided for traditional JEE Application Servers, a **Rich Internet Application** (**RIA**) is provided for Oracle Event Processing, called the **Visualizer**:

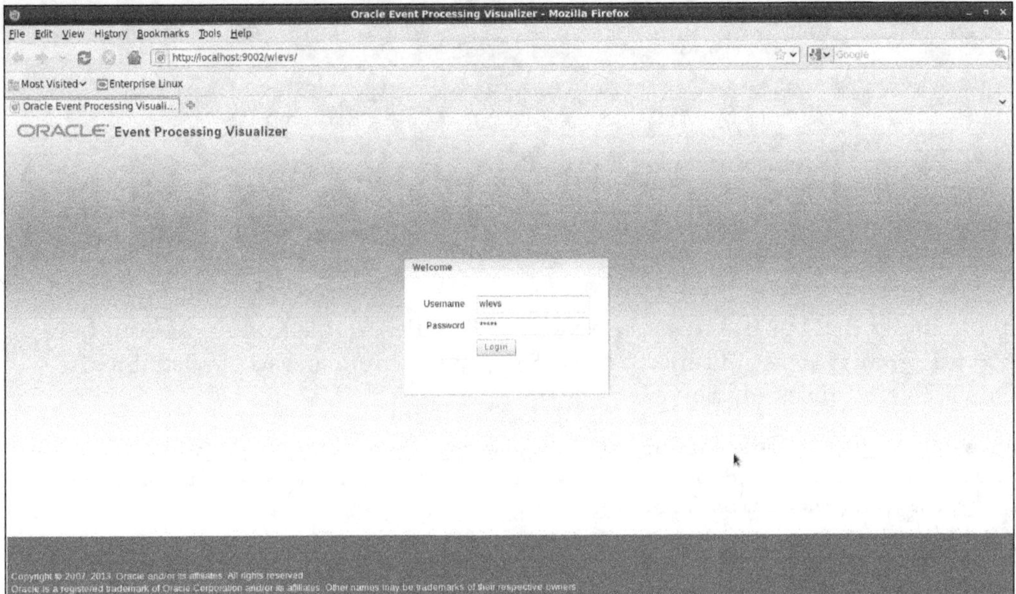

Using the URL indicated in the preceding screenshot, the browser user can use the Visualizer to effectively observe all of the major aspects of the executing Oracle Event Processing Server(s), configure, and manipulate that runtime environment.

The default user ID and password for the Visualizer are `wlevs` and `wlevs`.

The features and capabilities are significant. So in this section, we will focus on some of the typical uses of this tool with a typical usage pattern and leave you with enough details to explore in more depth using the available product documentation.

A good starting point when using the Visualizer is to review the actual published (deployed) Event Processing Network of the application currently executing on the Oracle Event Processing Server.

This is achieved, by expanding the visual nodes available on the left-hand side navigation tree and then under the **Applications** node selecting the application of interest. On the right-hand side of the Visualizer, you can select the **Event Processing Network** tab at the top of the window.

This representation of the EPN will mirror the visualization of the EPN that was created in the development environment; the difference is that what is shown in the Visualizer is the actual application deployed which can be manipulated during its execution:

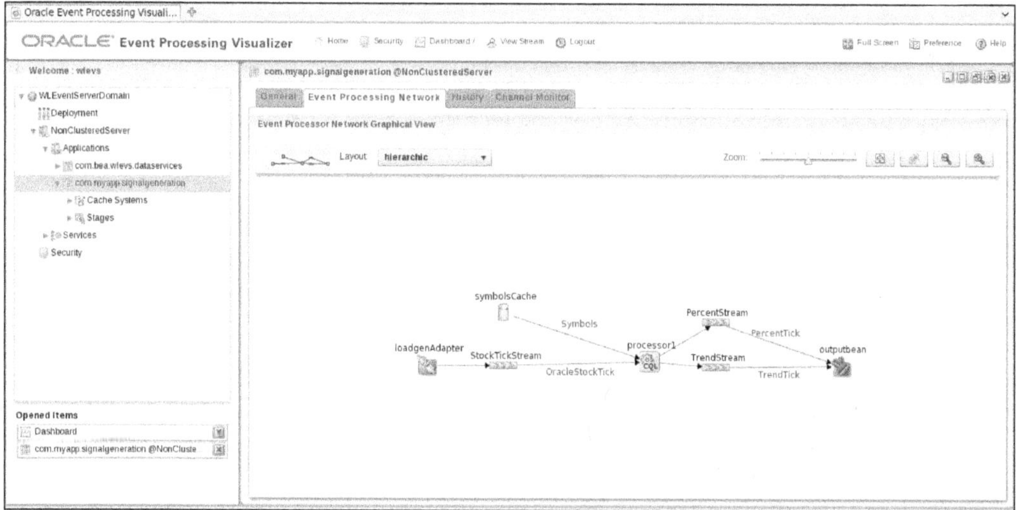

Now we can review an application executing, we can manipulate its processing dynamically using the Visualizer. For example, let's change the CQL query that is currently executing in the processor, by right-clicking on the processor node:

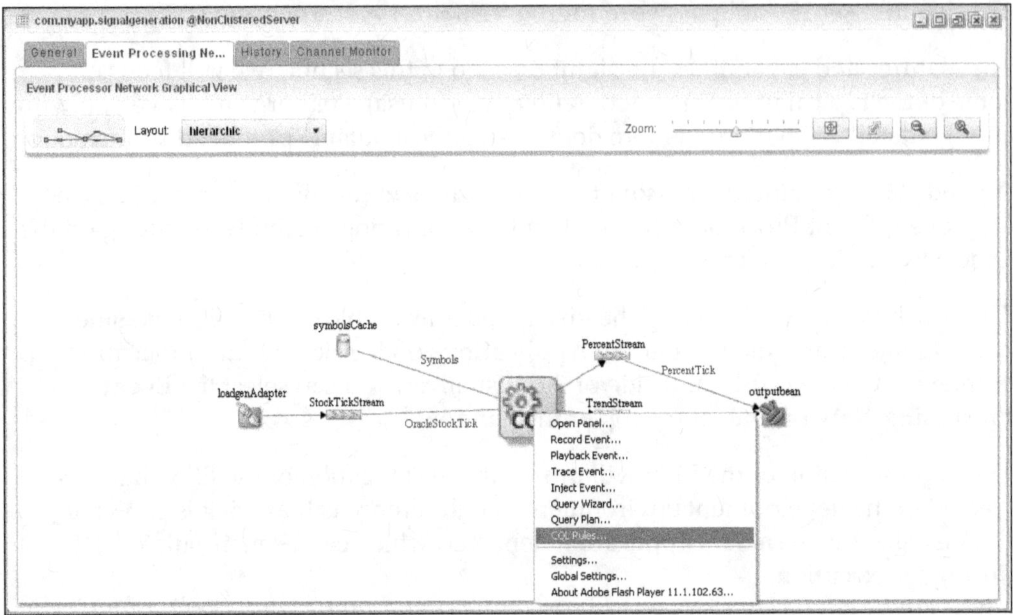

Select the **CQL Rules** option from the context menu and press *Enter*. In a tabular format, the Visualizer will show the existing CQL queries in that processor. To see a more visual representation of a query, select the query with a **Rule ID** of **percent**, and then press the **Query Wizard** button:

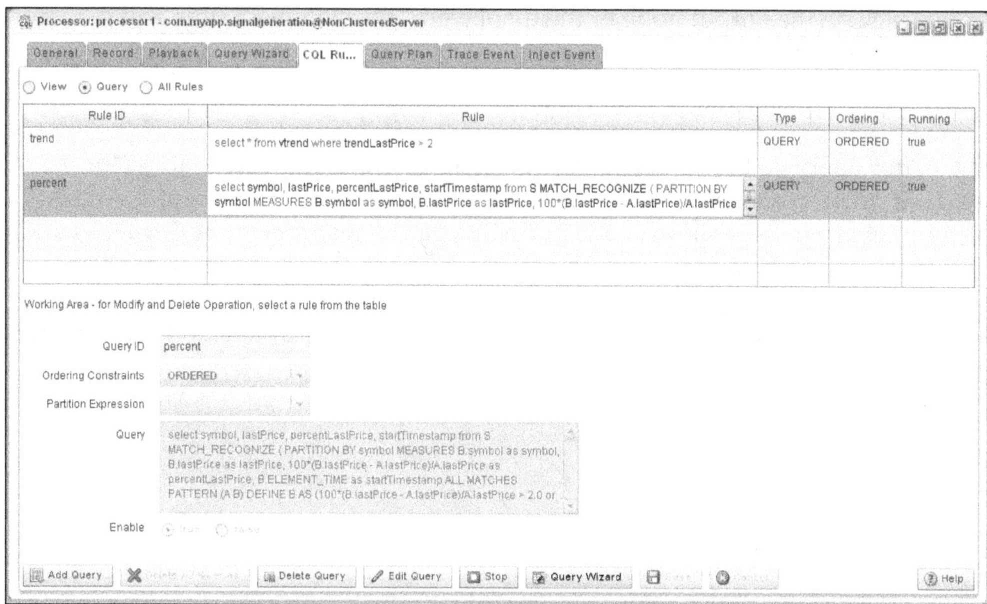

The **Query Wizard** tab can be used to visually manipulate and construct CQL that can be deployed to the processors found in an application. For now, we will use this capability to change some of the parameters of the already defined CQL which will dynamically change the real-time analysis and results provided by the application:

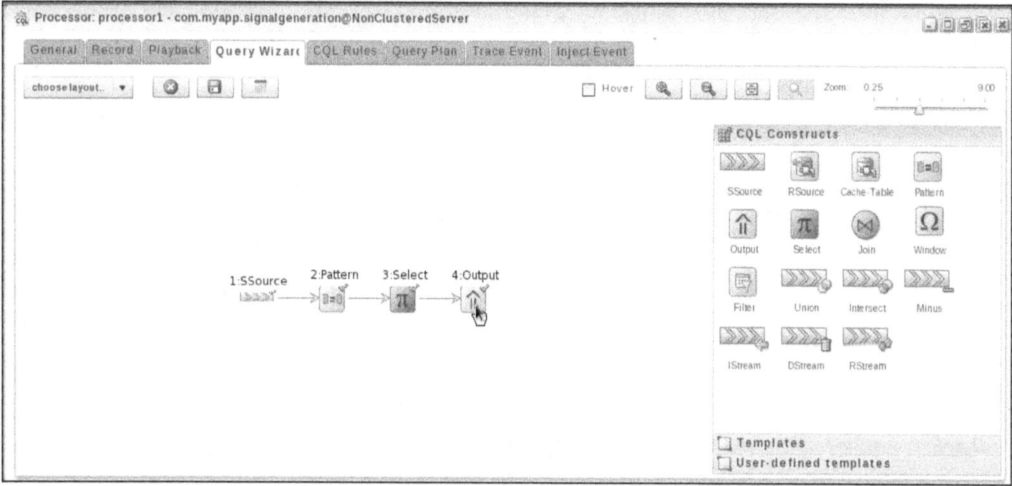

Double-click on the output node of the displayed CQL statement; this will display the generated and available query, which can now be modified as desired.

Change the parameters indicated. What are you doing?

Well, in this query you are changing the percentage change spread analysis for the displayed stock symbol event data shown on the user interface dashboard. At this point, our goal here is to show you how easily you can manipulate CQL queries and immediately inject them for execution in the processors. In our subsequent chapters, we will focus a lot of attention on the semantics and clauses of the Continuous Query Language, so you can learn in more detail how to build and understand these queries:

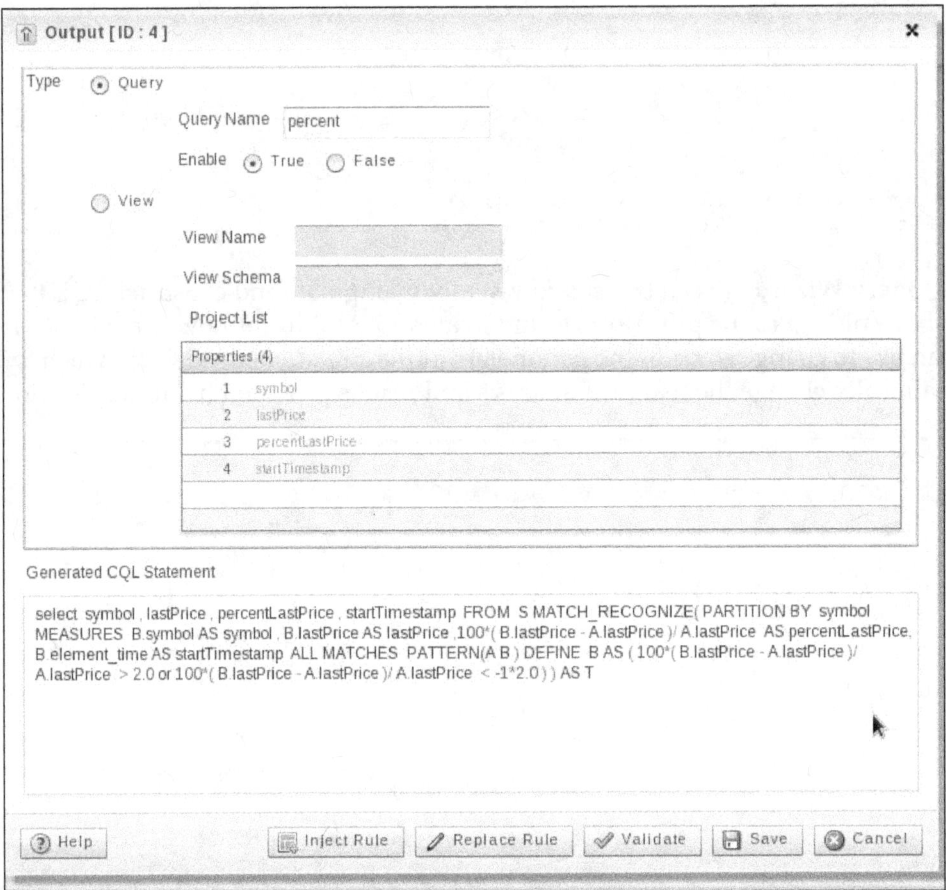

Once you have modified the values, in this case, change from `2` to `5`, in the two required locations, you should press the **Validate** button and, if the validation is successful, then press the **Replace Rule** button, to immediately influence the processor:

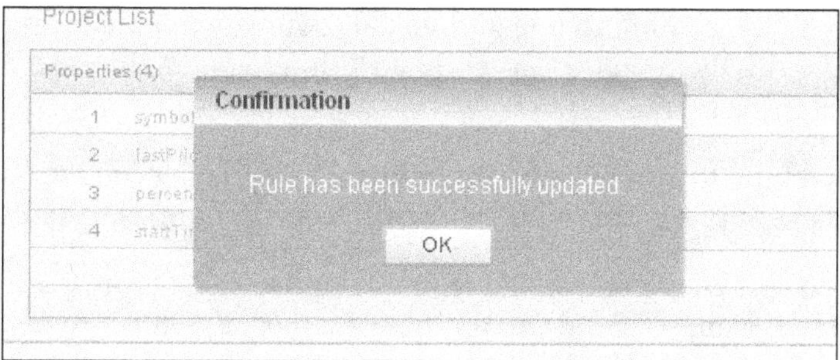

A message box will be displayed to indicate that the injection process has completed. The Visualizer, under the cover, uses the Oracle Event Processing JMX framework to implement this functionality and in fact, this can also be done programmatically as you learn more of the capabilities of this event-driven platform:

Percentage Change

Time	Symbol	Price	Change
10:36:34	FRG	$38.51	6.68
09:42:16	PPV.H	$18.23	-7.41
09:35:32	GIF	$22.22	-6.01
09:28:31	MRM	$10.85	-6.79
09:09:06	EML	$8.57	-5.20
08:07:57	QLD	$36.53	5.76
07:09:06	SND	$22.85	5.06
06:03:07	DTY	$30.86	-6.48
05:53:03	PEJ	$27.30	5.32
05:24:24	AMS	$21.89	-7.56

Finally, as you return to reviewing the provided Signal Generation Dashboard, you will observe that under the **Change** column on the left-hand side of the display, the stock symbols that have had a change spread greater or less than five percent are only shown. Importantly to note, is that your sample application continued to execute without the need to stop and restart.

Summary

We have described in this chapter the history behind the technology, the basic architecture of the Oracle Event Processing event-driven platform, and how you can leverage both the command line and visual tooling available to create application bundles and execute them on the server, in addition to managing and monitoring the environment of the server.

Also we learned how to dynamically manipulate a CQL query in the Visualizer and update an event processor, while the application continues to execute.

Over the subsequent chapters, we take you through a much more detailed review of the major artifacts, elements, and capabilities of Oracle Event Processing, focusing next on how to define and adapt the use of events in your event-driven applications.

3 Adapting Events for OEP

The first step in processing events is to set up adapters that receive and prepare the events for processing. Adapters are the event sources and event sinks at the beginning and the end of an application. This chapter explains how to use the out-of-the-box adapters (such as JMS, CSV, and HTTP pub-sub) and also how to create your own adapter for other protocols. We also demonstrate how you can enable re-use by packaging events and adapters in a separate bundle.

This chapter will cover the following topics:

- Creating and converting events
- Event type system
- Platform adapters
- Configuring your own custom adapter

Creating and converting events

One of the first tasks when writing an OEP application is to get the event data into our application. We classify any streaming input data that we would like to use in our application as an event. Each event will have a name and attributes with defined data types.

Event type system

Every OEP application needs a way to specify how the incoming data will be processed in a manner that the OEP container understands.

There are two main ways of accomplishing this:

- One way is to define all of the details regarding the specification of your events purely in XML within the application's spring assembly file. By using this method, you can define event types as either: a Java bean, `java.util.Map`, or tuple.
- The other way is to create a **Plain Old Java Object** (**POJO**) and map the class name to the name that you provide for the event. We will look at each of these ways in more detail.

The first main way to declare events is to explicitly define the event name, its properties, and data types in the spring assembly file of the application. You would define a `type-name` attribute for your event and then the properties, as shown in the following example:

```
<wlevs:event-type-repository>
    <wlevs:event-type type-name="ShipPos">
        <wlevs:properties type="tuple">
            <wlevs:property name="shipId" type="int" />
            <wlevs:property name="seq" type="int" />
            <wlevs:property name="latitude" type="double" />
            <wlevs:property name="longitude" type="double" />
            <wlevs:property name="info" type="char" length="256" />
        </wlevs:properties>
    </wlevs:event-type>
```

Using the OEP Java data cartridge, you can use Java class `event-type` definitions within Java bean event definitions, as shown here:

```
<event-type-repository>
    <event-type name="Customer">
        <property name="name" type="char"/>
        <property name="address" type="Address"/>
    </event-type>

    <event-type name="Address">
        <class-name>postal.Address</class-name>
    </event-type>
<event-type-repository>
```

The more common way to define an event is to provide a Java class that has the attributes that you would like to use. You need to generate the getter and setter methods for each attribute.

You can easily generate the getters and setters using a feature in Eclipse, which can be accessed from the **Source** menu with the **Generate Getters and Setters** option:

ShipPosEvent.java

```
package com.oracle.cep.event;

public class ShipPosEvent {

    private int shipId ;
    private int seq ;
    private double latitude ;
    private double longitude ;
    private String info ;

    public int getShipId() {
        return shipId;
    }
    public void setShipId(int shipId) {
        this.shipId = shipId;
    }
    public int getSeq() {
        return seq;
    }
    public void setSeq(int seq) {
        this.seq = seq;
    }
    public double getLatitude() {
        return latitude;
    }
    public void setLatitude(double latitude) {
        this.latitude = latitude;
    }
```

It is also a good idea to generate a `toString()` method with your POJO. This can be helpful in logging event output, especially during application development. Again, the Eclipse IDE has an option to generate this for you.

Once you've created your Java class, you simply reference it in the application's spring assembly file, as shown in the following code snippet:

```
<wlevs:event-type-repository>

    <wlevs:event-type type-name="ShipPosEvent">
        <wlevs:class>com.oracle.cep.event.ShipPosEvent</wlevs:class>
    </wlevs:event-type>
```

An important point to keep in mind is that event type names are global to the server, so you want to make sure that you don't duplicate event type names and or definitions with another application running on the same server. If this is a possibility for your environment or you are considering a large-scale deployment of OEP applications, it is recommended that you package events in their own bundle. This will be explained later in this chapter.

Platform adapters

The platform adapters are out-of-the-box adapters, which you can use to receive data and create events without having to write your own Java code. They provide you with technical implementations of specific protocols while still giving you the flexibility to convert data as you wish, if necessary.

The JMS adapter

One of the most common ways to receive and send events into your OEP application is to set up a JMS adapter. OEP does not have the JMS server capabilities, but it does have all of the WebLogic JMS client libraries readily available for use.

The JMS adapter will create events from JMS map messages when you specify the name of the event that you would like to create. It will look for names in the JMS map message that correspond exactly to attribute names in your event type and map the values accordingly. Likewise, in the case of an outbound JMS adapter, it will take the attributes for the event that you specify and create a JMS map message that has a set of names and values according to the attributes and values of the outgoing event.

When the incoming JMS message type is not a `Map` message, you can still use the JMS adapter, but you should use a converter to convert the incoming type to the desired event type using a few lines of your own Java code. For example, the incoming JMS message could be a text message in an XML format. You would supply a converter bean that had a few lines of code, which parsed the XML, and created the desired event. You return that list of events in the `convert` method of the inbound converter.

You simply define the converter bean in the spring assembly file and pass it as an attribute of the JMS adapter.

Here is an example of the configuration for an input JMS adapter that uses a converter bean to convert an XML message to an event. In the assembly file, specify the adapter configuration and the converter bean definition:

```
<wlevs:adapter id="GPSPositionsJMSInputAdapter" provider="jms-inbound">
    <wlevs:instance-property name="converterBean"
        ref="InboundJmsJaxbMessageConverter" />
    <wlevs:listener ref="ShipPosEventChannel" />
</wlevs:adapter>

<bean id="InboundJmsJaxbMessageConverter" class="com.oracle.cep.adapter.InboundJmsJaxbMessageConverter"/>
```

The converter bean will contain the code to convert the XML to your event type using the `convert` method:

```
public class InboundJmsJaxbMessageConverter implements InboundMessageConverter, InitializingBean {

    Log log_ = LogFactory.getLog(InboundJmsJaxbMessageConverter.class);
    private JAXBContext jaxbContext_;
    private Unmarshaller unmarshaller_;
    private Marshaller marshaller_;

    @SuppressWarnings("rawtypes")
    public List convert(Message message) throws MessageConverterException {

        if (log_.isDebugEnabled()){
            log_.info("convert(): RECEIVED MESSAGE!");
        }

        List result = null;
        if (message instanceof TextMessage) {
            result = handleMessage((TextMessage) message);
        } else {
            log_.warn("onMessage():skipping unexpected message type:" + message.toString());
            result = Collections.EMPTY_LIST;
        }
        return result;
    }
```

For the JMS adapter, we must supply the configuration that provides the details about the JMS server and the JNDI names of the queues or topics, the connection factory, and any usernames and passwords, if necessary.

In the `wlevs` folder under `META-INF`, we can add to an existing configuration file or supply a new configuration file specific to adapter configuration that contains the configuration of our input adapter. If you need a new configuration file to place in the `wlevs` folder, you can easily generate a template for one using the **New** option under the **File** menu. You will find an option to generate a configuration file under the **Oracle Event Processing** section:

```
AdapterConfig.xml
<?xml version="1.0" encoding="UTF-8"?>
<wlevs:config xmlns:wlevs="http://www.bea.com/ns/wlevs/config/application">

    <jms-adapter>
        <name>GPSPositionsJMSInputAdapter</name>
        <jndi-provider-url>t3://localhost:7001</jndi-provider-url>
        <connection-jndi-name>jms/SpatialDemoConnectionFactory</connection-jndi-name>
        <destination-jndi-name>jms/GPSPositionsInputQueue</destination-jndi-name>
        <user>weblogic</user>
        <password>welcome1</password>
        <work-manager>JettyWorkManager</work-manager>
    </jms-adapter>
```

In order to use the JMS adapters in our application, we must import the following additional packages in our manifest file:

```
com.bea.wlevs.adapters.jms;version="11.1.1.7_0",
com.bea.wlevs.adapters.jms.api;version="11.1.1.7_0",
```

The CSV adapter

The CSV adapter is a great, simple way to start creating and getting data into your OEP application. It allows you to create a simple comma-delimited file as the input to your application and have it processed in a predictable manner according to the timing settings that you specify. This is extremely helpful, since a lot of OEP applications are time-sensitive. The output of an application can often be highly dependent on the rate upon which the data is received.

The three important instance properties to specify when defining the CSV adapter are the `port`, `eventTypeName`, and `eventPropertyNames` properties. The CSV adapter is a type of socket adapter. When an OEP application starts with an adapter having the provider name `csvgen`, it will open a server socket connection on the specified port number. The adapter will attempt to create an event with the specified `eventTypeNames` property. The mapping between the data in the CSV file and the attributes of the event is determined by the order in which you specify the `eventPropertyNames` property for each of the attributes that you would like to populate from the file.

First, create a CSV file with the data you want to read. You can do this with a simple text editor. Then simply create a properties file that specifies, among other things, the name of the CSV file that you want read. Use one of the existing CSV properties files from the samples as an example.

Here is an example of a `csvgen` adapter configuration:

```
<wlevs:adapter id="ShipPositionGen" provider="csvgen">
    <wlevs:instance-property name="port" value="9022"/>
    <wlevs:instance-property name="eventTypeName" value="ShipPos"/>
    <wlevs:instance-property name="eventPropertyNames" value="shipId,seq,latitude,longitude"/>
    <wlevs:listener ref="ShipPosChannel"/>
</wlevs:adapter>
```

In this example, an adapter called `ShipPositionGen` will open a socket connection on port `9022` and will create events of type `ShipPos`, which must be defined in the event type repository. It will map the first data element in the file to the `shipID` attribute, the second to `seq`, and the third and fourth to `latitude` and `longitude` respectively.

Make sure that the attributes defined in the `eventPropertyNames` property are in the same order as the data that you provide in your CSV file.

Here's an example of the CSV file for the preceding adapter configuration:

ship_positions.csv

```
1,1,47.564797356181465,-52.701759338378906
2,1,45.4578,-50.1234
3,1,44.4578,-50.1234
4,1,43.4578,-50.8878
5,1,40.4578,-45.8878
1,2,47.565376500673430,-51.673091888427734
5,1,40.1578,-45.1878
1,3,46.55182284141726,-50.6380729675293
1,4,45.54857871070855,-49.60923385620117
1,5,44.123456,-48.123456
1,6,43.123456,-47.123456
1,7,42.123456,-46.923456
1,8,42.123456,-46.123456
1,9,42.123456,-44.823456
1,10.42.123456,-44.123456
1,11,42.123456,-43.823456
1,12,42.123456,-42.823456
```

The `loadgen` utility will read from the CSV file and try to connect to the TCP/IP socket by using the port number, which is provided as a property of the properties file that is passed to the `loadgen` utility as an argument. In addition to the name of the CSV file and the port number, there are some other useful properties to set.

Here is an example of a properties file for the `csvgen` adapter:

ship_positions.prop

```
# name of file containing your test data
test.csvDataFile=ship_positions.csv
# port the server will listen on for client connection
test.port=9022
# server host (localhost if not specified)
#test.host=
# do not change the packetType
test.packetType=CSV
test.loopBack=false
test.secs=90
test.rate=1

#test.mode=client
#test.senders=1
#test.latencyStats=false
#test.statInterval=2000

```

Notice, in the preceding example, that you can set how long the load generator should run (`test.secs`) and the rate at which it should send messages in seconds (`test.rate`). It's also possible to run the load generator for an OEP instance that is running on another server, simply set the host property (`test.host`) to the host that is running OEP.

A CSV adapter can be useful for getting started before connections to the actual data source are available. It is also helpful for testing various speeds by configuring the `loadgen` properties file accordingly.

The `loadgen` utility is the driver for the CSV adapter. The `loadgen` utility can be found in `\ocep11.1\utils\load-generator`.

HTTP pub-sub adapter

OEP includes a pub-sub server that programmers can use to implement HTTP publish-subscribe functionality in their applications.

The HTTP pub-sub adapter is an adapter that is designed to allow you to take advantage of the pub-sub capabilities provided by the OEP server, which leverage the Bayeux protocol from the cometd project. This is an HTTP protocol that maintains an open HTTP connection. This is much more efficient than plain HTTP since the connection is not continually opened and closed between messages. This is not to be confused with implementing REST. This is a protocol designed to help you build dynamic web pages.

By default, the HTTP pub-sub adapter will communicate by using **Java Script Object Notation (JSON)**. It works in a manner similar to the JMS adapter described earlier, in the sense that it will automatically map JSON to the event attributes (in the case of an inbound adapter) or automatically generate JSON according to the attribute names of the event you are sending (outbound).

The OEP Visualizer has some useful tools for helping you both send HTTP pub-sub messages to be received by your configured inbound HTTP pub-sub adapter and to view the events that are generated by your outbound adapter.

Here is an example of an adapter within an OEP application that is used to subscribe to a HTTP pub-sub channel:

```
<wlevs:adapter id="GPSPositionsHTTPSubAdapter" provider="httpsub">
    <wlevs:listener ref="ShipPosEventChannel" />
</wlevs:adapter>
```

Notice that the `provider` attribute is set to `httpsub`, because this will be an adapter that subscribes to a server to receive events into our OEP application.

The possible configuration for this adapter looks as follows:

```
<http-pub-sub-adapter>
    <name>GPSPositionsHTTPSubAdapter</name>
    <server-url>http://localhost:9002/pubsub</server-url>
    <channel>/ship/shippos</channel>
    <event-type>ShipPosEvent</event-type>
</http-pub-sub-adapter>
```

This configuration shows a server URL, which references the local host, but it could refer to an external server that implements the Bayeux protocol. In this case, you could also simply use `/pubsub` since the server is the local OEP server.

To test sending events into our application, we can use the **View Stream** feature of the OEP Visualizer. Remember to first initialize the client, select the channel to which you would like to publish the event, insert the JSON string (with attributes that correspond to the event you are creating) into the box provided, and click on the **Publish** button to publish the event:

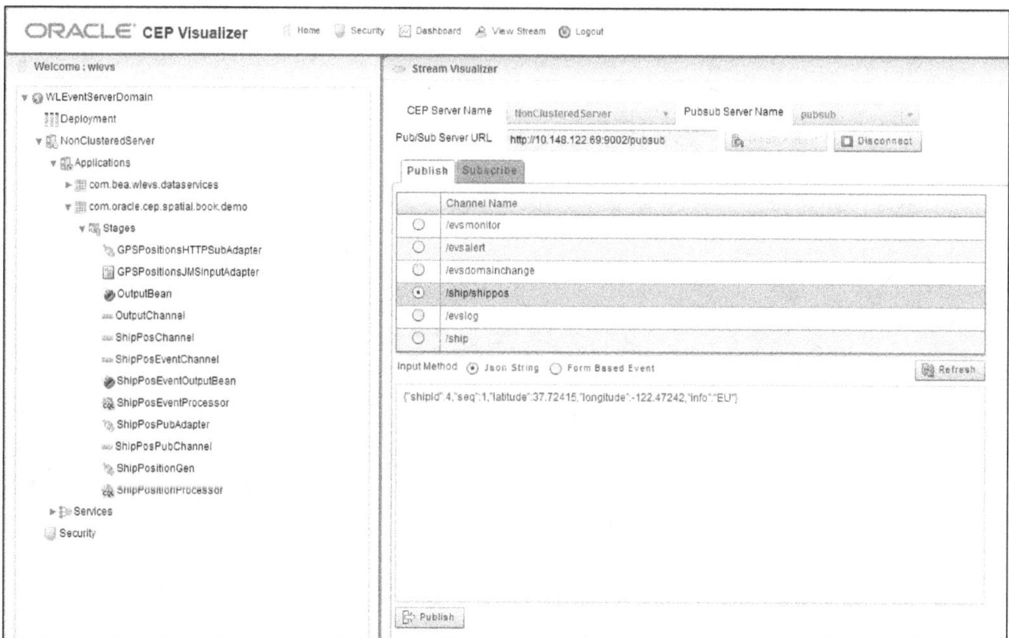

More commonly, you would use the HTTP pub-sub adapter to publish messages to a web-based client in the latter part of your event processing network as an event sink.

Let's look at how to create this adapter by using the Eclipse IDE tools. From within the **EPN Editor** screen, right-click and select **New**, then **Adapter**. A wizard will appear, which allows you to name the adapter and fill in the configuration details, as shown in the following screenshot:

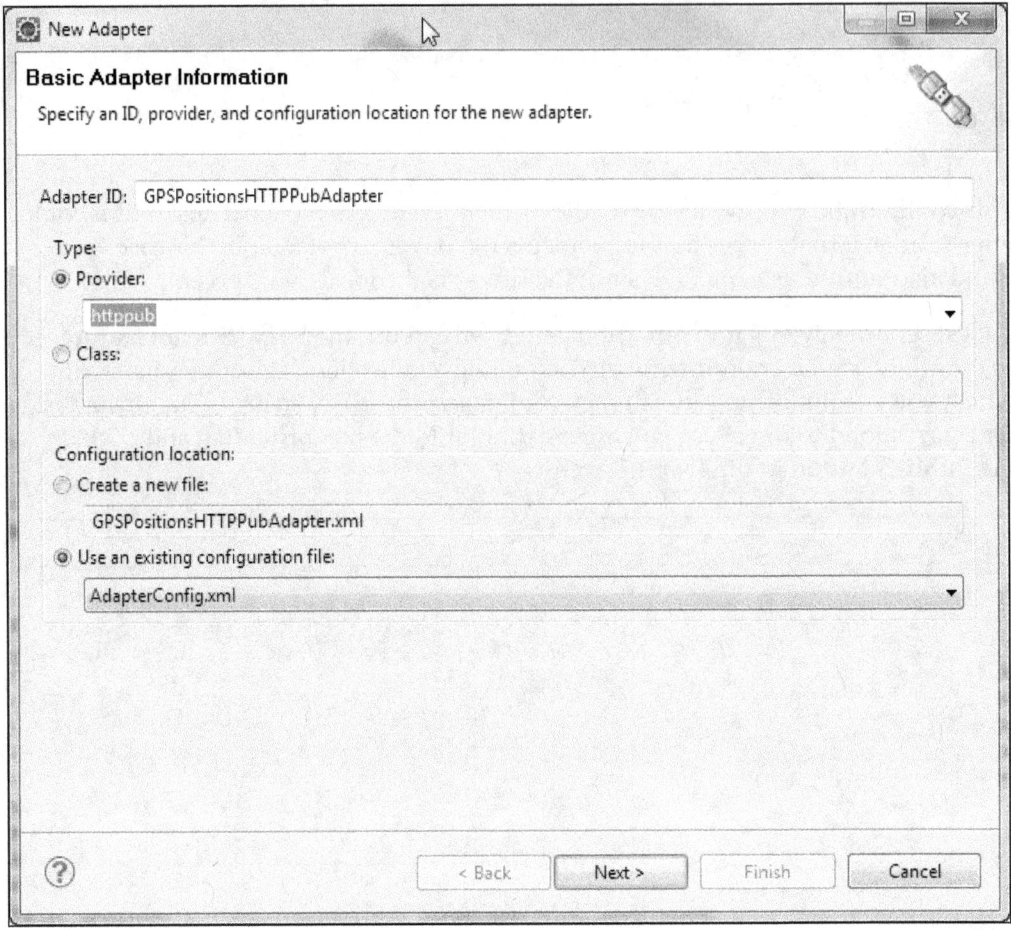

Select **httppub** as the provider and choose to create a new configuration file specific to this adapter or include it in an existing configuration file, perhaps one that contains all of your other adapter configurations. Click on the **Next** button to fill in the specific configuration information for the new adapter:

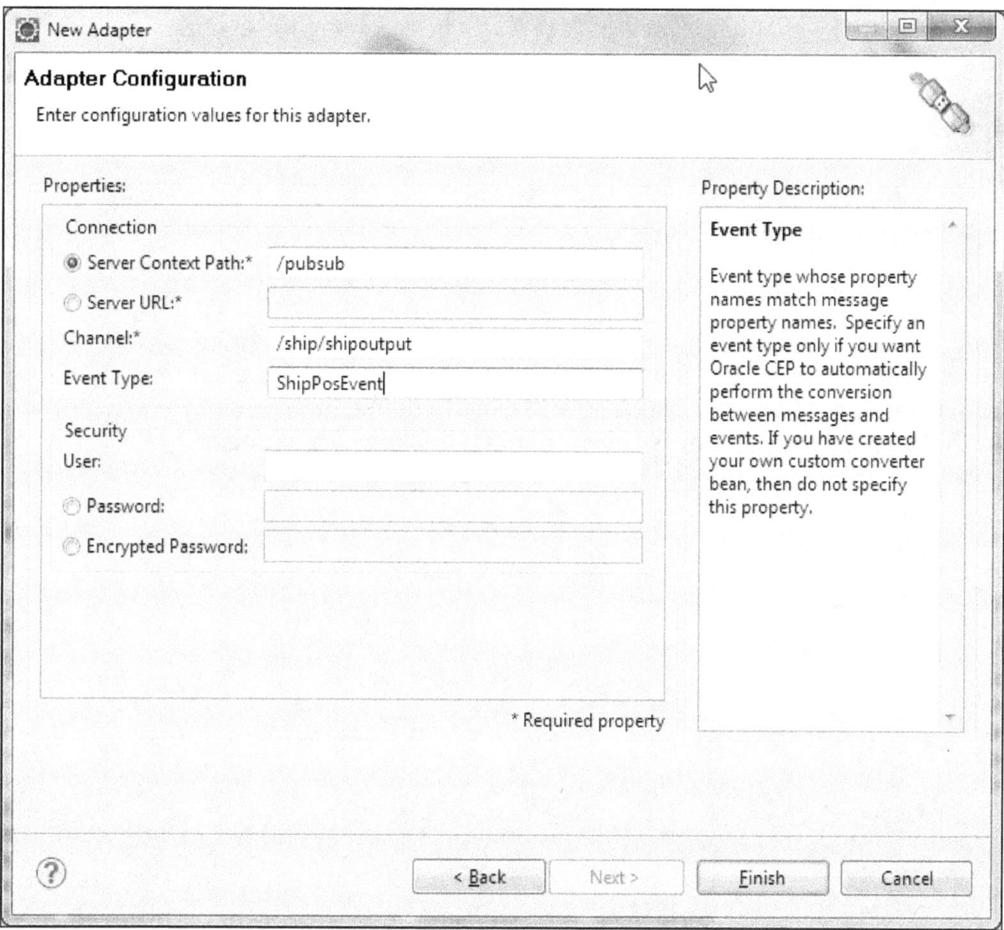

This time we will publish the events to the local pub-sub server implementation that is included with OEP. Use `/pubsub` to reference the local server's context path. Also, enter the name of the HTTP pub-sub channel and the type of event you are publishing. When you are ready with the configuration, click on the **Finish** button and the configuration XML will be generated for you. Be sure to connect the adapter in the EPN to the channel from which you will be receiving the events:

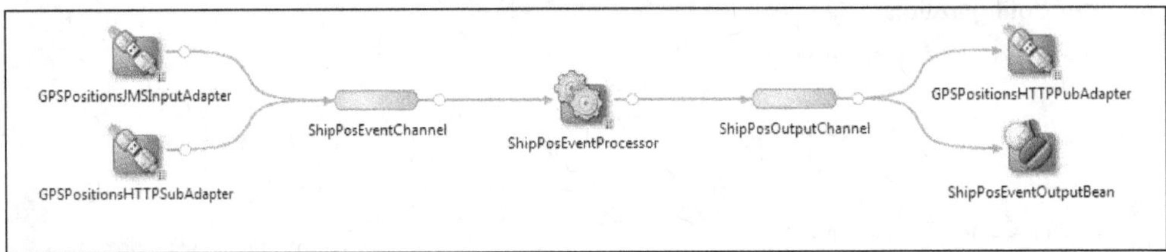

Make sure that you have the necessary pub-sub channels configured in the server's `config.xml` configuration file (that is, the configuration file for the domain, not the application's configuration file). You will need to define the channel pattern within the `<http-pubsub>` section, as shown in the following code snippet:

```
<http-pubsub>
  <name>pubsub</name>
  <path>/pubsub</path>
  <pub-sub-bean>
    <server-config>
      <supported-transport>
        <types>
          <element>long-polling</element>
        </types>
      </supported-transport>
      <publish-without-connect-allowed>true</publish-without-connect-allowed>
    </server-config>
    <channels>
      <element>
        <channel-pattern>/evsmonitor</channel-pattern>
      </element>
      <element>
        <channel-pattern>/evsalert</channel-pattern>
      </element>
      <element>
        <channel-pattern>/evsdomainchange</channel-pattern>
      </element>
      <element>
        <channel-pattern>/ship/shippos</channel-pattern>
      </element>
      <element>
        <channel-pattern>/ship/shipoutput</channel-pattern>
      </element>
    </channels>
  </pub-sub-bean>
</http-pubsub>
```

You can use the OEP Visualizer to see the output of the pub-sub adapter.

From the **View Stream** section, initialize the client, choose the channel that you are interested in, and click on the **Subscribe** button. After you've published the events, you should see the results:

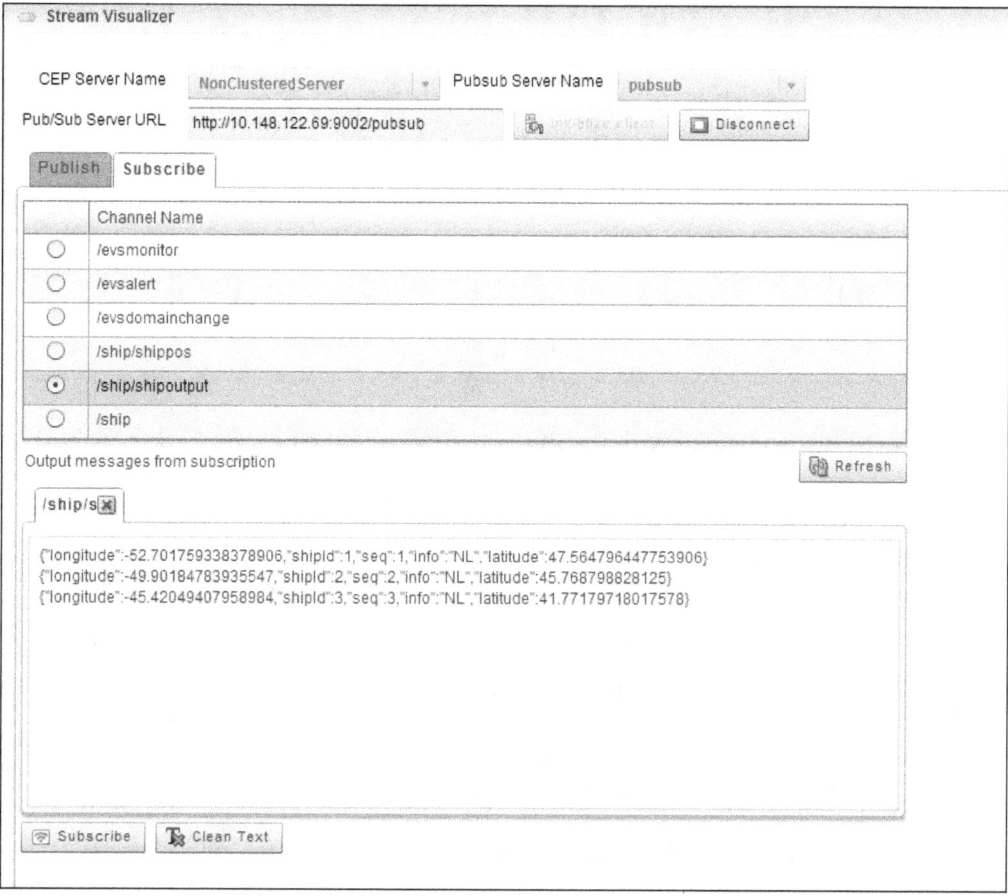

This will not affect your other clients from getting the results. Any other client subscribing to the same HTTP pub sub channel will receive the same events.

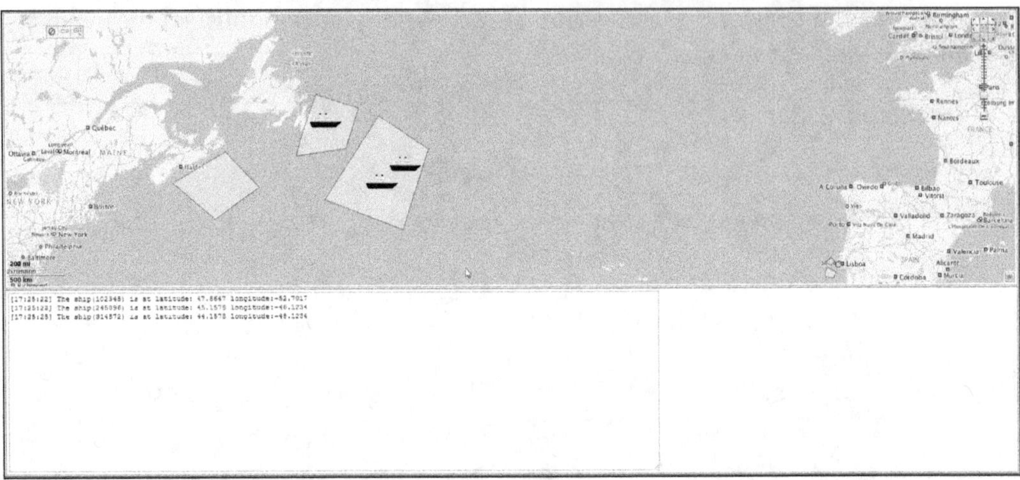

To implement this web page with the map (as shown in the preceding screenshot), we used the **Oracle MapViewer**. We will cover the Oracle Spatial capabilities integrated with OEP in more detail in a later chapter.

Remember, if you stop your OEP server, you may need to reconnect the subscribed clients. This can be done by simply refreshing the page in the browser.

Configuring your own custom adapter

OEP allows you to easily add your own custom adapter code. You shouldn't be afraid of the idea of creating your own adapter. It can be as simple as creating a single Java class. An adapter has optional APIs provided for life cycle notifications, allocating an execute thread, injecting service references, and receiving events.

Before creating your own adapter, you should review the OEP adapter APIs.

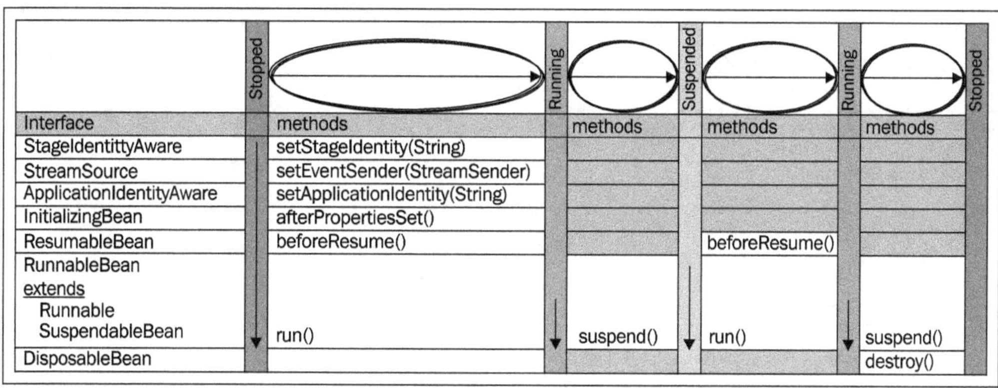

Interface	Role
`StageIdentityAware`	Provides a reference to the name of this node.
`StreamSource`	Allows you to get a reference to the downstream listeners.
`ApplicationIdentityAware`	Provides a reference to the name of the application.
`InitializingBean`	Provides you with access to the adapter after the properties have been set, so that you can do your own initialization.
`ResumableBean`	Provides you with an opportunity to perform the tasks that should be done to allow the adapter to start functioning again after it has been suspended.
`RunnableBean`	Provides you with a thread to execute the main processing logic of your adapter.
`DisposableBean`	Provides you with an opportunity to do any necessary cleanup or closing of connections before the adapter is shut down.

The sample `HelloWorld` application contains an example of a custom OEP adapter. It is an adapter that is generating its own event data. While it is more common to receive data from an outside source, it shows you how easily you can create an adapter of your own with a few lines of Java code:

```
package com.bea.wlevs.adapter.example.helloworld;

import java.text.DateFormat;

public class HelloWorldAdapter implements RunnableBean, StreamSource {

    private static final int SLEEP_MILLIS = 300;

    private DateFormat dateFormat;
    private String message;
    private boolean suspended;

    private StreamSender eventSender;

    public HelloWorldAdapter() {
        super();
        dateFormat = DateFormat.getTimeInstance();
    }

    /* (non-Javadoc)
     * @see java.lang.Runnable#run()
     */
    public void run() {
        suspended = false;
        while (!isSuspended()) { // Generate messages forever...

            generateHelloMessage();

            try {
                synchronized (this) {
                    wait(SLEEP_MILLIS);
                }
            } catch (InterruptedException e) {
                e.printStackTrace();
            }
        }
    }
```

As you can see in the preceding code snippet, `HelloWorldAdapter` implements `RunnableBean` and `StreamSource` from the `com.bea.wlevs.ede.api` package. `StreamSource` allows you to send events downstream by calling the `sendInsertEvent` method. `RunnableBean` is where you will implement the code to receive the events. In this case, the adapter is generating its own events for simplicity. Also notice that you must implement a `suspend` method when using `RunnableBean`. Here is where you will provide the logic to help suspend the receiving of events in order to temporarily stop your adapter when the user makes a request to suspend it (for example, via the OEP Visualizer):

```
    public void setMessage(String message) {
        this.message = message;
    }

    private void generateHelloMessage() {
        String message = this.message + dateFormat.format(new Date());
        HelloWorldEvent event = new HelloWorldEvent();
        event.setMessage(message);
        eventSender.sendInsertEvent(event);
    }

    /* (non-Javadoc)
     * @see com.bea.wlevs.ede.api.StreamSource#setEventSender(com.bea.wlevs.ede.api.StreamSender)
     */
    public void setEventSender(StreamSender sender) {
        eventSender = sender;
    }

    /*
    /* (non-Javadoc)
     * @see com.bea.wlevs.ede.api.SuspendableBean#suspend()
     */
    public synchronized void suspend() {
        suspended = true;
    }

    private synchronized boolean isSuspended() {
        return suspended;
    }
}
```

The `setEventSender` method is the mechanism used to connect the adapters to downstream listeners.

Leveraging OSGi services to create an adapter

Since OEP is an OSGi-based platform, a useful thing to do is to inject OSGi service references into your adapter. A common reason to do this is to implement a simple HTTP adapter.

To do this, we add `org.osgi.service.http` to the list of imports in the application's manifest file (`MANIFEST.MF`). You will also need `javax.servlet` and `javax.servlet.http`. By using annotations, set the reference to the OSGi HTTPService, as shown in the following code snippet:

```
public class ClearAdapter extends HttpServlet implements StreamSource {

    private static final long serialVersionUID = -6615297520746961297L;

    private StreamSender eventSender;

    private String contextString;

    public void setContextString(String contextString) {
        this.contextString = contextString;
    }

    public void setEventSender(StreamSender sender) {
        this.eventSender = sender;
    }

    @Service(serviceType = HttpService.class)
    public void setHttpService(HttpService httpService) {
        try {
            httpService.registerServlet(contextString, this, null, null);
        } catch (ServletException e) {
            System.out.println("ERROR: Could not register servlet: "
                    + e.getMessage());
            e.printStackTrace();
        } catch (NamespaceException e) {
            System.out.println("ERROR: Could not register servlet: "
                    + e.getMessage());
            e.printStackTrace();
        }
    }


    public void doGet(HttpServletRequest request, HttpServletResponse response)
    throws IOException {
        doAny(request, response);
```

Define your adapter by using the `class` attribute. Perhaps you will like to set the HTTP context string here as well:

```
<wlevs:adapter id="HTTPAdapter" class="com.oracle.cep.cache.ClearAdapter">
    <wlevs:instance-property name="contextString" value="/clear" />
    <wlevs:listener ref="ClearChannel" />
</wlevs:adapter>
```

Packaging custom adapters

In some cases, it may be useful to package adapters separately so that they can easily be re-used across multiple applications on the same server or across multiple OEP servers.

Let's take a look at the `HelloWorld` application and see how we can repackage it so that the adapter and the associated events are in a separate bundle. Then we will modify the application so that it uses the separately packaged adapter and event types.

First, we'll create a new OEP application project. Let's call it `com.oracle.cep.helloworld.adapter`.

Create a package called `com.oracle.cep.helloworld.event` and move `HelloWorldEvent` from the sample. Let's put our adapter code in a package called `com.oracle.cep.helloworld.adapter` and move the code from the `HelloWorld` example. Fix the package references as appropriate.

Now make `HelloWorldAdapter` implement the `Adapter` interface `com.bea.wlevs.ede.api.Adapter`:

```
package com.oracle.cep.helloworld.adapter;

import java.text.DateFormat;
import java.util.Date;

import com.bea.wlevs.ede.api.Adapter;
import com.bea.wlevs.ede.api.RunnableBean;
import com.bea.wlevs.ede.api.StreamSender;
import com.bea.wlevs.ede.api.StreamSource;
import com.oracle.cep.helloworld.event.HelloWorldEvent;

public class HelloWorldAdapter implements Adapter, RunnableBean, StreamSource {

    private static final int SLEEP_MILLIS = 300;

    private DateFormat dateFormat;
    private String message;
    private boolean suspended;

    private StreamSender eventSender;

    public HelloWorldAdapter() {
        super();
        dateFormat = DateFormat.getTimeInstance();
    }
```

To use the adapter in a separate bundle, we need to create an adapter factory. In the adapter package, create a new class called `HelloWorldAdapterFactory`. It should implement the `com.bea.wlevs.ede.api.AdapterFactory` interface. You'll need to implement the `create` method to return an instance of `HelloWorldAdapter`:

```
package com.oracle.cep.helloworld.adapter;

import com.bea.wlevs.ede.api.Adapter;
import com.bea.wlevs.ede.api.AdapterFactory;

public class HelloWorldAdapterFactory implements AdapterFactory {

    @Override
    public Adapter create() throws IllegalArgumentException {

        return new HelloWorldAdapter();
    }

}
```

In the spring context file for this bundle, we need to define the event type and the adapter:

```
com.oracle.cep.helloworld.adapter.context.xml
<?xml version="1.0" encoding="UTF-8"?>
<beans xmlns="http://www.springframework.org/schema/beans"
       xmlns:xsi="http://www.w3.org/2001/XMLSchema-instance"
       xmlns:osgi="http://www.springframework.org/schema/osgi"
       xmlns:wlevs="http://www.bea.com/ns/wlevs/spring"
       xsi:schemaLocation="
  http://www.springframework.org/schema/beans
  http://www.springframework.org/schema/beans/spring-beans.xsd
  http://www.springframework.org/schema/osgi
  http://www.springframework.org/schema/osgi/spring-osgi.xsd
  http://www.bea.com/ns/wlevs/spring
  http://www.bea.com/ns/wlevs/spring/spring-wlevs-v11_1_1_7.xsd">


    <wlevs:event-type-repository>
        <wlevs:event-type type-name="HelloWorldEvent">
            <wlevs:class>com.oracle.cep.helloworld.event.HelloWorldEvent</wlevs:class>
        </wlevs:event-type>
    </wlevs:event-type-repository>


    <osgi:service interface="com.bea.wlevs.ede.api.AdapterFactory">
        <osgi:service-properties>
            <entry key="type" value="myHelloAdapter"></entry>
        </osgi:service-properties>
        <bean class="com.oracle.cep.helloworld.adapter.HelloWorldAdapterFactory" />
    </osgi:service>


</beans>
Design Source
```

Notice that we used the OSGi service tags `<osgi:service>` to define the adapter factory.

In the manifest file (`MANIFEST.MF`), we'll want to export the `com.oracle.cep.helloworld.event` and `com.oracle.cep.helloworld.adapter` packages. To do this, go to the **Runtime** tab of the manifest editor and in the **Exported Packages** section, use the **Add** button to add these packages:

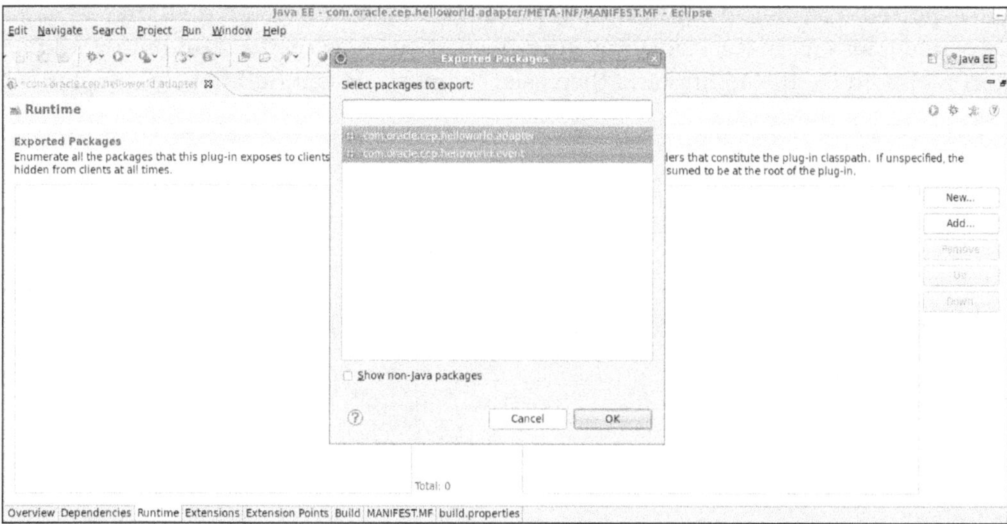

Export the bundle to the `user_projects\domains\<domain_name>\<servername>\modules` directory within your OEP server installation. Use the **File** menu to select **Export** and select **Oracle Event Processing Applications**; the following dialog window will be displayed:

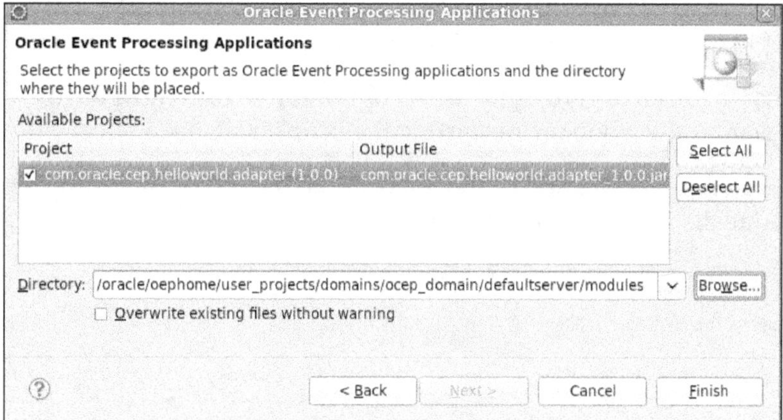

If the server is started, you'll need to stop and restart it before you can deploy any application that uses this bundle.

Now let's create a new application. We will call it `com.oracle.cep.helloworld.application`. This time we won't use the `HelloWorld` application template, so we start with an empty EPN.

We'll need to add a required bundle to this manifest file for the bundle that we just exported. For the new application, use the manifest editor and go to the **Dependencies** tab. In the **Required Plug-ins** section, click on the **Add** button and start typing in the box to find and then select **com.oracle.cep.helloworld.adapter**:

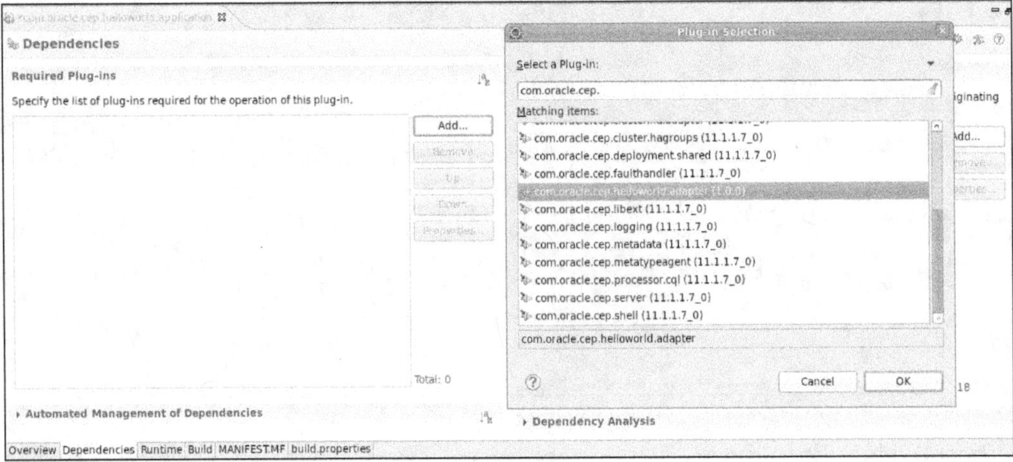

Be sure to save this change after you click **OK**.

Create a new package called `com.oracle.cep.helloworld.bean`. Copy the `HelloWorld` bean from the example. Change the import of the event to `com.oracle.cep.helloworld.event.HelloWorldEvent`.

If you are having trouble getting the new application to recognize the dependency on the adapter bundle, then try re-starting the Eclipse IDE.

Let's configure this new version of the application. Instead of providing a class name to define the adapter, use the following:

```
type="myHelloAdapter"
```

There is no need for an event-type repository definition since the only event that we are using is defined within the event-type repository section of the adapter package. The rest of the configuration is the same, with the exception of the change in the package name of the output bean. Make sure to include the processor configuration from the `wlevs` folder.

Use the same CQL Processor configuration, as in the example:

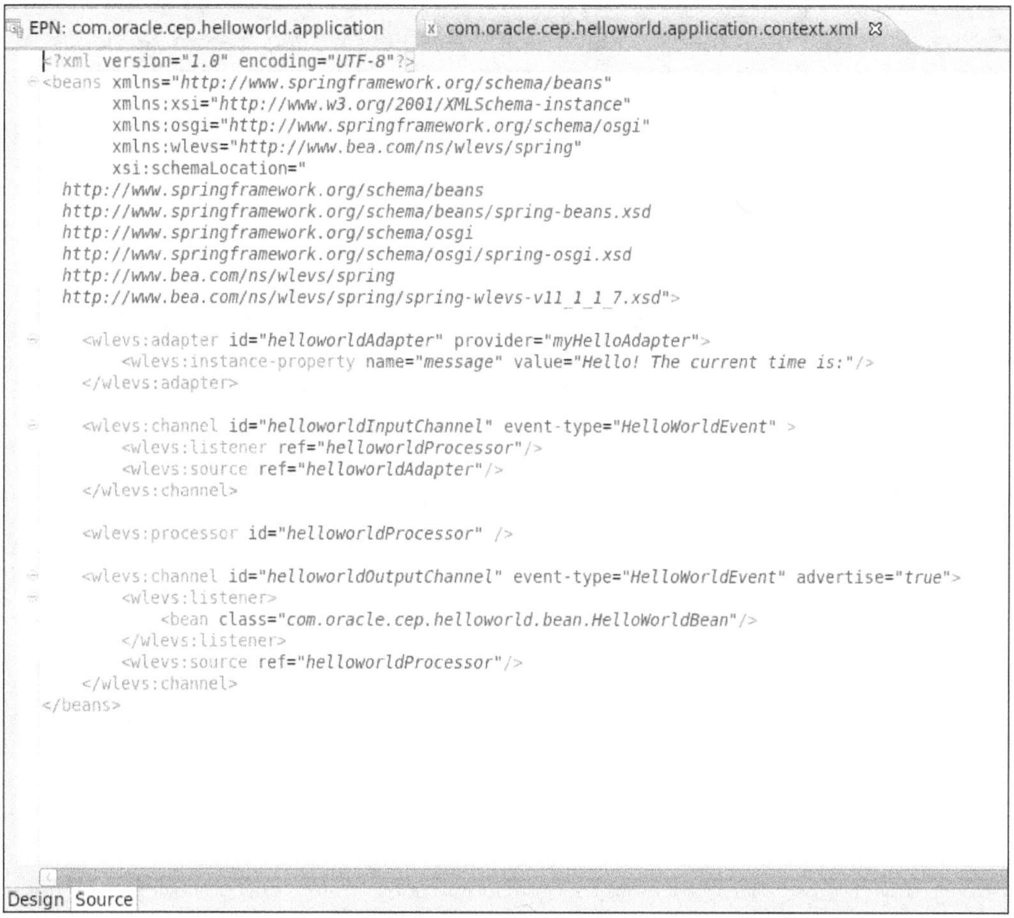

EPN: com.oracle.cep.helloworld.application   com.oracle.cep.helloworld.application.context.xml

```
<?xml version="1.0" encoding="UTF-8"?>
<beans xmlns="http://www.springframework.org/schema/beans"
        xmlns:xsi="http://www.w3.org/2001/XMLSchema-instance"
        xmlns:osgi="http://www.springframework.org/schema/osgi"
        xmlns:wlevs="http://www.bea.com/ns/wlevs/spring"
        xsi:schemaLocation="
  http://www.springframework.org/schema/beans
  http://www.springframework.org/schema/beans/spring-beans.xsd
  http://www.springframework.org/schema/osgi
  http://www.springframework.org/schema/osgi/spring-osgi.xsd
  http://www.bea.com/ns/wlevs/spring
  http://www.bea.com/ns/wlevs/spring/spring-wlevs-v11_1_1_7.xsd">

    <wlevs:adapter id="helloworldAdapter" provider="myHelloAdapter">
        <wlevs:instance-property name="message" value="Hello! The current time is:"/>
    </wlevs:adapter>

    <wlevs:channel id="helloworldInputChannel" event-type="HelloWorldEvent" >
        <wlevs:listener ref="helloworldProcessor"/>
        <wlevs:source ref="helloworldAdapter"/>
    </wlevs:channel>

    <wlevs:processor id="helloworldProcessor" />

    <wlevs:channel id="helloworldOutputChannel" event-type="HelloWorldEvent" advertise="true">
        <wlevs:listener>
            <bean class="com.oracle.cep.helloworld.bean.HelloWorldBean"/>
        </wlevs:listener>
        <wlevs:source ref="helloworldProcessor"/>
    </wlevs:channel>
</beans>
```

Design Source

We will discuss coding CQL in more detail in *Chapter 5, Coding with CQL*.

Summary

In this chapter you learned how to receive data into your application in the form of an event. You've seen the different ways an event and its attributes with types can be defined in XML or associated with a simple Java class.

We saw how to define a name for each event and discussed how events have a global scope in the entire OEP server on which they are deployed.

We looked at the out-of-the-box adapters and saw how we can customize them with a converter class to implement any specific data conversion logic that we may need while still leveraging the adapter's protocol capabilities.

We showed how easy it is to create your own adapter and how you take advantage of the lifecycle of an adapter to implement specific features of your adapter at the appropriate time. We also looked at how to leverage OSGi services when implementing our own custom adapter.

Finally, we looked at how we can package adapters and events separately from the main application so that they could be re-used. It is a good idea to package your events as separate bundles when you have large systems that are likely to have multiple applications that will be required to share the same event types.

In the next chapter, we will cover assembling and configuring Oracle applications. This includes creating an Event Processing Network (EPN), which defines the structure and flow of events for your application. We'll also look at both application and server configuration.

4

Assembling and Configuring OEP Applications

In *Chapter 2, An Overview of Oracle Event Processing*, we learned about the Oracle Event Processing development environment for Eclipse. This included importing, deploying, and running a sample application. In *Chapter 3, Adapting Events for OEP*, we learned about one of the most fundamental parts of any OEP application, namely, creating adapters for OEP so that you can receive data into your application.

In this chapter, we will look more closely at other elements of an OEP application and explain in detail the Event Processing Network (EPN). The EPN defines the flow of events through your application and contains various nodes that control the flow and perform different types of processing. We will explain each of the types of nodes, discuss why they are used, and demonstrate how they are connected to form your own application. Each of these nodes can also have associated configuration elements. We will explore the configuration of the various components and investigate how we can extend the configuration for cases where we would like to further customize the components to make them more easily configurable.

OEP applications may also rely on configurations that are defined at the server level. We will look at the server configuration elements and some of the more commonly used additions to the standard server configuration file.

This chapter will cover the following topics:

- Implementing the component model
- Exploring the EPN extensions
- Understanding the application configuration
- Defining resources in the server configuration
- Extending the component type infrastructure

Implementing the component model

OEP leverages the Spring development framework for developing applications. The EPN is documented in the form of a Spring assembly file. This chapter doesn't cover the Spring Framework in great detail, but we will mention a couple of important points that you will need to know in order to develop an OEP application. An in-depth knowledge of Spring is not necessary in order to build an OEP application, but we encourage you to read more on your own as you become more proficient in building OEP applications.

One important point to remember about the Spring framework is that it allows you to instantiate components by expressing them in the XML configuration file. This component could be an adapter or CQL processor.

Another important point is that you can set or inject values into your components using the XML configuration. For example, you may have a Java class that could potentially be used more than once to listen for events. Perhaps this class uses a TCP/IP socket connection that requires a server name and port number. Rather than hardcoding this information into the adapter itself, it can be supplied via the Spring configuration so that it is set when the adapter is instantiated. In this way, you will be able to re-use the same Java code to create multiple socket connections with varying server and port numbers.

You may have noticed by now that the EPN, while visible using the EPN Editor within the Eclipse environment, is expressed in XML that resides in the `spring` folder within `META-INF` in the project's structure.

Exploring the EPN extensions

In this section we will explore all of the elements of an EPN that we can use to build our application. You can find the schema that contains the EPN extension elements at `<MIDDLEWARE_HOME>\ocep_11.1\xsd\spring-wlevs-v11_1_1_7.xsd`.

Defining a simple Spring bean

The simplest element that you can define within an EPN is a Spring bean. This is not an EPN extension, but we wanted to point out that you may still use this element. It can be defined at the top level within your EPN XML file, as done in the following example for a converter bean:

```
<bean id="InboundJmsJaxbMessageConverter" class="com.oracle.cep.
adapter.InboundJmsJaxbMessageConverter"/>
```

You can also define it within a listener element to act as the listener for processing the output:

```
<wlevs:listener>
  <bean class="com.oracle.cep.listener.EventListener">
    <property name="nodeName" value="TransactionChannel" />
  </bean>
</wlevs:listener>
```

You'll notice that the elements which make up the set of extensions for EPN have the `wlevs` prefix.

Creating the event type repository

We saw in the previous chapter that an important part of any application is the definition of events which are used in an OEP application. The event type repository contains all of the event definitions that are used within any OEP application running on that server. As we saw in the previous chapter, event definitions are global to the server, so we can define an event in a separate bundle and use it from one or more applications running on the same server.

To define an event type repository, we use the `<wlevs:event-type-repository>` element. Within the repository definition, we supply the event type definitions. For this we use the `<wlevs:event-type>` element. These elements have a `type-name` attribute defining the name that will be used throughout the rest of the application when referring to this event type. As we saw in the previous chapter, there are several ways to define an event, the most common being to use `<wlevs:class>` and specify the class which represents that event.

Setting up the adapters

One or more adapters are usually the starting point for an OCEP application. We create an adapter either graphically, using the EPN Editor in Eclipse, or manually, by specifying the `<wlevs:adapter>` tag in the spring assembly file of our application. An adapter should always have an ID and have either a class or a provider. In the case of the out-of-the-box adapters, you specify the `provider` attribute. If you were to create your own adapter for which the custom Java code was provided within your application, you could simply use the `class` attribute and supply the name of the Java class including the package name.

A common requirement of many adapters is to use `<wlevs:instance-property>` to specify properties which the adapter requires. You will need to supply the name of the property that you are setting and either a `value` or a reference (`ref`) to a `<bean>` element, which is also defined in the Spring assembly file, whichever is appropriate for that specific property that you are setting.

To connect the adapter to downstream components, you need to supply one or more `<wlevs:listener>` elements to express where the output events from the adapter should go next to be processed. For the listener elements, you supply a reference (`ref`) to another node defined in the EPN.

Besides setting some properties here, you can also supply some optional configuration, which can override the configuration that is supplied in the Spring assembly file. As we've seen in the previous chapter, adapters have specific configuration associated with them depending upon the type of adapter. This configuration resides in the `wlevs` folder under `META-INF`. We'll cover that in more detail in the next section.

Configuring channels

A **channel** represents the physical conduit through which events flow between other types of components. When using channels in conjunction with a CQL processor, the channels must specify a single event type. We create a channel by creating a `<wlevs:channel>` element in our Spring assembly file. You will supply an `id` attribute and, in most cases, and an `event-type`. You can also supply the `max-size` and `max-threads` attributes, but these are probably best left for the optional configuration of a channel, which we will cover in the next section. Also note that instead of a channel getting its input data from an adapter or other node specifying it as a listener, a channel can have a `<wlevs:source>` configured to integrate a source. For example, `<wlevs:source ref="MyAdapter" />`.

A very interesting aspect of OEP is its ability to give developer control to the application over the concept of time. When beginning to use OEP, you may simply want to let the system control the concept of time. Here, the server assigns a timestamp to each event, which is received on the channel, by using `System.nanoTime()`. Optionally, you can specify the time by providing the optional `<wlevs:application-timestamped>` element and by specifying an expression to use for the time using one of the attributes in your event within the `<wlevs:expression>` element, as shown in the following code snippet:

```
  <wlevs:channel id="evEventStream" event-type="EvseEvent">
<wlevs:listener ref="EVProcessor" />
```

```
    <wlevs:application-timestamped>
      <wlevs:expression>myTimeAttribute</wlevs:expression>
    </wlevs:application-timestamped>
  </wlevs:channel>
```

This allows the concept of time to be driven by your event data. This can be very important when you want to create applications that are capable of doing a what-if analysis over a long time frame of data and you wish to run data through the system at a rate faster than it naturally would. It's also useful when you have very precise system timing requirements and would like to get exact results from two different servers even if their system clocks can differ from each other slightly. Therefore, for very precise HA across multiple physical systems, you may wish to use channels that are application time-stamped.

Implementing event-beans

The distinguishing factor in event-beans is that they are able to both receive events and send events to downstream listeners. They are primarily used for putting your own Java code in the middle of an EPN. For many reasons, it is often best to try to express your logic in CQL within a CQL processor. This is because logic within a CQL processor can be dynamically modified even when the application is running, (without needing to redeploy the application or restart the server. Changing Java logic within an event-bean will require you to redeploy the application). But there are many cases where you would want to include some custom Java logic within an EPN. You may have something involving many steps, which are quite complex (especially when this logic is not likely to change very often). Another reason might be to access one or more Coherence Java APIs in a way that is not supported with the out-of-the-box OEP-Coherence integration features or would be difficult to model in CQL. While Coherence is a separate product within Oracle, the JAR files are bundled in OSGi format with OEP. Many applications use Coherence features within their application, because Coherence, among other things, is great at holding large amounts of data in-memory across multiple JVMs. Often OEP applications need low-latency access to reference data while processing incoming data streams. OEP integration with Coherence will be discussed later in the chapter and in more detail in later chapters.

To use an event-bean within an application, you would supply the `<wlevs:event-bean>` tag, We will need to supply the `id` attribute and the class containing the Java implementation.

Enabling the power of CQL processors

We have dedicated an entire chapter to cover CQL processing in great detail (*Chapter 5, Coding with CQL*). For now, we will note that you define a CQL processor by specifying the `<wlevs:processor>` tag. We provide the `id` attribute to define the name of the CQL processor. We will most certainly have channels with a defined event-type supplying data to the CQL processors and also have `<wlevs:listener>` elements defined within the CQL processor definition to indicate where the resulting output events should be sent.

While the definition of the CQL processor is quite simple within the EPN, the real power comes from defining the specific CQL queries, which is done using the standard OEP application configuration files placed in the `wlevs` folder. Like other configuration files, the name of the file itself doesn't matter as long as it has an `.xml` extension. It is a common practice to name the XML file after the name of the CQL processor.

Defining a database table

We can integrate database tables within the EPN by introducing the `<wlevs:table>` element. You need to define a data source in the server's configuration file. We will discuss this later in this chapter. For this element, you would define the `id`, `event-type`, and the `data-source` attributes. For example:

```
<wlevs:table id="RegistrationTable" event-type="RegistrationEvent"
data-source="RegistrationDataSource"/>
```

Once this configuration is in place, you can join a data stream with a table in a manner similar to joining two database tables.

This can be useful for joining an incoming event from a data stream with its related reference data, but you might want to consider using a cache for better performance.

Using caching

Cache components can also be integrated with the EPN. This is useful in many ways. It can be used to connect to reference data for your CQL queries to join incoming data streams with more static data that is needed for either the CQL logic or the output messages. It can also be used to store data for future use or, in the case of a Coherence cache, be used to send data to the database in a simple low-latency way so that the OEP processing threads are made available for processing more incoming data without the need to wait for commits to occur against the database.

We can include caching within our application by first defining a caching system using the `<wlevs:caching-system>` tag. For this we use the `id` attribute to define the name and the `provider` attribute to specify which caching implementation is used. Oracle Event Processing contains a local cache implementation, supports Coherence, and allows for integration of third-party caches. If you are not familiar with the Oracle Coherence product, you should read a little about it because it contains useful features that can help you complete your OEP application.

To declare a caching system that uses the OEP implementation declaratively in the EPN assembly file, use the `<wlevs:caching-system>` element without any additional attributes. Since the local cache implementation is the default provider, you can simply specify the `id` attribute for the cache:

```
<wlevs:caching-system id="LocalCache"/>
```

Oracle Event Processing contains specific integration features for integration with Coherence. To use Coherence for development, there's nothing extra that you need to install. The Coherence libraries are included with the OEP install as OSGi bundles. To implement Coherence, you simply need to supply `coherence` as the provider when you define the caching system.. For example:

```
<wlevs:caching-system id="MyCachingSystem" provider="coherence"
advertise="true"/>
```

Of course, Coherence requires some configuration files. We will provide the same Coherence cache configuration files that we would supply to any other Coherence client JVM. We will discuss this further in the chapter.

Once we have a caching system defined, we can then define some specific caches using the `<wlevs:cache>` element. We will provide an `id` attribute to name our cache, the `caching-system` attribute to refer to the caching system defined earlier, the `value-type` attribute referring to an event type defined in the event type repository, and either the `key-properties` or `key-class` attribute depending on which one you are using to define the key for this cache. For `key-properties`, you supply one of more attributes of the event that will serve as the key. With `key-class`, you supply the name of the Java class that is implementing the key.

We will also stress here that the value-type used for our cache should be defined in the event type repository. This is a common mistake when configuring a cache. Also, the Java class used here needs to implement `java.io.Serializable` or for a better performing serialization when using Coherence as the provider, use the `PortableObjectFormat` Coherence.

Especially during development, it is often useful to define a cache listener using `<wlevs:cache-listener>` with a reference to a bean that implements the cache listener logic. The cache listener should implement the appropriate listener for the caching implementation. In the case of Coherence, it should implement `com.tangosol.util.MapListener`.

Here's an example of the configuration of a Coherence caching system and a cache with a cache listener:

```
    <!-- Caching Configuration -->
  <wlevs:caching-system id="CoherenceCachingSystem"
provider="coherence" advertise="true"/>

   <wlevs:cache id="AccountCache" caching-system="CoherenceCachingSys
tem"
    value-type="Account" key-properties="accountID">
    <wlevs:cache-listener ref="CacheListener"/>
  </wlevs:cache>

      <bean id="CacheListener" class="com.oracle.cep.listener.
CacheListener"/>
```

Understanding the application configuration

The components within an application are configurable with parameters that either configures the technical properties of an adapter, such as a port number, some custom application logic such as a message to display to the user or some application-tuning parameters.

The entire application-specific configuration resides within the `wlevs` folder in the `META-INF` directory. It is important to note that the names of the files in this folder are not important, you can use any naming convention that you feel would be most convenient for your application. The only rule to follow is that the file names should have an `.xml` extension.

Adapter configuration

In *Chapter 3, Adapting Events for OEP,* we covered getting started with OEP by explaining how to define events and implement the various types of adapters, including explaining the configuration for each.

When we created an adapter, we specified the configuration that is appropriate for that adapter. Recall that wizards in the Eclipse IDE can not only help you define the adapter in the Spring assembly file, but also help you complete the specific configuration.

Channel configuration

The default channel configuration is typically adequate for most applications. However, if you want to change this configuration, you must create a channel element in a component configuration file. In this channel element, you can specify channel configuration that overrides the defaults. Let's take a look at the possible configuration elements of a channel.

You can specify the `max-size` configuration element when you want to allow the channel to hold events in the event that they cannot be processed immediately. This will cause the events to be placed in a queue and processed by a new thread. The default configuration value for this element is `0`, which implies there will not be a thread context switch and that processing will continue on the current thread. You should specify a value greater than `0` when you want to allow events to queue here, if necessary, and asynchronously process events from this point using one or more threads. You specify the maximum number of threads to use in this case using the `max-threads` attribute. Keep in mind that setting `max-threads` to a value greater than `1` can lead to the possibility of events being processed out of order depending upon what is happening after this channel. Also note that setting `max-threads` greater than `0` without specifying a `max-size` element other than `0` will have no effect.

Another important configuration of channels is the ability to control from where inputs are received when preceded by a CQL processor. The `selector` element allows you to choose which queries will provide input to this channel.

For this example, imagine that there are two queries within the same processor and the downstream channels are `TotalTypeChannel` and `TotalChannel`. If you wanted the results of `TypeTotalQuery` to go on the `TotalTypeChannel` and the results of `TwentyFourHourTotalQuery` to go on the `TotalChannel`, you would use a configuration like this:

```
<channel>
  <name>TotalTypeChannel</name>
  <max-size>10000</max-size>
  <max-threads>2</max-threads>
  <selector>TypeTotalQuery</selector>
</channel>
```

```
<channel>
  <name>TotalChannel</name>
  <max-size>10000</max-size>
  <max-threads>2</max-threads>
  <selector>TwentyFourHourTotalQuery</selector>
</channel>
```

Cache configuration

To configure a local cache, we provide some caching-system configuration within a configuration file in the `META-INF\wlevs` directory.

For the OEP caching implementation, you can optionally configure these elements:

- `max-size`: The number of cache elements in memory after which eviction occurs.
- `eviction-policy`: The eviction policy to use when `max-size` is reached. Supported values are: FIFO, LRU, LFU, and NRU; default value is LFU.
- `time-to-live`: The maximum amount of time, in milliseconds, that an entry is cached. Default value is infinite.
- `idle-time`: Amount of time, in milliseconds, after which cached entries are actively removed from the cache. Default value is infinite.
- `work-manager-name`: The work manager to be used for all asynchronous operations. The value of this element corresponds to the name child element of the `work-manager` element in the server's `config.xml` configuration file. We will discuss the server configuration file later in this chapter.

Here is an example of the configuration for an OEP caching system implementation:

```
<caching-system>
  <name>LocalCache</name>
  <cache>
    <name>DrawDownStatusCache</name>
    <max-size>1000</max-size>
  </cache>
</caching-system>
```

When using Coherence, you provide the same configuration files as you would for any other Coherence JVM. The important thing to note when configuring OEP as a member of the Coherence cluster is that there is a simple way to allow the server to find the configuration files. You simply create a folder called `coherence` in the `META-INF\wlevs` folder and use the default names `coherence-cache-config.xml` and optionally `tangosol-coherence-override.xml`.

Coherence cache configuration is a complex topic by itself. You can learn more about Coherence on OTN at `http://www.oracle.com/technetwork/middleware/coherence/overview/index.html`.

Defining resources in the server configuration

The OEP server configuration contains many important elements that you should be aware of.

Here's where you will find the name of the domain. The default is `WLEventServerDomain`:

```
<domain>
    <name>WLEventServerDomain</name>
</domain>
```

A very important configuration element is `netio`. This is where you will find the default port number and the SSL port numbers configured:

```
<netio>
  <name>NetIO</name>
  <port>9002</port>
</netio>

<netio>
  <name>sslNetIo</name>
  <ssl-config-bean-name>sslConfig</ssl-config-bean-name>
  <port>9003</port>
</netio>
```

The default work manager is called `JettyWorkManager`. Here is where you can tune the minimum and maximum number of threads to be made available to adapters and other components that use work managers:

```
<work-manager>
  <name>JettyWorkManager</name>
  <min-threads-constraint>5</min-threads-constraint>
  <max-threads-constraint>10</max-threads-constraint>
</work-manager>
```

OEP comes bundled with the Jetty web server. The server's configuration file allows you to configure it:

```
<jetty>
    <name>JettyServer</name>
```

```
    <network-io-name>NetIO</network-io-name>
    <work-manager-name>JettyWorkManager</work-manager-name>
    <scratch-directory>Jetty</scratch-directory>
    <secure-network-io-name>sslNetIo</secure-network-io-name>
  </jetty>
```

There are configuration elements that allow you to configure RMI, the JNDI context, JMX, and SSL.

You can optionally define a `data-source` element if you need to use it in your application. Here is an example of the `data-source` configuration; you can also configure connection pool and driver details:

```
    <data-source>
        <name>oracledb</name>
        <data-source-params>
            <global-transactions-protocol>None</global-transactions-
protocol>
        </data-source-params>
        <connection-pool-params>
            <test-table-name>SQL SELECT 1 FROM DUAL</test-table-name>
            <initial-capacity>2</initial-capacity>
            <max-capacity>10</max-capacity>
        </connection-pool-params>
        <driver-params>
            <url>jdbc:oracle:thin:@localhost:1521/lloywill.us.oracle.
com</url>
            <driver-name>oracle.jdbc.driver.OracleDriver</driver-name>
            <properties>
                <element>
                    <name>user</name>
                    <value>ocep</value>
                </element>
                <element>
                    <name>password</name>
                    <value>password</value>
                </element>
            </properties>
            <use-xa-data-source-interface>false</use-xa-data-source-
interface>
        </driver-params>
    </data-source>
```

If you are configuring the record and playback capability, you will need a data source, but you might want to use an embedded database such as derby. Here is an example of this configuration:

```
<!--  start config for record playback -->
<data-source>
  <name>derby1</name>
  <connection-pool-params>
    <initial-capacity>15</initial-capacity>
    <max-capacity>50</max-capacity>
  </connection-pool-params>
  <driver-params>
    <url>jdbc:derby:dbtest1;create=true</url>
    <driver-name>org.apache.derby.jdbc.EmbeddedDriver</driver-name>
  </driver-params>
</data-source>
<rdbms-event-store-provider>
  <name>test-rdbms-provider</name>
  <data-source-name>derby1</data-source-name>
</rdbms-event-store-provider>
<!-- end config for record playback -->
```

If necessary, configure transaction managers in the server configuration file:

```
<transaction-manager>
    <name>TM</name>
    <rmi-service-name>RMI</rmi-service-name>
</transaction-manager>
```

We discussed in *Chapter 3, Adapting Events for OEP*, the HTTP pub-sub adapter. The server configuration file allows you to configure the pub-sub server. The default server is called `pubsub` with the path as `/pubsub`. If you decide to use the pub-sub capability in your own application, you can add additional pub-sub servers or extend the default one with additional channels by providing more channel elements as in the following example. Here, we provide three additional channels for a ship tracking application:

```
<http-pubsub>
  <name>pubsub</name>
  <path>/pubsub</path>
  <pub-sub-bean>
    <server-config>
      <supported-transport>
```

```
            <types>
              <element>long-polling</element>
            </types>
          </supported-transport>
          <publish-without-connect-allowed>true</publish-without-
connect-allowed>
        </server-config>
        <channels>
          <element>
            <channel-pattern>/evsmonitor</channel-pattern>
          </element>
          <element>
            <channel-pattern>/evsalert</channel-pattern>
          </element>
          <element>
            <channel-pattern>/evsdomainchange</channel-pattern>
          </element>
          <element>
            <channel-pattern>/ship/shippos</channel-pattern>
          </element>
          <element>
            <channel-pattern>/ship/shipoutput</channel-pattern>
          </element>
          <element>
            <channel-pattern>/ship/shiparrival</channel-pattern>
          </element>
        </channels>
      </pub-sub-bean>
    </http-pubsub>
```

The server's configuration file also allows you to configure clustering. The clustering capability can use Coherence, in which case you would provide some cache configuration details and add the Coherence configuration files to the server's configuration directory:

```
<cluster>
      <server-name>myServer1</server-name>
      <multicast-address>239.255.0.1</multicast-address>
      <identity>1</identity>
      <enabled>coherence</enabled>
      <security>encrypt</security>
</cluster>
```

Finally, the server configuration allows you to control logging. Add additional entries as needed. You may choose to log a particular class by including the full class name including the package:

```
<logging-service>
  <name>myLogService</name>
  <log-file-config>myFileConfig</log-file-config>
  <stdout-config>myStdoutConfig</stdout-config>
  <logger-severity>Notice</logger-severity>
  <logger-severity-properties>
    <entry>
      <key>LifeCycle</key>
      <value>Notice</value>
    </entry>
    <entry>
      <key>Management</key>
      <value>Notice</value>
    </entry>
    <entry>
      <key>CQLProcessor</key>
      <value>Notice</value>
    </entry>
    <entry>
      <key>EplProcessor</key>
      <value>Notice</value>
    </entry>
    <entry>
      <key>Stream</key>
      <value>Notice</value>
    </entry>
    <entry>
      <key>Ede</key>
      <value>Notice</value>
    </entry>
    <entry>
      <key>Cache</key>
      <value>Notice</value>
    </entry>
    <entry>
      <key>Adapters</key>
      <value>Notice</value>
    </entry>
    <entry>
      <key>Spring</key>
```

```
        <value>Notice</value>
      </entry>
      <entry>
        <key>Channel</key>
        <value>Notice</value>
      </entry>
      <entry>
        <key>Recplay</key>
        <value>Notice</value>
      </entry>
      <entry>
        <key>Monitor</key>
        <value>Notice</value>
      </entry>
      <entry>
        <key>Server</key>
        <value>Notice</value>
      </entry>
      <entry>
        <key>Deployment</key>
        <value>Notice</value>
      </entry>
      <entry>
        <key>EventTrace</key>
        <value>Notice</value>
      </entry>
      <entry>
        <key>XMLOutputChannel</key>
        <value>Debug</value>
      </entry>
      <entry>
        <key>AreaChangeEvents</key>
        <value>Debug</value>
      </entry>
      <entry>
        <key>AreaDefinitionEventChannel</key>
        <value>Debug</value>
      </entry>
      <entry>
        <key>ShipArrivalOutputChannel</key>
        <value>Debug</value>
      </entry>
    </logger-severity-properties>
  </logging-service>
```

By default, the logfile configuration keeps all of the logfiles on your system. Especially during development, you may wish to change the logging to a strategy that keeps only the last few logfiles and automatically rotates the logfiles for you, so that you don't have logfiles, which you no longer need taking up disk space on your system:

```
<log-file>
    <name>myFileConfig</name>
    <number-of-files-limited>true</number-of-files-limited>
    <rotated-file-count>4</rotated-file-count>
    <rotate-log-on-startup-enabled>true</rotate-log-on-startup-
enabled>
    <log-file-severity>Debug</log-file-severity>
    <log-file-rotation-dir>logs</log-file-rotation-dir>
</log-file>
```

Also, configure the log level severity that's best for your standard output:

```
<log-stdout>
  <name>myStdoutConfig</name>
  <stdout-severity>Debug</stdout-severity>
</log-stdout>
```

Extending the component type infrastructure

It is possible to extend the configurability of various components of your application by performing custom extensions of the XML schema. This is often very important for adapters. We discussed how you could use the Spring framework to inject a configuration value into our adapter. Often you want not only to set these values in the EPN so that you can re-use the adapter, but you would like to make them as optional configuration that can be changed after the application has been initially deployed successfully.

We should take a moment to discuss an important feature of OEP related to deployment. When an application is developed, it is packaged into a single JAR file. This is often referred to as a module or OSGi bundle. Upon successful deployment, a folder is created in the server's `applications` directory and this JAR file is deployed there. It is important to note that at this time all the configuration files in the `META-INF\wlevs` directory are extracted and deployed here as well. This is the configuration that the server will use when it starts. This is a useful feature, because if you need to change a configuration attribute of an adapter, you can stop the server, make the change to the appropriate file that is already extracted and available, and re-start the server. You need not worry about going back to the development environment to make changes to the application, re-package and re-deploy it.

When you have your own adapters with their own configurable properties, you may like to have this same level of flexibility that you have out-of-the-box with the adapters that are provided. The idea is to make any custom attributes configurable from files in the `wlevs` folder.

Take, for example, the `helloworld` sample. It allows you to set the message that is displayed each time the time interval for generating a message has elapsed. We set this message using the `<wlevs:instance-property>` element in the EPN. We can easily re-use this adapter within the same application and have different messages by setting a different message for a second instance of the same adapter. But what if we wanted to change the message that is displayed after the application is deployed the first time. We would need to re-build the JAR file with a change to the EPN. If we were able to make the message property configurable as an attribute in the `wlevs` folder, we wouldn't need to do that. We could simply change the configuration file and, in this case, restart the server to pick up the change. Of course, in this example, you might want to consider a better way of implementing this using CQL so that you don't need to restart the server at all.

Another better example would be if you had a socket adapter that used a hostname and a port number. If, for some reason, the host or the port number for the socket connection changed, it would be easy to make that change to a text file that is already extracted rather than needing to repackage the application's JAR file.

Summary

You have already learned how to implement the structure of an OEP application according to the programming model. In this chapter, you learned a great deal about application configuration and server configuration. By now, you should be able to see how flexible an OEP application can be. You can design it to accomplish any type of event processing use case and integrate with other systems in many different ways. There are also many performance-tuning options available to you for your application and for the server.

In the next chapter, we will cover CQL processing in great detail. This is one of the most important aspects of the product. It will allow you to easily program complex constructs into your application logic.

5
Coding with CQL

In this chapter, you will learn how to program with CQL, Oracle event processing language. CQL provides a high-level descriptive language for performing event processing tasks such as event filtering and event summarisation. Further, it is highly optimised and extremely efficient, therefore allowing your application to handle the ever increasing volume of events in today's systems. Some of the topics we will cover are as follows:

- Introducing CQL
- CQL fundamentals
- The structure and semantics of event processing
- SQL as a foundation
- Typing and expressions
- Timing models

Introducing CQL

As you have learned so far, one of the main components of Oracle Event Processing is the CQL processor. The CQL processor is the brain of the EPN. In the CQL processor, you will code rules that determine the processing of the events. Common examples are rules that perform filtering of the events, or that aggregate input events into summary output events. The following diagram shows a CQL processor in an EPN:

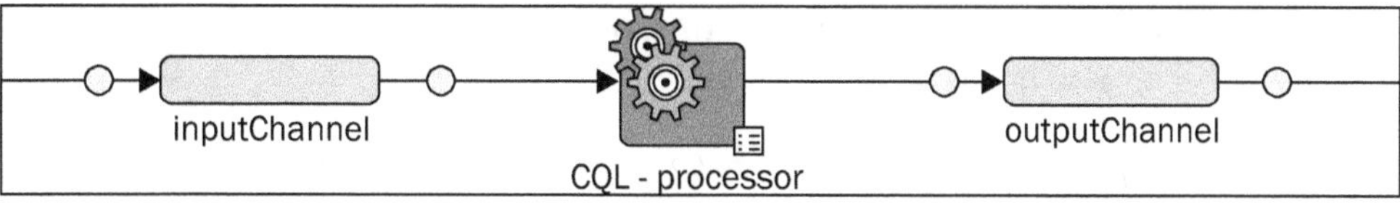

The CQL processor is programmed using a language called **Continuous Query Language (CQL)**. This may sound a bit odd, but the rationale for the name will become apparent later on when we understand the proper semantics of CQL.

CQL is an extension to SQL, the common language of databases. These extensions, as you shall see in the next sections, deal with additional logic for handling time and events that are not part of the standard SQL.

Without further ado, let's immerge into the interesting world of CQL, which many may find to be a paradigm shift in the way they think about programming. We start by looking at the basic concepts.

Understanding CQL fundamentals

The starting point for CQL is the **CQL query**. A CQL query is a single statement that defines how **input events** are to be processed and transformed into **output events**.

Oracle Event Processing considers an event as a collection of named key-value pairs. This is sometimes known as tuples. Each one of these pairs defines an attribute or property of the event, so henceforth we shall refer to them as **event properties**. Considering this, a better definition of a CQL query is that it specifies how particular properties of the input events are processed and result into output events with their own set of properties.

Let's take a look at an example. Consider an event `e1` that contains two properties, `p1` and `p2`, whose values are respectively set to `1` and `"hi"`. We will represent this event as follows:

```
e1 => {p1 = 1, p2 = "hi"}
```

Next, the CQL query `Q1` simply transforms this input event into an output event containing just `p1` and dropping `p2`. So, the output for the input `e1` is `e2`, where `e2` is represented as follows:

```
e2 => {p1 = 1}
```

This is a very simple naive example, but highlights the behavior of a valid CQL query.

The name and data type of the set of all event properties of an event is called its **event type**. For example, for `e1`, its event type, which we shall name `InputEventType`, which can be defined as:

```
InputEventType = { p1 = Integer, p2 = String}
```

Next, let's take a look at how a query receives the input events and where the output events are dispatched.

Establishing your sources and destinations

The input events arrive from a set of named and typed **sources**, and conversely are output to a set of named and typed **destinations**.

The sources and destinations of a query are defined by the EPN where the CQL processor containing the query resides. More precisely, it is defined by the adjacent components in the EPN to the CQL processor in question. For example, consider the following diagram for source and destinations for Q1:

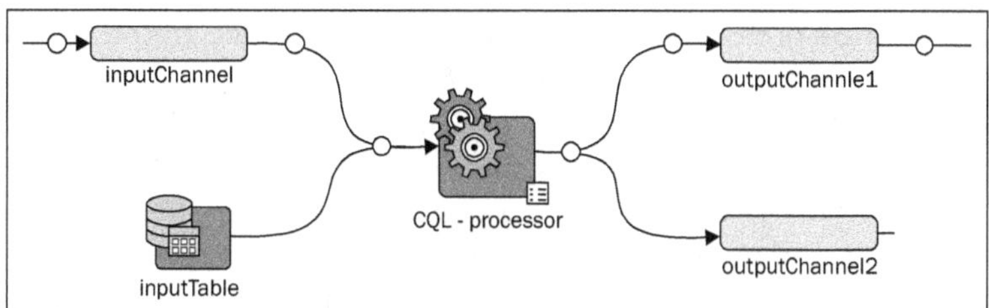

In this case, the channel `inputChannel` and the table `inputTable` are the potential sources for query `Q1`, where as the channel `outputChannel1` and `outputChannel2` are the potential destinations.

Why potential? The EPN gives us all the components of the application and their connections, but the CQL query can further narrow down this list by specifying which one of the connected components are being used. You shall see this in the next section, but for the time being we are interested in understanding the concepts that make up CQL rather than defining precisely how they can be used.

The type of the source and of the destination defines the type of the event. If a channel named `inputChannel` is of the event type `InputEventType`, events that flow through `inputChannelto` the query are of this type. This determines the metadata that the query can make use of. For example, consider the `InputEventType` defined previously as:

- p1 = Integer
- p2 = String

This means that the query `Q1` only sees the event properties `p1` and `p2`, and that they are respectively defined as being an `Integer` and a `String`. We discuss the supported data types later on in this chapter in the *Typing and expressions* section.

In addition to the event type, a source and a destination define the **model of processing** of an event, which is explained in the next section.

Processing models

The model of processing demonstrates how events should be interpreted so that they can be processed correctly in some systematic form. For CEP, which deals with a timed continuous flow of events, this translates to how events are seen when in an ever-changing collection. There are two ways of interpreting this continuous flow of events:

- The flow of events form a **stream**
- The flow of events contribute to a **relation**

A stream is a collection of events where the events are inserted into the collection, that is, the stream, at a particular moment in time. In this **conceptional** model, the events are never deleted from the stream (don't worry about implementation details such as running out of memory!). In other words, once inserted into the stream, the events live forever and are never dropped or even changed. For example, event `e1` is added to the stream at time `t = 0`, and event `e2` is added to the stream at time `t = 1`:

A relation is a collection of events that supports the operations of insertion, deletion, and update. In this sense, a relation is very similar to a standard database table. In other words, you can add event `e1` to the relation; you can change it, and then delete the event. The only difference between a standard table and our concept of a relation is that a relation must always be referenced at a particular instance of time. For example, considering the previous case, at time `t = 0`, the relation is empty, at time `t = 1`, the relation has event `e1`, and at time `t = 2`, the relation is again empty:

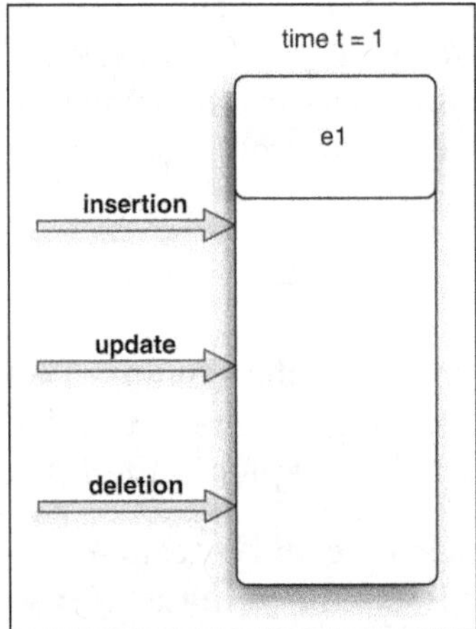

Understanding these two concepts is absolutely fundamental to understanding how CQL works. So let's spend a bit more time on this, and try to relate it to some other more common day-to-day ideas. Say we have a swimming pool that gets filled up from a water hose coming from the public water system in the street.

What we want to do is to clean the water by adding chlorine to it. To do this, you can't just place the chlorine in the water hose; you have to place the chlorine in the swimming pool.

Another way of looking into this is that the water hose is our stream of water, or stream of *water events*. Water flows continuously through it. A particular liter of water flowed through the hose at a particular time of the day. Once that happens, you can't really change this fact. You can't go back in time and change that liter of water. Further, trying to remove that liter of water from the hose makes no sense; there is no such concept.

Conversely, the swimming pool is like a relation of water. Water is continuously added to it, up to a point where the pool gets fool and water starts splashing out of the pool. But at a particular time, we know precisely the amount of water in the pool, and we can change it, as we will. In fact, we can process the water in the pool, which we do by adding chlorine to it. In other words, the pool gives us a bounded amount of water that can be worked on, transformed, filtered, and so on.

CEP as a technology is the same thing. The enterprise is a world of events; it is a hose where events flow continuously. CEP gives us the ability of pooling these events into relations and henceforth being able to process it effectively in real time.

You now understand the basic concepts. Next, let's look at the syntax or structure of CQL queries.

The structure and semantics of event processing

The structure of CQL queries is very similar to that of SQL. In fact, CQL is based on a subset of SQL99. Let's revisit the simple example from the beginning of the previous section:

```
SELECT p1
FROM inputChannel
```

In this case, the `FROM inputChannel` clause informs the query that the input events arrive from the source called `inputChannel`, which happens to be the upstream channel to this CQL processor in the EPN. Further, the `SELECT p1` clause states that the query is selecting only the event property `p1` for output. The behavior of this query is best described with the following table:

Timet	Input event	Output event
0	{p1 = 1, p2 = "hi"}	{p1 = 1}

In other words, at time `t = 0`, we receive event `{p1 = 1, p2 = "hi"}` and output event `{p1 = 1}`. For the time being, ignore the time-related aspect of processing.

Here is a slightly more complicated case:

```
SELECT p2
FROM inputChannel
WHERE p1 = 1
```

In this second query, we make use of a `WHERE` clause. This clause is used to specify a predicate condition that must be met before the input event is selected for output. In this case, the predicate condition is that the property `p1` of the input event must be equal to the value `1`. The following table provides an example of the application of this second query:

Time	Input event	Output event
0	{p1 = 1, p2 = "hi"}	{p2 = "hi"}
1	{p1 = 2, p2 = "bye"}	

In this example, the interesting aspect is that there is no output for the second event, as its property `p1` does not evaluate to `true` for the predicate condition. When this happens, the event is essentially filtered out of the output.

Next, let's introduce the notion of time to the CQL queries.

Restricting streams with Windows

So far we have dealt directly with processing events from a stream, that is, an event arrives, we process it, and we immediately output its result. Due to the nature of the processing done so far, we have been able to perform it directly in events on a stream without having to rely on the notion of relations. Next, let's tackle the contrary.

Say we want to find out the average value of an event property. For example, we could be receiving stock prices from a *stream* of market stock feed and we are interested on finding the average price of a particular stock.

The first question that comes up is that, as we have learned, a stream is unbounded, that is, it has no end, and therefore we couldn't simply find the average price for all possible events that flowed through it at all possible time. At least, not effectively! Instead, we need to define some kind of window that contains the events that are of interest to us. For example, let's assume we are interested on finding the average of the price for the last minute of events from the market feed stream. We can state this in CQL by using a window operator, as follows:

```
SELECT AVG(price)
FROM marketFeed [RANGE 1 MINUTE]
```

First, we receive the events from the `marketFeed` stream; next we convert this stream into a relation that contains a range of 1-minute of events. Why do we need to do this? By creating a relation, we can now apply the average operation on it. An average of a relation is a well-defined operation; it is after all just like applying an average on a bag of tuples of a standard RDBMS table. Further, by having a relation, we can now add and remove events to it, whereas we can't remove events from a stream, as we learned in the previous sections. For example, as time progresses, we can now delete an event from the relation when it expires past the 1-minute window.

Before we go on, we need to establish a few assumptions for the purpose of simplifying the examples. These are as follows:

- The system ticks in seconds
- We only receive one input event at every tick, unless otherwise noted
- Initially we will only show the new values in the output, that is, we don't show the delete of the old value

Later, when we discuss outputs and application time-stamped systems, the rationale for these assumptions will be clear.

The following table illustrates an example of processing for this query:

Time (in secs)	Input event	Output event
`00`		`{AVG(price) = 0.0}`
`01`	`{symbol = "aaa", price = 4.0}`	`{AVG(price) = 4.0}`
`10`	`{symbol = "bbb", price = 2.0}`	`{AVG(price) = 3.0}`

Time (in secs)	Input event	Output event
59	{symbol = "aaa", price = 5.0}	{AVG(price) = 3.6}
61		{AVG(price) = 3.5}
70		{AVG(price) = 5.0}
80	{symbol = "aaa", price = 6.0}	{AVG(price) = 5.5}

At time `t = 0`, there are no input events, yet the query still outputs a value of 0 for the average. You may find this odd, but the reason for this is that, as in a database, the defined value for an average of an empty table is zero; hence CQL duplicates this same behavior.

At time `t = 1`, we have a single input event, and the output is its own value as the average. At time `t = 10`, the relation now contains two events, that is, `{symbol = "aaa", price = 4.0}` and `{symbol = "bbb", price = 2.0}`, so the average of the property price is *(4.0 + 2.0) / 2 = 3.0*. At time `t = 59`, the relation has three events and the average becomes *(4.0 + 2.0 + 5.0) / 3 = 3.6*.

At time `t = 60`, we get an output event, even though there is no input event. Why is that? The reason is that even though there is no input event, the CQL processor is still continuously working, and a change of an internal state has happened, which caused the state of the output to change. Specifically, at time `t = 60`, a one-minute interval has elapsed. That is, `t = 0`, `t = 1`, … `t = 60` is equal to *60 + 1* progress of time. When this happened, the relation is changed to a window starting (inclusive) at `01` to (inclusive) `60`, expiring any event that happened at `t = 00`, which in this case is none.

However, at `t = 61`, the relation now moved from 02 to 61, causing the event `{symbol = "aaa", price = 4.0}` to be expired from the relation. This means that the output state is no longer accurate, and thus an event with the new average is output, which is *(2.0 + 5.0) / 2 = 3.5*.

The following diagram demonstrates time-window expiration:

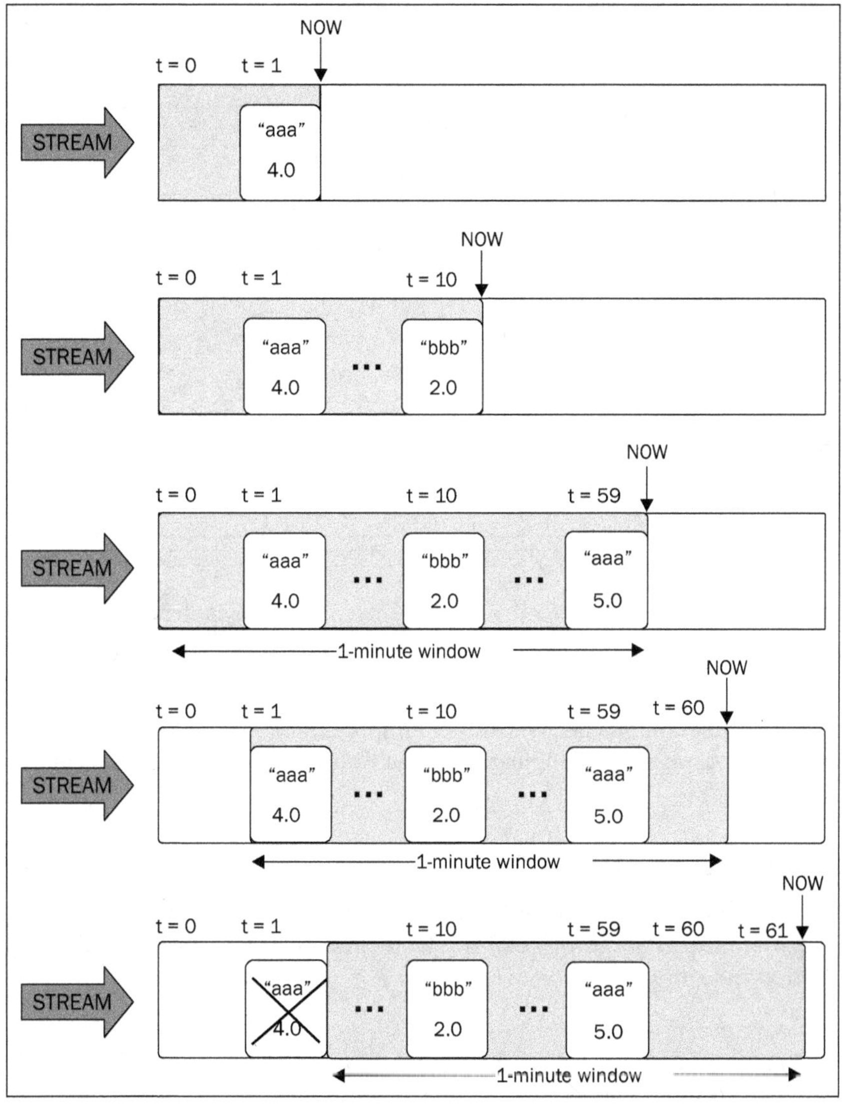

At time `t = 70`, the second event, `{symbol = "bbb", price = 2.0}`, expires from the window, therefore the new output becomes *5.0 / 1 = 5.0*. Finally, at time `t = 80`, there is a new input of `{symbol = "aaa", price = 6.0}`, and the output is *(5.0 + 6.0) / 2 = 5.5*. The following diagram shows the complete interaction for this scenario:

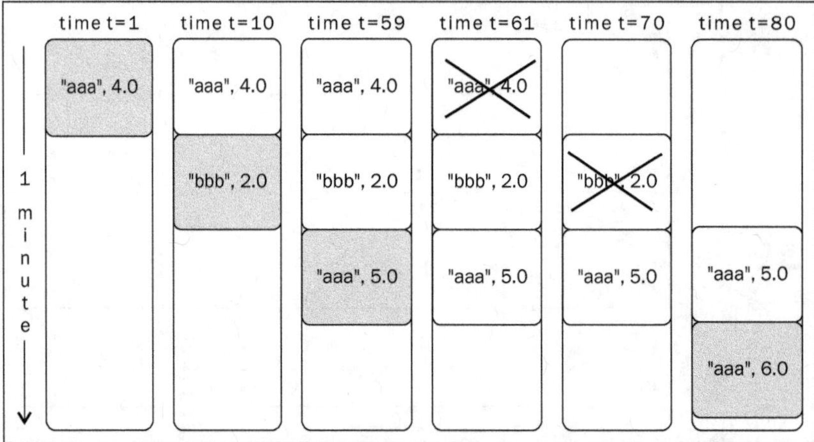

The `RANGE` operator is a time-based window operator, as it is driven by time. There are several other types of window operators, such as tuple-based and partitioned.

The continuous behavior is very important and the reason Oracle CEP's event processing language is called **Continuous Query Language**.

Tuple-based windows

A tuple-based window is a window that is driven by events. For example, say we want to calculate the average price of the last three events received. This can be done with the following query:

```
SELECT AVG(price)
FROM marketFeed [ROWS 3]
```

Let's take a look at the output resulting from this query using the same set of events from the last example:

Time	Input event	Output event
`00`		
`01`	`{symbol = "aaa", price = 4.0}`	`{AVG(price) = 0.0}, {AVG(price) = 4.0}`

Time	Input event	Output event
10	{symbol = "bbb", price = 2.0}	{AVG(price) = 3.0}
59	{symbol = "aaa", price = 5.0}	{AVG(price) = 3.6}
61		
70		
80	{symbol = "aaa", price = 6.0}	{AVG(price) = 4.3}

Note the difference where the query does not output any event in time `t = 61` and `t = 70`. The reason being is that in this case the relation is defined by a window containing 3 events, which don't expire any events until the fourth event arrives at time `t = 80`. At this point, the event {`symbol = "aaa", price = 4.0`} leaves the window and the event {`symbol = "aaa", price = 3.0`} enters the window, causing a state change at the output, which now has the average of *(2.0 + 5.0 + 6.0) / 3 = 4.3*.

There is also another minor difference; the first event of {`AVG(price) = 0.0`} is only output when the first event arrives. The reason for this is that the window relation only starts working when it is trigged by an event. In the case of a time-window, this start event is the first instance of time. However, in the case of tuple-window, the start event is the arrival of the first tuple:

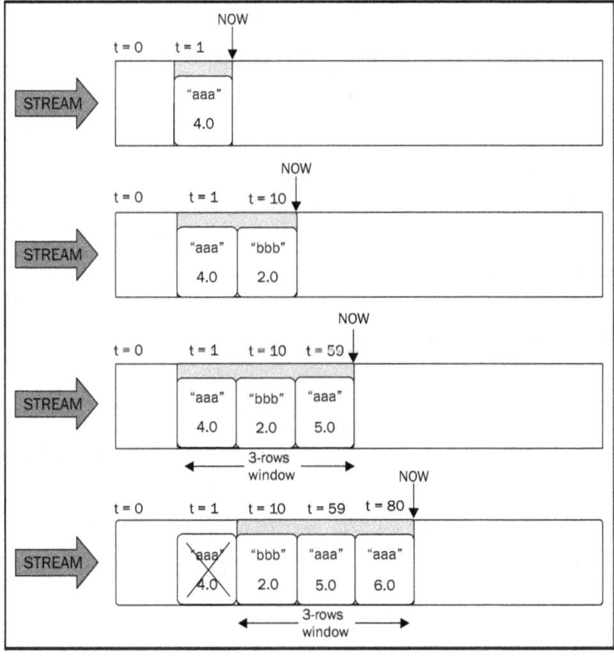

There is subtle problem with these last two queries; the average output is of all the events and not of the events relating to a particular symbol, which would be the most common scenario. In other words, we are getting the average price regardless of the stock, where what we really want is the average for symbol `"aaa"` separately from symbol `"bbb"`. The following query fixes this:

```
SELECT AVG(price), symbol
FROM marketFeed [ROWS 3]
GROUP BY symbol
```

Here is the output table for this case:

Time	Input event	Output event
00		
01	{symbol = "aaa", price = 4.0}	{AVG(price) = 4.0, symbol = "aaa"}
10	{symbol = "bbb", price = 2.0}	{AVG(price) = 2.0, symbol = "bbb"}
59	{symbol = "aaa", price = 5.0}	{AVG(price) = 4.5, symbol = "aaa"}
61		
70		
80	{symbol = "aaa", price = 6.0}	{AVG(price) = 4.5, symbol = "aaa"}

The `GROUP BY` clause works as in a regular RDBMS. It groups the content of the window relation, which happens to contain the last 3 events, per the property symbol. So, at time `t = 1`, we get the average for symbol `"aaa"`, which is *4.0/1 = 4.0*. At time `t = 10`, we get the average for `"bbb"`, which is *2.0/1 = 2.0*. Note how this already differs from the previous case, where at time `t = 10`, we had got 3.0 as the average. At time `t = 59`, the average for `"aaa"` becomes *(4.0 + 5.0)/2 = 4.5*. One crucial note is that at this time we only get the output for `"aaa"`, as only the `"aaa"` tuple changed, that is, the average for `"bbb"` does not change, and therefore is not output at this time. Finally, at time `t = 80`, the output is *(5.0 + 6.0)/2 = 5.5*.

The astute reader should ask, "why 5.5 and not *(4.0 + 5.0 + 6.0)/3 = 5.0* instead? Aren't we supposed to keep the last three events?" This is a very good question, what is happening is that our relation window does keep the last three events, however it is doing it for the last three events regardless of the `GROUP BY` expression. In other words, at time `t = 80`, the content of the window relation is:

```
{{symbol = "bbb", price = 2.0},
 {symbol = "aaa", price = 5.0},
 {symbol = "aaa", price = 6.0}}
```

We need to fix this, as it is obviously not what we intended. You can do so by using a partitioned window.

Partitioned windows

Partitioned windows are easier to understand by following an example:

```
SELECT AVG(price), symbol
FROM marketFeed [PARTITION BY symbol ROWS 3]
GROUP BY symbol
```

If you run the same set of inputs, we get the following result:

Time	Input event	Output event
00		
01	{symbol = "aaa", price = 4.0}	{AVG(price) = 4.0, symbol = "aaa"}
10	{symbol = "bbb", price = 2.0}	{AVG(price) = 2.0, symbol = "bbb"}
59	{symbol = "aaa", price = 5.0}	{AVG(price) = 4.5, symbol = "aaa"}
61		
70		
80	{symbol = "aaa", price = 6.0}	{AVG(price) = 5.0, symbol = "aaa"}

Notice how this query outputs the expected result of 5.0 at time `t = 80`. A partitioned window creates separate relation-windows for each partition. In this case, a separate partition is created for symbol `"aaa"` and another for symbol `"bbb"`. By segregating the events into separate partitions, we make sure that the windows are only filled by the right events.

Each distinct value of the partition by property uses a distinct window, increasing memory usage.

The following diagram shows how the partitions look at time `t = 80`:

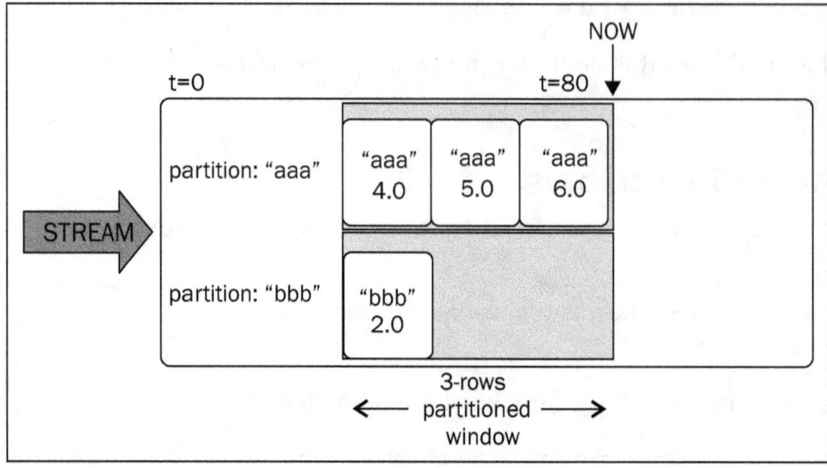

In the next section, let's revisit how the events are output.

Output

Previously in this chapter, you learned that sources and destinations have an event-type and are defined as being either a stream or a relation. You also learned that the source of events are specified using the `FROM` clause in a CQL query. However, how is the destination specified in CQL? The destination is whatever is being output by the query, which is roughly specified by the `SELECT` clause.

Consider the following query you looked in the beginning of this section:

```
SELECT AVG(price)
FROM marketFeed [RANGE 1 MINUTE]
```

In this case, the output consists of the single event property `AVG(price)`, and the processing model for this output is of a relation. Why a relation and not a stream? The query outputs a relation because the Window operator `[RANGE 1 MINUTE]`, which happens to be the last operator to be executed before the projection, generates a relation. This is easier to understand when looking at the logical query plan that represents the execution of this query:

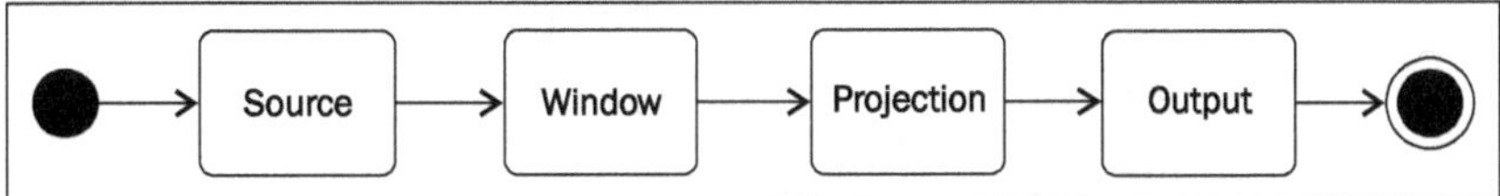

The query starts with a Source operator that receives the events as a stream, then a Window operator that converts the stream into a relation, a Projection operator that maintains the relation, and finally the Output operator that emits the resulting relation to the next downstream node in the EPN.

Because the query outputs a relation, there is only need to emit an event out when the relation changes. In other words, if the query receives an event that does not cause the average to change, then there is no need to output an event, as the content of the relation is still valid. However, if the average changes, the query sends a delete event to remove the previous average, and then an insert event to add the new average into the relation.

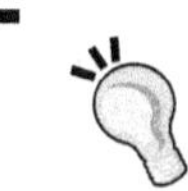

If the destination is indexed, the query can output an update event instead of a delete followed by an insert event.

By definition, CQL does a value comparison between the events to determine if something changed. In this previous example, our relation always contains a single row (or event) with a single column (or event property), named AVG.

You can change the name of the output event property by using the `AS` expression, as in the following example:

```
SELECT AVG(price) AS avgPrice …
```

There are cases when you want to always output an event, regardless if the value changed, or you may want to output only if a value has been inserted, or only if a value has been deleted from the relation. This can be accomplished by converting the output from a relation to a stream. CQL defines three operators that convert relations to streams; these are the `ISTREAM` (insert stream), the `DSTREAM` (delete stream), and the `RSTREAM` (relation stream) operators.

`RANGE` and `ROW` are stream-to-relation operators. `ISTREAM`, `DSTREAM`, and `RSTREAM` are relation-to-stream operators.

The ISTREAM operator converts a relation to a stream in such a way that only the insert events are considered. In other words, every time an event is inserted into the input relation, the ISTREAM operator generates an insert event in the output stream. Events being deleted or updated in the relation are ignored.

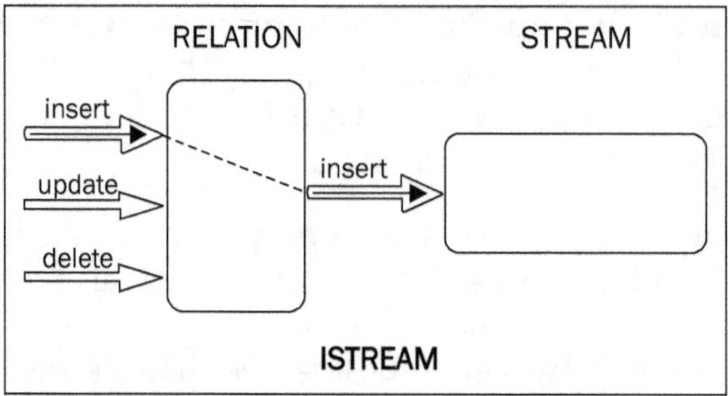

Another way of looking at this is that the output stream only contains events that exist at time *t* in the input relation, but do not exist at time *t - 1* in the input relation. The following query, which have used previously, provides an example of the ISTREAM operator being used:

```
ISTREAM (SELECT AVG(price)
FROM marketFeed [RANGE 1 MINUTE])
```

To better understand this example, take a look at the following table. Insert events are represented by a leading + (plus sign), and delete events are represented by a leading - (minus sign).

Time	Input event	WINDOW output	ISTREAM (query) output
00		+{AVG(price) = 0.0}	+{AVG(price) = 0.0}
01	+{price = 4.0}	-{AVG(price) = 0.0}, +{AVG(price) = 4.0}	+{AVG(price) = 4.0}
10	+{price = 2.0}	-{AVG(price) = 4.0}, +{AVG(price) = 3.0}	+{AVG(price) = 3.0}

Time	Input event	WINDOW output	ISTREAM (query) output
59	+{price = 5.0}	-{AVG(price) = 3.0}, +{AVG(price) = 3.6}	+{AVG(price) = 3.6}
61		-{AVG(price) = 3.6}, +{AVG(price) = 3.5}	+{AVG(price) = 3.5}
70		-{AVG(price) = 3.5}, +{AVG(price) = 5.0}	+{AVG(price) = 5.0}
80	+{price = 6.0}	-{AVG(price) = 5.0}, +{AVG(price) = 5.5}	+{AVG(price) = 5.5}

Remember that the previous examples ignored the delete events. This was done for simplification purpose. In reality, the output of the query 5.X in section 5.X should be similar to the WINDOW output in this example.

Next, let's consider the `DSTREAM` operator. As expected, in this case the operator generates an (insert) event into the output stream only when a delete event happens in the input relation. Events being inserted or updated in the relation are ignored. Another way of looking into this is that the output stream only contains events that exist at time *t - 1* in the input relation, but do not exist at time *t* in the input relation.

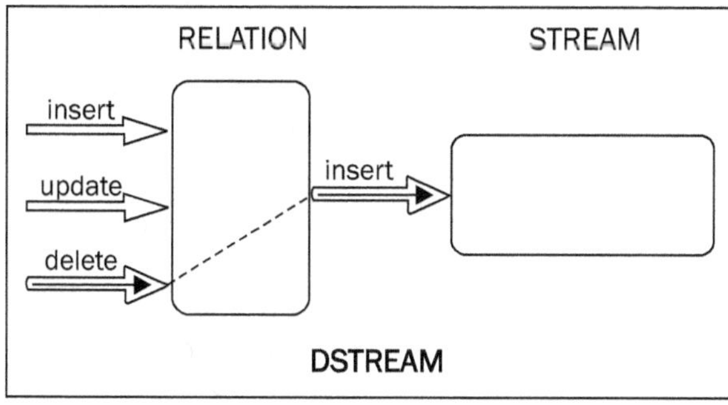

When would this be useful? The `DSTREAM` operator is useful when you want to find out when a situation is no longer valid. For example, consider a query that calculates special discounts for items being sold by a store. In this case, you want to be informed when a discount for an item is no longer valid, even if a new discount is not available.

The following query provides an example of the `DSTREAM` operator being used:

```
DSTREAM (SELECT AVG(price)
FROM marketFeed [RANGE 1 MINUTE])
```

The corresponding input and output events are provided in the following table:

Time	Input event	WINDOW output	DSTREAM (query) output
00		+{AVG(price) = 0.0}	
01	+{price = 4.0}	-{AVG(price) = 0.0}, +{AVG(price) = 4.0}	+{AVG(price) = 0.0}
10	+{price = 2.0}	-{AVG(price) = 4.0}, +{AVG(price) = 3.0}	+{AVG(price) = 4.0}
59	+{price = 5.0}	-{AVG(price) = 3.0}, +{AVG(price) = 3.6}	+{AVG(price) = 3.0}
61		-{AVG(price) = 3.6}, +{AVG(price) = 3.5}	+{AVG(price) = 3.6}
70		-{AVG(price) = 3.5}, +{AVG(price) = 5.0}	+{AVG(price) = 3.5}
80	+{price = 6.0}	-{AVG(price) = 5.0}, +{AVG(price) = 5.5}	+{AVG(price) = 5.0}

Finally, the `RSTREAM` operator outputs the whole relation as insert events in the stream. In other words, the `RSTREAM` operator generates insert events for the current state of the input relation. The outcome of this is that the query emits events even when the window's relation does not change. This is useful when you need to react in the downstream system for every input, in spite of the input causing a change to the output value.

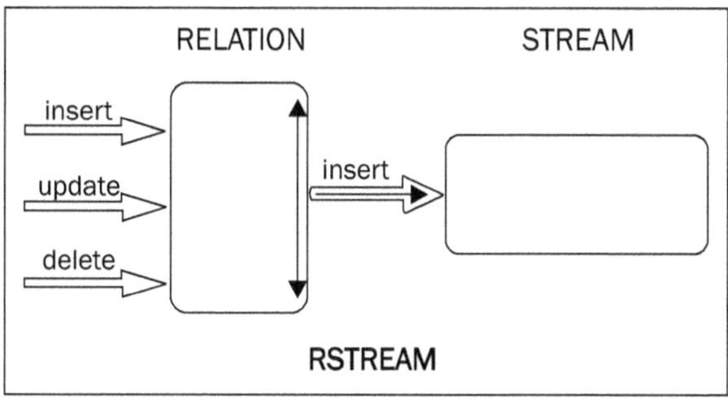

To understand the `RSTREAM`, let's use a different query and set of input events, which demonstrates this operator a little better. The new query is as follows:

```
RSTREAM (SELECT *
FROM marketFeed [ROWS 2])
```

Next, consider the following input/output table:

Input event	WINDOW output	RSTREAM (query) output
`+{price = 1.0}`	`+{price = 1.0}`	`+{price = 1.0}`
`+{price = 2.0}`	`+{price = 1.0},` `+{price = 2.0}`	`+{price = 1.0},` `+{price = 2.0}`
`+{price = 3.0}`	`-{price = 1.0},` `+{price = 3.0}`	`+{price = 2.0},` `+{price = 3.0}`
`+{price = 3.0}`	`-{price = 1.0},` `+{price = 3.0}`	`+{price = 3.0},` `+{price = 3.0}`
`+{price - 3.0}`		`+{price = 3.0},` `+{price = 3.0}`

Now, contrast the output for the three relation-to-stream operators for the same set of inputs:

Input event	ISTREAM	DSTREAM	RSTREAM
`+{price = 1.0}`	`+{price = 1.0}`		`+{price = 1.0}`
`+{price = 2.0}`	`+{price = 2.0}`		`+{price = 1.0},` `+{price = 2.0}`
`+{price = 3.0}`	`+{price = 3.0}`	`+{price = 1.0}`	`+{price = 2.0},` `+{price = 3.0}`
`+{price = 3.0}`	`+{price = 3.0}`	`+{price = 2.0}`	`+{price = 3.0},` `+{price = 3.0}`
`+{price = 3.0}`			`+{price = 3.0},` `+{price = 3.0}`
`+{price = 3.0}`			`+{price = 3.0},` `+{price = 3.0}`

As you can see, CQL provides a lot of flexibility on defining exactly the events to be output. Next, let's take a look at another dimension of processing, how to control the rate of the output.

Controlling output with slides

In the examples from the previous sub-section, the CQL queries output the changes to the window's relation immediately as they happen. This is not always desirable, for example if you have a very fast paced input, you may end up outputting more events that the CQL destination can cope with. One way of avoiding this is to batch the output events, and send them at a later time. In CQL, you can do this by using the `SLIDE` subclause in the Window specification.

The `SLIDE` subclause delays the output from the Window operator until either a certain number of events have been received in a row-based Window, or until *t* time units have progressed in a time-based Window. For example, consider the following query:

```
SELECT * FROM marketFeed[ROWS 3 SLIDE 2]
```

Next, let's take a look at its input/output table for some sample inputs:

Input event	Output events
+{price = 1.0}	
+{price = 2.0}	+{price = 1.0}, +{price = 2.0}
+{price = 3.0}	
+{price = 4.0}	- {price = 1.0}, +{price = 3.0}, +{price = 4.0}

Note how this query does not output events for the first and third input events. The `[ROW r SLIDE n]` window only outputs events every *n* events. So, in this case, at *n* = 2, 4, 6, 8,....

Further, for the fourth input event, it not only outputs two insert events, that is for `{price = 3.0}` and `{price = 4.0}`, but it also outputs the delete event of `{price = 1.0}`. Yet, it does not output the delete event of `{price = 2.0}`.

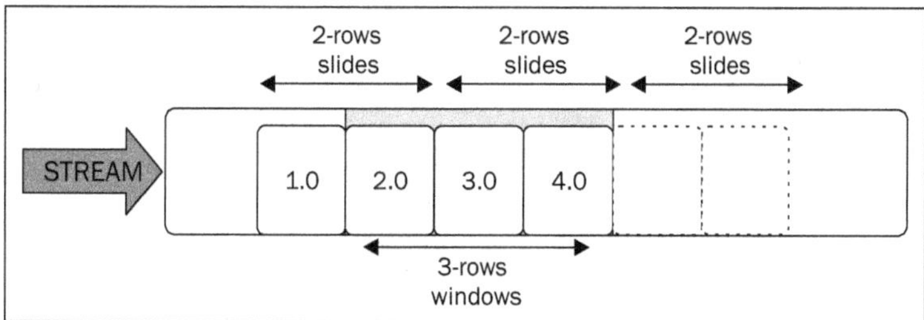

The reason being is that even though the slide changes when the events are output, it does not influence the actual state of the window's relation, which in this case still maintains three events. This is easier to see when a `RSTREAM` operator is used:

```
RSTREAM(SELECT * FROM marketFeed[ROWS 3 SLIDE 2])
```

In this case, the input/output table is:

Input event	Output events
+{price = 1.0}	
+{price = 2.0}	+{price = 1.0}, +{price = 2.0}
+{price = 3.0}	
+{price = 4.0}	+ {price = 2.0}, +{price = 3.0}, +{price = 4.0}

The `SLIDE` subclause works similarly with time windows, except for the first batch. Say you have specified a slide of 10 seconds, and the first event received is at time `t = 03`. It would be odd if the first output is emitted at time `t = 13` seconds and henceforth the batch is at `t = 23, 33, 43,...`. Instead, CQL tries to keep the output at time that is a multiple of the slide specification. So, in this case, the output should be at time *t = 10, 20, 30, 40,...*. This means that the first batch is actually smaller and only contains events from the time interval from time `t = 03` to `t = 10`, but the following batches would include the full 10 seconds of events. Formally, the output batch time (`batchTime`) is defined (in Java) as:

```
timeInterval = actualTime / slideSpecification
if((actualTime % slideSpecification) == 0) //no remainder
  batchTime = timeInterval * slideSpecification
else
  batchTime = (timeInterval + 1) * slideSpecification
```

There is one final caveat regarding range windows with slides—it is an error to specify a slide larger than the range value.

> When a slide value is not specified, it assumes the default value of 1 row for tuple-based windows and 1 time tick for time-based windows. This is the reason that the previous examples worked even when no slides were specified.
>
> On a separate topic, CQL's default time tick unit is a nanosecond. In the Application-time section, we explore this subject in details.

Next, we take a look a few special cases of windows.

The unbounded window

You can specify a window as unbounded so as that it never expires any events. This is useful only when using aggregation functions that are incremental in nature, such as average, as in this case there is no need to keep the entire history of events to calculate the result. Otherwise, unbounded windows should be used with care, as they can be extremely heavy. The following example specifies an unbounded window:

```
SELECT AVG(price) FROM marketFeed[RANGE UNBOUNDED]
```

Note that even though this is specified as a range window, it has the same effect as if it were tuple-based.

The constant value range window

A constant value range window is a window that maintains the events in the window based on the difference between an event property value and a constant value.

For example, let's say you want to keep only the events in the window whose prices are less than 10 dollars a part. You can do this with the following query:

```
SELECT * FROM marketFeed[RANGE 10 ON price]
```

Here is the input/output table for the preceding query:

Input event	Output events
`+{price = 1.0}`	`+{price = 1.0}`
`+{price = 4.0}`	`+{price = 4.0}`
`+{price = 11.0}`	`-{price = 1.0}, +{price = 11.0}`
`+{price = 12.0}`	`+{price = 12.0}+{price = 5.0},` `+{price = 5.0}`
`+{price = 14.0}`	`-{price = 14.0}, +{price = 14.0}`

The first two events are inserted and kept in the window, then when the query receives the event `{price = 11.0}`, the difference between the price of the third event `(11.0)` and the first event `(1.0)` is not less than `10` (*11.0 – 1.0 = 10.0*) and therefore the first event is removed from the window. Following, the next two events are inserted and do not cause any events to be deleted, as *12.0 – 4.0 < 10.0* and |*5.0 – 12.0*| < *10.0*. However, when the event `{price = 14.0}` is received, then the second event is removed from the window as *14.0 – 4.0 = > 10.0*.

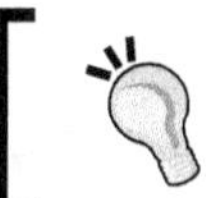

Constant value range windows may grow very large if the event properties cause the events to never expire!

Interestingly, you can specify a timestamp or an interval as the constant, as in the following example:

```
SELECT * FROM marketFeed[RANGE INTERVAL "0 0:10:0.0DAY TO SECOND
ONtimestampProperty]
```

By doing this, and using a time-stamped event property, you can create your own time-based window implementation.

The NOW window and the Last Event window

The NOW window contains the event that happened at the last tick of the system. Let's look at the syntax of the NOW window through the following example:

```
SELECT * FROM marketFeed[NOW]
```

Although this sounds simple enough, it should be observed that the event of the last tick is not necessarily the last input event! The system moves continuously, therefore an input may be received now at the last known tick, and then it is immediately removed in the next time tick, as it is no longer "now". The best way of understanding this is to compare the previously defined [NOW] query with the following query:

```
SELECT * FROM marketFeed[ROWS 1]
```

This latter query indeed functions as the last event received. Let's take a look at their input/output table:

Time	Input event	[NOW] output	[ROWS 1] output
00			
01	+{price = 1.0}	+{price = 1.0}	+{price = 1.0}
02		-{price = 1.0}	
03			
04	+{price = 2.0}	+{price = 2.0}	-{price = 1.0}, +{price = 2.0}
05		-{price = 2.0}	

As it can be seen, dealing with time has its caveats!

So far, we have gone through several ways of converting the streaming model to the relational model. In the next section, we explore more ways of leveraging the relational model in Oracle CQL.

SQL as a foundation

You have learned how to transform a stream into a relation by using WINDOW operators, and then how to convert a relation back to a stream by using the ISTREAM/DSTREAM/RSTREAM family of operators. But why do we convert to relations to begin with? By converting streams to relations, you can leverage the full power of SQL, as we are used to it in a database. After all, SQL works directly on top of relations.

CQL supports most of the SQL99 commands, which we explore in this section.

Joins

In CQL, you can join multiple sources, but all sources must be relations or streams that have been converted to relations using a window operator.

Joins are very useful as a mechanism for enriching events with contextual data that don't change often. For example, consider the following query that enriches a stock market feed event with the full address of the said stock:

```
SELECT
  S1.symbol as symbol
  fullName
FROM
  reutersMarketFeed[RANGE 60 SECONDS] AS S1,
  tickerListing AS R1
WHERE
  S1.symbol = R1.tickerSymbol
```

Assume that the `tickerListing` relation contains the following rows (events):

tickerSymbol	**fullName**
ORCL	Oracle Corp
IBM	International Business Machine Corp
MSFT	Microsoft Corp.

Here is an example of the input/output events for this example query:

Time	Input S1 (Reuters	Output
00	+{symbol = ORCL, price = 29.0}	+{symbol = ORCL, fullName = 'Oracle Corp'}
30	+{symbol = IBM, price = 100.0	+{symbol = ORCL fullName = 'International Business Machine Corp'}

The following diagram shows how the rows of the different sources are joined together:

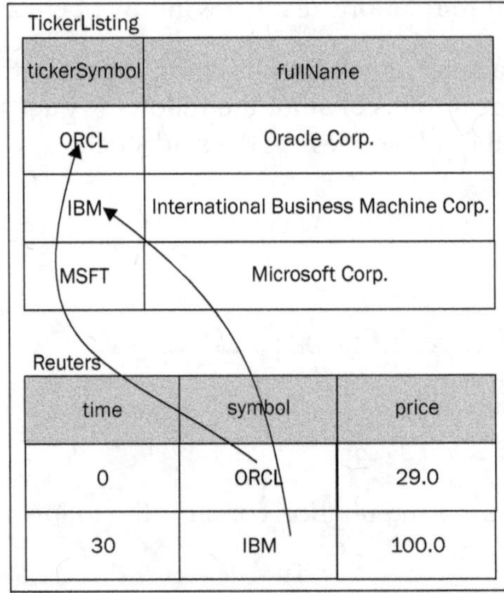

CQL joins are not limited only to joining events and data across two sources. You can join an arbitrary number of sources, making this feature a very powerful and usable one. Here is an example of a join across three sources:

```
SELECT
  S1.price AS price1,
  S2.price AS price2,
  fullName
FROM
  reutersMarketFeed[RANGE 60 SECONDS] AS S1,
  bloombergFeed[RANGE 60 SECONDS] AS S2,
  tickerListing AS R1
WHERE
  S1.symbol = S2.symbol AND
  S2.symbol = R1.tickerSymbol
```

In this case, we have two streams that contain market feeds, one coming from Reuters, and another from Bloomberg, and the same relation called `tickerListing` that contains the company details for a particular stock symbol (for example, ORCL), such as the company's full name (for example, Oracle Corporation) and address. The query converts the two streams to a relation using the `RANGE` operator, and then joins all three resulting relations using the join condition specified in the `WHERE` clause. The join condition links the events that have the same symbol together. Finally, the `SELECT` clause projects properties from all three relations, namely the `price` property from the streams `reutersMarketFeed` and `bloombergeFeed`, and the `fullName` property from `tickerListing`.

When the names of the event properties coming from different sources collide, they must be prefixed by the source name.

In the previous example, both the Reuters and the Bloomberg feeds have a `price` property; therefore references to this property must be prefixed by `s1` or `s2`, or by the source name (for example, `bloombergFeed.price`). One important difference between a regular RDBMS and CEP is that in the latter case the queries are run in a continuous mode, this means that as the window in the relations slide, you will get a continuous flow of output.

An example of the input/output events for this example query is as follows:

Time	Input S1 (Reuters)	Input S2 (Bloomberg)	Output
00	+{symbol = ORCL, price = 29.0}	+{symbol = ORCL price = 29.5}	+{price1 = 29.0, price2 = 29.5, fullName = 'Oracle Corp'}

Time	Input S1 (Reuters)	Input S2 (Bloomberg)	Output
30	+{symbol = ORCL price = 28.5	+{symbol = ORCL, price = 30.0}	+{price1 =28.5, price2 = 29.5 fullName = 'Oracle Corp'}, +{price1 = 28.5, price2 = 30.0, fullName = 'Oracle Corp'}, +{price1 = 29.0, price2 = 30.0 fullName = 'Oracle Corp'}
60	+{symbol = IBM, price = 100.0}		-{price1 = 29.0, price2 = 29.5, fullName = 'Oracle Corp'}, -{price1 = 28.5, price2 = 29.5, fullName = 'Oracle Corp'}, -{price1 = 29.0, price2 = 29.5, fullName = 'Oracle Corp'}

Continuous joins may not be so intuitive to grasp. Note how at time `t = 30` there are three output events! The reason being is that at this time the total number of events that match the join condition across all sources are *2 (for S1) x 2 (for S2) x 1 (for S3) = 4* rows. However, the output relation already contains one row, which was output at time `t = 00`, therefore we only need to insert three additional outputs at time `t = 30`.

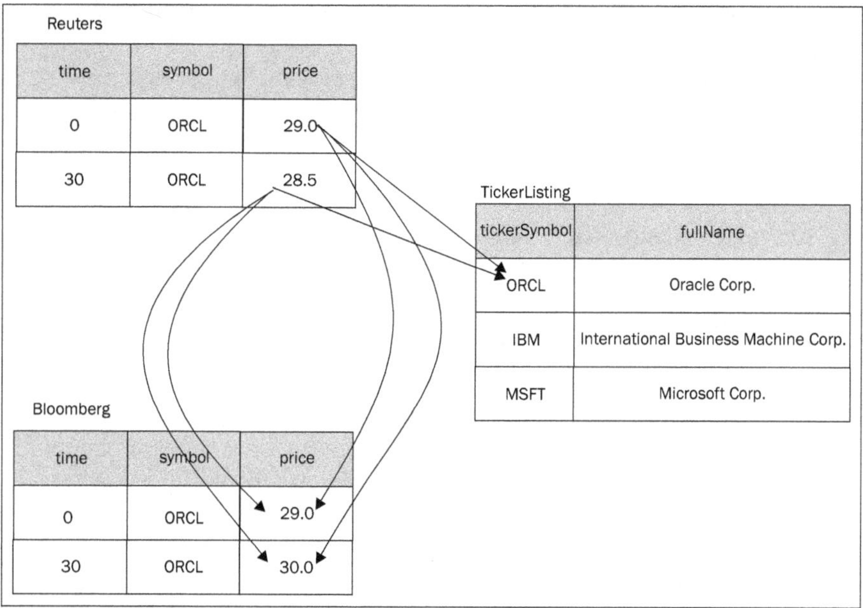

At time `t = 60`, the first event from `S1` and `S2` have expired, and the new event from `S2` does not match the join criteria, therefore we need to remove three events from the output relation and maintain only the event `{price1= 28.5, price2 = 30.0, …}`.

This type of join is called an inner join. CQL also supports left and right outer joins, but those are outside the scope of this book.

External sources

So far, all the sources we have used in the examples of this chapter are streaming sources. Sources that actively send events are streaming sources and generally map to channels in the EPN. However, there is also the case of regular pull-based sources. Examples of pull-based sources are a table from an external database, or a cache from a caching system like Coherence. These two examples of pull-based sources map respectively to a table and a cache component in the EPN. As these sources are maintained by an external system, they are called external sources. You will have a in-depth look into the usage of external sources in *Chapter 7, Using Tables and Caches for Contextual Data*.

CQL supports joins between streaming sources (like we have seen in the previous examples) and external sources. These external sources are generally more static, and provide data to be used for enriching the events. When joining to external sources, the external sources are (logically) pulled every time a new event arrives that needs data from this external source.

> A CQL join must have at least one streaming source. In other words, you cannot define a CQL query that is composed of only external sources, as it would become a strictly pull-based query, contrary to CQL's continuous nature.

Next, let's look how aggregations are realized in CQL.

Aggregations

In past sections, you have already seen the usage of the AVG function, which is an example of an aggregation function. CQL supports other standard aggregation functions, such as `COUNT`, `SUM`, `MAX`, and `MIN`. The aggregate functions `AVG`, `COUNT`, and `SUM` are calculated incrementally, however the `MAX` and `MIN` functions are not incremental, so beware when using these latter two with large windows.

As in SQL, you can check for conditions on the aggregate results by using the HAVING clause, as in the following example:

```
SELECT AVG(price) FROM marketFeed[RANGE 1 HOUR]
HAVING AVG(price) > 10
```

In this case, only averages that is higher than 10 will be output. Note that you cannot specify this condition in the `WHERE` clause as the `WHERE` clause is processed before the average can be calculated.

Further, CQL supports a plethora of additional math and statistical related aggregate functions provided by the built-in COLT open-source library. These include `mean`, `median`, `variance`, and so on. Please take a look at COLT's website for further details.

Ordering

You can order the result of a query's relation output by using the `ORDER BY property [ASC|DESC] ROWS n` clause. In this case, the relation is ordered using the specified event property (row attribute) in ascending or descending order, and only the top *n* events are output. By default it is ordered in ascending order.

It is mandatory to specify the top *n* rows when ordering a relation output. The reason being is that a relation may be very large, and therefore the top *n* rows help restrict the processing.

Let's take a look at an example to better understand this:

```
SELECT price FROM marketFeed[ROWS 4]
ORDER BY price DESC ROWS 2
```

This query is stating that you are interested in ordering the results from the `marketFeed` window in descending order of price (from largest price to smallest price) and to only keep the two largest results. Next, consider the input/output table for this query:

Input event	Output events
`+{price = 5.0}`	`+{price = 5.0}`
`+{price = 3.0}`	`+{price = 3.0}`
`+{price = 4.0}`	`-{price = 3.0}, +{price = 4.0}`
`+{price = 6.0}`	`-{price = 4.0}, +{price = 6.0}`
`+{price = 0.0}`	`-{price = 5.0}, +{price = 4.0}`

The first two sets of input/output are clear, but it starts getting interesting from there on. When the query receives the third input event, the `marketFeed` window relation is updated to:

```
Window: {{price = 5.0}, {price = 3.0}, {price = 4.0}}
```

In this window, `{price = 3.0}` is no longer part of the two top prices, so it is removed from the output relation and replaced with `{price = 4.0}`. In other words, the ordered output relation has become:

```
Output: {{price = 5.0}, {price = 4.0}}
```

Likewise, when the query receives the event `{price = 6.0}`, the window relation is updated to:

```
Window: {{price = 5.0}, {price = 3.0}, {price = 4.0}, {price = 6.0}}
```

For this window, the ordered output relation is changed to:

```
Output: {{price = 6.0}, {price = 5.0}}
```

Finally, when the query receives the last event, its window output becomes:

```
Window: {price = 3.0}, {price = 4.0}, {price = 6.0}, {price = 0.0}}
```

In other words, the first event of `{price = 5.0}` is expired from the `[ROWS 4]` window. Now, the ordered output is changed to:

```
Output: {{price = 6.0}, {price = 4.0}}
```

Note how the event `{price = 4.0}` is moved back into the ordered output with the absence of the event `{price = 5.0}` from the window relation.

> The change of the location (order) of the rows in a relation does not cause its update. In other words, when comparing the relation `{{price = 5.0}, {price = 4.0}}` and the relation `{{price = 6.0}, {price = 5.0}}`, the (set) difference is that the event `{price = 4.0}` has been removed and the event `{price = 6.0}` has been added. The fact that event `{price = 5.0}` has moved from the first to the second location is not considered a change.

In the `ORDER BY` clause, you can specify multiple properties. This means that should there be multiple rows with the same value for a property, then these rows are ordered using the second specified property, and so on.

Furthermore, you can specify the location of the event property in the event type definition rather than its name. The location starts at `1`. Let's extend the previous query to make use of both of these two features:

```
SELECT price, symbol FROM marketFeed[ROWS 4]
ORDER BY 1 DESC, symbol ASC ROWS 2
```

In this case, events that have the same price are further ordered by their symbol in ascending order.

So far, you have seen how to use the `ORDER BY` clause on top of relations. Yet, CQL also supports `ORDER BY` with streams. You may find this strange, as we have always seen a single output per time `t` for a stream. However, this has been for simplification purpose of the examples used so far, CQL can output more than a single event in the same time *t*. These are called simultaneous events. The `ORDER BY` clause can be used to order simultaneous events.

Here is a simple example:

```
SELECT price FROM marketFeed
ORDER BY price DESC
```

We have a sample input/output table for this query:

Time	Input event	Output events
`00`	`+{price = 5.0}`	
`00`	`+{price = 10.0}`	
`00`	`+{price = 1.0}`	

`01`		`+{price = 10.0},`
		`+{price = 5.0},`
		`+{price 1.0}`

In this case, note how the event `{price = 10.0}` is output first before the event `{price = 5.0}`, even though the former was received after the latter.

When used with streams, it is not mandatory to specify the top *n* events in the `ORDER BY` clause. This is so because it is expected that the number of simultaneous events is not large.

It is worth noting that the output only happens after the time *t* has moved from 0 to 1. This is necessary for CQL to know that no more events with time `t = 0` will be received. We explore CQL's timing model in details in a later section in this chapter.

Views

CQL queries, similarly to SQL, can get overwhelming very quickly, so there is a need to be able to compose queries together in an efficient and productive form. This is solved in CQL by using views. A view is a CQL statement that can be re-used by different CQL queries. You can make use of the full CQL syntax in a view, except that views can only be used as sources of a query. In other words, views do not output events directly out of a CQL processor, but only to other CQL queries.

Let's take a look at an example of a view:

```
SELECT price FROM marketFeed
```

The name of this view is `MarketFeedView`.

Next, let's define two queries that re-use this view:

- `SELECT price FROM MarketFeedView WHERE price > 10.0`
- `SELECT price FROM MarketFeedView WHERE price < 5.0`

From the perspective of the queries, the `MarketFeedView` view behaves just like any other source, and therefore can emit either streams or relations.

However, it is important to make sure the views and the queries type-check correctly. In other words, if a view is projecting a `price` string property, then the query must use only a `price` string property when referencing the view source. For example, the following view and query fail to compile:

```
View V1:  SELECT symbol FROM marketFeed
Query Q1: SELECT price FROM V1
```

In this case, `Q1` is referencing to a `price` property that has not been projected by the `V1` view, even though it may exist in the original `marketFeed` source.

Set operations

CQL supports the usual set operations between relations, such as `EXCEPT`, `MINUS`, `INTERSECT`, `UNION`, `UNION ALL`, `IN`, and `NOT IN`.

These operators are binary and need to reference queries (or views) in both their left and right hand-side. To better understand their usage, consider the following two views:

```
View V1:   SELECT symbol
      FROM reutersMarketFeed[RANGE 1 MINUTE]
View V2:  SELECT symbol
      FROM bloombergMarketFeed[RANGE 1 MINUTE]
```

Next, consider the following queries:

```
Query Q1: V1 EXCEPT V2
Query Q2: V1 MINUS V2
Query Q3: V1 INTERSECT V2
Query Q4: V1 UNION V2
Query Q5: V1 IN V2
```

Finally, let us assume that the feeds `reutersMarketFeed` and `bloombergMarketFeed` respectively output the following events in the last minute:

```
reutersMarketFeed:
  {symbol = "ORCL"},{symbol = "IBM"},{symbol = "ORCL"}
bloombergMarketFeed:
  {symbol = "IBM"},{symbol = "MSFT"}
```

In this case, the result from the previous `Q1` to `Q5` queries at the end of the one-minute period is:

```
Q1: {symbol = "ORCL"}
Q2: {symbol = "ORCL"}
Q3: {symbol = "IBM"}
Q4: {symbol = "ORCL"},{symbol = "IBM"},{symbol = "MSFT"}
Q5: {symbol = "IBM"}
```

Remember that comparison between events is done based upon their value. All of the previous operators remove duplicates, hence the reason that query `Q1` only outputs a single `{symbol = "ORCL"}` event, even though the `reutersMarketFeed` stream received two such events in the last minute of execution.

`UNION ALL` is slightly different; it does not remove duplicates. More importantly, it can be used directly with streams. Consider the following set of statements that make use of `UNION ALL`:

```
View V1:    SELECT symbol AS ticker
      FROM reutersMarketFeed
View V2:   SELECT symbol
      FROM bloombergMarketFeed
Query Q1:   V1 UNION ALL V2
```

Here is a sample input/output table for these statements:

Time	V1 output	V2 output	Q1 output
00	+{ticker = "ORCL"}		+{ticker = "ORCL"}
01	+{ticker = "ORCL"}	+{symbol = "IBM"}	+{ticker = "ORCL"}, +{ticker = "IBM"}

Time	V1 output	V2 output	Q1 output
02		+{symbol = "MSFT"}	+{ticker = "MSFT"}
03	+{ticker = "ORCL"}	+{symbol = "ORCL"}	+{ticker = "ORCL"}, +{ticker = "ORCL"}

As noted, the interesting behavior of this example is that at time `t = 03`, the query outputs two simultaneous events that are equal. This is only possible as we are outputting a stream, otherwise the two similar events would have been considered as if they were the same in the case of a relation, and the second one wouldn't have been output.

Further, notice how the output property is always called `ticker`, rather than `symbol`, which happens to be the event property name for the relation at the left-hand side of the `UNION ALL`. For all binary set operators in CQL (and SQL for that matter), the schema of the left-hand side and of the right-hand side relations must match in number and type, and the properties (row attributes) of the output events are named using the name of the event properties of the left-hand side relation.

The type of a property is very important not only for these set operators, but also in general to dictate what kind of operations is supported with a particular data. In the next section, we explore CQL's type system.

Typing and expressions

CQL native types are similar to Java with some additional RDBMS types. They are defined as follows:

- `BIGINT`: This is equivalent to Java `long`
- `BOOLEAN`: This is equivalent to Java `boolean`
- `BYTE(size)`: This is equivalent to an array of Java `byte`
- `CHAR(size)`: This is equivalent to a Java `String` or an array of Java `char`
- `DOUBLE`: This is equivalent to Java `double`
- `FLOAT`: This is equivalent to Java `float`
- `INTEGER`: This is equivalent to Java `int`
- `INTERVAL`: This represents an interval of time, and is similar to Oracle RDBMS interval data type
- `TIMESTAMP`: This is equivalent to Java `DateTime` class
- `XMLTYPE`: This represents XML data

The numeric data types of `bigint`, `double`, and `integer` support the following comparison operators:

- = (equality)
- <> (inequality)
- < (greater than)
- > (less than)
- <= (greater than or equal)
- >= (less than or equal)
- Range

Most of these are intuitive, except for range. Range is true if the value is in between a range, as in the following example:

```
WHERE price BETWEEN 10 AND 30
```

The `char` type supports the `like` operator, which allows you to match a String with another String or even to a regular expression. Here is an example:

```
WHERE symbol LIKE "ORCL"
WHERE symbol LIKE "[A-C][A-C]"
```

This latter case matches symbol to "AA", "AC", but not to "DD", or "AAA".

Explaining the full syntax of regular expressions is beyond the scope of this book.

The date-time types `timestamp` and `interval` likewise support all the previous comparison operators. Here is an example:

```
WHERE INTERVAL "1 12:00:30" DAY TO SECOND > INTERVAL "1 12:00:00" DAY
TO SECOND
```

You can construct compound comparisons by combining terms with the AND, OR, NOT, and XOR. Here is a simple example:

```
WHERE (price = 10 AND symbol like "ORCL")
OR (price between 100 and 200 and symbol like "IBM")
```

This matches events whose price are `10` and symbol is `"ORCL"` or events whose prices are in between the values `100` and `200` and the symbol is `"IBM"`.

You can also check with an event property is null by using `is [not] null` operator, as in the following example:

```
WHERE symbol is not null
```

In most cases, you won't need to worry about all this different data types, as the server will take care of converting Java to CQL types automatically. You can also explicit convert the data-types by using the following cast functions:

- `to_bigint()`
- `to_boolean()`
- `to_char()`
- `to_double()`
- `to_float()`
- `to_timestamp()`

In future chapters, you will learn more about how to use Java with CQL, and about the XML data type.

Timing models

As you have without a doubt realized, time is an essential part of CQL. It dictates how the streams are computed, how the windows behave, and ultimately the continuous nature of Oracle CEP.

Oracle CEP supports two different timing models:

- System time-stamped streams
- Application time-stamped streams

In system time-stamped streams, the system automatically timestamps the events as the events arrive. The CQL processor does this as events arrive from upstream channels. This is the default modus operandi. In this mode, time is measured in nanoseconds.

In application time-stamped streams, it is the responsibility of the application to provide a timestamp. Placing the timestamp in an event property does this. In this mode, it is up to the application to define how time progresses, and time is measured in application time ticks. An application could determine that every one hour of wall-clock time equals to one application time tick, and so on. For example, consider an event whose `ts` property is the application time-stamped property, and a query as the following:

```
SELECT * FROM S[range 2 nanoseconds].
```

At lunch time, you send your first event as `{ts = 0, id = 1}`, and you will get the following output:

```
+{ts = 0, id = 1}
```

Later, at midday, you send another event as `{ts = 1, id = 2}`. The output is:

```
+{ts = 1, id = 2}
```

At night, you send the event `{ts = 2, id = 3}`. The output now is:

```
-{ts = 0, id = 1}
+{ts = 2, id = 3}
```

So even though several hours progressed on the wall-clock, in your application only three nanoseconds have gone by.

The timing model you choose also has two other implications. First, in system time-stamped streams, if no events arrive, the progress of time can be trigged by periodic heartbeats. For example, considering still the same query as previously, even if no events arrive after 3 nanoseconds, the server knows that the system time has progressed by looking at the CPU clock, and so can automatically generate the delete event `-{ts = 0, id = 1}` when necessary. This doesn't work for application time-stamped streams, as the server cannot assume that the application time has moved by looking at the CPU clock. The implication of this is that there is no heartbeat for application time-stamped streams.

> You can configure the periodicity of the heartbeat for system time-stamped streams using the following MBean operation: `com.bea.wlevs.management.configuration.EventChannelMBean.setHeartbeatTimeout(long)`

The second implication is that in system time-stamped streams, you may get more than one event in a single tick. However, in application time-stamped streams, the application can determine if every event in the stream arrives with a different increasing time-stamp. This property of having strictly increasing time-stamps is called a **total ordered time-stamped stream**. By informing the CQL processor that a stream is totally ordered, it allows the CQL processor to perform optimizations.

> You can configure an application time-stamped stream as total-order by setting the XML attribute of a channel `is-total-order` to true in the EPN assembly

One optimization is that the CQL processor does not have to wait for the next time-stamp before being able to assume that time has progressed. For example, still considering the same query, take a look at the input/output table for the application time-stamped stream `S1` that is not totally ordered, and for the application time-stamped stream `S2` that is totally ordered:

Time	Input Event	Output S1	Output S2
0	`+{ts = 0, id = 1}`	`+{ts = 0, id = 1}`	`+{ts = 0, id = 1}`
1	`+{ts = 1, id = 2}`	`+{ts = 1, id = 2}`	`+{ts = 1, id = 2},` `-{ts = 0, id = 1}`
2	`+{ts = 2, id = 3}`	`-{ts = 0, id = 1},` `+{ts = 2, id = 3}`	`+{ts = 2, id = 3},` `-{ts = 1, id = 2}`

As you can see, dealing with time is not exactly trivial, but its understanding is crucial in CEP systems.

Summary

CQL is a powerful language for performing event processing. In this chapter, you learned the foundations of CEP, one important aspect of which is the difference between streams and relations. You can now convert a stream to a relation by applying window operations. CQL supports several useful Window operators such as tuple-based windows, time-based windows, and partitioned windows. You can also convert a relation to a stream by using the `ISTREAM`, `DSTREAM`, and `RSTREAM` operations.

When using relations, you can apply most SQL operations, such as joins, aggregations, and ordering. The main difference is that these operations are executed in a continuous form.

We also learned how CQL native types are similar to that of Java and the RDBMS, and provide several functions for casting.

Finally, we looked into how CQL interprets time and different timing models supported, such as system time-stamped and application time-stamped streams.

In the next chapter we will be moving onto how to manage, monitor, and test Oracle OEP applications.

6

Managing and Monitoring Applications

In the previous chapters, you learned how to develop and run OEP applications. For example, you learned how to develop CQL queries and configure adapters that receive events. Next, you learned how to deploy these applications. In this chapter, you will learn how to manage and monitor these deployed running applications to make sure they are functioning correctly and to tune them as the load in your system changes.

Specifically, you will learn how to:

- Enable and check log messages for OEP server components
- Deploying, suspending, resuming, and undeploying applications through the Visualizer
- Dynamically manage the configuration of EPN adapters, channels, and processors
- Dynamically manage the configuration of OEP server-wide services, such as the embedded Jetty HTTP server, and data sources
- Monitor the throughput and latency of OEP applications

Configuring the logging service

The first step in managing and debugging a running application is to selectively enable logging for the different OEP server components and check their log records. You can do this by using the Visualizer.

Start an OEP server in the `helloworld` sample domain. You have learned how to do this in the previous chapters, but as a recap, here are the detailed steps in a Unix-based environment:

1. Execute the following command:

   ```
   cd Oracle/Middleware/ocep_11.1/samples/domains/helloworld_domain/
   defaultserver
   ./startwlevs.sh
   ```

2. Next, log into the Visualizer through your web browser. Remember, that by default the URL should be `http://localhost:9002/wlevs`, and the user ID and password are both `wlevs`.
3. Next, select your server in the **Domain Browser** window, which is located in the left panel. The **Domain Browser** window allows you to explore all the servers of your domain. By default, a domain contains a single server called **NonClusteredServer**. Within each server, you can see all the applications that are deployed. Within each application, you can further drill-down in all the stages of the application, that is, the EPN nodes. The next screenshot shows the **Domain Browser** window for the sample `hello-world` domain included in the product:

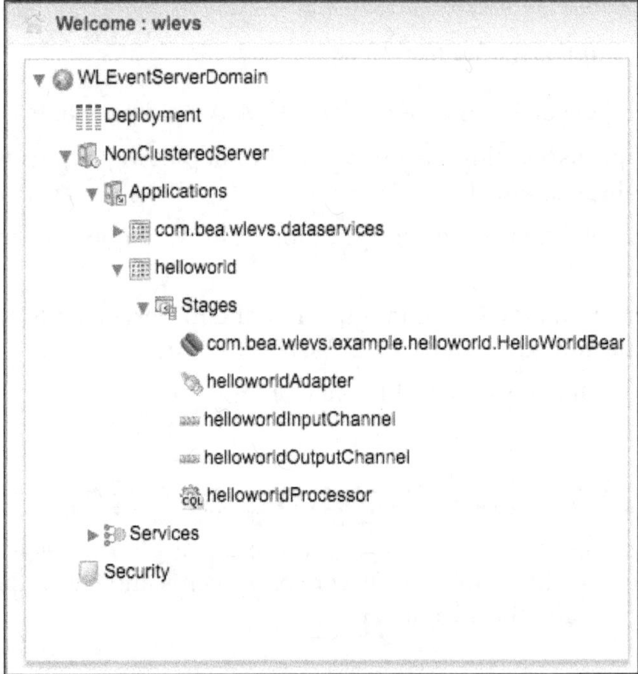

4. Further, when you select a server, you will get several tabbed panels in the right-hand window representing the different services you can manage. Select the **Logging** tab. This is shown in the following screenshot:

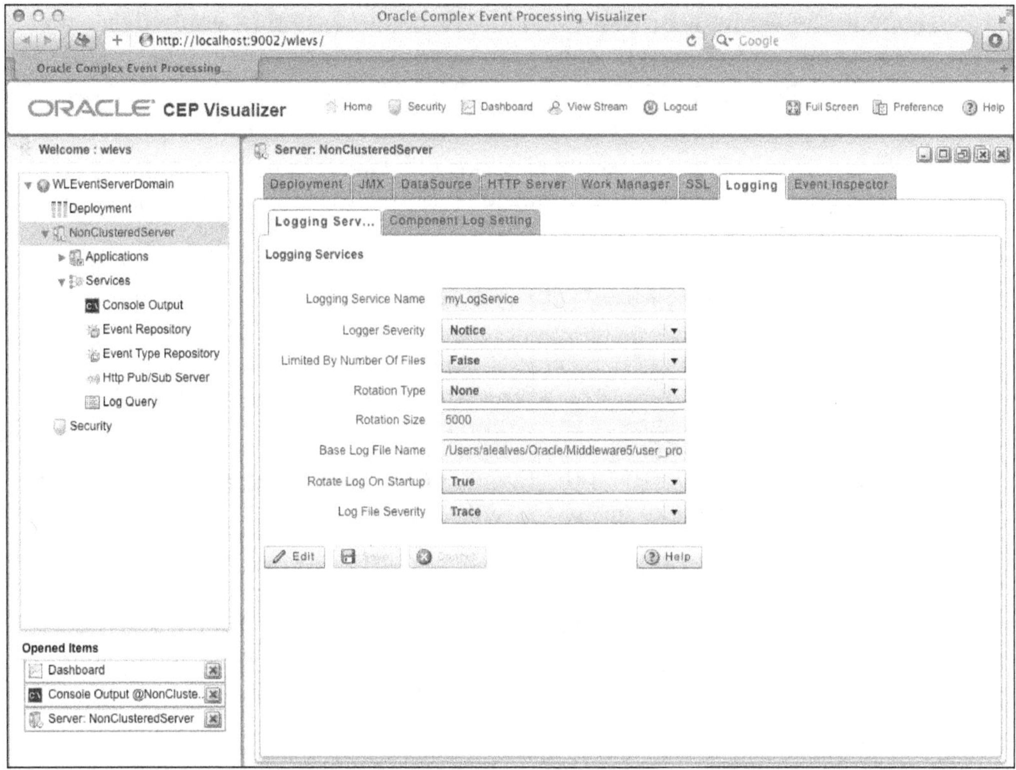

5. Next, select the sub-panel titled **Component Log Setting**. This provides a list of all the available components of the server. For example, the **Channel** component can be used to control the log messages for channels in the EPN. Similarly, the **CQLProcessor** component controls logging for CQL processors in the EPN. By default, all of the logging components are set to severity **Notice**. This means that only logs whose severity are **Notice** or of higher severity, such as **Warning**, **Error**, **Critical**, **Alert**, or **Emergency** are logged.

6. Select the **EventTrace** component, then press the **Edit** button, and change its severity to **Info**.

7. The **EventTrace** component is a very useful log category. It allows you to trace the events as they flow through the EPN. Let's take a look at how it works. You can check all the log messages that are being output to the console by selecting the **NonClusteredServer/Services/Console Output** node in the **Domain Browser** window. When you do this, you will see the console output in the right-hand side window. For example, you should see the following log messages:

```
Message: HelloWorld - the current time is:11:26:53 AM

<Jul 6, 2012 11:26:53 AM PDT> <Info> <EventTrace> <BEA-000000>
<Application [helloworld], Stage [helloworldInputChannel] received
insert event>

<Jul 6, 2012 11:26:53 AM PDT> <Info> <EventTrace> <BEA-000000>
<Application [helloworld], Stage [helloworldProcessor] received
insert event>

 <Jul 6, 2012 11:26:53 AM PDT> <Info> <EventTrace> <BEA-000000>
<Application [helloworld], Stage [helloworldOutputChannel]
received insert event>
```

8. If you change the severity of the **EventTrace** component back to **Notice**, the previous `<EventTrace>` messages will no longer be output.
9. Let's try a different category. Change the severity of **CQLProcessor** category to **DEBUG**. The **DEBUG** severity is useful when problems arise, and you need a finer grain of details showing what's happening. Also, if you run into a bug, Oracle support may enquire that you send a debug-level logging file. The following is an example of the **CQLProcessor** component's debug logging messages:

```
<Nov 22, 2012 1:47:32 PM EST> <Debug> <CQLProcessor> <BEA-
000000> <Event com.bea.wlevs.event.example.helloworld.
HelloWorldEvent@4a8e91eb incoming to processor:
helloworldProcessor>

<Nov 22, 2012 1:47:32 PM EST> <Debug> <CQLProcessor> <BEA-000000>
<onEvent [eventType=HelloWorldEvent object=helloworldInputChannel
kind=PLUS time=0 _this=com.bea.wlevs.event.example.helloworld.
HelloWorldEvent@4a8e91eb, message=HelloWorld - the current time
is:1:47:32 PM isTotalOrderGuarantee=false] to helloworld_$ocep$_
helloworldProcessor_$ocep$__s1640586218>

<Nov 22, 2012 1:47:32 PM EST> <Debug> <CQLProcessor> <BEA-
000000> <processor [helloworldProcessor] output tuple =
object=helloworldRule kind=null time=1353610052612109000
helloworldInputChannel._this=com.bea.wlevs.event.example.
helloworld.HelloWorldEvent@4a8e91eb, helloworldInputChannel.
message=HelloWorld - the current time is:1:47:32 PM
isTotalOrderGuarantee=true isBatchDestination=false
propagateHeartbeat=false>
```

10. Finally, in the **Logging Service** sub-panel, you have several logging service properties, such as the location of the logfile name, and the rotation size of the file.

In the next section, you will learn how to manage the deployment of applications.

Provisioning applications

In the previous chapters, you deployed and undeployed applications using the Integrated Development Environment (IDE). This is the norm when you are developing the applications and need to test them. However, after development, you will generally deploy and manage your deployed applications in your production environment using the Visualizer.

Let's start by using the `helloworld` sample domain. Log into the Visualizer as usual, and navigate to the **Deployment** node, which is the first node underneath **WLEventServerDomain** in the **Domain Browser** panel. In the right-hand panel, you will see a list of all the deployed applications, the first of which is the **helloworld** application. This is demonstrated in the following screenshot:

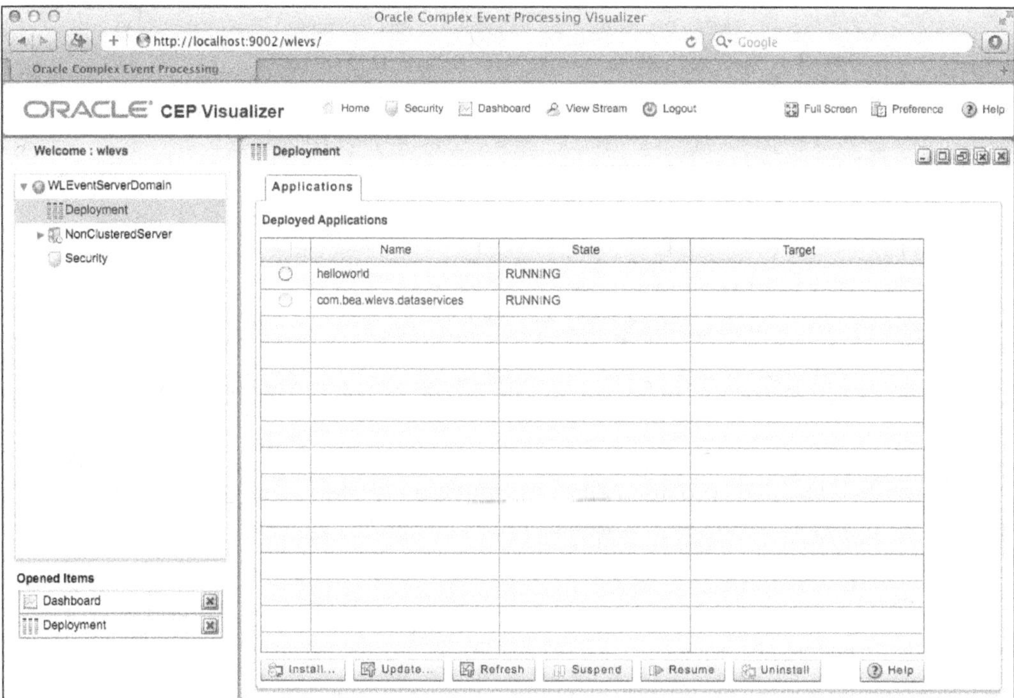

Next, select the **helloworld** application, and then click on the **Suspend** button in the bottom of the window. Go back to the **Console Output** node, and you should see the following log message:

```
<Jul 7, 2012 10:17:47 AM PDT> <Notice> <Spring> <BEA-2047005> <The
application context "helloworld" was suspended successfully>
```

You can also go to the server's dashboard, by selecting the **Home** shortcut at the top of the window. In the dashboard, there is a **Management Events** window that shows all the management-related log messages. This is demonstrated in the next screenshot:

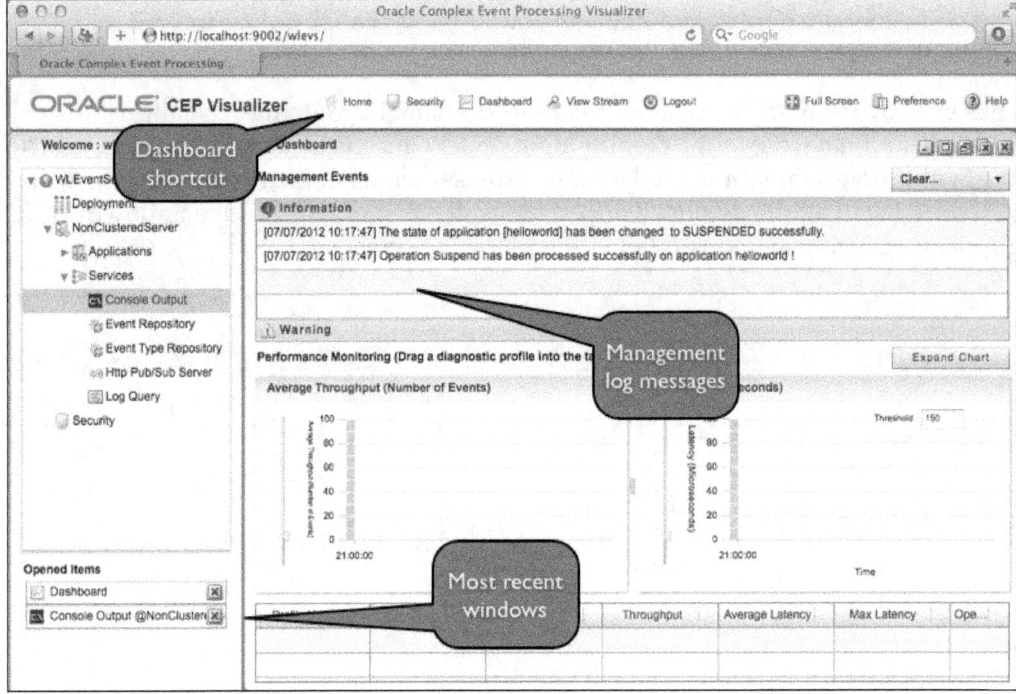

Notice how there is also a shortcut at the bottom-left corner for all recent windows you have selected so far. For example, you will see the **Console Output** window there, as you had just used it previously.

You can resume your **helloworld** application by going back to the **Deployment** window, selecting the **helloworld** application, and then clicking on the **Resume** button.

When you suspend and resume an application, the application is informed of this action so that it can take the appropriate actions, such as releasing and acquiring resources. A stage in the EPN that wishes to be informed of these actions must respectively implement the `com.bea.wlevs.ede.api.SuspendableBean` and `com.bea.wlevs.ede.api.ResumableBean.java` interfaces.

Next, undeploy the `helloworld` application by selecting the `helloworld` application and clicking on the **Uninstall** button. It will be undeployed and no longer part of the deployed applications list.

You can redeploy the `helloworld` application by clicking on the **Install** button. The first step to deploy an application is to upload its JAR file to the server. You do this by choosing a file in your local file-system by clicking on the **...** button. Navigate to the source location of the `helloworld` application, and select the JAR file in the `dist` directory.

The sources for all samples are located at `Oracle/Middleware/ocep_11.1/samples/source/applications` in Unix and `Oracle\Middleware\ocep_11.1\samples\sources\applications` in Windows.

To build an application from its source, make sure you have Ant and Java in your environment path, and run Ant from the root location of the sample. For example, for the `helloworld` application, the steps are:

```
cd Oracle/Middleware/ocep_11.1/samples/source/applications/helloworld
ant
```

The output JAR file is placed in the `dist` directory.

Next, click on the **Upload** button. The JAR file will be uploaded to the server, and a new window is shown. Select the uploaded JAR file and click **Deploy**. This is shown in the next screenshot:

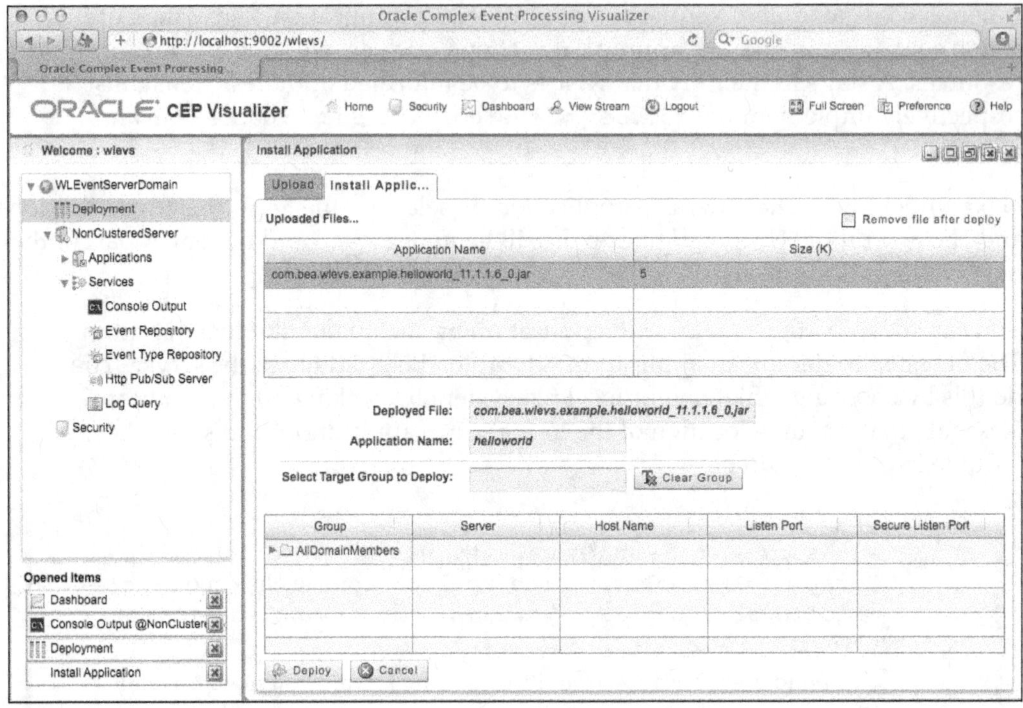

Finally, confirm by clicking on the **Ok** button, and the `helloworld` application will be deployed and its status shown as **Running** in the list of deployed applications.

By now, you are able to deploy, suspend, resume, and undeploy applications. In the next section, let's explore what other management actions you can do on a deployed application.

Changing application configuration

The Visualizer not only allows you to manage the server, but also to change the configuration of the deployed applications. In the **Domain Browser** window, select the **helloworld** node under **NonClusteredServer/Applications**. You will get a general description of the application in the panel that appears on the right. Next, select the **Event Processing Network** tab, which shows you a graphical representation of the application's EPN. This is demonstrated in the next screenshot:

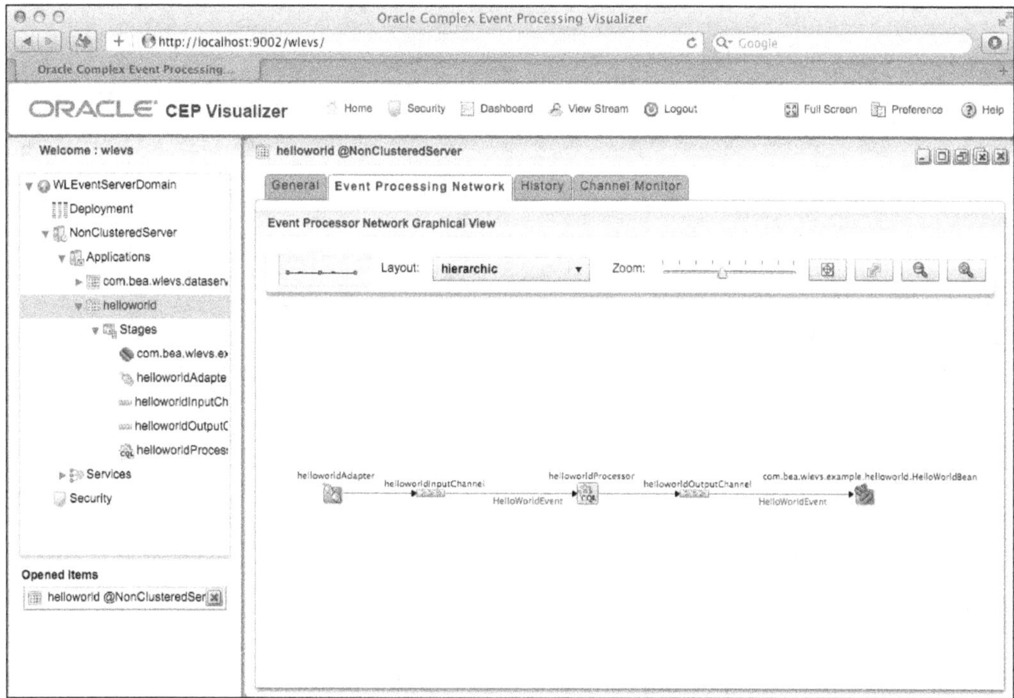

This graphical view is not only a useful visualization aid for understanding the EPN, but also allows you to easily select any of the stages of the EPN.

As you have learned, the EPN is a directed graph representing the flow of events from left to right. The first stage, which is the left-most upstream node in the graph, is **helloworldAdapter**. Double-click this node and you will get a new panel with the adapter's configuration, as is shown in the next screenshot:

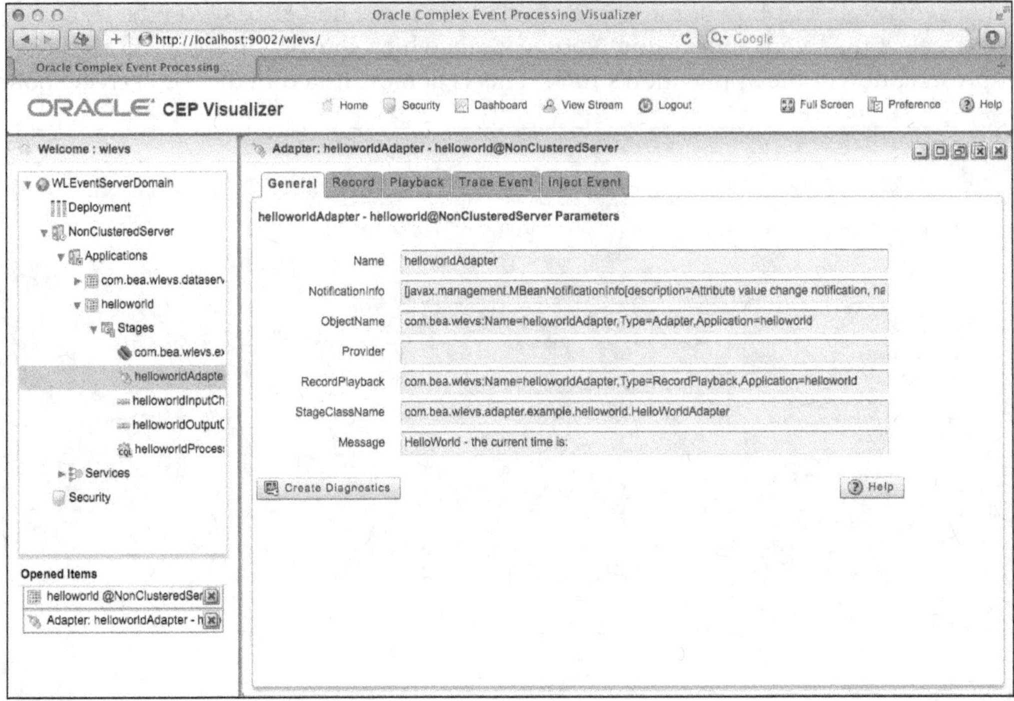

The `helloworldAdapter` has a lot of interesting properties, particularly the last one, which is called the `Message` property. This property has the content of the message that is being printed.

Different adapters have different properties. For example, the CSV adapter has a `port`, `eventPropertyNames`, and `eventTypeName` properties.

The `helloworldAdapter` doesn't have any configuration that can be changed dynamically, therefore there is no **Edit** button. However, this is not the case for some of the other adapters, which can have editable configurations.

Next, go back to the EPN view, and double-click the **helloworldInputChannel** channel. You will see all the properties of a channel in the **General** tab. This is shown in the next screenshot:

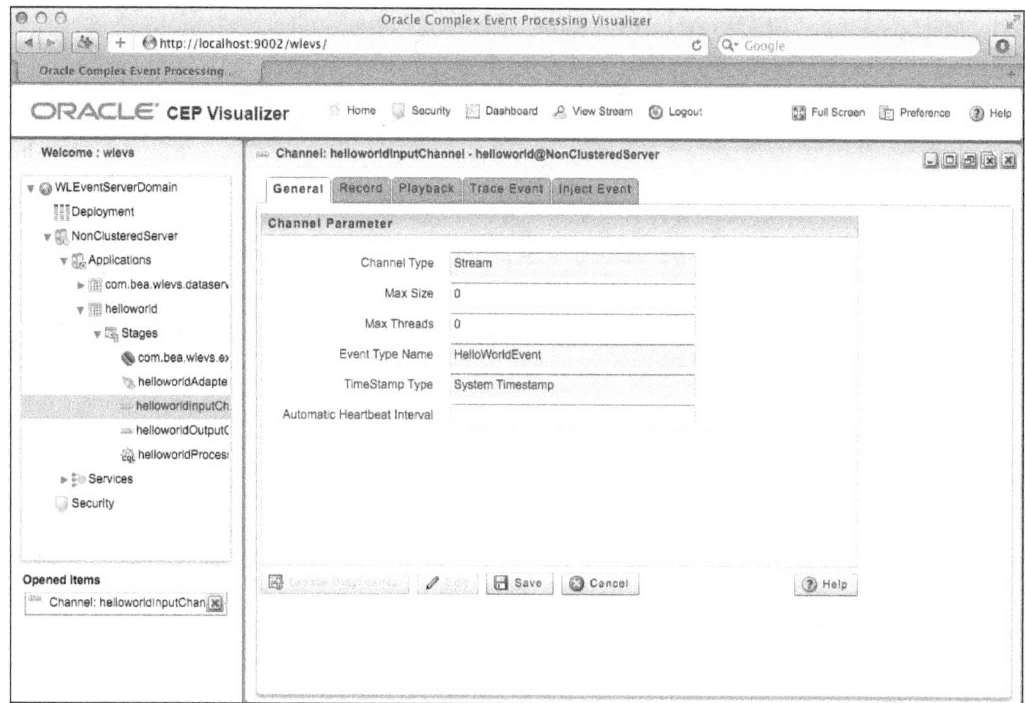

A channel does have editable properties, such as the **Max Size**, **Max Threads**, and **Automatic Heartbeat Interval** properties. You can see this by clicking on the **Edit** button. The **Max Size** and **Max Threads** properties control the concurrency behavior of the channel. You can change any of these properties and then press the **Save** button for the change to take effect. A full description of these attributes can be found in *Chapter 9, Implementing Performance Scaling, Concurrency, and High-Availability for Oracle Event Processing*.

Next, select the CQL processor. You have seen this before in *Chapter 2, An Overview of Oracle Event Processing*. The CQL processor has a lot of changeable configuration, the most important of which is the actual configuration of the CQL queries being executed. Select the **CQL Rules** tab. Next, select the **Query ratio** button in the upper right-hand side, and then the **Edit Query** button. This is shown in the next screenshot:

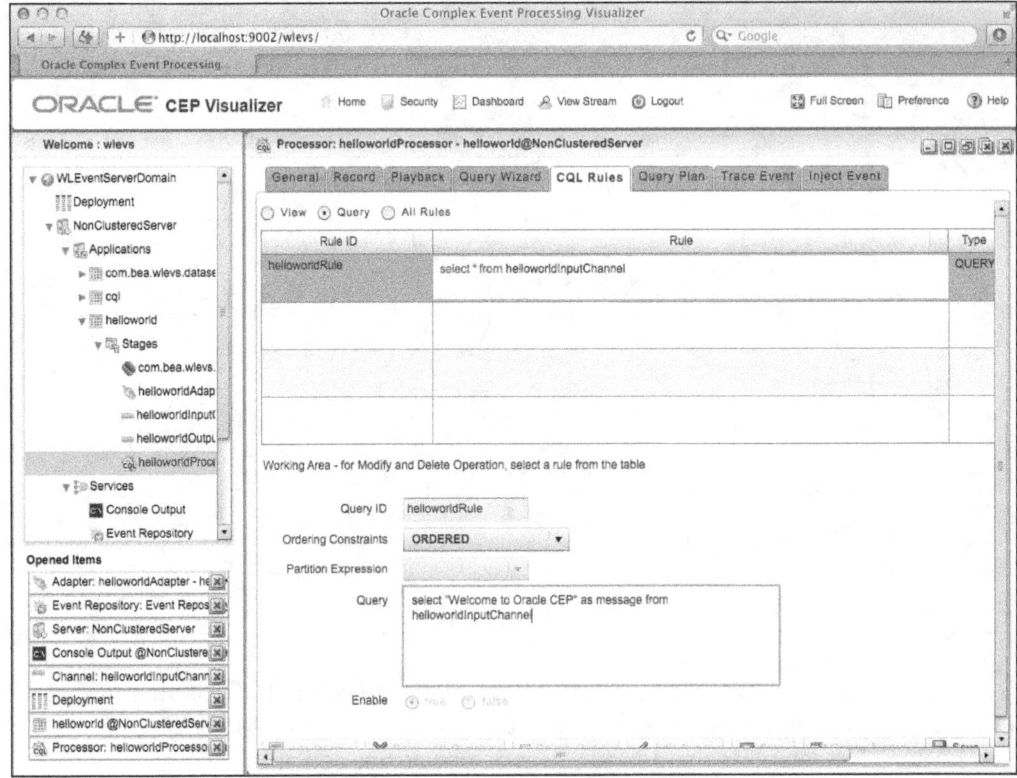

Type the following CQL query in the **Query** window:

```
select 'Welcome to Oracle CEP' as message
from helloworldInputChannel
```

Finally, press the **Save** button. Go back to the **Console Output** window and confirm that the message has been changed.

In the next section, you will learn how to manage the server-wide configuration, such as data sources, work managers, and the event type repository.

Managing server-wide configuration

There are a number of configurations that are related to server-wide services. Let's start with **work managers**.

Controlling concurrency with work managers

Work managers are responsible for controlling the threading behavior of the server, such as the thread pool size. By default, there is a single work manager that is associated to the embedded Jetty web server. The Jetty web server is used to service HTTP requests for all HTTP servlets that may be deployed in the OEP server. The Jetty web server is also used by the deployment service, when you deploy an application. However, as you will learn in *Chapter 9, Implementing Performance Scaling, Concurrency, and High-Availability for Oracle Event Processing*, the concurrency established by a channel is not directly related to a work manager.

You can find its description by selecting the server in the **Domain Browser** window, and then opening the **HTTP Server** tab in the service panel. This is the same panel where we previously selected the logging service. This panel is shown in the next screenshot:

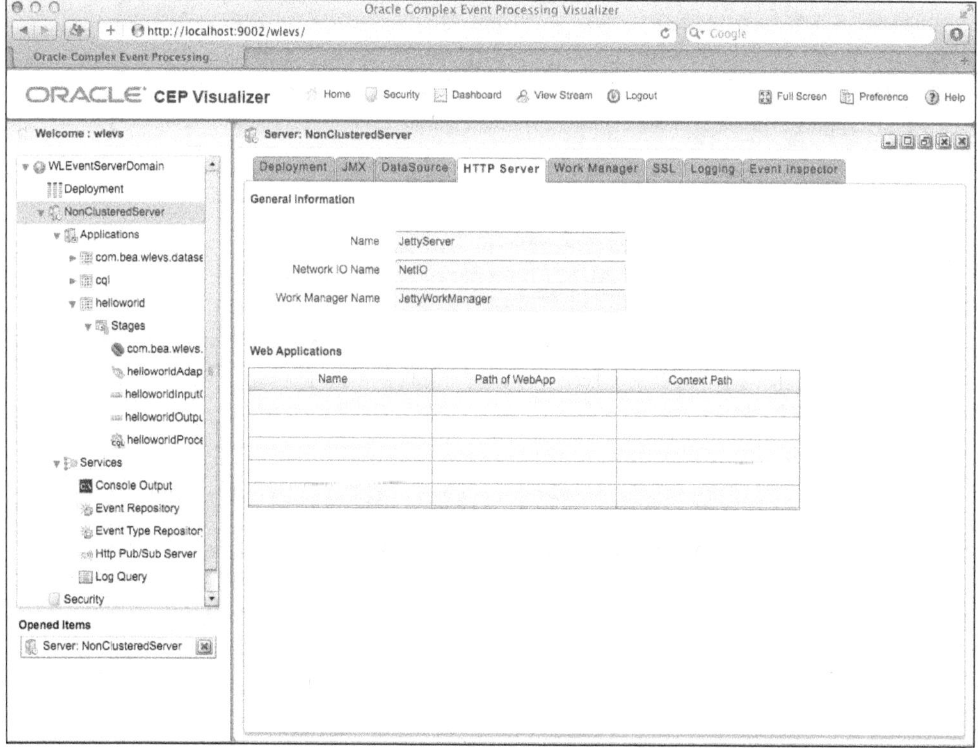

You will notice that the Jetty server is associated to a work manager named **JettyWorkManaager**. Next, select the **Work Manager** tab. This tab lists all the available work managers in the server. Select **JettyWorkManager** and click on the **Edit** button. You will be able to edit the **Min Threads** and **Max Threads** properties. These are used to respectively limit the minimum and maximum number of threads available in this work manager. You can change these values, and then save them by clicking on the **Save** button, as shown in the next screenshot:

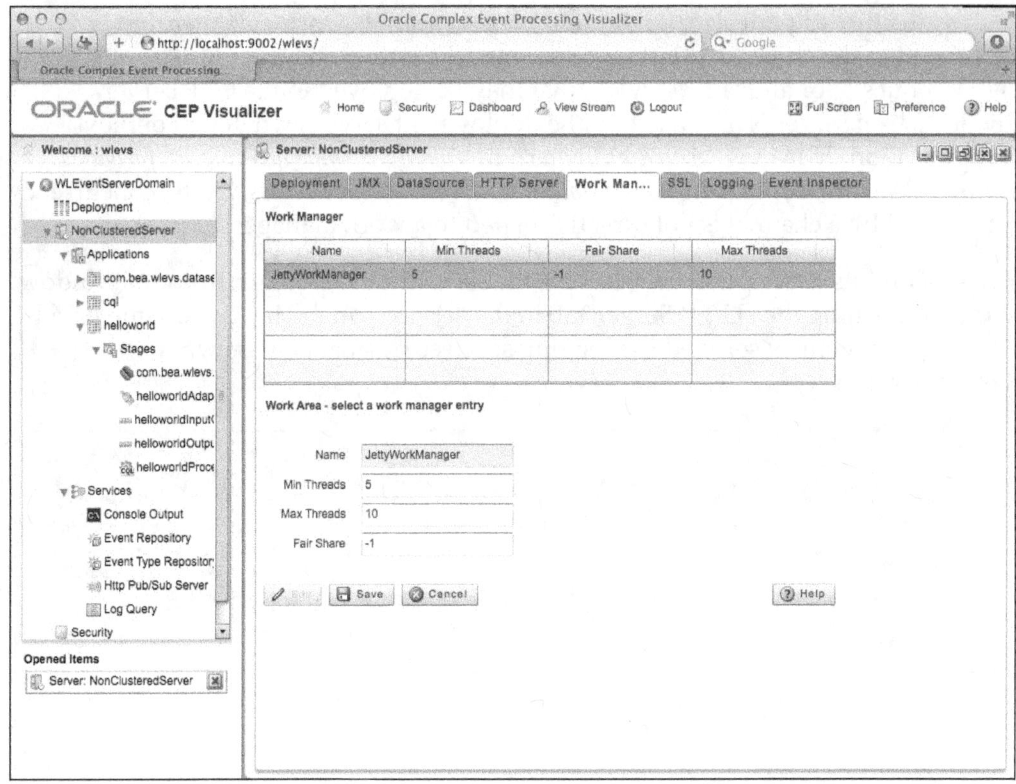

Next, let's take a look at data sources.

Accessing contextual data with data sources

Data sources represent connections to databases, and therefore are very useful. In later chapters, you will learn how to create CQL queries, which enrich events with contextual data that lives in database tables, however before you can do that, you need to configure data sources to their respective relational database systems.

In the Visualizer, you can add a data source by selecting the **DataSource** tab in the **Service** panel, which is the tab just prior to the **HTTP Server** tab you used previously. You will see a list of data sources, which by default is empty. Click on the **Add** button. You will be presented with three panels, where you can respectively set the data source parameters, the connection pool parameters, and the database driver parameters. Let's go through a simple scenario where you add a data source to a Oracle database. In the first panel, set a name for the data source, such as `myDataSource`. Generally, you don't need to set a JNDI name. This is shown in the next screenshot:

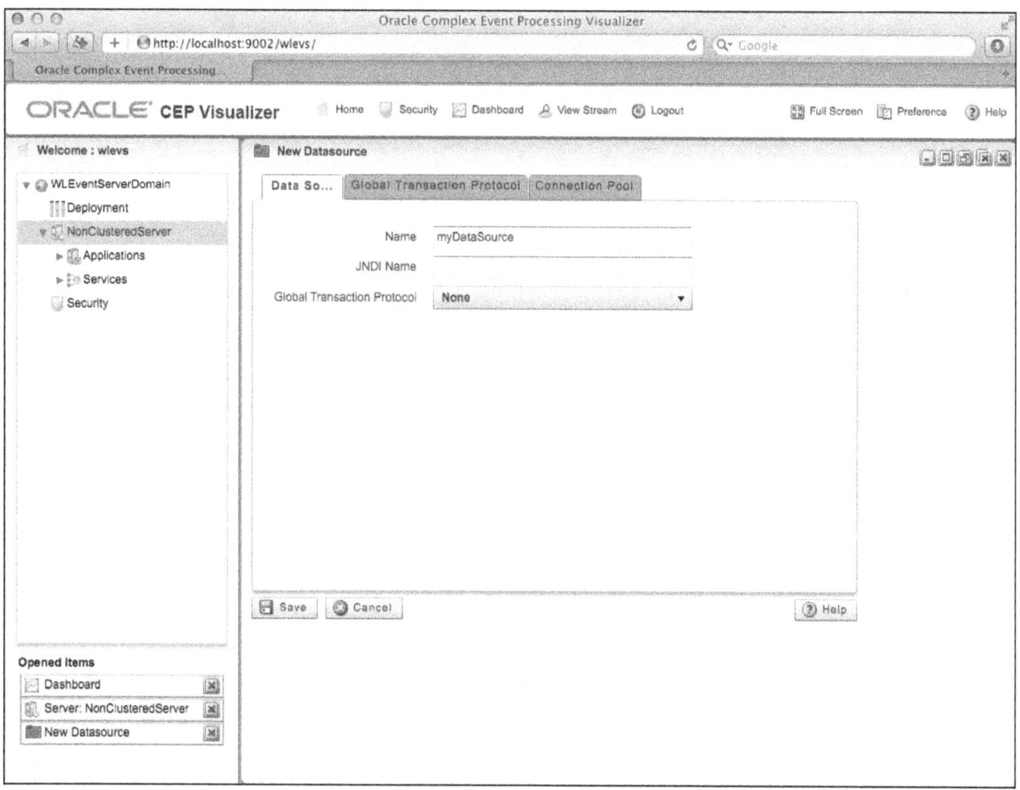

Select the **Global Transactions Protocol** tab. In the **Database Type** drop-down list, select **Oracle**. The URL is configured for a default installation of an Oracle database, change it if necessary. Finally, set the username and password in the **User Name** and **Password** fields respectively, and optionally set the **Use XA** property to **false**. This is shown in the next screeshot:

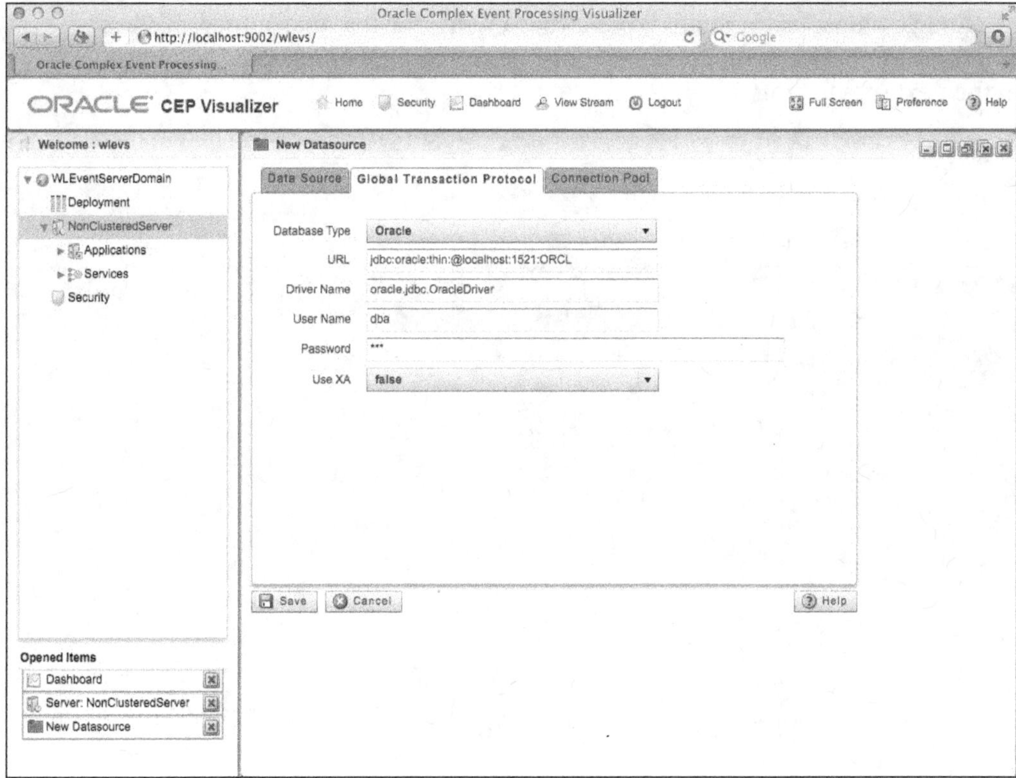

Finally, in the **Connection Pool** tab, you can keep the default configuration, and click on the **Save** button to add the data source to the sever. A noteworthy mention is the **Test** option, which allows you to specify a SQL statement to be used as a sanity check when a connection is first established to the database. This is shown in the following screenshot:

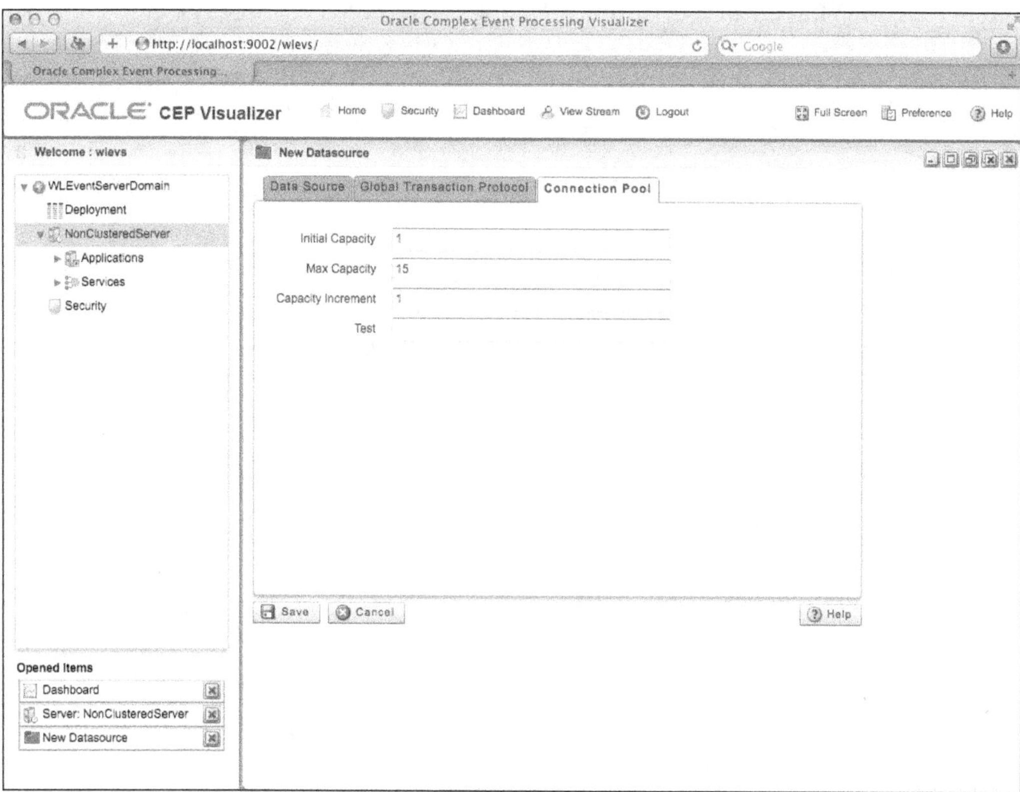

Data sources are global, and can be used by one or more applications.

There are several other useful server-wide services. One of them is the event type repository service, which we take a look at next.

Browsing metadata with the event type repository

The **event type repository** is a server-wide repository that contains all registered event types by all deployed applications. You can inspect it by navigating to **WLEventServerDomain** | **NonClusteredServer** | **Services** | **Event Type Repository**. You can select an event type, and see a short description of its event properties and their types, as shown in the following screenshot:

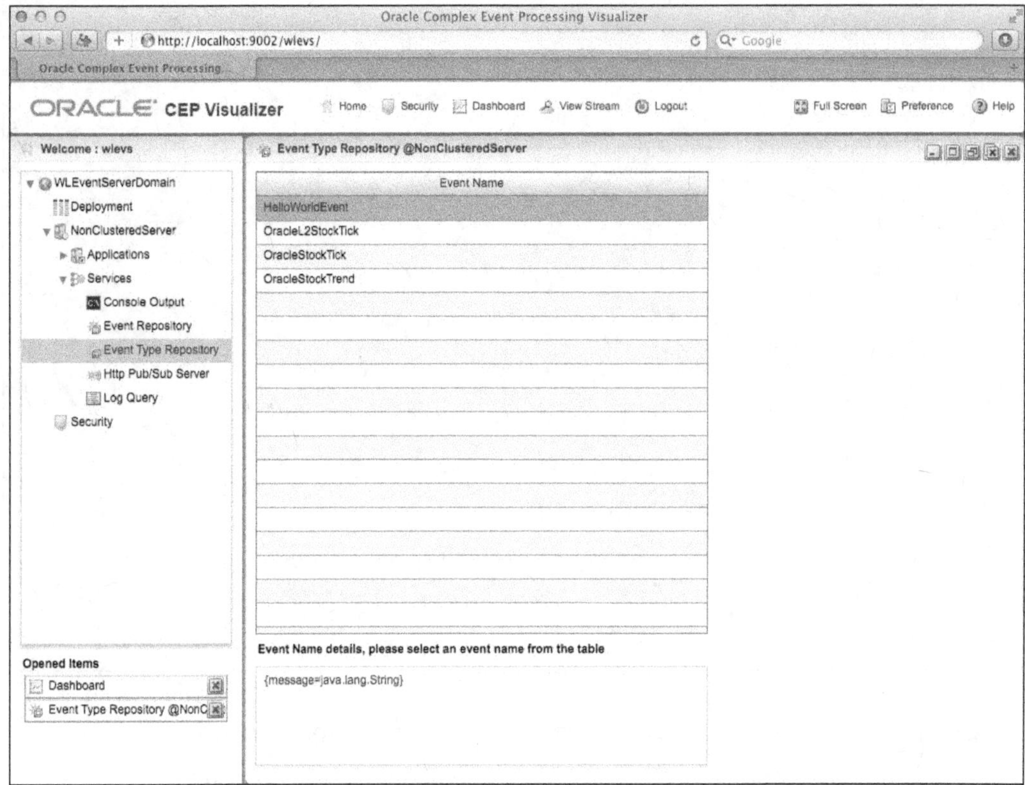

So far, you have learned how to configure the server, how to deploy applications, and how to configure them. In the next section, you learn how to monitor the running applications.

Monitoring progress

When your application is in production, one of the major tasks is to make sure that your applications are running as expected. You can verify this by monitoring the throughput and the latency of the events being processed by your applications.

In the Visualizer, first select the application and the stage that you wish to monitor in the **Domain Browser** window. For example, let's select **helloworldAdapter**. Next, click on the **Create Diagnostics** button, which is shown in the following screenshot:

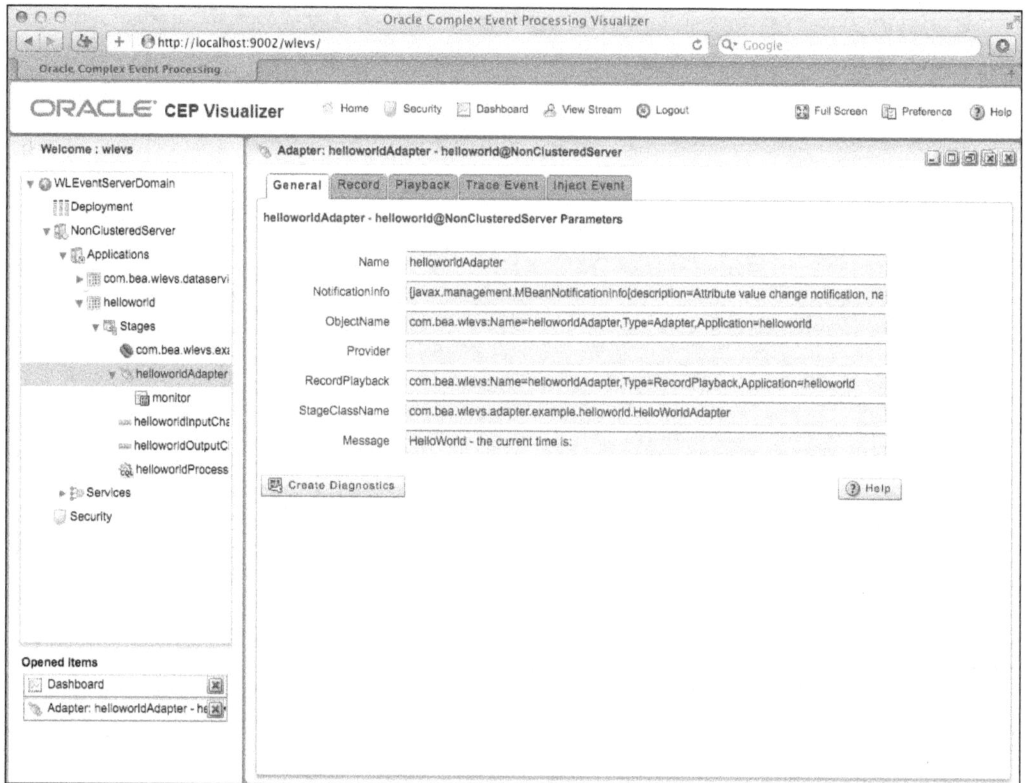

When you do this, a new panel with three sections named **Profile Information**, **Latency**, and **Throughput** shows up. In the **Profile Information** section, you need to give your monitoring profile a name, and optionally set the **State** option to **On**. Keep in mind that a profile can monitor both latency and throughput. Next, we show how to monitor latency:

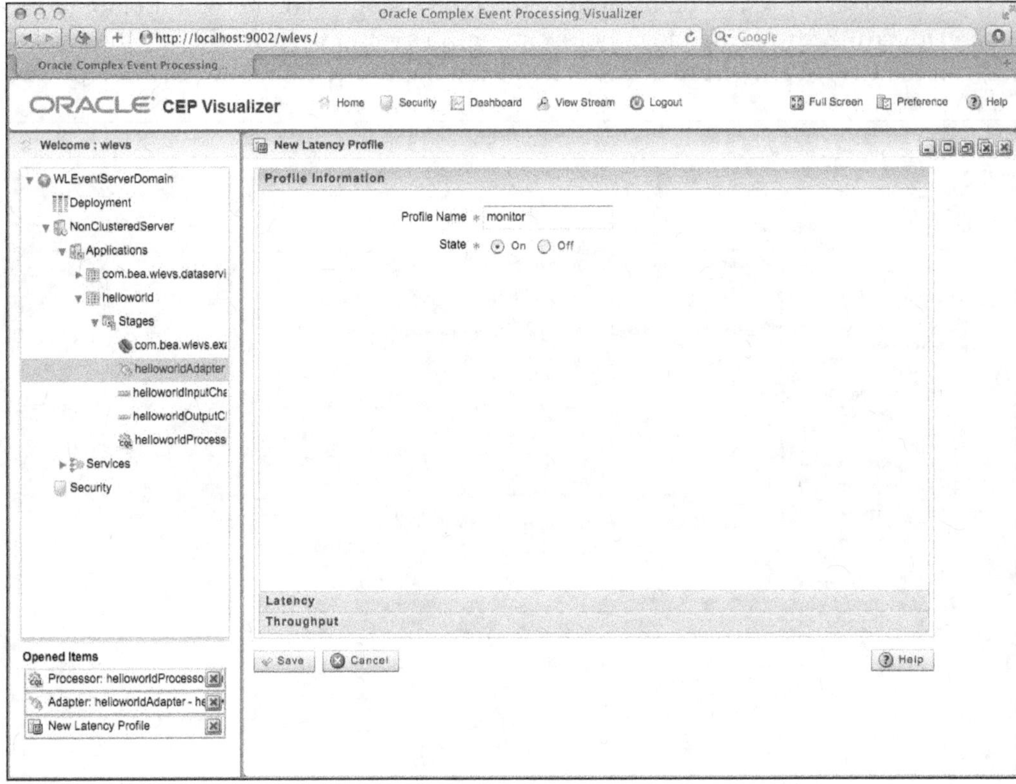

Next, select the **Latency** section. In this section, you can enable the monitoring of the latency of the events that flow through the EPN. The latency of an event is the time it takes to go from point A to point B. In our case, points A and B are the stages in the EPN. This is called a **path** in the EPN. In the **Latency** section, first select if you are interested in the maximum latency or the average latency. Next, you need to specify the collection interval. For example, should the server check the latency every second, every ten seconds, and so on. Finally, go to the **Path Information** sub-section, and specify the starting point and the ending point used for determining the latency. All this is shown in the next screenshot:

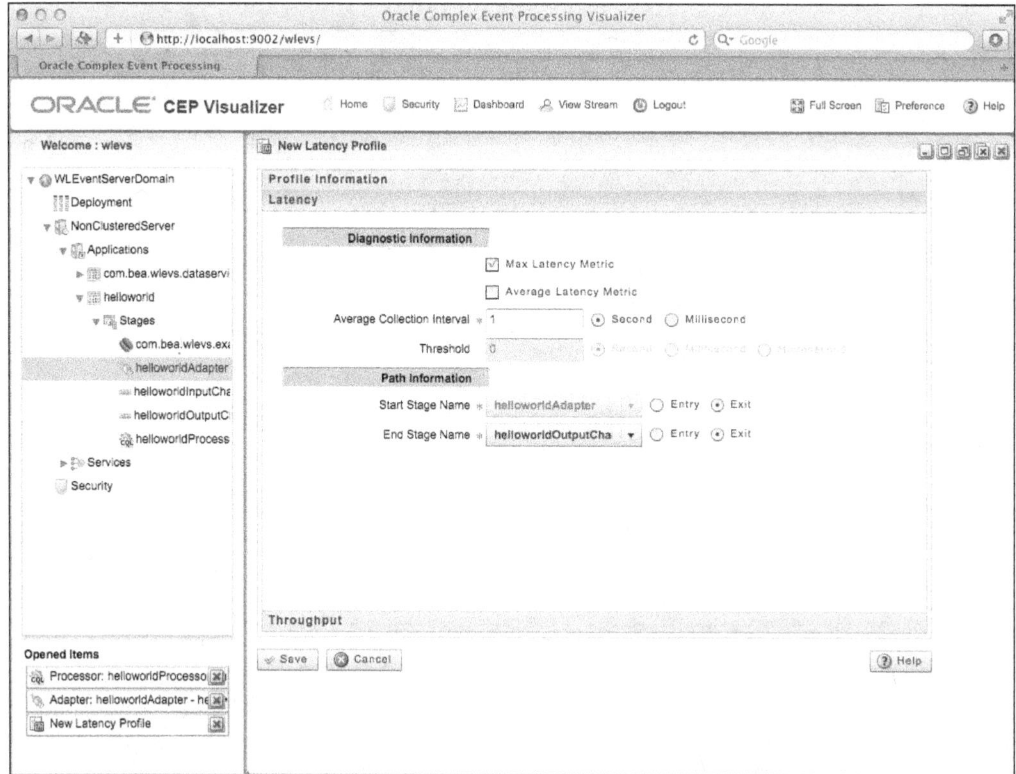

You have configured how to monitor the latency, next you can optionally configure how to monitor the throughput. The throughput is the number of events that flow through a particular stage per some interval of time. For example, if an adapter is sending 10 events every millisecond, then its throughput is of 10 events per millisecond, or 10000 events per second. This is shown in the next screenshot:

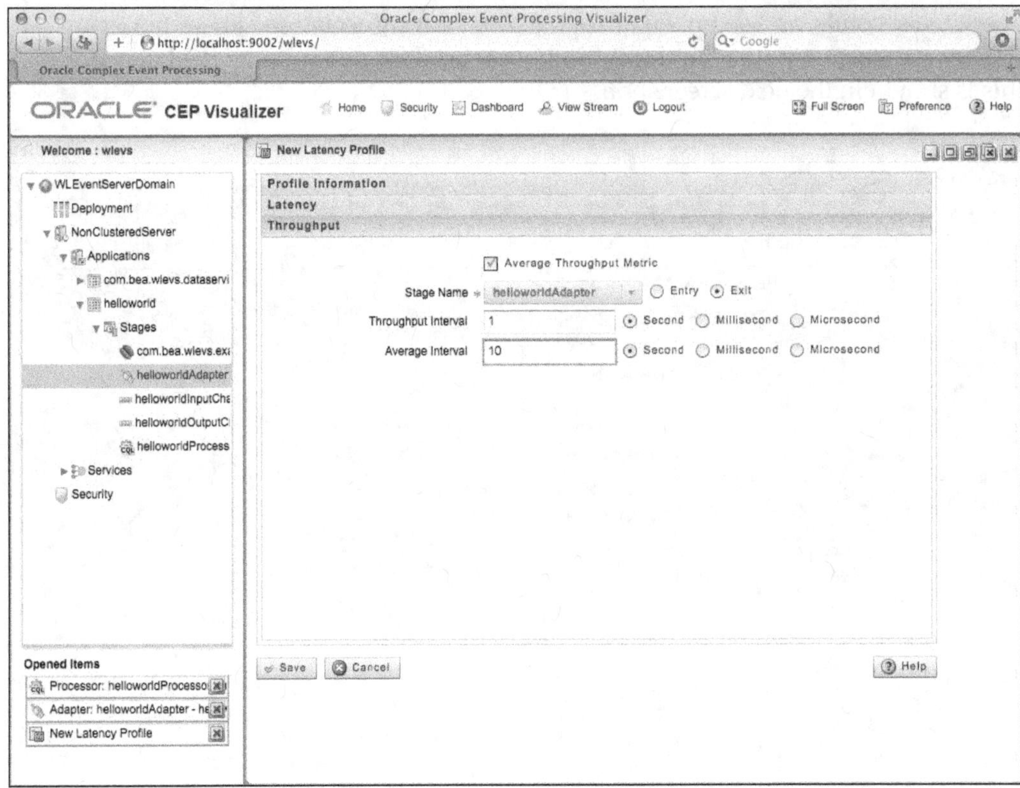

You are now ready to save this monitoring profile. You can do this by clicking on the **Save** button. To see the profile in action, you need to drag it into the dashboard. Go back to the main dashboard window by clicking on the **Home** button. In the **Domain Browser** window, you should see the profile you created named **monitor** underneath **helloworldAdapter**. Drag it into the **Profile Table** in the lower-bottom area of the window. When you do this, the latency and throughput graphs will get populated with the monitoring results as specified in your profile. This is shown in the next screenshot:

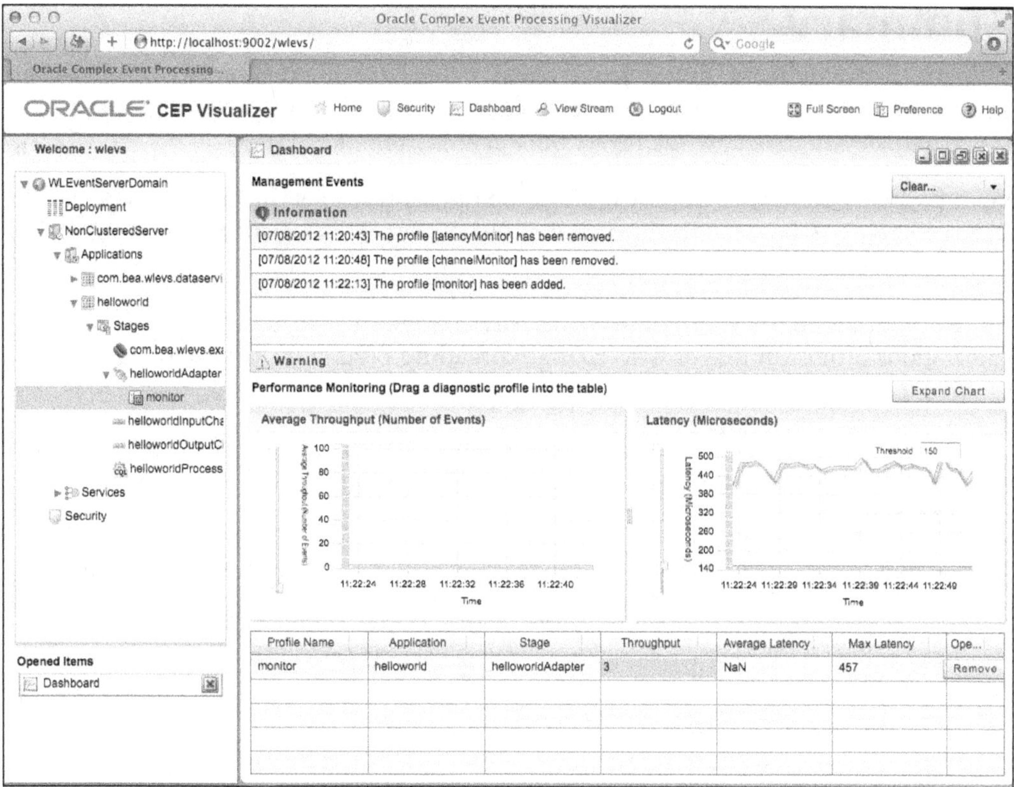

The graphs are updated in real time, as the application is running. You can create multiple profiles, and monitor different stages of your EPN. Further, you can also define thresholds that cause management events to be raised when crossed.

> Monitoring the throughput and the latency of an application consumes CPU, therefore be conscious and monitor your application only when needed.

In the next section, you will learn how to manage and monitor your applications using JMX rather than going through the Visualizer. Using the JMX API gives you additional flexibility, and allows you to create your own manager for OEP servers.

Summary

In this section, you learned how to enable and check the log messages of OEP server components. A useful log component or category is the **EventTrace** component, which allows you to follow the flow of the events in the EPN.

Next, you learned how to deploy and undeploy applications through the Visualizer without having to use the development environment. This is especially useful when moving applications from a testing environment to your production environment.

You learned how to view and to dynamically change the configuration of deployed applications. For example, how to change threading behavior of channels, and how to add and remove CQL queries in CQL processors.

You learned how to view and to dynamically change the configuration of server-wide services, such as work managers, the embedded HTTP server, and how to add new data sources.

Finally, you learned how to monitor the latency and the throughput of the events being processed by a running application.

7

Using Tables and Caches for Contextual Data

So far we've learned how to create events, assemble, and configure Oracle Event Processing applications. You've learned how CQL is used to process incoming data streams. Sometimes incoming data streams do not contain all of the information that we need for the business logic. In most instances, incoming data streams contain some information about a current transaction, but other information such as customer alert preferences are contained elsewhere. This contextual information is often held in a database table and ideally for low latency applications, pushed to an in-memory cache. It is also sometimes convenient to have application-specific thresholds or other contextual information in a cache as well for lower latency access to drive better application performance.

This chapter will cover the following topics:

- Setting up JDBC data sources
- Enriching events using a database table
- Setting up caching systems
- Enriching events using a cache
- Using caches as event sources and event sinks
- Implementing an event bean to access a cache
- Monitoring Coherence in the Visualizer

Setting up JDBC data sources

In *Chapter 4, Assembling and Configuring OEP Applications*, we discussed the event server's configuration file (`config.xml`). One of the sections of this file is used for making connections to a database. We'll review this configuration as it relates to including a reference to a table in our application.

Let's suppose that we have a reference database that has a table containing customer information, such as their name and their loyalty program status.

To make the connection to a data source, you define the data source along with its connection pool and driver parameters as in the following example:

```
<data-source>
<name>ReferenceDB</name>
<data-source-params>
<jndi-names>
<element>ReferenceDB</element>
</jndi-names>
<global-transactions-protocol>None</global-transactions-protocol>
</data-source-params>
<connection-pool-params>
<credential-mapping-enabled></credential-mapping-enabled>
<test-table-name>
SQL SELECT 1 FROM MYREFERENCETABLE
</test-table-name>
<initial-capacity>1</initial-capacity>
<max-capacity>15</max-capacity>
<capacity-increment>1</capacity-increment>
</connection-pool-params>

<driver-params>
<use-xa-data-source-interface>false</use-xa-data-source-interface>
<driver-name>oracle.jdbc.OracleDriver</driver-name>
      <url>jdbc:oracle:thin:@localhost:1521:XE</url>
       <properties>
<element>
<value>refuser</value>
<name>user</name>
</element>
<element>
<value>password1</value>
<name>password</name>
</element>
</properties>
</driver-params>
</data-source>
```

Enriching events using a database table

Now that you have a JDBC connection in place in the server's configuration file, you can use this to join to a table. Suppose that we have an OEP application that is processing the key attributes of a customer's complaints. We may want to evaluate the important details of each complaint in real time to establish the priority of each complaint in order to provide better customer service. To do this, we will want to include a reference to the customer table in our application.

You would use the `<wlevs:table>` tag to include a table within your EPN. For example:

```
<wlevs:table id="CUSTOMER" event-type="CustomerData" data-
source="ReferenceDB"/>
```

Of course, you would need to define an event type with the appropriate attributes corresponding to the columns in the `CUSTOMER` table.

You must then specify the table as a `<wlevs:table-source>` for a processor that requires the data:

```
<wlevs:processor id="CustomerComplaintProcessor">
  <wlevs:listener ref="ComplaintEventChannel " />
  <wlevs:table-source ref="CUSTOMER"/>
</wlevs:processor>
```

We want to find the customer's information, including the name and loyalty program status, corresponding to the complaint.

Within the processor that has the table source defined, you can create CQL to join the event stream to the database table in the same manner as you would if you were joining two tables in SQL, as in the following example:

```
<processor>
<name>CustomerComplaintProcessor</name>
<rules>
<query id="LoyaltyStatusQuery">
<![CDATA[
SELECT E.customerID,
 E.complaint,
E.employeeID,
E.location,
C.loyaltyStatus,
C.firstname,
```

```
C.lastname
FROM ComplaintEventChannel [NOW] as E, CUSTOMER as C
WHERE E.customerID = C.customerID
]]>
</query>
</rules>
</processor>
```

The resulting output event will now contain both the desired attributes from the event stream and the selected columns from the database table. This allows us to take action immediately on complaints from customers with a particular loyalty status. When the most loyal customers have a complaint, it is best to address it as soon as possible since they represent important repeat business for the company, which could be lost if not addressed in a timely manner.

Setting up caching systems

A cache is an in-memory storage area. In OEP, a cache is often used to store events. While it is not strictly necessary to use a cache in your application, it can significantly improve performance over retrieving data from the database.

In *Chapter 4, Assembling and Configuring OEP Applications*, we briefly looked at how to set up a caching system. Now we'll cover that in a little more detail.

A caching system is a configured instance of a caching implementation. A caching system includes the configuration information needed to connect to one or more named caches defined in the caching system. Setting up Coherence requires specific configuration files which must also be made available to the OEP JVM, just as they would need to be part of the configuration of any Coherence JVM that is part of the cluster. This is a rich topic which you should learn more about if you plan to implement caching within OEP. A good place to start to experiment with the different configurations of caching systems is to extract the example cache configuration file from the Coherence JAR file. It contains comments explaining the logic behind each type of sample configuration.

OEP supports a local in-memory single-JVM cache as well as Oracle Coherence. Oracle Coherence is a JCache-compliant in-memory distributed data grid solution for clustered applications and application servers. The main advantages of Coherence are that it coordinates updates to the data using cluster-wide concurrency control, replicates data modifications across the cluster using the highest performing clustered protocol available, and delivers notifications of data modifications to any servers that request them. Oracle Coherence uses the standard Java collections API to access and modify data, and uses the standard Java Bean event model to receive data change notifications.

Since this book is not intended to teach you all the aspects of Coherence, we recommend that you do your own research on how to develop an application using Coherence. In this section, we will specifically point out areas that are specific to integrating with OEP.

We'll start with looking at an example of setting up a caching system. One best practice to consider implementing is the creation of a separate JAR file for the classes that relate to Coherence. The reason for doing this is so that these classes can be easily added to both the OEP application and the classpath of the Coherence server. A good way to implement this is to have an Ant script that not only builds the JAR file but also updates the OEP application project and copies the file to any other locations you want to update.

An important point to consider is getting any Coherence **Portable Object Format** (**POF**) configuration files in the classpath, especially the OEP application's classpath. One way to do this is to place the configuration files in the JAR file. You can add them to your source folder and make sure that your Ant script includes them in the creation of the JAR file.

Now that you have a JAR file with the required Coherence classes, you should include it in your OEP application. A simple way to do this is to add a folder to your OEP application, such as `lib` and then add it to the `Bundle-Classpath` in the `MANIFEST.MF` file:

```
Bundle-ClassPath: .,
 lib/creditcard-demo-cache.jar,
```

The Eclipse editor for the manifest will easily help you do this from the **Runtime** tab after you double-click the `MANFEST.MF` file, which is under `META-INF`.

Next, you'll want to configure your cache. As mentioned in *Chapter 4, Assembling and Configuring OEP Applications*, you need to define a caching system and a cache using the `<wlevs:caching-system>` and `<wlevs:cache>` tags:

```
<!-- Caching Configuration -->
<wlevs:caching-system id="CoherenceCachingSystem" provider="coherence"
/>
<wlevs:cache id="DeviceCache"
caching-system="CoherenceCachingSystem"
value-type="Device" key-properties="deviceID">
</wlevs:cache>
```

Once this is done, you have a cache set up and ready to use. The next few sections will show you some examples on how you can use the cache.

Enriching events using a cache

Once the caching system and cache is in place, one common use case is to use it to enrich events. In most cases, applications are designed so that the incoming event contains the key that you'll need to access the cache. Just as you've seen previously how a database table can be incorporated into the EPN, a cache is also a first-class citizen in an OEP application. Once we've linked the cache to the CQL processor as a source, you can refer to it in the CQL in the same way that you referenced the database table in the previous section. This will allow you to join an event stream on an incoming channel with its associated cached attributes.

You will use the key attribute from the incoming data stream to join to the cache just like you would do if you were making a join between two tables in SQL.

Let's take a look at some examples. Suppose you are collecting data from various types of devices. The data stream may simply send you the device ID and the measured value. You may need to determine if the measured value has exceeded a predefined threshold depending upon the type of device. The Coherence cache may contain the device IDs and their types as well as other information that may be of interest to business users that doesn't get sent with each event, such as the device location.

As we receive each event (for example, D100, 70.3), where D100 is the device ID and 70.3 is a temperature reading, we need to enrich the event with the device type and location. Subsequently, we can evaluate whether to send an alert. We can join the incoming data stream to the cache using CQL and extract the additional information. A good idea might be to use a CQL view to do this, and then execute queries against the view.

First, you'll need to inject the cache as a source for the processor using `<wlevs:cachesource>`. The processor now has access to the cache:

```
<wlevs:processor id="DeviceProcessor">
<wlevs:listener ref="DeviceAlertOutput" />
<wlevs:cache-source ref="DeviceCache" />
</wlevs:processor>
```

Then you can join incoming event streams with configured cache sources as in this example:

```
<processor>
<name>DeviceProcessor</name>
<rules>
<query id="DeviceTypeQuery">
<![CDATA[
SELECT M.deviceID,
```

```
 M.measuredValue,
D.location,
D.deviceType
FROM MeasurementEventChannel [NOW] as M, Device as D
WHERE M.deviceID = D.deviceID
]]>
</query>
</rules>
</processor>
```

The resulting output event will have the measured values as well as the location and device type.

Using caches as event sources and sinks

Besides using a cache for contextual data, another good use is to use it as the supplier of input data or as the final event sink for processed results.

The Oracle Coherence cache has a simple way for you to listen for changes that occur. By implementing a Map Listener interface, you can receive data into your OEP application and then connect a channel so that it acts similar to how an input adapter would.

At the end of an EPN, you could use a cache as the result sink. This provides a low latency way to output your events.

First, let's look at using the cache in place of an input adapter to supply events to your application as an event source. You need to set up the caching system as described at the beginning of this chapter, but you will make one important addition to the configuration. You will use `<wlevs:cache-listener>` to set up an event-bean class that implements `MapListener` and `StreamSource`, which can listen for changes in the cache and forward events to downstream channels:

```
<wlevs:cache id="CardTransactionCache" caching-
system="CoherenceCachingSystem" value-type="CardTransactionEvent"
key-properties="cardID">
<wlevs:cache-listener ref="TransactionCacheListener"/>
</wlevs:cache>
```

Create a class that receives events from the cache, performs any necessary logic, and sends the events to downstream channels:

```
<wlevs:event-bean id="TransactionCacheListener" class="com.oracle.cep.
listener.TransactionCacheListener">
      <wlevs:listener ref="CardTransactionChannel"/>
 </wlevs:event-bean>
```

Here is an example:

```
import com.tangosol.util.MapEvent;
import com.tangosol.util.MapListener;

import com.bea.wlevs.ede.api.StreamSender;
import com.bea.wlevs.ede.api.StreamSource;;

/**
 * This class implements the cache listener
 *
 */
public class TransactionCacheListener implements MapListener, StreamSource {

    private StreamSender streamSender_;

    public void setEventSender(StreamSender sender) {
        streamSender_ = sender;
    }

    public TransactionCacheListener() {
    }

    public void entryDeleted(MapEvent event) {
        System.out.println("entryDeleted: " + event.getOldValue());
    }

    public void entryInserted(MapEvent event) {
        System.out.println("entryInserted: " + event.getNewValue());
        streamSender_.sendInsertEvent(event);

    }

    public void entryUpdated(MapEvent event) {
        System.out.println("entryUpdated: OLD: " + event.getOldValue() + " NEW: " + event.getNewValue());
    }
```

This configuration will notify your application of any changes in the cache. Let's assume that another application is putting credit card transaction events into `CardTransactionCache`. There may be a number of reasons to do this. Perhaps there is logic that needs to occur as these events are placed into the cache. Coherence can replicate these events to provide reliability in the event of a hardware failure and help batch insert them into a database. Other applications may also be interested in subscribing to these events. There may also be a need to insert these events into a database. This is something that Coherence can help do more efficiently versus inserting them a single transaction at a time. Coherence-specific implementation parameters should be taken into consideration to manage how long these events stay in cache. Also cache sizing should be planned appropriately.

By using the `sendInsertEvent()` method, you have made the events available to any channels configured as listeners to this `wlevs:event-bean`.

Another useful role for the cache is to receive the alerts or other events that are to be processed downstream. The cache is used in this case for a number of reasons. It provides a low latency way for the OEP application to distribute events to other applications. The cache can be configured to replicate the events, so that this valuable information, which we have learned, is not lost in the event of a system failure. If this information needs to be written to the database, Coherence can perform this functionality thereby freeing up the OEP application thread from the responsibility of making sure that the database transaction commits successfully. Coherence also has other features that could potentially be beneficial when writing the results to the database.

OEP provides Coherence integration features that assist the application developer with inserting the output events into Coherence as an event sink. It is sufficient to configure the channel receiving the events to be put into cache with a cache as a listener. The OEP infrastructure will automatically perform the `put()` operation. There is no need to explicitly write code to do this. For very high-performance situations, you may want to explicitly batch the insert of events into the cache using the `putAll()` operation or modify your cache configuration to have Coherence handle this automatically using a preconfigured time interval for batching events.

Using the cache as an event sink can be as simple as supplying the cache as a listener to a channel that has the correct event type to be cached:

```
<wlevs:channel id="AccountChannel" event-type="Account">
<wlevs:listener ref="AccountCache"/>
</wlevs:channel>
```

Implementing an event bean to access a cache

Sometimes the logic that you want to implement goes beyond simply joining to the cache using CQL or listening for and pushing events to the cache. Perhaps, you want to implement one or more of the Java APIs for Coherence. A common example is to implement an invoke operation on the cache. You can do this by implementing an <wlevs:event-bean> event bean. The event bean implements both the `StreamSource` and `StreamSink` interfaces, so that you can receive incoming events, do whatever logic you need using the Coherence cache APIs, and then create your outgoing events to downstream channels. Here is an example of the event bean configuration:

```
<wlevs:event-bean id="GetAccountCustomers"
    class="com.oracle.cep.eventbean.GetCustomersForAccount">
```

```
    <wlevs:listener ref="CustomerThresholdChannel"/>
    <wlevs:instance-property name="accountCache" ref="AccountCache" />
</wlevs:event-bean>
```

One important point to notice is that we are able to set a reference to the cache using the `<wlevs:instance-property>` tag. This allows us to use the Spring framework to set the reference to the cache.

Define an attribute of type `java.util.Map` for the cache and an appropriate setter method:

```
private Map accountCache;
public void setAccountCache(Map accountCache)
{
this.accountCache = accountCache; }
```

A common reason to use an event bean to access the Coherence cache is to take advantage of the Coherence entry processor pattern.

You need to implement a class that extends `com.tangosol.util.processor.AbstractProcessor`.

Be sure to add the appropriate dependency entries in the `MANIFEST.MF` file or you will get an error when you deploy the application and start the server.

In the `process()` method, you can check if an entry is present based upon the key and perform any logic you need performed within the cache. You can then return any object you desire to OEP for further processing by sending the existing or any new event to downstream listeners of your event bean. This is useful in cases where you are checking for entries in the cache (such as cases where you want to check if an alert has already been sent) or performing complex logic that would best be done within the cache. Keep in mind that you should always try to keep logic that may need to change frequently within OEP since application logic within CQL processors can easily be updated.

Here is an example of using the Coherence entry processor functionality within an OEP event bean to check if an entry is present for a key. If the entry is not present, the object is added to the cache. If an entry is present, the cache is updated, but the old entry is returned to the OEP application so that CQL logic downstream of the event bean can compare the old and the new entries and perform some business logic.

```
AgentStateCacheInvoke.java    AgentStateUpdater.java
    }

    public void onInsertEvent(Object event) throws EventRejectedException {

        if (event != null){

            if (log_.isDebugEnabled()){
                log_.debug("CEP CACHE INVOKE: Received event!");
            }

            if (event instanceof AgentStateData){
                AgentStateData e = (AgentStateData)event ;

                String key = e.getAgentID();
                AgentStateChange change = addToCache(key, e);

                if (change != null){

                    if (!change.getOldState().contentEquals(change.getNewState())){
                        streamSender_.sendInsertEvent(change);
                    }
                }
            }

        }

    }

    public AgentStateChange addToCache(String key, AgentStateData event) throws EventRejectedException {


        NamedCache cache = (NamedCache)agentStateCache ;

        AgentStateUpdater updater = new AgentStateUpdater(event);
        Object old = cache.invoke(key, updater);

        if (old != null){

            //get an event with new and previous in it
            if (old instanceof AgentStateData){

                AgentStateData oldState = (AgentStateData)old ;
                AgentStateChange change = new AgentStateChange(event, oldState);

                return change ;
            }

        }

        return null ;

    }
```

The following code runs within the Coherence cache to process incoming data and compare it with a previous entry for the same key if it exists:

```
AgentStateCacheInvoke.java    AgentStateUpdater.java

    // ----- constructors ------------------------------------------------

    public AgentStateUpdater(){
    }

    public AgentStateUpdater(AgentStateData data){

        this.data = data ;

        System.out.println("CACHE: Incoming data: " + data.toString());
    }

    // ----- InvocableMap.EntryProcessor interface ------------------

    public Object process(InvocableMap.Entry entry) {

        if (entry.isPresent())
          {

            //System.out.println("Entry is Present! " + data.toString());
            // do update
            AgentStateData prev = (AgentStateData) entry.getValue();

            //replace the old entry with the new entry in the cache
            entry.setValue(data);

            //pass back the old entry
            return prev ;

          }
          else
          {

            System.out.println("CACHE: No Entry Yet. Add it: " + data.toString());
            entry.setValue(data);
            return null ;

          }

    }

    public void readExternal(PofReader in) throws IOException {
        this.data = (AgentStateData) in.readObject(0);
    }

    public void writeExternal(PofWriter out) throws IOException {
        out.writeObject(0, this.data);
    }

}
```

There are many reasons to do something like this. One example would be in a healthcare application where the CQL logic is not simply about whether values have crossed a specific threshold, but rather attempts to determine if a patient's condition is getting worse.

Monitoring Coherence in the Visualizer

Although it is possible to configure a cache entirely within an OEP application, it is best to configure the cache at the server level (in the server's `config.xml` file). When this is done, the ability to monitor the cache within the OEP Visualizer tool is available.

This is an interesting feature of the product as it will enable you to view important statistics at runtime including cache misses, hit statistics, total requests, cache size, coherence topologies, and packet traffic.

Summary

In this chapter, you learned about configuring a database and using it to connect to a table within CQL. You also learned about configuring a cache in your application and the many ways that you could use it. We used it as a data source for contextual information in a manner similar to joining to a database table, but we also used it as a source of events and as an event sink for output to other systems. We saw how implementing an event sink within the application and using that to access the Oracle Coherence APIs can be a very interesting and useful design pattern. While we learned a little about Oracle Coherence here, it is a very in-depth topic that you should continue to explore.

In the next chapter, we will cover blending CQL with Java. This will provide you even more ways to leverage the flexibility that developing business logic in CQL provides for your application.

8

Pattern Matching with CQL

In *Chapter 5, Coding with CQL*, you learned the basics of event processing languages with CQL and how it relates with SQL. In this chapter, you will learn advanced event processing features such as pattern matching, and further learn how to intermingle CQL with Java and XML.

Specifically, you will learn how to:

- Extend CQL with OEP cartridges
- Blend CQL with the Java programming language
- Process XML documents with CQL
- Perform pattern matching on events

Extending CQL with OEP cartridges

As we have learned, CQL is a very powerful, declarative language for processing events; however sometimes you may need to do simple programming tasks such as string manipulation, and for those cases you may find that CQL is just too high-level. These types of tasks are commonly called programming in the small, and are best done with imperative languages, such as Java. Fortunately, Oracle CEP provides a framework that can be used to extend the CQL language itself. This is done through the plugin of Oracle CEP cartridges.

By default, Oracle CEP comes installed with several cartridges, as shown in the following diagram:

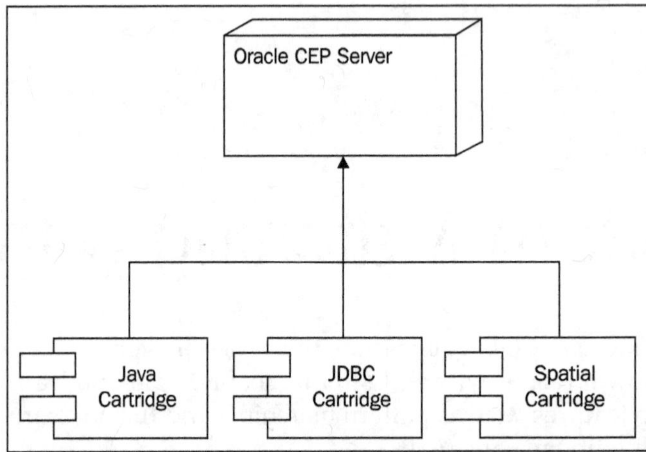

The pre-installed Java cartridge seamlessly blends CQL with the Java language. In the next section, we take a look at how to program day-to-day tasks in CQL by leveraging Java.

Blending CQL and Java

We explore the CQL and Java integration by walking through several scenarios. Let's start with a simple scenario, where we want to get a sub-string from the `symbol` event property, whose type is the `CHAR` native type. This is illustrated in the following example:

```
SELECT symbol.substring(0,2)
FROM marketFeed
```

First, CQL performs an implicit conversion between the CQL native `CHAR` data type and the Java `String` class. Next, you can invoke an instance method of a Java class instance in CQL by using the `.` (dot) operator, very much like you would do normally in Java. In other words, the expression `symbol.substring(...)` invokes the method `String java.lang.String.substring(intbeginIndex, intendIndex)` in the object represented by the property symbol. You can even go further, and nest invocations as in the following example:

```
SELECT symbol.substring(0,2).toUpperCase()
FROM marketFeed
```

In this case, you first invoke the `substring()` method, and then invoke the `toUpperCase()` method in the returning String object.

Next, let's say you want to create a new Java `String` object and use it in CQL. This is done in the following example:

```
SELECT symbol.substring(0,2).toUpperCase()
FROM marketFeed
WHERE symbol.startsWith(String("ORCL"))
= true
)
```

The creation of a new Java `String` happens on line three, in the expression `String("ORCL")`. In this case, there is a difference to the Java language. In CQL, there is no need of a new keyword. Instead, CQL determines that a constructor is being invoked by considering the context of usage.

Functions are an intrinsic core piece of CQL. This is one reason why there is no need for a new keyword in CQL and instead a Java class constructor is invoked as if it is a function.

Further, note how the result of the `startsWith()` method returns a Java `Boolean` native type, which is automatically converted to a CQL `boolean` and compared with the CQL literal `true`. This implicit conversion back and forth between CQL and Java types greatly improves usability.

Let's look at another example of data type conversions:

```
SELECT symbol
FROM marketFeed
WHERE Integer.valueOf(priceAsStringValue) > 10
```

Assume that the incoming event in the `marketFeedstream` has a `CHAR` (for example, `String`) property named `priceAsStringValue` that contains the symbol's price and you want to filter out all events whose price are less than or equal to 10. Because `priceAsStringValue` is a `CHAR` type, you need first to convert it to a native CQL `integer` type. You could do this by using the built-in casting function called `intto_int(CHAR)`. However, an arguably simpler approach for Java developer would be to use the static method `Integer Integer.valueOf(String)`. This returns an Integer object, which is automatically unboxed as a native Java integer, and following converted to a native CQL integer for the comparison evaluation.

CQL literals are not converted to Java literals. For example, the following expression is illegal:

```
SELECT "hi".toUpperCase() …
```

So far you have invoked Java instance methods, static methods, and constructors. There are two remaining cases to be looked at, which is that of field reference and that of arrays. These are explored in the following example:

```
SELECT
address.zipcode as zipcode,
address.phones[0] as mainPhone
FROM marketFeed
```

In this case, consider that the type of the address property is the following Java class:

```
package myorg.app1;

public class Address
{
  public String city;
  public String state;
  public String zipcode;
  public String [] phones;
}
```

So, as expected, field referencing and array indexing in CQL is also no different than in Java.

Oracle CEP 11*g* does not support instantiation of array objects in CQL. For example, the following is illegal:

```
SELECT String[0] {"ORCL"} FROM marketFeed
```

In the beginning of this section, the queries were referencing to JDK types such as `Integer` and `String`, which are always present in the classpath. However, this is not the case for this last example, where the query is using the user-defined class called `Address`. How is the CQL processor able to load this class? Next, we answer this question by looking into the class-loading rules for accessing Java classes in CQL.

Class loading in CQL

The class loading rules for accessing Java classes in CQL is determined by the Oracle CEP application that defines the CQL queries (or views) that reference to these Java classes.

By default, a CQL query has the same class-path visibility as of its defining application.

For example, say we have three applications, named A1, A2, and A3. Application A1 defines and exports the `myorg.app1.Address` class, application A2 imports this class and also defines and exports the `myorg.app2.Book` class, and application A3 defines and does not export the `myorg.app3.Student` class. A3 also doesn't import either `myorg.app1.Address`, or `myorg.app2.Book`. This is illustrated in the following diagram:

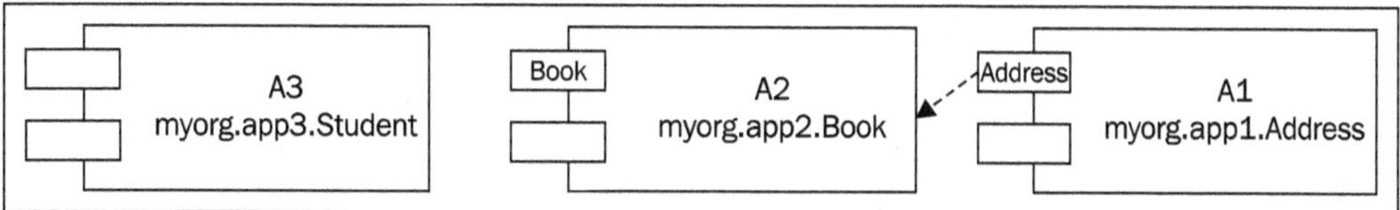

In this case, CQL queries (and views) in application A1 can make use of the `myorg.app1.Address` class, but cannot make use of the `myorg.app2.Book` and `myorg.app3.Student` classes, whereas the application A2 can make use of `myorg.app1.Address myorg.app2.Book`. Finally, application A3 can only make use of the `myorg.app3.Student` class.

As the `myorg.app1.Address` class is defined by A1, it is clear why CQL queries in A1 can load this class, but why can also A2 load it? A2 can also load it because A1 is exporting it and A2 is importing it. This is done respectively by the `Export-Package` and `Import-Package` OSGi manifest header entries in these applications.

> Oracle Event Processing makes extensive use of the OSGi technology (`www.osgi.org`) for its deployment model, application modularity, and service abstraction. It is beyond the scope of this book to describe OSGi, please refer to the OEP documentation or the OSGi documentation for further details around OEP's usage of the OSGi technology.

Here is an example of application A2's manifest file:

```
Bundle-ManifestVersion: 2
Bundle-SymbolicName: A2
Import-Package: myorg.app1
```

Conversely, A3 is not importing this class and therefore cannot use it. Its queries can only load the class it defines, which is the `myorg.app3.Student` class.

This default policy is called the **application class-space** policy. Oracle CEP also defines an alternative policy called **server class-space** policy. You can enable this policy by including the following manifest header entry in the application's manifest file:

```
OCEP_JAVA_CARTRIDGE_CLASS_SPACE: SERVER_CLASS_SPACE
```

In the case of the server class-space policy, a CQL query can load all Java classes being exported by all Oracle CEP applications and libraries.

Considering the previous example, if applications A1, A2, and A3 should all be changed to use the server class-space policy, then applications A1, A2, and A3 will be able to access the classes `myorg.app1.Address` and `myorg.app2.Book`, as these classes are being exported to all components in the Oracle CEP server. However, even with the server class-space policy, still only application A3 is able to access the `myorg.app3.Student` class, as this class (or rather its package) is not being exported by the A3 application.

The following table summarizes these results:

Query visibility for:	A1	A2	A3
`App class space`	`Address`	`Address, Book`	`Student`
`Server class space`	`Address, Book`	`Address, Book`	`Address, Book, Student`

The added visibility provided by the server class-space policy doesn't come without a price. This policy breaks modularity, doesn't react well to application updates, and performs worse, and therefore should generally be avoided aside when testing.

Avoid the server class-space policy in production systems.

Now, you understand the visibility of Java classes in CQL, however it still remains to be seen how you should be referencing to these classes, should you be including the full Java class name or just its simple name? In other words, should it be `java.lang.String` and `myorg.app1.Address` or just `String` and `Address`?

Generally, you should use the full Java class name, which consists of the package name and the actual class name, such as in `myorg.app1.Address`. For example, if you need to create a new `Address` class in a query, you should do it like this:

```
SELECT myorg.app1.Address() as address …
```

However, there are a couple of exceptions created to improve usability. First, you don't need to specify the package name if it is `java.lang`. That's the reason why the previous examples referencing to the class `Integer` and `String` worked as it is.

Furthermore, if you are using the default application class-space policy, then the Java cartridge automatically looks into your `Import-Package` definitions and checks if the referenced classes could be loaded by using these in an unambiguous form. For example, application A2 imports the package `myorg.app1`, and therefore its queries could use the simple class name of `Address`, as in the following example:

```
SELECT Address() as address …
```

Yet application A1 does not import this package, and even though the class is defined in its own application, its queries would need to use the full Java class name `myorg.app1.Address`.

This auto-importing only works if it can be done in an unambiguous form. Should application A2 also have defined a class named `Address` in its `myorg.app2` package, then the Java cartridge wouldn't be able to infer if the expression `Address()` is related to `myorg.app1.Address` or `myorg.app2.Address` and would return it as an error. In this case, you would need to specify the full Java class name in the query.

Finally, you can disable the auto-import by specifying the following manifest header entry in the application:

```
OCEP_JAVA_CARTRIDGE_CLASS_SPACE:
APPLICATION_NO_AUTO_IMPORT_CLASS_SPACE
```

This option forces the CQL queries to hard-code the full Java class name and therefore avoids confusion and ambiguities.

Speaking of ambiguities, in addition to determining the Java class to load, there are other cases where ambiguities may arise when working with Java in CQL. This is covered in the next section.

Handling ambiguities between Java and CQL

Consider an application that defines the following class in the default package:

```
public class S
{
  public static String myProp;
}
```

Next, let's say that we are sending an event containing a single property called `myProp` to the following query:

```
SELECT S.myProp
FROM S
```

Does `S.myProp` refer to the static property in the class named `S` or does it refer to the `myProp` event property from the stream `S`? The expression `S.myProp` actually refers to the latter case, that is, `S` maps to the stream `S` and `myProp` to an event property.

Whenever there is an ambiguity, CQL symbols, such as the event source name, have preference over Java-cartridge symbols, such as Java class methods, fields, and constructors.

What if the ambiguity is only related to Java? For example, consider a class that overloads several of its methods, as following:

```
public class Address
{
  voidsetNumber(Integer) {...}
  voidsetNumber(Object) {...}
  voidsetNumber(int) {...}
  voidsetNumber(long) {...}
}
```

And the following expression:

```
... address.setNumber(10) ...
```

Which method gets invoked? The Java cartridge follows the rules for method resolution as determined by the **Java Language Specification** (**JLS**).

> The Java Cartridge supports all forms of method overloading, except overloading based on variable arity.

So, in this example, the resolution would be (in order of precedence):

- `setNumber(int)`
- `setNumber(long)`
- `setNumber(Integer)`
- `setNumber(Object)`

As you can see, the Java cartridge follows the JLS. Furthermore, it also allows you to use the Java-Bean coding-style conventions, as you shall see next.

Using the JavaBeans conventions in CQL

The Java cartridge also supports the JavaBeans coding-style conventions, allowing the CQL queries to be further simplified. In a nutshell, the JavaBeans specification says that the Java methods `getName()` and `setName()` can be interpreted respectively as implicit getters and setters for a JavaBean property called `name`. Further, should name be of Boolean type, you can also use the convention of `isName()` as the getter.

For example, consider the following query:

```
SELECT
  student.getAddress().getState() as state
FROM R
WHERE student.isRegistered() = true
```

Using the JavaBeans conventions, this can be changed to:

```
SELECT
  student.address.state as state
FROM R
WHERE student.registered = true
```

This is a great improvement to the readability of the CQL queries, preserving their declarative aspect, and therefore the preferred approach.

Keep in mind that in terms of precedence, CQL first checks for a stream or relation name, then for an event property (column) name, only then for a Java property. However, Java properties do have precedence over Java fields. In other words, an expression such as `student.address` would prefer a method `Student.getAddress()` over a public field `Student.address` should both be present.

> The Java cartridge does not support indexed, bound, or constrained JavaBean properties.

The blending of Java with CQL is a powerful tool for performing event processing in Oracle CEP, as it allows the user to not only program the structure of the processing using CQL, but also to perform day-to-day tasks better done in Java all together in the same environment. Next, we take a look at how to expand CQL to also include processing of events that include XML documents.

Processing XML with CQL

With the progress of web services and XML technologies, it is not uncommon for an Oracle CEP application to have to receive and output XML documents as part of event processing. Let's start our study of how to work with XML in CQL by first tackling the case where queries need to output strings containing valid XML documents.

> **XML Primer**
>
> Here is a quick primer on the XML vocabulary. Using the following XML as a reference:
>
> ```
> <docElem>
>   <elementAattributeA="v1">content</elementA>
>   <elementBattributeB="v2">content</elementB>
> </docElem>
> ```
>
> The tags `<docElem>`, `<elementA>`, and `<elementB>` are called XML elements. XML elements contain content between their start (`<elementA>`) and end tag (`</elementA>`), which can be other XML elements, or just character data.
>
> The tag `<docElem>` is the root of the document and is called the document element. Proper XML documents must have a single root. Unrooted XML are called **XML fragments**. XML fragments with multiple roots are called XML forests.
>
> The keys `attributeA` and `attributeB` are called XML attributes. XML attributes have values, as `v1` and `v2`.

Consider the case where a query receives stock tickers, as you have seen in the past, and it needs to output the following XML for each symbol it receives:

```
<stock>
<symbol>ORCL</symbol>
<price>30.0</price>
</stock>
```

To be able to do this, you can use the built-in XML function `xmlelement`, as in the following example:

```
SELECT
XMLELEMENT(
    NAME "stock",
    XMLELEMENT(NAME "symbol", symbol),
    XMLELEMENT(NAME "price", price)
  ) as xml
FROM marketFeed
```

Initially, this may look a bit elaborate, but it is mostly because we had to nest calls to several `xmlelement` functions together. If you take a single expression such as `XMLELEMENT(NAME "price", price)`, it boils down to specifying the name of the XML element and its value. The value is a standard CQL expression, and in most cases it is just a reference to an event property, but potentially it could be expressions containing calls to other XML functions.

Let's say that the `marketFeed` stream receives the events as shown in the following table:

Time	Input event
0	{symbol = "AAA", price = 10.0}
1	{symbol = "BBB", price = 100.0}

In this case, the output of the query is:

Time	Input event
0	{xml = "<stock><symbol>AAA</symbol><price>10.0</price></stock>"}
1	{xml = "<stock><symbol>BBB</symbol><price>100.0</price></stock>"}

The type of the event property `xml` is the native CQL data type called `XMLTYPE`. When converted to Java, it becomes a Java `String` type.

Next, let's say we want to change the output XML fragment to:

```
<stock symbol="ORCL" price="30.0" />
```

This is done with the following query:

```
SELECT
XMLELEMENT(
    NAME "stock",
    XMLATTRIBUTE(symbol AS "symbol"),
    XMLATTRIBUTE(price AS "price")
  ) as xml
FROM marketFeed
```

No surprises here, you just replace the inner elements by `xmlattribute` functions.

One other variation is to output an XML forest instead of a XML document, as we have done in the previous example. The reason you may want to do this is because each output event may be collated together as content for a parent global element. Here is an example of an XML forest output:

```
<symbol>"ORCL"</symbol>
<price>"30.0"</price>
```

You can achieve this by using the following query:

```
SELECT
XMLFOREST(
    XMLELEMENT(NAME "symbol", symbol),
    XMLELEMENT(NAME "price", price)
  ) as xml
FROM marketFeed
```

Finally, let's say that rather than outputting individually each stock as a separate XML document, we would like to aggregate them all together and output a single document, as in the following example:

```
<stocks>
<stock>
<symbol>AAA</symbol>
<price>10.0</price>
</stock>
<stock>
<symbol>BBB</symbol>
<price>15.0</price>
</stock>
</stocks>
```

The following query generates the desired outcome:

```
SELECT
  XMLELEMENT(NAME "stocks",
    XMLAGG(
  XMLELEMENT(
    NAME "stock",
          XMLELEMENT(NAME "symbol", symbol),
          XMLELEMENT(NAME "price", price)
  )) as xml
FROM marketFeed [RANGE 10 MINUTES SLIDE 10 MINUTES]
```

This is no different than using any other aggregation function, such as `avg`, `max`, and `min`. First, we need to convert the stream to a relation, and then we can apply the `xmlagg` function. Instead of summarizing the aggregated rows as a single value, the `xmlagg` function generates an XML fragment for each aggregated row. In this particular case, the query generates an XML document containing the last 10 minutes of stocks every 10 minutes coming from the `markedFeed` stream.

So far, you have seen how to generate XML documents. In the next section, you will learn how to process events that contain XML documents.

Handling XML document sources

The `xmltable` function is a function that returns a relation from a source event property. Because it returns a relation, that is, a collection of rows or events, such functions are called table functions.

Let's use the xmltable to revert what we have done in the previous example. That is, say we receive an event that has a property called stocks of type xmltype with the following content:

```
<stocks>
<stock>
<symbol price="10.0">AAA</symbol>
</stock>
<stock>
<symbol price="15.0">BBB</symbol>
</stock>
</stocks>
```

The following query receives its input as an XML document and generates separate events representing the individual stocks:

```
SELECT
  R.sym, R.pri
```

```
FROM
stocksXmlFeed
  XMLTABLE (
    "/stocks/stock"
    PASSING BY VALUE
      stocksXmlFeed.stocks as "."
    COLUMNS
      sym char(16) PATH "fn:data(symbol)",
      pri float PATH "fn:data(@price)"
  ) as R
```

As `xmltable` is a table function, it can only be used in the `FROM` clause, as a relation source. The first task you have is to establish which event property contains the XML document and how you want to set it as the context node. The context node is your root node against which you will later execute XPath (and XQuery) functions. This is done with the `PASSING BY VALUE` clause in line 7 and 8 in the preceding example. In our case, we state that the `stocks` property in the `stocksXmlFeed` source contains the XML document and that its root, using the expression `"."`, is the context node.

Next, you need to establish the rows you will be working with. This is done by querying the context node with the `XPath` expression `"/stocks/stock"`, this is done in line 6 in our example. In our case, remember that the context node is the whole document. The `XPath` expression `"/stocks/stock"` then returns a forest containing the two stock elements. Had we changed the context node to `"/stocks"`, we could have achieved the same result by using the expression `"/stock"`.

Finally, we need to assign each element from the returned forest to one or more properties. We do this with the `COLUMNS` clause. In our example, we had got two `stock` elements in the previous step. Now we will assign the returning node from the expression `"symbol"` to the `sym` property, and the returning node from the expression `"@price"` to the `pri` property. Both of these properties are properties of the `R` relation, which contains two rows. The `"symbol" XPath` expression returns the inner symbol element. The `"@price" XPath` expression returns the XML attribute called price in the `stock` element.

> In XPath and XQuery, XML attributes must referenced by using the `@` prefix.

At the end, running this query against a single input event with the stocks property containing the given XML document generates the following two events:

```
{sym = "AAA", pri = 10.0}
{sym = "BBB", pri = 15.0}
```

By now you have learned how to use all the major CQL data types. In the next section, we take a look at the one remaining key CQL feature, that of pattern matching.

Pattern matching

One of the main features of CEP is the ability to detect patterns of events directly on a stream, even complex conditions such as sequences, alternations, and non-events (missing events). For example, detect if a particular event is followed by another event within some time period. This feature is generally called **pattern matching**.

In CQL, pattern matching is realized through the `MATCH_RECOGNIZE` operator. Being a streaming-processing related feature, `MATCH_RECOGNIZE` is a stream-to-stream operator, meaning that it applies directly to a stream, without the need to convert it to a relation using a Window operator as you have done in the past for some of the other features like joins.

Let's take a look at the basic skeleton for `MATCH_RECOGNIZE` with the following example:

```
SELECT M.goingUpPrice
FROM marketFeed
MATCH_RECOGNIZE (
  MEASURES
    B.price as goingUpPrice
  PATTERN (A B)
  DEFINE
    A as price < 29.0,
    B as price > 30.0
) as M
```

The skeleton is rather large, but as you will see, it is mostly intuitive. Let's start with the subclause `PATTERN`. This is at the heart of pattern matching, and defines the general pattern of events that must be matched. In this case, we are stating that some event, which henceforth is named `A`, is followed by another event, named `B`. The identifiers `A` and `B` are called **correlation variables**. A sequence of events in the input stream that satisfies the correlation variables is considered a match of the pattern.

We then define exactly what `A` and `B` are by using the `DEFINE` clause. You can use any regular CQL expression in the define clause. In this query, we define that `A` is an event whose `price` property is less than `29.0`, and `B` is an event whose `price` is larger than `30.0`.

A correlation variable that is not defined is always true for all input events.

When the pattern is matched, we need a way of referencing to these matched events. This is the role of the `MEASURES` subclause. For this particular case, the `MEASURES` is very simple, it just names the `price` of the matched event `B` as `goingUpPrice`. The whole result of the pattern matching is associated to the `M` alias, which can then be used in the `SELECT` clause, as we have done with `M.goingUpPrice`.

The input/output table for the pattern-matching query is as follows:

Number	Input event	Output event
1	`+{symbol = 'ORCL', price = '28.0'}`	
2	`+{symbol = 'ORCL', price = '31.0'}`	`+{M.goingUpPrice = 31.0}`
3	`+{symbol = 'ORCL', price = '28.0'}`	
4	`+{symbol = 'ORCL', price = '28.0'}`	
5	`+{symbol = 'ORCL', price = '31.0'}`	`+{M.goingUpPrice = 31.0}`
6	`+{symbol = 'ORCL', price = '28.0'}`	
7	`+{symbol = 'ORCL', price = '29.5'}`	
8	`+{symbol = 'ORCL', price = '31.0'}`	

When the query receives the first event, it is able to match the correlation variable `A`. You can think of this as a state machine, as shown in the following diagram:

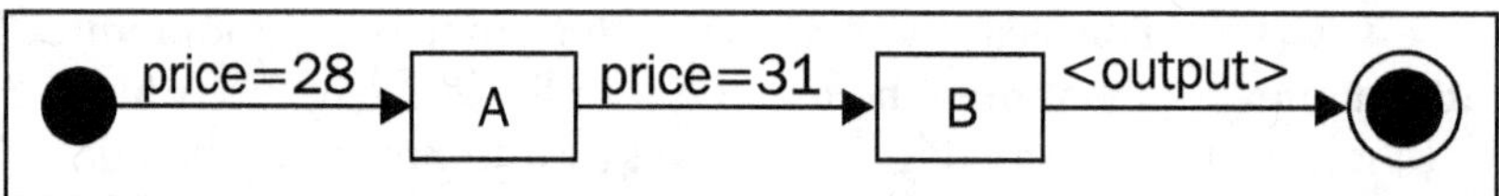

When we match correlation variable `A`, we move to state A. When the query receives the second event, the state machine moves to state B, and hence the pattern is considered complete, and an output is emitted.

Next, the query clears both correlation variables and starts a new instance of the state machine. When it receives the third event, it again moves to state A. However, when it receives the forth event, it doesn't match with `B`, as the `price` is not higher than `30.0`, so it remains in state A. In fact, because our pattern states that the next immediate event must match correlation `B`, this state machine instance will never be realized, and terminates. However, at the same time this instance terminates, a new instance of the state machine is created, as the fourth event does match the correlation variable `A`. When the query receives the fifth event, the state machine moves to state B, sends an output, and terminates successfully. This scenario is illustrated in the following diagram:

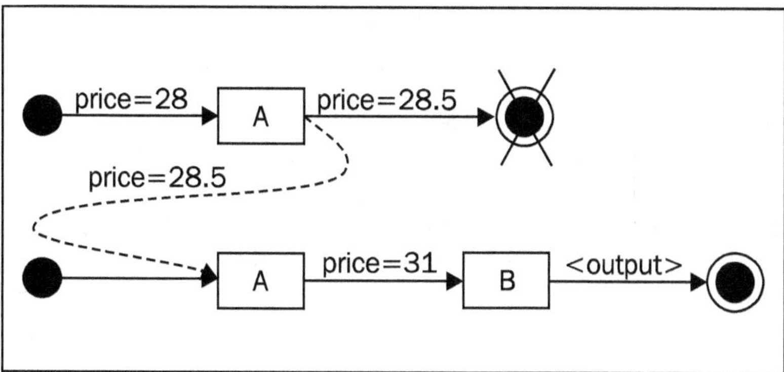

Finally, the query receives event six and starts a new instance of the state machine in state A. When it receives the seventh event, it doesn't match with correlation variable `B`, thus terminating the current machine. Likewise, seventh event doesn't match with correlation variable `A`, therefore not triggering the creation of a new state machine instance. When event eight arrives, it would have matched with correlation variable `B` if there had been a state machine in state A. But as there is none, the event is simply discarded.

Think of pattern matching as instances of state machines where each state is defined by a correlation variable.

The `MATCH_RECOGNIZE` clause is similar to a sub-query in the way that it defines a new source. In the case of the previous example, it is called `M`. However, the original source is no longer available, so it would be an error to try to use the properties `price` or `symbol` in the `select` or `where` clause, as they are no longer available. Only the properties explicitly defined as measures of `M` can now be used in the `select` or in the `where` clause of the outer query. In other words, in the previous case, only the `goingUpPrice` property from the base source can be projected in the output. Further, keep in mind that the `where` clause is applied after the pattern matching has occurred. If you need to apply it before, define a view and use it in the view, and then have the `MATCH_RECOGNIZE` clause reference the view.

In the next section, you will learn how to improve this example.

Partitioning events for matching

In the previous example, we made no distinction around a stock's symbol, but, as we have done in the case of a partitioned window, we should likewise partition the stream so that the query is looking at the variation of price for a particular company. Luckily, this is easily done with the `PARTITION BY` subclause, as shown in the following example:

```
SELECT M.goingUpPrice
FROM marketFeed
MATCH_RECOGNIZE (
  PARTITION BY symbol
  MEASURES
    B.price as goingUpPrice
  PATTERN (A B)
  DEFINE
    A as price < 29.0,
    B as price > 30.0
) as M
```

This query matches the `goingUpPrice` per partition of symbol.

Be conscious of the use of the `PARTITION BY` clause, as a separate partition is created for each distinct value of the partition by property, therefore potentially being a resource drain if the matches are very long.

Next, let's say that rather than hard coding the prices `29` and `30`, you would like to find out if the price is going up, in other words, if there is an upward trend in the price.

To do this, we need to improve two aspects of the query: we need a more elaborate pattern that matches more than a single event, and a way of referencing to previous events in the `define` clause. In other words, a mechanism for using aggregate functions in the `define` clause. Let's tackle the first problem in the next section.

Patterns as regular expressions

CQL has a rich set of pattern operators that can be used to specify pattern expressions, as regular expressions. These are called **pattern quantifiers** and are defined as follows:

- `*`: Zero or more events
- `+`: One or more events
- `?`: Zero or one event
- `|`: Alternation (or)
- `()`: Grouping

> Supporting regular expressions in the pattern sub-clause makes sense as the `match recognize` clause can be visualized as an evaluation of state machine.

Most of these are very intuitive, and should be familiar to those used to working with regular expressions. Let's walk through a couple of examples. However, before we start, let's put in place a simple convention. Uppercase letters represent a correlation variable, and a corresponding lowercase letter corresponds to an event that matches the condition defined for the uppercase letter's condition. Now consider the following example:

```
PATTERN (A+ B*)
```

This pattern matches with the following sequence of events:

- `a`
- `aa`
- `ab`
- `aabb`

But, it fails to match the following sequences:

- `b`
- `bb`
- `acb`

Next, consider the following pattern:

```
PATTERN ( (A B?) | (B A?) )
```

Examples of sequences that match this pattern are:

- `a`
- `ab`
- `b`
- `ba`

Examples that fail to match are:

- `abb`
- `baa`

As you can see, the alternation operator is useful when you need to match permutations, such as `(A B) | (B A)`, which means either `A` followed `B`, or `B` followed by `A`.

Controlling the number of matches

When performing a pattern match, a query may either try to match the longest set of events as possible, or match the smallest set and terminate as soon as possible. The former case is known as a **greedy match**, and the latter as a **reluctant match**. Let's take a look at a simple example:

```
PATTERN (A+)
DEFINE
  A as val like 'a'
```

Next, say the query receives the following sequence of events:

```
aaab
```

The pattern is greedy and therefore matches the sequence of events `aaa` at the time it receives event `b`. Why only when it receives event `b`? Because only when it receives event `b`, it will know that no other longer match can be realized.

You can configure a pattern as reluctant by appending the `?` character to a pattern match operator. For example, consider the following reluctant pattern:

```
PATTERN (A+?)
DEFINE
   A as val like 'a'
```

Also, consider that this query receives the same sequence of events as the previous case:

```
aaab
```

The pattern is reluctant and therefore matches the sequence of events `aa` as soon as it is seen. In other words, the query won't try to match `aaa`, and instead is contented on matching the smaller set of `aa`.

Next, let's take a look at a more elaborate scenario. Say that a correlation variable `BandC` establishes conditions that can be matched by both events `B` and for events `C`. Next, say we have the following sequence of events:

```
abcc
```

The pattern `(A BandC+ C+)` is greedy; therefore the correlation variable `BandC` would try to maximize the number of events it matches. In this case, `BandC` would be correlated with the sequence `bc` and `C` would correlate to `c`.

However, if we change the pattern to be reluctant, as in `(A BandC+? C+)`, then `BandC` would correlate to the minimum sequence of `b` and `C` would correlate to `cc`.

Yet, what if you are interesting on finding out all results, in other words, both the reluctant matches, as well as the greedy ones? Rather than creating two queries, one that is reluctant, and another that is greedy, you can use the `ALL MATCHES` subclause.

Again, considering the previous example, let's change it to:

```
SELECT M.countOfBandC, M.countOfC
FROM stream
MATCH_RECOGNIZE (
  MEASURES
    count(BandC.*) as countOfBandC,
    count(C.*) as countOfC
    ALL MATCHES
    PATTERN (A BandC+ C+)
    DEFINE
    A as val like 'a'
    BandC as val like 'b' or val like 'c'
    C as val like 'c'
) as M
```

The input/output table for this query is shown in the following table:

Number	Input event	Output events
1	`+{val = "a"}`	
2	`+{val = "b"}`	
3	`+{val = "c"}`	`+{countOfBandC = 1, countOfC = 1}`
4	`+{val = "c"}`	`+{countOfBandC = 2, countOfC = 1}, +{countOfBandC = 1, countOfC = 2}`

As expected, there are no outputs for the first two events. When the query receives the third event, the sequence becomes `abc`, which does match with the `pattern (A BandC C)`. Now comes the interesting part—when the query receives the fourth event, the query emits two output events. In the first one, the correlation variable `BandC` matches to `bc` and `C` matches to `c`. In the second one, `BandC` matches to `b` and `C` matches to `bc`.

The `ALL MATCHES` subclause matches not only to the maximum and minimum cases, but actually to all possible cases. For example, if you send one additional event whose value is `c`, the query emits three events as follows:

```
+{countOfBandC = 3, countOfC = 1},
+{countOfBandC = 2, countOfC = 2},
+{countOfBandC = 1, countOfC = 3}
```

This is equivalent to the following matches to the correlation variables:

```
BanC = "bcc", C = "c"
BanC = "bc" , C = "cc"
BanC = "b"  , C = "bcc"
```

As it should be obvious, there is no need to specify the reluctant operator (`?`) when using the `ALL MATCHES` subclause.

Now that you have learned how to create complex patterns, and correlate multiple events to a single correlation variable, you need a way to reference to a particular event within a correlation variable group, as we have done with the `count` function in the previous example. This is explained in the next section.

Working with correlation groups

Correlation variables can match to a single event, or to a group of events. One example of the former case is a pattern such as `(A)`; this type of correlation variables is called singleton correlation variables. One example of the latter case is a pattern such as `(A*)`. Specifically, for this latter case, the correlation variable may correlate to a group (or bag) of events. These are called **correlation variable groups**.

A correlation variable (both singletons and groups) may be used in the context of three different scopes:

- In the `DEFINE` clause, while it is being defined. For example, this is the case of correlation variable `A` in `A as A.price = 10`. In this case, the correlation variable is still matching, that is, it is still running.
- In the `DEFINE` clause, by a different correlation variable. For example, this is the case of correlation variable `A` in `B as B.price>A.price`. Likewise, in this case, the correlation variables are still running.
- In the `MEASURES` clause. In this case, the correlation variables have already matched and are final.

Next, let's explore the semantics of referencing correlation variables in these three different scopes.

If you are referencing a singleton correlation variable, then the semantics is simple. For the first case, that is, referencing a correlation variable in a `define` clause while it is being defined, the correlation variable points to the current event. For example, in the case `A as A.price = 10`, the identifier `A` points to the current event being evaluated. This is similar to specifying `A as price = 10`, as in this case the non-qualified `price` identifier points to the current event in the input source stream.

For the latter two cases, the correlation variable points to the single event that matched the correlation conditions. For example, consider the following query fragment:

```
DEFINE
  A as A.price = 10
  B as B.price>A.price
```

As we have understood this before intuitively, the identifier `A.price` in the definition of `B` points to the event that matched correlation variable `A`, which is essentially the event whose `price` is `10`.

Next, let's consider the case of correlation variable groups. As we are now working with aggregates, we need to either aggregate the value of the group, or use an aggregate function that returns a particular event within the group. For this purpose, in addition to the standard aggregate functions we learned about previously, `avg`, `max`, `min`, and `count`; when working with `match_recognize`, you can also make use of the following new aggregates:

- `first`: This returns the first event of a correlation variable group. If you optionally specify an integer, which works as an offset from the first event.
- `last`: This returns the last event of a correlation variable group. If the correlation variable is running (which is the case of scopes two and three), then be aware that this value changes as new events are received. Likewise you can specify an integer, which works as an offset from the last event.
- `prev`: This returns the last event matched in the correlation variable group. This can only be used in the case of the first scope, that is, while the correlation is being defined. `prev()` returns null if there is no previous event.

Summing up the rules, when referencing to a correlation variable group, you need to use an aggregate function. There is one exception to this rule. If you are in the context of the first scope, that is, when defining the correlation variable on its own term, you may also reference the current event that is being matched.

Finally, remember that for running correlation variables, the value returned by an aggregate may change as new events are matched. Next, let's consider an example:

```
PATTERN (A B+ C+ D)
DEFINE
  A as price = 10,
  B as B.price>A.price,
  C as C.price<avg(B.price),
  D as D.price>prev(D.price)
```

Let's explore the `define` statements one by one. The first statement is a simple case of a singleton correlation variable being defined.

The second statement is a case of a group correlation variable, as `B` is defined with a quantifier (+). In its condition, we first reference `B.price`. This normally would be illegal as we are trying to reference a single event in a group, however in this particular case it is allowed as it is done in the definition of `B` itself, and therefore applies to the current event. Next, we reference to `A.price`, this is likewise valid as `A` is a singleton.

In the third statement, we can't reference to `B.price` any longer, as `B` is a group. So instead we use an aggregate function that returns the average for the current events that have matched so far in the correlation group `B`.

Finally, in the fourth statement, we make use of `prev`, which returns the previous event in the `D` group. Note that we would not have been able to use `prev` to reference any other correlation variables such as `A`, `B`, or `C`, as `prev` can only be used with the definition of the correlation variable itself.

The count aggregate also has special meaning within `match_recognize`:

- `count(*)` returns the total number of events received by the input source.
- `count(A.*)` returns the total number of events so far in the correlation variable group named A.
- `count(A.p)` returns the total number of events so far in the correlation variable group named A whose property `p` is not null.

Having understood all the scoping and referencing rules, let's improve our pattern-matching query from the beginning of this section. Let's try a more elaborate scenario where you want to detect a down-trend followed by an up-trend. This can be done with the following query:

```
SELECT M.downTrendPrice, M.upTrendPrice
FROM marketFeed
MATCH_RECOGNIZE (
  PARTITION BY symbol
  MEASURES
    FIRST(A.price) as downTrendPrice,
    LAST(B.price) as upTrendPrice
  PATTERN (A+ B+)
  DEFINE
    A as A.price < prev(price),
      B as B.price > prev(price)
) as M
```

For an example of its execution, consider the following input/output table:

Input event	Output event
`+{symbol = "ORCL", price = 30.0}`	
`+{symbol = "ORCL", price = 29.0}`	
`+{symbol = "ORCL", price = 30.0}`	

Input event	Output event
`+{symbol = "ORCL", price = 31.0}`	
`+{symbol = "ORCL", price = 30.5}`	`+{downTrendPrice = 29.0, upTrendPrice = 31.0}`

The first event kicks off the pattern match, however it is not included in the matched correlation variable A, as, per definition, the `prev()` function returns null when there are no previous events, therefore excluding the first event from the group. The third event terminates the match for correlation variable A and starts the matching for correlation variable B, which is terminated by the fifth event. Interestingly, because of its greedy pattern, you need at least 5 events to match the query.

Furthermore, you can group the correlation variables together creating larger groups. This is done using the `SUBSET` clause. For example, in the previous query, we are using the highest price of the correlation variable B. However, this is not necessarily the highest price overall as the down-trend could actually have started with a higher price than the highest price of the up-trend. Should we want to find the highest price overall, we would need to consider both correlation variables A and B. So rather than doing it separately for correlation variable A and then for B, you can group them together and then apply the maximum aggregation function in this new set, which contains the union of all events from A and B. This is shown in the next example:

```
SELECT M.maxUpPrice
FROM marketFeed
MATCH_RECOGNIZE (
  PARTITION BY symbol
  MEASURES
    MAX(AB.price) as maxUpPrice
  PATTERN (A+ B+)
  SUBSET AB = (A,B)
  DEFINE
      A as A.price < prev(price),
      B as B.price > prev(price)
) as M
```

You can create multiple subsets, as in the following example:

```
SUBSET S1 = (A,B) S2 = (C,D) S3 = (E,F)
```

Let's say that our stock goes up forever, then when would we terminate this pattern matching? Should we just let it run unbounded forever? In most real scenarios, you do want to restrict the amount of time that a pattern matching has. This is the subject of the next section.

Expiring patterns

There are two situations where you may need to limit the execution time of a pattern match. The first case is when you want to terminate any ongoing matching because some period of time has already elapsed. The previous query is one such case; for example, if the stocks continue to go up, simply terminate the matching after an hour. You can do this using the `within` subclause, as in the following example:

```
SELECT M.maxUpPrice
FROM marketFeed
MATCH_RECOGNIZE (
  PARTITION BY symbol
  MEASURES
    MAX(AB.price) as maxUpPrice
  PATTERN (A+ B+) WITHIN 1 HOUR
  SUBSET AB = (A,B)
  DEFINE
      A as A.price < prev(price),
      B as B.price > prev(price)
) as M
```

Essentially, you are telling the query that it needs to match within a time period, otherwise simply terminate any ongoing potential matches.

The second case is the opposite, that is, you want to match if a pattern is still valid (has potential matches) after some duration of time. For example, still considering our up-trend pattern, let's say rather than terminating the query, we want to be notified with an event if the up-trend continues even after 10 minutes. In other words, let us know if an up-trend started and a down-price event does not happen after the duration of 10 minutes. You can do this with the `duration` subclause, as in the following example:

```
SELECT M.maxUpPrice
FROM marketFeed
MATCH_RECOGNIZE (
  PARTITION BY symbol
  MEASURES
    MAX(AB.price) as maxUpPrice
  INCLUDE TIMER EVENTS
  PATTERN (A+ B+) DURATION 10 MINUTES
  SUBSET AB = (A,B)
  DEFINE
      A as A.price < prev(price),
      B as B.price > prev(price)
) as M
```

In this case, you will receive the `maxUpPrice` event after 10 minutes even if the correlation variable `B` never matches. Another way of looking into this is that the `DURATION` subclause allows us to detect missing events. In this case, the missing event is the lack of the down-price event.

> The `DURATION` subclause must always be accompanied with the include timer events subclause. This is needed because this pattern matches with timer events in addition to input events from the stream source.

We can even go further, and state that we want to be continuously notified every 10 minutes while the up-trend continues and no down-event is received. This is done with the addition of the `multiple of` option in the `duration` sub-clause, as in the following example:

```
SELECT M.maxUpPrice
FROM marketFeed
MATCH_RECOGNIZE (
  PARTITION BY symbol
  MEASURES
    MAX(AB.price) as maxUpPrice
  INCLUDE TIMER EVENTS
  PATTERN (A+ B+) DURATION MULTIPLE OF 10 MINUTES
  SUBSET AB = (A,B)
  DEFINE
      A as A.price < prev(price),
      B as B.price > prev(price)
) as M
```

Note that the query terminates without an output event as soon as the down-event occurs.

We have gone through all the major features of this incredible world of event processing with CQL. If you are feeling a bit overwhelmed, do not worry. As with most new languages, it takes some time for the concepts and ideas to sink in!

Summary

In this chapter, we learned that CQL is extensible using cartridges, and that it comes with a Java cartridge, which allows CQL to be seamlessly blended with Java.

The syntax for using Java in CQL is very similar to plain programming in Java. CQL also supports the JavaBeans programming conventions.

CQL has several functions for processing XML, you can break XML documents into events using the `xmltable` function, and you can generate XML documents using the `xmlelement` and `xmlattribute` functions.

One of the most important features in CQL is pattern matching, which allows you to find patterns in a stream. Pattern matching is realized through the `match_recognize` clause, and supports the specification of regular expressions. It also supports the definition of a within and duration time.

In the next chapter, we move on to learning how to scale Oracle CEP applications.

9

Implementing Performance Scaling, Concurrency, and High Availability for Oracle Event Processing

You've learned how to build OEP applications, but now it's time to discuss some important topics relating to making them production ready. We'll look at the factors involved in scaling your application, concurrency, and making your application highly available.

In this chapter, we will consider the issues and challenges involved in creating high-performance applications using Oracle Event Processing and describe some of the many ways in which this technology can be tailored to meet the needs of any Use Case. The topics we will cover are as follows:

- Scalability versus high availability
- Understanding performance and ways to influence
- Scaling Oracle Event Processing
- Using concurrency with processors
- High availability in Oracle Event Processing
- A sample HA Oracle Event Processing application

Scalability versus high availability

When approaching scalability and high availability, many people often discuss them with a goal to accomplish both at the same time but often use these words and concepts interchangeably. While the presence of state in Oracle Event Processing can make it more challenging to tackle these issues concurrently, particularly HA, we will now discuss how these requirements can be addressed and successfully implemented.

Like any computing resource, Oracle Event Processing servers can be subject to both hardware and software faults that can lead to temporarily unavailability of services and/or loss of data. OEP high availability features give you the capability to mitigate both of these possibilities at a level of reliability that suits your application requirements.

OEP supports an "active/active" high availability architecture; meaning the additional servers in the architecture are in an active state in the event that there is a failure, but both (or all of the servers, if there are multiple backup/secondary servers) are processing all of the incoming events. This approach was chosen because it provides a simple way to achieve extremely high performance and short failover time, and also because OEP applications often hold complex states in memory. This state could take significant time to re-build if a passive architecture was used. As usual, the beauty of OEP is that it is an open, flexible event-processing platform, so it is possible to implement many types of high-availability architectures.

When you require that your application be highly available, you should deploy it to an OEP cluster configured with two or more server instances (ideally running on separate hardware). OEP will automatically choose one server in the group to be the active "primary". The remaining servers become active "secondary" servers. This means that all servers are running processing input events. You want to configure the deployment architecture so that both servers are processing *all of the same input events*. This is so if one server fails, another one can become the primary and begin correctly sending the output events. You can choose one of several available quality-of-service options depending upon your specific application requirements; for example, tolerance for duplicates or missing events.

Secondary servers don't generate output events, as this would create duplicate data in downstream systems. OEP provide a mechanism for secondary servers to buffer their output events using in-memory queues and the primary server keeps the secondary servers up-to-date with which events the primary has already output. In the event of a failure, you can have the secondary server that automatically becomes primary pick-up sending output events in exactly the place where the primary left off before it failed.

In this chapter, we'll discuss various qualities of service for high availability. These involve a variety of strategies for sharing state and have implications on scalability.

Understanding performance and ways to influence

As we turn to the topics that focus on the performance, availability, failover, and application scaling in event stream processing, we start to address a very important domain that in essence should be covered in other publications since there is a wealth of important concepts to be addressed. In this chapter we will focus on the major areas of interest and concern, and provide you with the solid foundation to fully understand and implement various performance optimization related techniques.

The "out-of-the-box" pre-configured Oracle Event Processing platform provides a comprehensive collection of default settings and options, so that even basic event-driven applications will execute at high speed, with in most cases, acceptable latencies. However, these types of applications do have fairly unique performance challenges that differ from general JEE application server workloads. These can be a combination of any of the following:

- Very high streaming data rates (that could exceed 100,000 events/second)
- Low and deterministic application latency
- Determinism requirements on worst case (or 99.999 percentile) latencies
- Ordered processing within streams

Millisecond or lower latency can be a competitive differentiator for many businesses and work has progressed to provide a significantly increased performance on the Oracle Engineered Systems, and in particular, Exalogic. While benchmark use cases can be very subjective, a relatively common and often referenced sample the "signal generation" application was used to give a reasonable baseline to indicate possible performance numbers. With a slight implementation variation, this application, which receives simulated market data and verifies if the price of a security has fluctuated more than 2 percent, and also detects if there is a **trend** occurring by keeping a track of the successive stock prices for a particular symbol, was executed on a single node achieving impressive results, processing 1 million events per second. The fully documented scenario, hardware and software configurations, tuning options used and more, can all be found in an Oracle Event Processing whitepaper on the Oracle Technology Network (OTN) website.

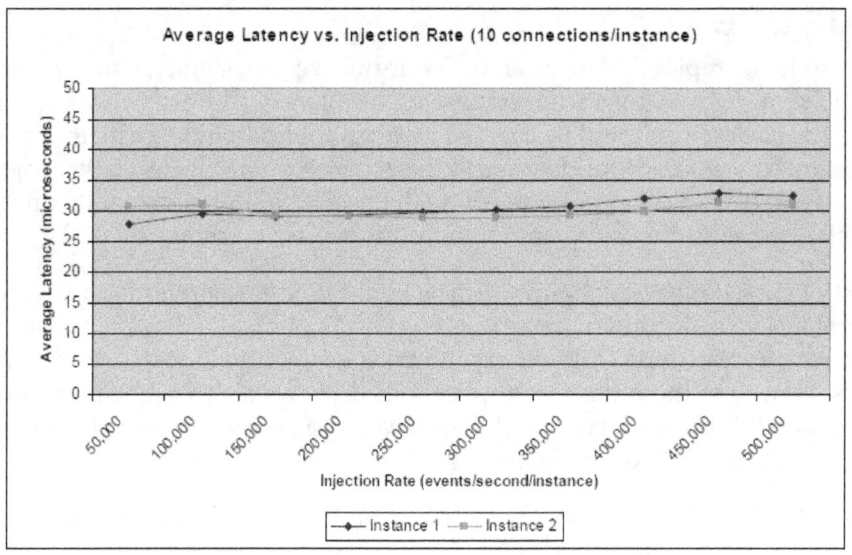

With the application deployed as two instances on one Exalogic node, the result was a constant latency rate of around 30 microseconds, which remained relatively flat throughout the ramping up of the load. With all of the nodes available in a full rack Exalogic machine, it might be possible to enable the processing of 30 million events per second and beyond while obtaining the same extremely low latencies. The application latency was measured from the point the events entered the input adapter (at the start of the EPN) until the matched results were posted to an output bean (at the end of the EPN).

While all benchmarks are subjective and very Use-Case specific, this example shows the impressive potential performance capability of Oracle Event Processing, which in a distributed architecture makes its scaling possibilities phenomenal.

We will now explore in more detail on how you can effectively impact the performance of your own Oracle Event Processing applications.

Scaling Oracle Event Processing

Unlike other event-stream processing products on the market, which are effectively "closed black-box" platforms, Oracle Event Processing facilitates performance-scaling optimization for your applications in many ways using many available attributes and options, to scale up and scale out. In this next section, we will describe and recommend some techniques to help you implement these powerful capabilities.

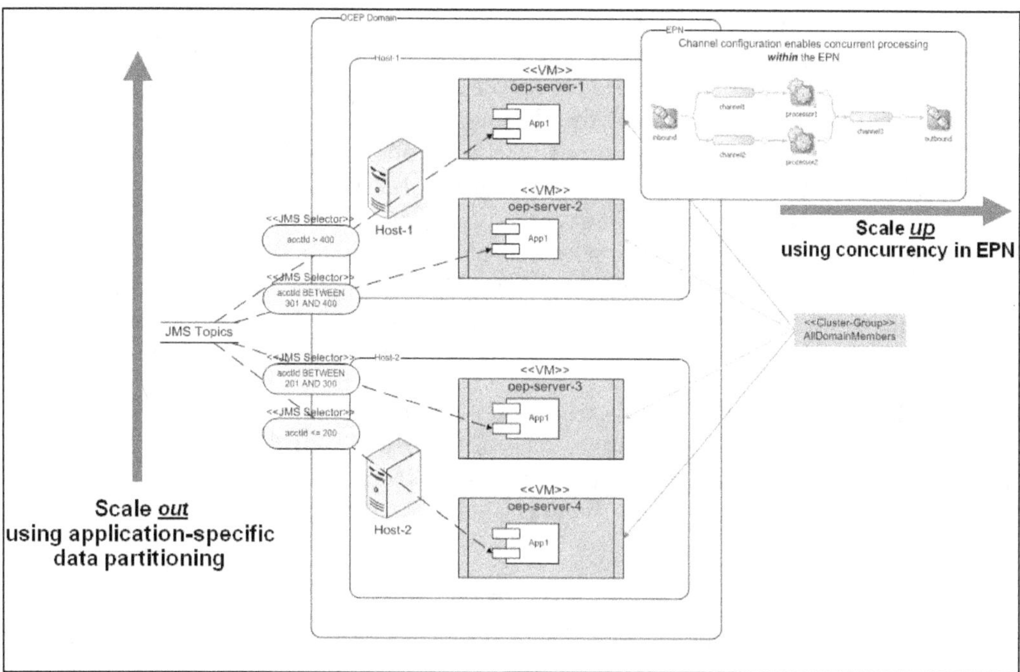

The threading model

A clear understanding of Oracle Event Processing threading and how threads interact within the EPN is fundamental to performance optimization. Threads can originate:

- In input adapters
- In beans/adapters implementing `RunnableBean` (The Oracle Event Processing runtime will call the `run` method)

- In channels
- From work managers such as `java.util.concurrent.Executor`

It is important to understand where threads originate in your EPN. Threading is easily configurable for your application and is an area where you can significantly influence the performance of your applications.

Optimizing threading in channels

So let's focus now on threading in channels. There are many different ways to configure an event channel that will impact the control flow. If the `max-size` and `max-threads` attributes of a channel are set to `0` (or if no *max-size/max-threads* attributes are specified at all), this channel will act as a pass-through channel. In this case, you will have one or more producer threads going into the channel, and a given thread will simply call into the channel and pass through the channel calling any listeners that are configured on the channel in sequence. Alternatively, it is possible to configure a queue and a thread pool on a channel by setting the `max-size` and `max-threads` attributes to values greater than `0`. This provides a classic producer/consumer model where you can have asynchronous execution and create a higher level of concurrency downstream which can improve the throughput and parallelism, but it does not guarantee the ordering of events because there is no way to know which consumer threads will get which events.

There is also an opportunity for partitioning within the channel, which allows you to specify an event property that you want to use to partition on at the channel level. Instead of the channel broadcasting the event to all its listeners and calling them in sequence, a given event will get routed to a single listener based on the value of the property.

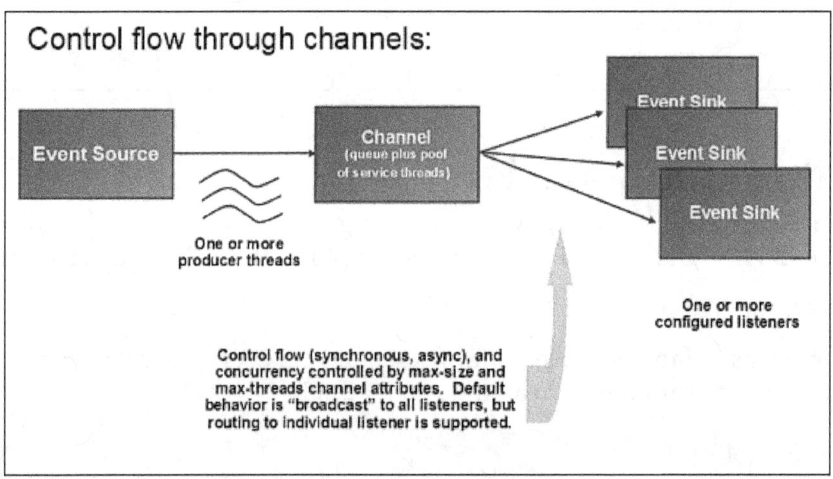

The primary related function of channel components is to create and control concurrency.

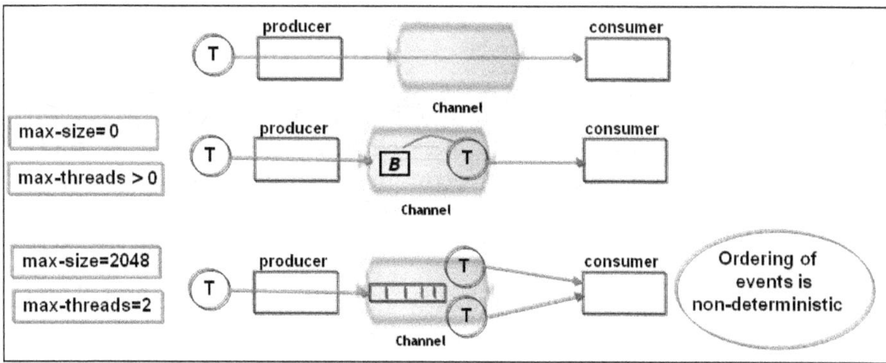

There are three basic types that are configured in the Spring configuration files or dynamically in the component's `config` file:

- **Pass Through (max-threads=0, max-size=0)**: Continue to run on the callers thread.
- **Synchronous Handoff (max-threads>0, max-size=0)**: Synchronous handoff from callers thread to thread pool associated with the channel. The caller thread is blocked until the event is schedule by the pool.
- **Concurrent Queue (max-threads>0, max-size>0)**: Asynchronous queuing onto queue of specified size, serviced by thread pool.

Note that the use of the `EventPartitioner` property as described above is orthogonal to the configuration of threading/queuing via the `max-threads` and `max-size` values, and that also helps with the concurrency in your application. In many cases, it is sufficient to the use the default, "Pass Through" option but under certain circumstances as described below, you may be able to get better performance using the "Concurrent Queue" capability.

Now armed with this knowledge, let's understand recommended approaches on when to use each type of channel configuration. Your goal is to get as much concurrency in the system while still honoring any ordering requirements in your application.

If the parallelism in your EPN is sufficient coming into channel (for example, multiple upstream threads) and you are not seeing low CPU utilization, the default, pass-through option may be the best choice for low latency. You do not need a thread pool to create more concurrency and having thread scheduling on the channel will just add more latency.

If your application requires ordering your queries, you do not want multiple threads servicing the queue, potentially allowing the events to get out of sequence downstream then you can specify a queue with `max-threads=1` which provides pipelined model which allows concurrency between producer and consumer while preserving ordering.

If ordering is unimportant downstream from the channel, the CPU utilization is too low, you are not seeing the concurrency required and there are a small number of producer threads, we would recommend using a larger number of threads (`max-threads > 0`).

The main purpose of the channel queue itself is to act as a buffer, balancing the relative rates of the producer and consumer. While manipulating the threading can assist in this process, if the rates vary over time, a large queue size can mitigate this performance issue. Try to never put a large queue in a latency critical path and if queue is consistently empty or consistently full, it is not going to help and if it is consistently full you may lose events.

Try to address the bottleneck in producer or consumer to get better balance. In general, while there is no upper limit on the queue size (only limit would be your hardware and operating system resources available), it is recommended that you do not exceed a value of more than 2000, otherwise it will be using memory and increasing latencies unnecessarily, and in practice you should be tuning elsewhere.

As a side note, using the Visualizer tooling or the JMX API framework programmatically could be the methods that you employ to monitor the channels and their related queue sizes and facilitate the tuning process.

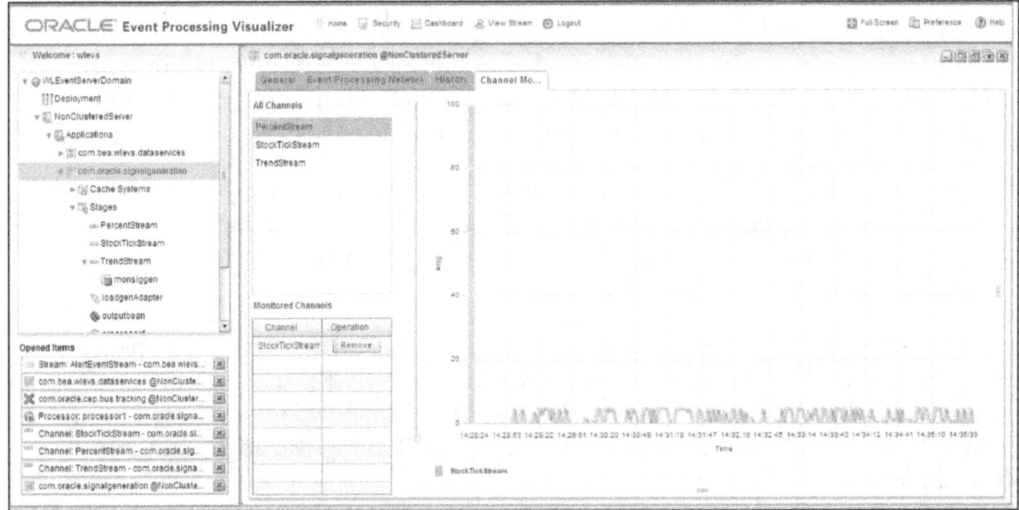

The EventPartitioner example

While the use of an `EventPartitioner` has been superseded to some extent with the newer capabilities in Oracle Event Processing for enabling concurrency in a single event processor instance, it is still worthwhile mentioning this important capability.

Typically, you can partition events onto threads upstream to the channel, and in the following example, we have two threads each carrying a subset of the input "stock symbols". In this particular case, the channel partitions the input events by hashing the specified property "symbol". This means that events containing the same value for symbol will be partitioned always to the same processor. The hash function used is one that minimizes the number of collisions. The result of the hash is then divided by the number of listeners and the remainder used to select the proper listener. This can effectively reduce lock contention in the processors because each one will get fewer events, and there is no lock shared across processor instances'. This works best if you can bind these threads to the partition's upstream data so the same thread is always carrying the same set of "symbols" in the same partition of the data. In which case, you can completely eliminate the contention in the processors in many cases.

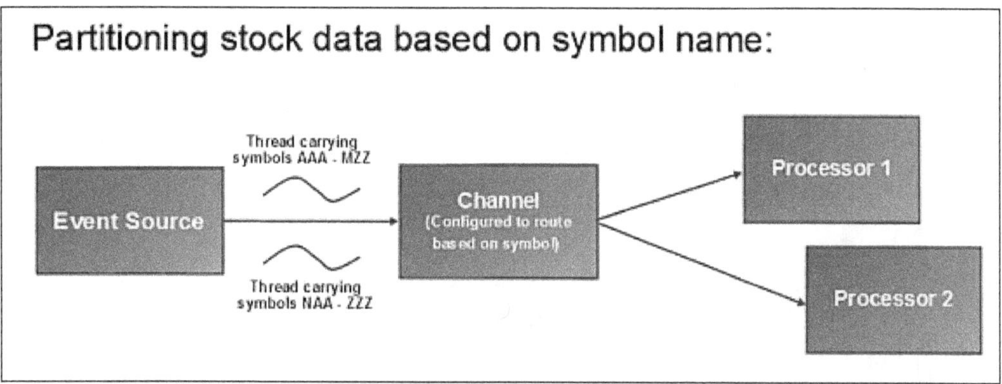

To set up event partitioning in an event channel, you must configure the instance property `partitionByEventProperty`, as shown in the following example:

```
<wlevs:channel id="MyChannel" event-type="MyChannelEventType" >
<wlevs:instance-property name="partitionByEventProperty"
value="symbol" />
<wlevs:channel>
```

Using concurrency with processors

We will turn now to improving the performance in your Event Processors using the concurrency feature with the **Continuous Query Language** (CQL). For CQL queries that requiring ordering, the CQL engine uses internal locks, as you would expect to maintain integrity, however this can result in lock contention and slower performance if multiple threads are active in a single processor instance.

In Oracle Event Processing 11.1.1.6 and later releases, the support for parallelism in the CQL engine has been enhanced, allowing lock contention to be minimized or eliminated for CQL queries with specific types of ordering constraints. This capability is implemented using the `ordering-constraint` attribute.

```
<query id="symbolanalysis" ordering-constraint="PARTITION_ORDERED" partitioning-expression="symbol">
        SELECT
           COUNT(*) as c, symbol
        FROM
        S[RANGE 1 minute]
        GROUP BY
        symbol
</query>
```

Use `ordering-constraint="UNORDERED"` for stateless queries where order doesn't matter (filtering). This will allow your application to scale to large number of threads/CPU cores without contention.

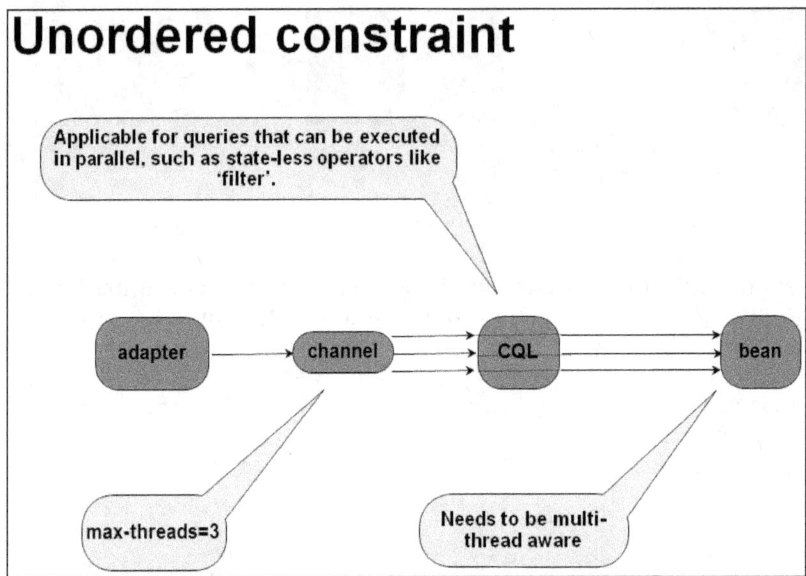

Use `ordering-constraint="PARTITION ORDERED"` guarantees that ordering will be maintained within any given partition of the input data (based on a user-specified partitioning key), but events from different partitions are not guaranteed to be ordered. Relaxing the ordering constraint of the query in this way allows the CQL engine to reduce its locking and provide a greater level of concurrency (essentially threads handling events from different partitions can run in parallel).

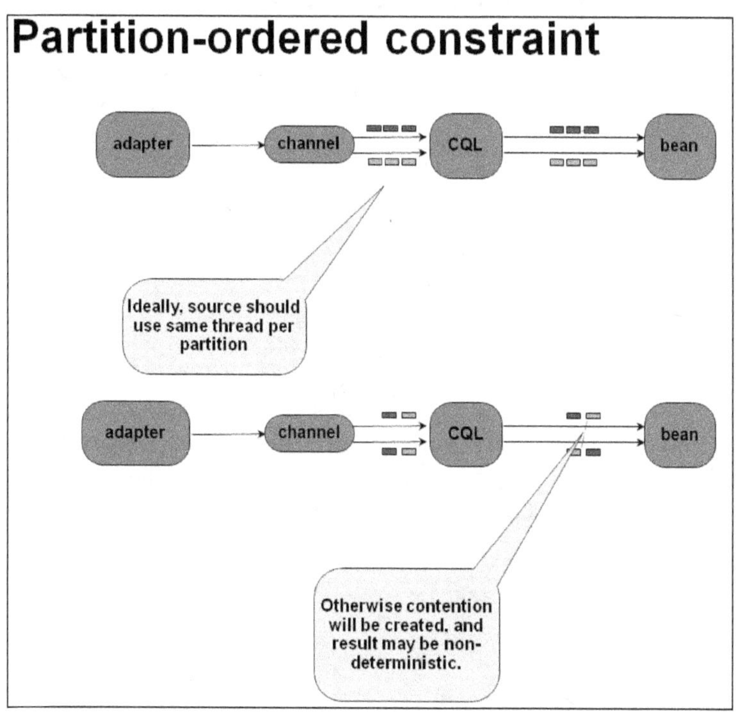

This option will allow your application to scale well when there are large numbers of partitions in the input data (unique partition keys).

An additional capability that is documented but easy to miss is the `partition-order-capacity` property used on input channel to the processor. This is applicable only when using queries that specify an ordering constraint `PARTITION ORDERED`. In concept, this will specify the number of unique partition buckets that will be allocated in the processor, which determines the locking granularity or the degree of parallelism you can expect from the processor. The default value is `4`, but if you still see contention on a processor instance you can increase this value and it is not too "expensive" to make it a fairly high value, for example 64. Internally, it requires just a few additional data structures that will be allocated for the processor and it will give you more unique locks and associated partition buckets so therefore less contention.

Use `ordering-constraint="ORDERED"`, which is the default option and is specified for queries that require all events in a given processor be handled in order (not partitionable). As you would expect, this requires the most locking in the CQL engine.

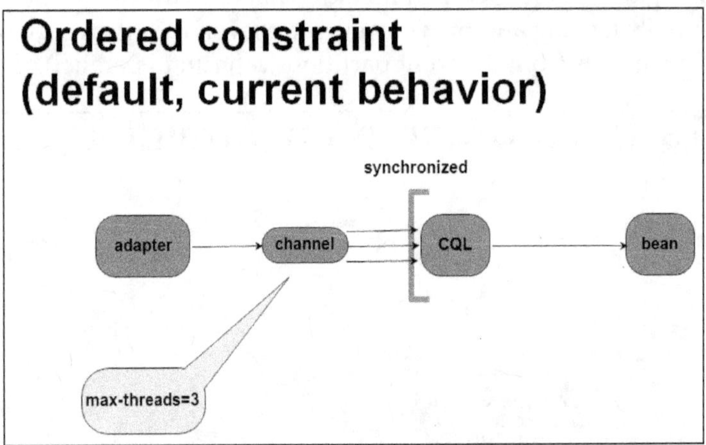

The use of processor parallelism can have a substantial effort of overall performance of your application. To emphasize the performance implications of this type of capability, Oracle created an event processing application with an EPN that included an event processor created with a collection of queries using the default `ORDERED` execution.

```
<query id="q0" ordering-constraint="ORDERED">
  <![CDATA[ select eventCount as id, ELEMENT_TIME as startTime, filter from inchannel where filter = 0 ]]>
</query>
<query id="q1" ordering-constraint="ORDERED">
  <![CDATA[ select eventCount as id, ELEMENT_TIME as startTime, filter from inchannel where filter = 1 ]]>
</query>
<query id="q2" ordering-constraint="ORDERED">
  <![CDATA[ select eventCount as id, ELEMENT_TIME as startTime, filter from inchannel where filter = 2 ]]>
</query>
<query id="q3" ordering-constraint="ORDERED">
  <![CDATA[ select eventCount as id, ELEMENT_TIME as startTime, filter from inchannel where filter = 3 ]]>
</query>
<query id="q4" ordering-constraint="ORDERED">
  <![CDATA[ select eventCount as id, ELEMENT_TIME as startTime, filter from inchannel where filter = 4 ]]>
</query>
<query id="q5" ordering-constraint="ORDERED">
  <![CDATA[ select eventCount as id, ELEMENT_TIME as startTime, filter from inchannel where filter = 5 ]]>
</query>
<query id="q6" ordering-constraint="ORDERED">
  <![CDATA[ select eventCount as id, ELEMENT_TIME as startTime, filter from inchannel where filter = 6 ]]>
</query>
<query id="q7" ordering-constraint="ORDERED">
  <![CDATA[ select eventCount as id, ELEMENT_TIME as startTime, filter from inchannel where filter = 7 ]]>
</query>
<query id="q8" ordering-constraint="ORDERED">
  <![CDATA[ select eventCount as id, ELEMENT_TIME as startTime, filter from inchannel where filter = 8 ]]>
</query>
<query id="q10" ordering-constraint="ORDERED">
  <![CDATA[ rstream(select eventCount as id, ELEMENT_TIME as startTime, filter, filterRelation.description
                from inchannel[now], filterRelation where filter = filterRelation.id) ]]>
</query>
```

With an input event source streaming 3000 events, and using a `max-threads=5` on the channel attribute on a 4-CPU processor, the total processing time amounts to 605 milliseconds.

```
<query id="q0" ordering-constraint="UNORDERED">
  <![CDATA[ select eventCount as id, ELEMENT_TIME as startTime, filter from inchannel where filter = 0 ]]>
</query>
<query id="q1" ordering-constraint="UNORDERED">
  <![CDATA[ select eventCount as id, ELEMENT_TIME as startTime, filter from inchannel where filter = 1 ]]>
</query>
<query id="q2" ordering-constraint="UNORDERED">
  <![CDATA[ select eventCount as id, ELEMENT_TIME as startTime, filter from inchannel where filter = 2 ]]>
</query>
<query id="q3" ordering-constraint="UNORDERED">
  <![CDATA[ select eventCount as id, ELEMENT_TIME as startTime, filter from inchannel where filter = 3 ]]>
</query>
<query id="q4" ordering-constraint="UNORDERED">
  <![CDATA[ select eventCount as id, ELEMENT_TIME as startTime, filter from inchannel where filter = 4 ]]>
</query>
<query id="q5" ordering-constraint="UNORDERED">
  <![CDATA[ select eventCount as id, ELEMENT_TIME as startTime, filter from inchannel where filter = 5 ]]>
</query>
<query id="q6" ordering-constraint="UNORDERED">
  <![CDATA[ select eventCount as id, ELEMENT_TIME as startTime, filter from inchannel where filter = 6 ]]>
</query>
<query id="q7" ordering-constraint="UNORDERED">
  <![CDATA[ select eventCount as id, ELEMENT_TIME as startTime, filter from inchannel where filter = 7 ]]>
</query>
<query id="q8" ordering-constraint="ORDERED">
  <![CDATA[ select eventCount as id, ELEMENT_TIME as startTime, filter from inchannel where filter = 8 ]]>
</query>
<query id="q10" ordering-constraint="ORDERED">
  <![CDATA[ rstream(select eventCount as id, ELEMENT_TIME as startTime, filter, filterRelation.description
              from inchannel[now], filterRelation where filter = filterRelation.id) ]]>
</query>
```

When the same application, modified with the `UNORDERED` option, is run again using the same criteria, the performance result is significant. It takes just 204 milliseconds to process all the events.

Once again the results of this kind or implementation is very subjective, but is provided to give an indication of the performance gains possible using these tuning attributes and options.

Partitioned versus pipelined parallelism

There are conceptually a couple of dimensions to understand related to improving performance through the implementation of parallelism. Let us delve into the aspects of partitioned and pipelined parallelism and clarify the differences.

Partitioned parallelism, will partition input events into independent streams that don't require shared state or ordering among events in different streams. Partitioning can achieve parallelism within an EPN or even across a cluster.

Pipelined parallelism executes different stages within the EPN on separate threads (for example, by using channels with `max-threads > 0`) to achieve parallelism within each stream. Note if ordering is required, each stage in pipeline should run on a single thread (`channel max-threads=1`).

In general, partitioning is a better approach when the application use case can support this type of implementation. Pipelining is a poor choice for latency sensitive applications because of thread switching.

Improving performance with batching

Another concept to address is end-to-end event batching which can also provide performance advantages, and is now supported in Oracle Event Processing. Java code implemented in custom adapters or event beans can be used to send/receive batches in your application EPN using the `BatchStreamSender` API and implementing `BatchStreamSink` (and respectively `BatchRelationSender` and `BatchRelationSink` for relations). Event channels will keep batches intact, unless using the `EventPartitioner` capability as described earlier. The CQL processor will handle input events in batch, if the input channel is system time-stamped and it will batch output events with same timestamp if the "batching" attribute is set on processor's output channel.

Batching can improve application throughput and latency (but don't hold events in input adapters waiting for more to arrive). If ordered processing is required, use batching with extreme caution.

```
Collection<Object> events = new LinkedList<Object>();

String message = "Hi";
HelloWorldEvent event = new HelloWorldEvent();
event.setMessage(message);

events.add(event);

message = "Bye";
event = new HelloWorldEvent();
event.setMessage(message);

events.add(event);

eventSender.sendInsertEvents(events);
```

The preceding code fragment shows two events batched and sent together for processing.

General event processing, network performance tuning, and memory sizing observations

The recommended approach for best performance is to carefully consider the control flow and threading as part of your design process before you create the application. Map out and design the full control flow, giving thought to where threads start/pickup and handoff events, and how they flow through the EPN. Identify any latency critical paths through the EPN and keep the processing for the path on a single thread. Understand application ordering constraints and strive for as much parallelism as possible while honoring ordering requirements, and finally, and fairly obviously but try to reduce data volume (filter) as early as possible in the processing path.

In Oracle Event Processing the use of computing memory while generally internally optimized is used in some form across your entire EPN application and we address memory (heap) sizing based on the sum of short- and long-term allocations.

Long-term allocations are typically objects that live beyond a full JVM **Garbage Collection** (**GC**). These tend to be in a few specific places in most OEP applications.

The following are the three main areas:

- The event objects retained in CQL query windows
- Any data that is cached in the Coherence in-memory grid
- Any long-term allocations that you can write in custom beans (POJO code)

There can be a significant amount of short-term allocations associated with processing of events in transit through the EPN. This can be substantial for high-data rates.

In general terms, to estimate how much memory may be needed for capacity planning, it is recommended to use a baseline size of 200 MB for long-term allocations. In addition to this, use the size of your CQL windows and data rates to estimate how much data will be stored. You must also evaluate how much (reference) data you may be storing into any data grid (Coherence). This should allow you to predict what the long-term memory requirements may reach.

Short-term allocations are really proportional to input data rate, so the best way to get an estimate would be to measure the heap allocation rate under a fixed load.

So the general guidance for the heap sizes is to size the heap so that long-term data (live data after full GC) is no more than 40 percent of maximum heap size (or 30 percent if using JRockit JVM deterministic GC); avoid 64 bit-heaps if possible. For partitionable workloads it is generally better to run multiple clustered CEP instances each less than 4 GB. Finally, when sizing physical memory, allow for the JVM's non-heap memory requirements.

For the available Java Virtual Machines, there are many additional options to configure and optimize your Oracle Event Processing Platform. Over time, we see consistently improved performance being made available with optimized algorithms for handing garbage collection more efficiently.

High availability in Oracle Event Processing

Oracle Event Processing's **high availability** (**HA**) differs from other kinds of systems in that the data involved (events) is usually very dynamic, changing constantly. In a typical system, such as a database, the data is relatively static and HA systems, for example, both improve the reliability of the stored data and the availability of querying against that data. Since the Oracle Event Processing data changes so fast, storing it reliably can become problematic from a performance standpoint, or may even be pointless if the only relevant data is the latest data.

In a similar vein, Oracle Event Processing is often highly stateful, building up a historically influenced view of incoming event streams, and HA must take account of this statefulness. Of course, the state of the Oracle Event Processing is likely to be changing as rapidly as the incoming events are arriving and so preserving this state reliably and accurately can also be quite problematic. Typically, the problem of the statefulness of the system itself is solved in one of three ways:

- By replicating the behavior of the system—termed **active/active**
- By replicating the state of the system—termed **active/passive**
- By saving the stream of events that produced the state so that the state can be rebuilt in the event of failure—termed **upstream backup**

Oracle Event Processing supports an active/active HA architecture. The active/active approach has the advantages of high performance, simplicity, and short failover time relative to other approaches, as was mentioned previously. An Oracle Event Processing application that needs to be highly available is deployed to a group composed of two or more Oracle Event Processing server instances running in an Oracle Event Processing cluster. Oracle Event Processing will choose one server in the group to be the active primary. The remaining servers become active secondaries. It is not possible to specify the server that will be the initial primary as it is chosen automatically.

The number of active secondaries depends, of course, on the number of servers in the group hosting the application. If the group contains *n* server instances then there will be *n-1* secondary instances running the application. The number of secondaries in the group determines the number of concurrent server failures that the application can handle safely. A server failure may be due to either a software or hardware failure, which effectively causes termination of the server process. Note that most applications require just one or possibly two secondaries to ensure the required level of availability.

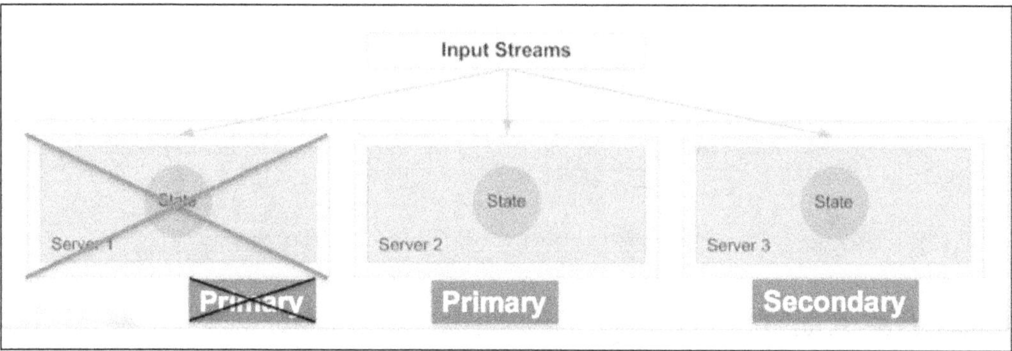

During normal operation—prior to a failure occurring—all server instances hosting the application process the same stream of input events. The active primary instance is responsible for sending output events to the downstream clients of the application. The active secondary instances, on the other hand, typically insert the output events that they generate into an in-memory queue. Events are buffered in the queue in the event that they are needed to recover from a failure of the active primary instance. Queued events are proactively discarded, or "trimmed", when Oracle Event Processing HA determines that they are no longer needed for recovery.

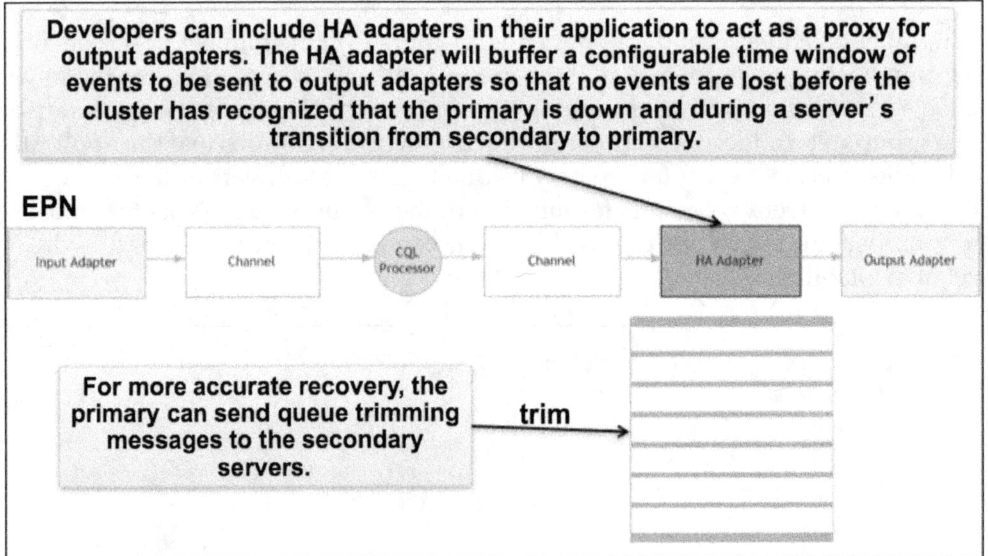

Failure scenarios

Failure of an active secondary instance does not cause any change in the behavior of the remaining instances in the group, but it does mean that there is one less secondary available in case the active primary instance should fail. The active primary continues to be responsible for sending output events to downstream clients, while the remaining active secondaries continue to enqueue their output events.

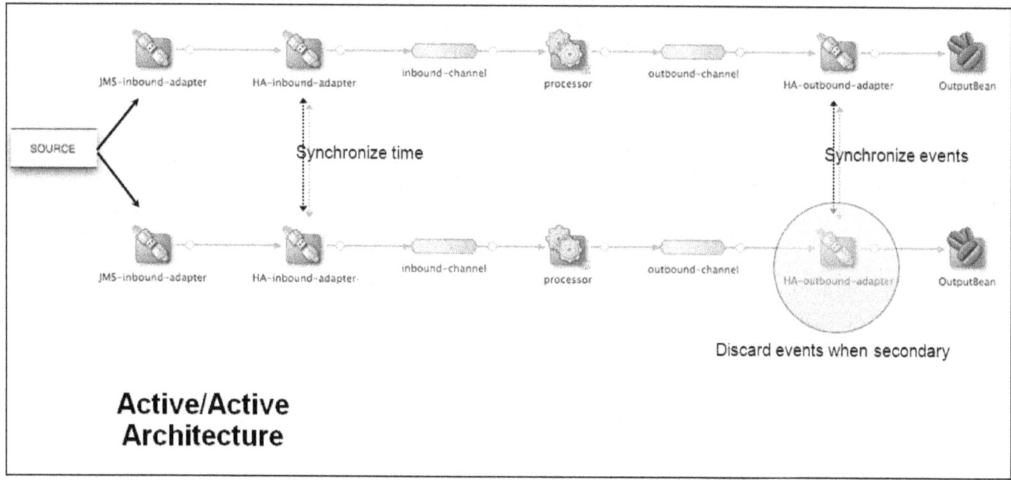

Failure of the active primary instance, on the other hand, results in failover to an active secondary instance. The secondary instance becomes the new active primary and takes over the responsibility of sending output events to downstream clients. The new active primary will begin by sending the output events that are currently contained in its output queue(s) before sending any new output events that are generated following failover.

A sample HA Event Processing application

Understanding the concepts and principles for high availability and zero event-loss failover with Oracle Event Processing can be daunting and sometimes confusing. During this chapter, we have described many of the aspects and various configuration options available, but to help simplify and bring together the basic requirements and implementation to get you "up and running" relatively quickly. We will now walk you through a very simple high availability configuration for the Oracle Event Processing platform.

As discussed earlier in this chapter, Oracle Event Processing supports the active/active model for high availability. In this type of configuration, a typical topology consists of a primary server and several secondary servers in the same cluster group, as you will encounter in our HA sample described in more detail below which has two servers are configured in a cluster group in a domain.

When the application is deployed to the cluster group, the server that is the first in the group will take the primary role. Both primary and secondary servers are able to receive events from upstream, but most applications only want the primary server that is able to forward events to downstream so that the receiving application does not receive duplicates, while the secondary servers need to cache the events in a queue to be able to recover correctly in the event of a failure and trim them according the trimming message from the primary server when it is determined that the receiving application has definitely received the corresponding event. When the primary fails for any reason, one of the secondary servers will take up the new primary role to continue processing events from the failure point.

The artifacts required for this scenario involve the Oracle Event Processing HA sample application, a JMS server (in this case we use the open source and freely available ActiveMQ technology0, and a JMS client that places a continuous stream of messages (events) onto a JMS topic to be processed by Oracle Event Processing.

High availability quality of services

Oracle Event Processing provides several HA adapters out of the box to allow you to create HA capable applications with different levels of precision and performance. After having understood Oracle Event Processing HA architecture, the next step is to learn Oracle Event Processing HA adapters and how to configure your desired quality of service.

Oracle Event Processing supports four active/active HA options with different quality of service (QoS) as follows:

- Simple failover
- Simple failover with buffering
- Light-weight queue trimming
- Precise recovery with JMS

These are detailed in the next sub-sections.

Simple failover

When configured for simple failover, there is negligible performance degradation, however your application may lose many events in case of a failure, and may receive a few duplicate events while recovering.

To configure for simple failover, you need to follow these steps:

1. Add a `ha-buffering` adapter to your EPN downstream to your output adapter. This is demonstrated in the following example:

```
<wlevs:channel id="helloworldOutputChannel"
     event-type="HelloWorldEvent" advertise="true">
     <wlevs:listener ref="myHaSlidingWindowAdapter"/>
     <wlevs:source ref="helloworldProcessor"/>
 </wlevs:channel>

 <wlevs:adapter id="myHaSlidingWindowAdapter" provider="ha-
buffering" >
     <wlevs:listener>
          <bean class="com.bea.wlevs.example.helloworld.
HelloWorldBean"/>
     </wlevs:listener>
 </wlevs:adapter>
```

2. Configure the `windowLength` property of the `ha-buffering` adapter to `0`. This is demonstrated in the following example:

```
<wlevs:adapter id="myHaSlidingWindowAdapter" provider="ha-
buffering" >
     <wlevs:listener>
          <bean class="com.bea.wlevs.example.helloworld.
HelloWorldBean"/>
     </wlevs:listener>
     <wlevs:instance-property name="windowLength" value="0"/>
 </wlevs:adapter>
```

3. Finally, there is a chance that the results output during the recovery may very slightly if the clustered nodes do not use the same time. So, to guarantee that the different nodes use the same timestamp, you can configure your input channel to use application timestamps.

This is demonstrated in the following example:

```
<wlevs:channel id="helloworldInputChannel" event-
type="HelloWorldEvent" >
      <wlevs:listener ref="helloworldProcessor"/>
      <wlevs:source ref="myHaInputAdapter"/>
         <wlevs:application-timestamped>
              <wlevs:expression>arrivalTime</wlevs:expression>
         </wlevs:application-timestamped>
   </wlevs:channel>
```

Keep in mind that you must be running a clustered Oracle Event Processing domain with at least two nodes, or as many nodes as you need to protect your system against simultaneous node failures.

Next, we take a look at the next quality of service for HA.

Simple failover with buffering

When configured for simple failover with buffering, there is some (low) performance degradation, however your application potentially loses less events in case of a failure. In fact, the number of events lost is proportional to the size of the buffering window configured. In other words, if the buffering window is configured to be high enough, then no events are lost.

For example, if your application receives 10 events per second, and the HA buffering window is configured to 500 milliseconds, then your application may potentially lose up to 5 events, that is, 1/2 second of events at the rate of 10 events per second.

You can configure the buffering size using the `windowLength` property as you have seen in the previous section.

Here is an example that sets the buffering window to `500` milliseconds:

```
<wlevs:instance-property name="windowLength" value="500"/>
```

The larger your `windowLength` configuration, the more memory is needed and the further performance degradation is seen, therefore choose wisely and always opt for the smallest window that still fulfills your application requirements.

In the next section, you learn how to configure Oracle Event Processing applications so that they do not lose events in case of a failure.

Lightweight queue trimming

This high availability quality of service is characterized by a low performance overhead with a relatively faster recovery time and increased data integrity (no missed events; but a few duplicate events are possible during failover).

The active primary server sends messages to secondary servers to notify them of the events that it has completely processed. This enables the secondary servers, which are holding buffers of events, to trim their buffers to only contain events that have not been sent by the primary. Events are only trimmed after they have been sent by the current primary; this allows the secondary servers to avoid missing sending the correct output events. If a fail-over occurs, that secondary becomes the primary.

The frequency with which the active primary sends queue trimming messages to active secondary servers is configurable to a certain number of event or a specific amount of time.

If it is configured to a use a number of events, this limits the number of duplicate output events at failover.

If it is configured to use a specific interval, the queue-trimming adapter requires a way to identify events consistently among the all of the servers. The recommended approach is to use application time to identify events, but any key value that uniquely identifies events will do.

The advantage of queue trimming is that output events are never lost. There is a slight performance overhead at the active primary, however, for sending the trimming messages and this overhead increases as the frequency of queue trimming messages increases.

To implement this high availability quality of service, you must configure your EPN with a high availability input adapter after each input adapter and a high availability broadcast output adapter before each output adapter.

The following code shows the configured inbound adapter sending messages to the HA inbound adapter:

```
<wlevs:adapter id="helloworldAdapter" class="com.bea.wlevs.adapter.
example.helloworld.HelloWorldAdapter" >
<wlevs:instance-property name="message" value="HelloWorld - the
current time is:"/>
    <wlevs:listener ref="myHaInputAdapter"/>
</wlevs:adapter>
```

The HA inbound adapter is part of the EPN and sends events to downstream processing:

```
    <wlevs:adapter id="myHaInputAdapter" provider="ha-inbound">
      <wlevs:instance-property name="timeProperty"
    value="arrivalTime"/>
    </wlevs:adapter>

<wlevs:channel id="helloworldInputChannel" event-
type="HelloWorldEvent" >
  <wlevs:listener ref="helloworldProcessor"/>
      <wlevs:source ref="myHaInputAdapter"/>
</wlevs:channel>
```

The final output channel is configured to send results to a `ha-broadcast` adapter:

```
<wlevs:channel id="helloworldOutputChannel" event-type="HelloWorldEven
t"advertise="true">
     <wlevs:listener ref="myHaBroadcastAdapter"/>
  <wlevs:source ref="helloworldProcessor"/>
</wlevs:channel>

    <wlevs:adapter id="myHaBroadcastAdapter" provider="ha-broadcast" >
  <wlevs:listener>
    <bean class=
"com.bea.wlevs.example.helloworld.HelloWorldBean"/>
  </wlevs:listener>
</wlevs:adapter>
```

Optionally, configure the component configuration file to include the OEP high availability input adapter and buffering output adapter:

```
<ha:ha-inbound-adapter>
  <name>myHaInputAdapter</name>
</ha:ha-inbound-adapter>

<ha:ha-broadcast-adapter>
  <name>myHaBroadcastAdapter</name>
  <trimming-interval units="events">10</trimming-interval>
</ha:ha-broadcast-adapter>
```

If your OEP application must generate exactly the same sequence of output events as existing secondary servers, you need to configure the warm-up-window-length for the broadcast output adapter. This ensures that, in the event of another failure, this server does not get chosen to become the primary until the adequate warm-up time has passed so that the state of the server is correct.

As always, the appropriate import package definitions must be included in the `MANIFEST.MF` file. In this case, the definitions are `com.bea.wlevs.ede.api.cluster`, `com.oracle.cep.cluster.hagroups`, `com.oracle.cep.cluster.ha.adapter`, and `com.oracle.cep.cluster.ha.api`.

Precise recovery with JMS

This quality of service has a high performance overhead (slower recovery time) but maximum data integrity (no missed events and no duplicate events during failover). It is only compatible JMS input and output adapters. It is not concerned with transactional guarantees along the event path for a single-server, but rather a single output from a set of servers. To achieve this, secondary servers listen, over JMS, to the event stream being published by the primary. This incoming event stream is essentially a source of reliable queue-trimming messages that the secondary servers use to trim their output queues.

If JMS is configured for reliable delivery, we can be sure that the stream of events seen by the secondary is precisely the stream of events output by the primary and thus failover will allow the new primary to output precisely those events not delivered by the old primary.

The JMS inbound adapter immediately sends events to the HA inbound adapter:

```
<wlevs:adapter id="JMSInboundAdapter" provider="jms-inbound">
     <wlevs:listener ref="myHaInputAdapter"/>
</wlevs:adapter>
```

The HA inbound adapter is configured with the key properties and the time properties:

```
<wlevs:adapter id="myHaInputAdapter" provider="ha-inbound" >
  <wlevs:instance-property name="keyProperties" value="sequenceNo"/>
  <wlevs:instance-property name="timeProperty" value="inboundTime"/>
</wlevs:adapter>
```

All of the CQL processing is type `application-timestamped` using the chosen time property:

```
<wlevs:channel id="channel1" event-type="StockTick">
  <wlevs:listener ref="processor1" />
     <wlevs:source ref="myHaInputAdapter"/>
     <wlevs:application-timestamped>
       <wlevs:expression>inboundTime</wlevs:expression>
     </wlevs:application-timestamped>
</wlevs:channel>
```

The HA correlating adapter is configured in the application with a correlated source that is receiving the queue-trimming messages from an inbound JMS adapter.

```
    <wlevs:adapter id="myHaCorrelatingAdapter" provider="ha-
    correlating" >
      <wlevs:instance-property name="correlatedSource" ref="clusterCor
    relatingOutstream"/>
   <wlevs:instance-property name="failOverDelay" value="2000"/>
   <wlevs:listener ref="JMSOutboundAdapter"/>
 </wlevs:adapter>

 <wlevs:channel id="channel2" event-type="StockTick">
   <wlevs:listener ref="myHaCorrelatingAdapter" />
 </wlevs:channel>

 <wlevs:adapter id="JMSOutboundAdapter" provider="jms-outbound"/>
 <wlevs:adapter id="JMSInboundAdapter2" provider="jms-inbound"/>

 <wlevs:channel id="clusterCorrelatingOutstream" event-type="StockTick"
 advertise="true">
   <wlevs:source ref="JMSInboundAdapter2"/>
 </wlevs:channel>
```

Use the same import package definitions mentioned in the previous section regarding lightweight queue trimming in the `MANIFEST.MF` file.

The HA application

At a high-conceptual level, the sample application receives events from JMS topic and populates output events to the downstream system. The basic EPN for this application is:

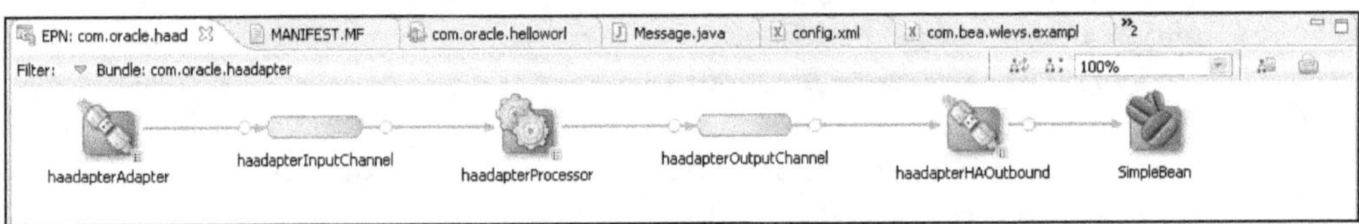

The JMS adapter is configured to connect to an ActiveMQ topic. The EPN HA adapter is a broadcast queue-trimming adapter. It can be configured to narrow down the number of lost events or duplicate events. On the primary server, the HA adapter forwards events to downstream and the events will be outputted at console by an output bean.

ActiveMQ server

This is a simplified version of ActiveMQ. The server is bound to the URL, `tcp://0.0.0.0:61616`, where `0.0.0.0` can be replaced with the hostname (for example, "localhost"). In this case, a JMS topic is defined with the JNDI name, `cepTopic`.

The JMS Message Client

This is used to send messages to the topic destination. Now the content and the format of the message are generated internally and can't be configured. This client is placed at the ActiveMQ's `bin` directory in order to simplify the configuration and the execution. It reads `jndi.properties` from the `conf` directory to retrieve the JNDI configuration of the topic. Thus, you can change the configuration of the JMS topic as you desire. In order to configure a cluster, we need to add the cluster configuration in the server's `config.xml` file. The configuration sample is shown in the following screenshot:

```
<?xml version="1.0" encoding="UTF-8" ?>
<!-- Sample XML file generated by XMLSpy v2007 sp2 (http://www.altova.com) -->
- <n1:config xsi:schemaLocation="http://www.bea.com/ns/wlevs/config/server wlevs_server_config.xsd"
    xmlns:n1="http://www.bea.com/ns/wlevs/config/server" xmlns:xsi="http://www.w3.org/2001/XMLSchema-instance">
  - <domain>
      <name>mydomain</name>
    </domain>
  - <cluster>
      <server-name>server1</server-name>
      <multicast-address>239.255.37.6</multicast-address>
      <identity>1</identity>
      <enabled>coherence</enabled>
      <groups>Group1</groups>
    </cluster>
  - <netio>
      <name>NetIO</name>
      <port>9002</port>
    </netio>
  - <netio>
      <name>sslNetIo</name>
      <ssl-config-bean-name>sslConfig</ssl-config-bean-name>
      <port>9003</port>
    </netio>
```

For other servers, the server name and identity should be different while the domain name, multicast address, cluster type, and groups remain the same. The cluster configuration is simple. In order to use ActiveMQ, the ActiveMQ libraries need to be added in the Oracle Event Processing server's bootstrap classpath in the server's startup script (for example, `startwlevs.sh`):

```
"%JAVA_HOME%\bin\java" %DGC% %DEBUG% -Xbootclasspath/a:activemq-all-
5.4.2.jar
```

For Windows, enter the following in `startwlevs.cmd`:

```
"%JAVA_HOME%\bin\java" %DGC% %DEBUG% -Xbootclasspath/a:activemq-all-
5.4.2.jar -Dorg.apache.commons.logging.Log=org.apache.commons.logging.
impl.SimpleLog -Dorg.apache.commons.logging.simplelog.defaultlog=error
-Dwlevs.home="%USER_INSTALL_DIR%" -Dbea.home="%BEA_HOME%" -jar "%USER_
INSTALL_DIR%\bin\wlevs.jar" %ARGS%
```

In the sample HA application, the JMS inbound adapter and HA adapter are configured as shown in the following screenshot:

```
<!-- Adapter can be created from a local class, without having to go through a adapter factory -->
<wlevs:adapter id="haadapterAdapter" provider="jms-inbound" >
<wlevs:instance-property name="customContextProperties">
    <props>
        <prop key="connectionFactoryNames">connectionFactory</prop>
        <prop key="topic.cepTopic">cepTopic</prop>
    </props>
</wlevs:instance-property>
</wlevs:adapter>

<wlevs:adapter id="haadapterHAOutbound" provider="ha-broadcast">
    <wlevs:listener ref="haadapterBean"/>
    <wlevs:instance-property name="keyProperties" value="messageId"/>
</wlevs:adapter>
```

Note that for ActiveMQ, `customContextProperties` is required for the extra configuration. The HA adapter is broadcast queue trimming adapter. The `keyProperties` property is required to identity the events it received.

In the application configuration file, more details of the components are provided:

```
  <jms-adapter>
    <name>haadapterAdapter</name>
    <event-type>Message</event-type>
    <jndi-provider-url>tcp://localhost:61616</jndi-provider-url>
    <jndi-factory>org.apache.activemq.jndi.ActiveMQInitialContextFactory</jndi-factory>
    <connection-jndi-name>connectionFactory</connection-jndi-name>
    <destination-jndi-name>cepTopic</destination-jndi-name>
    <user>system</user>
    <password>manager</password>
  </jms-adapter>

  <ha:ha-broadcast-adapter>
    <name>haadapterHAOutbound</name>
    <trimming-interval units="millis">100</trimming-interval>
  </ha:ha-broadcast-adapter>
</n1:config>
```

These configurations are persistent and can be changed from the Visualizer tooling or using a JMX client. The JMS adapter's `event-type` element specifies the event type to which the JMS adapter will convert the JMS messages. The `jndi-provider-url` is as configured in the ActiveMQ's `activemq.xml`. The HA adapter's element `trimming-interval` specifies that the primary server will send trimming message to secondary servers every 100 milliseconds.

Note that in the application's configuration file the cluster namespace is required to be included, the header should look similar to the following:

```
<?xml version="1.0" encoding="UTF-8"?>
<n1:config xsi:schemaLocation="http://www.bea.com/ns/wlevs/config/application wlevs_application_config.xsd"
xmlns:n1="http://www.bea.com/ns/wlevs/config/application"
xmlns:xsi="http://www.w3.org/2001/XMLSchema-instance"
xmlns:ha="http://www.oracle.com/ns/cep/config/cluster">
```

In the `MANIFEST.MF` file, the following packages are needed additionally to address the library dependency:

```
EPN: com.oracle.helloworldPS5   *EPN: com.oracle.haadapter   SimpleBean.java   MANIFEST.MF   com.c
Manifest-Version: 1.0
Bundle-ManifestVersion: 2
Bundle-Name: %project.name
Bundle-SymbolicName: com.oracle.haadapter
Bundle-Version: 1.0.0
Bundle-Localization: bundle
Bundle-Vendor: %project.vendor
Bundle-RequiredExecutionEnvironment: JavaSE-1.6
Bundle-ClassPath: .
Export-Package: com.bea.wlevs.event.example.haadapter;version="11.1.1",
 com.bea.wlevs.example.haadapter;version="11.1.1"
Import-Package: com.bea.wlevs.configuration;version="11.1.1",
 com.bea.wlevs.ede.api;version="11.1.1",
 com.bea.wlevs.ede.impl;version="11.1.1",
 com.bea.wlevs.ede.spi;version="11.1.1",
 com.bea.wlevs.ede;version="11.1.1",
 com.bea.wlevs.management.spi;version="11.1.1",
 com.bea.wlevs.spring.support;version="11.1.1",
 com.bea.wlevs.spring;version="11.1.1",
 com.bea.wlevs.util;version="11.1.1",
 org.apache.commons.logging;version="1.1.0",
 org.springframework.beans.factory.config;version="2.5.6",
 org.springframework.beans.factory;version="2.5.6",
 org.springframework.beans;version="2.5.6",
 org.springframework.core.annotation;version="2.5.6",
 org.springframework.osgi.context;version="1.2.0",
 org.springframework.osgi.extensions.annotation;version="1.2.0",
 org.springframework.osgi.service;version="1.2.0",
 org.springframework.util;version="2.5.6",
 com.bea.wlevs.configuration.application,
 com.bea.wlevs.management.configuration,
 com.bea.wlevs.ede.api.cluster,
 com.oracle.cep.cluster.ha.adapter,
 com.tangosol.util,
 com.tangosol.net,
 com.tangosol.net.cache,
 javax.jms
```

The `com.bea.wlevs.ede.api.cluster` package is required for cluster dependency, `com.oracle.cep.cluster.ha.adapter` is for HA adapters, `com.tangosol.*` packages are for coherence, while `javax.jms` is for JMS.

Running the HA solution sample

Follow these steps to run the sample:

1. To start the JMS server, open a terminal and change directory to `activemq/bin`. Run the following command:

   ```
   java -jar run.jar start
   ```

```
START_ACTIVEMQ - java -jar run.jar start
               2 File(s)         17,849 bytes
               2 Dir(s)   8,327,389,184 bytes free

D:\HA_DEMO\activemq\bin>java -jar run.jar start
Java Runtime: Sun Microsystems Inc. 1.6.0_23 E:\JAVA\jdk1.6.0_23\jre
  Heap sizes: current=15872k  free=15412k  max=253440k
    JVM args:
ACTIVEMQ_HOME: D:\HA_DEMO\activemq
ACTIVEMQ_BASE: D:\HA_DEMO\activemq
Loading message broker from: xbean:activemq.xml
Jan 10, 2013 10:38:31 PM org.springframework.context.support.AbstractApplicationContext prepareRefresh
INFO: Refreshing org.apache.activemq.xbean.XBeanBrokerFactory$1@85af80: startup date [Thu Jan 10 22:38:31 PST 2
013]; root of context hierarchy
Jan 10, 2013 10:38:32 PM org.springframework.beans.factory.xml.XmlBeanDefinitionReader loadBeanDefinitions
INFO: Loading XML bean definitions from class path resource [activemq.xml]
Jan 10, 2013 10:38:34 PM org.springframework.core.io.support.PropertiesLoaderSupport loadProperties
INFO: Loading properties file from URL [file:D:/HA_DEMO/activemq/conf/credentials.properties]
Jan 10, 2013 10:38:34 PM org.springframework.beans.factory.support.DefaultListableBeanFactory preInstantiateSin
gletons
INFO: Pre-instantiating singletons in org.springframework.beans.factory.support.DefaultListableBeanFactory@1df8
b99: defining beans [org.springframework.beans.factory.config.PropertyPlaceholderConfigurer#0,org.apache.active
mq.xbean.XBeanBrokerService#0]; root of factory hierarchy
Jan 10, 2013 10:38:35 PM org.apache.activemq.xbean.XBeanBrokerService setDestroyApplicationContextOnStop
WARNING: destroyApplicationContextOnStop parameter is deprecated, please use shutdown hooks instead
Jan 10, 2013 10:38:35 PM org.apache.activemq.store.kahadb.plist.PListStore doStart
INFO: PListStore:D:\HA_DEMO\activemq\data\localhost\tmp_storage started
Jan 10, 2013 10:38:35 PM org.apache.activemq.broker.BrokerService start
INFO: Using Persistence Adapter: KahaDBPersistenceAdapter[D:\HA_DEMO\activemq\data\kahadb]
Jan 10, 2013 10:38:39 PM org.apache.activemq.store.kahadb.MessageDatabase$Metadata read
INFO: KahaDB is version 3
Jan 10, 2013 10:38:39 PM org.apache.activemq.store.kahadb.MessageDatabase recover
INFO: Recovering from the journal ...
Jan 10, 2013 10:38:39 PM org.apache.activemq.store.kahadb.MessageDatabase recover
INFO: Recovery replayed 1 operations from the journal in 0.107 seconds.
Jan 10, 2013 10:38:39 PM org.apache.activemq.broker.BrokerService getBroker
INFO: ActiveMQ 5.4.2 JMS Message Broker (localhost) is starting
Jan 10, 2013 10:38:39 PM org.apache.activemq.broker.BrokerService getBroker
INFO: For help or more information please see: http://activemq.apache.org/
Jan 10, 2013 10:38:40 PM org.apache.activemq.transport.TransportServerThreadSupport doStart
INFO: Listening for connections at: tcp://xpone:61616
Jan 10, 2013 10:38:40 PM org.apache.activemq.broker.TransportConnector start
INFO: Connector openwire Started
Jan 10, 2013 10:38:40 PM org.apache.activemq.broker.BrokerService start
INFO: ActiveMQ JMS Message Broker (localhost, ID:xpone-1032-1357886320058-0:1) started
```

2. To start to feed messages to JMS server, open a terminal and change the directory to the `activemq/bin`. Run the following command:

   `java -jar jmsfeeder.jar`

```
ACTIVEMQ FEEDER - java -jar jmsfeeder.jar
Microsoft Windows XP [Version 5.1.2600]
(C) Copyright 1985-2001 Microsoft Corp.

D:\HA_DEMO\activemq\bin>dir
 Volume in drive D is VBOX_SHARED
 Volume Serial Number is E608-64B3

 Directory of D:\HA_DEMO\activemq\bin

07/23/2012  04:35 PM    <DIR>          .
07/23/2012  04:35 PM    <DIR>          ..
12/13/2010  05:57 PM             2,977 jmsfeeder.jar
11/26/2010  09:25 AM            14,872 run.jar
               2 File(s)         17,849 bytes
               2 Dir(s)   8,327,389,184 bytes free

D:\HA_DEMO\activemq\bin>java -jar jmsfeeder.jar
url: tcp://localhost:61616.
connection factory: connectionFactory.
topic: cepTopic.
Sent 20 messages
Sent 40 messages
Sent 60 messages
```

With the ActiveMQ Server started and the JMS client executing and sending messages to the topic, you should start the Oracle Event Processing Servers (Server1 and Server2).

If you observe the directory structures used in our sample, we have used the following to start each Oracle Event Processing Server:

```
${INSTALL_HOME}/ocep_11.1/samples/domains/ha_domain/server1


(similar for server2)
```

3. With the CMD, enter the following command:

```
startwlevs.cmd
```

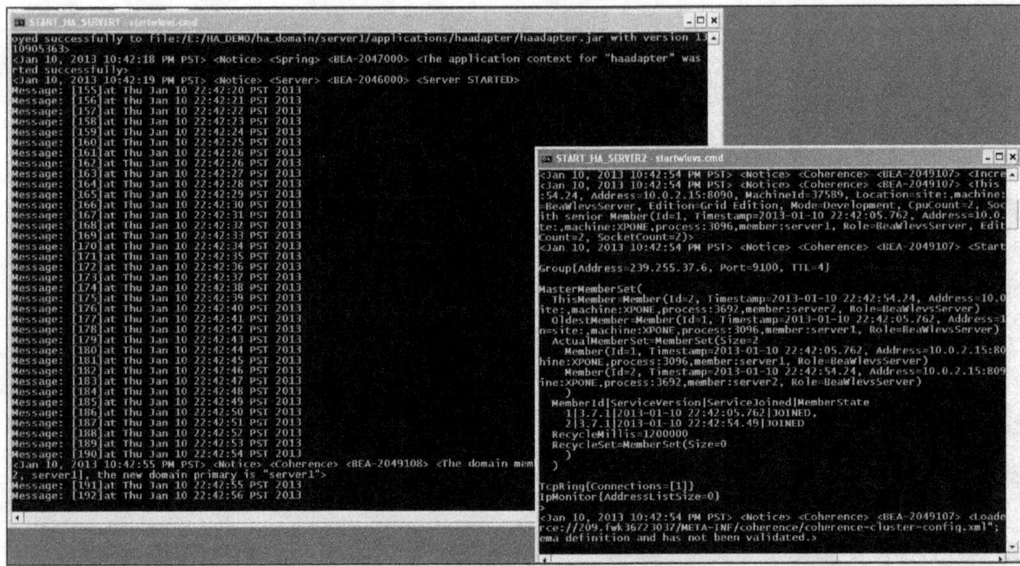

When the primary Oracle Event Processing server 1 "fails" (in this case we simply terminate the process), you can see that the secondary server immediately takes over and continues to process the events without any message loss.

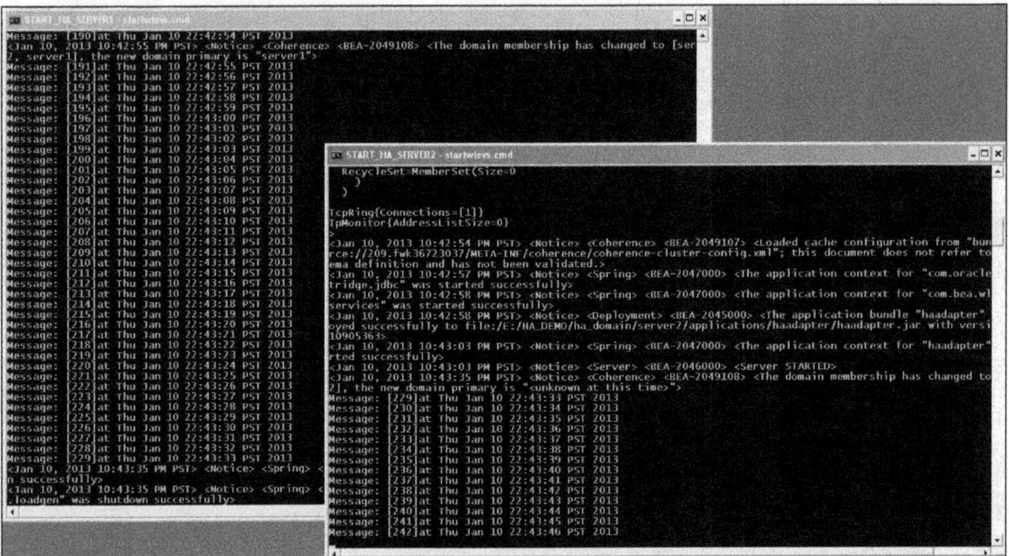

Studying the Visualizer tooling for HA implementation

As we conclude this chapter, we will review fairly quickly the use of the Visualizer tooling available with Oracle Event Processing and take a look at some of the information that is made available.

Let us take a look at the general configuration display that shows, in this case the two Oracle Event Processing Servers in a Cluster and associated configuration information:

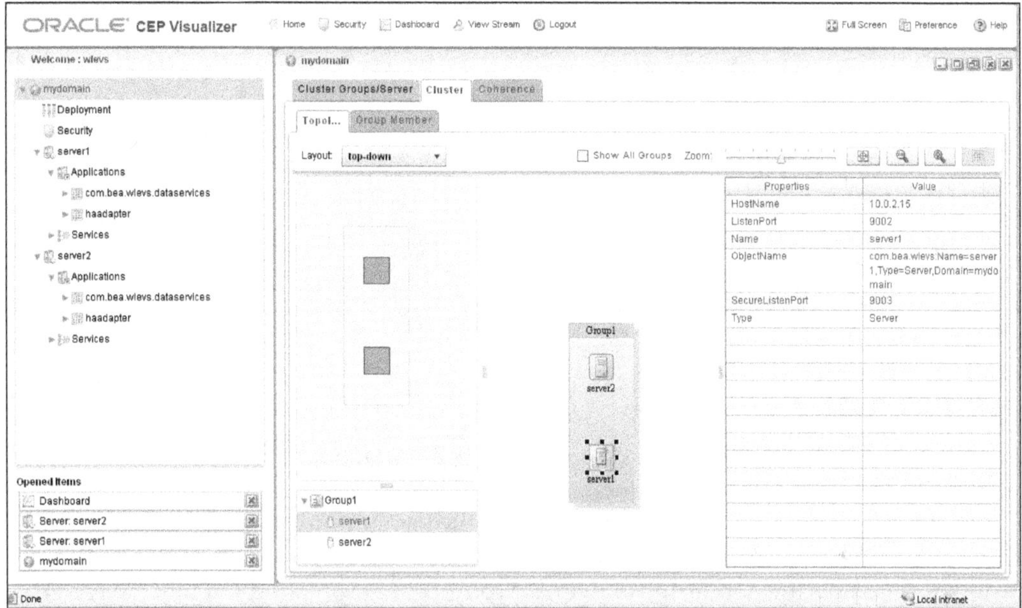

With Coherence providing in this configuration, the HA foundational technology to support this Oracle Event Processing implementation, the Visualizer tooling can also provide a wealth of statistics relating to its execution, to assist in tuning and optimization.

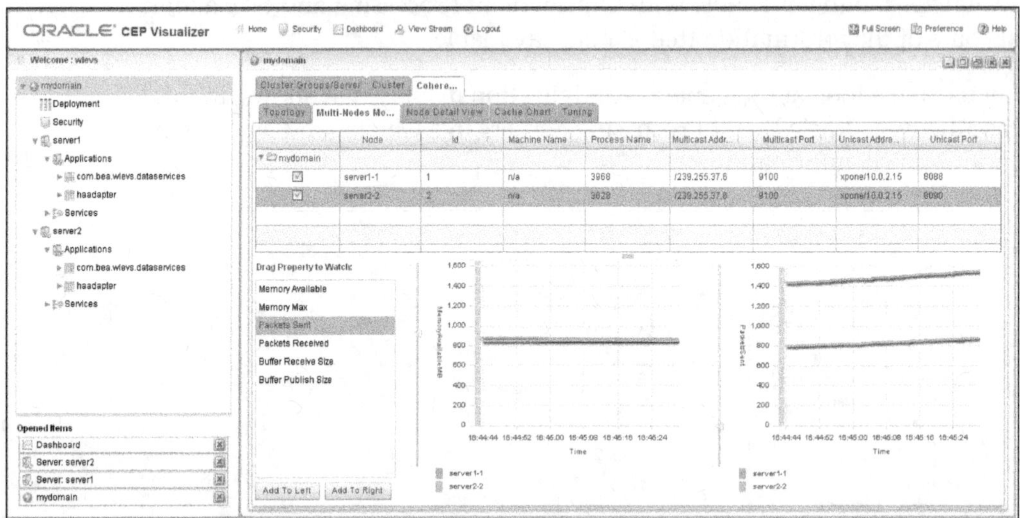

Summary

While generally a difficult subject to grasp, in this chapter we have covered the major issues of performance analysis and application-level optimization techniques, especially relevant to its relationship with event-driven requirements, guiding you through some of the aspects that can be configured and can influence how well your solutions perform in terms of event throughput and related latency. We have also introduced you to the general concepts and capabilities for implementing high availability and failover with the Oracle Event Processing platform.

As you gradually scale out your applications to multiple Oracle Event Processing servers using the clustering capabilities, it is highly recommended that you first evaluate fundamental configurations in a testing environment, in the same way as with the sample HA application and server infrastructure shown in this chapter to fully understand the best approaches for your specific application requirements.

In the next chapter, we will embark on a journey of understanding involving the world of geospatial real time event analysis. This topic covers the foundational information for creating Oracle Event Processing applications that can follow the movement patterns of any type of resource, and very importantly, how these resources are interacting with each other and with specific geographical areas of interest.

10
Introducing Spatial: A Telemetric Use Case

In this chapter, we will cover an overview of geospatial event processing real-time analysis, the spatial data cartridge integration approach, highlight basic real-time spatial features, and step through each fundamental requirement in creating and executing a real-world geo-streaming Oracle Event Processing Application. The topics we will cover are as follows:

- Introduction to Oracle Spatial with Oracle Event Processing
- Basic geospatial concepts and use cases
- The Oracle Spatial Data Cartridge
- Oracle geospatial features
- Tracking vehicles with an Oracle Event Processing application

Introduction to Oracle Spatial with Oracle Event Processing

As we delve more into the capabilities of Oracle Event Processing, one very important and unique collection of features apply to the real-time, location-based analysis of moving objects, geo-streaming, and their relationship to other objects whether they are fixed or dynamically created geographical areas, otherwise known as **geo-fencing**. Holistically, Oracle Event Processing provides a feature-rich platform for geospatial context-aware, real-time analysis.

The spatial capabilities of geo-streaming and geo-fencing are important for any Event Processing technology and provides the ability to constantly evaluate the continuous streaming events that arrive rapidly from **Global Positioning Systems (GPS)** enabled sensors in vehicles, or from many different mobile devices.

For example, by understanding the exact location of all the fire trucks in a given region and the current position of all the new fire outbreaks, Event Processing systems can immediately evaluate the best emergency resources to dispatch. This may not be a decision based only on which truck is close but also by added computing intelligence dynamically determining the skills of the firemen and the equipment available on the truck.

This additional complex analysis can be achieved by using profiling information that is either held in a database, big data stores or from an in-memory grid. The firemen and equipment profile data can be easily joined with the streaming location-based events and analyzed to enrich the events with information that describes each fireman's certified fire fighting capabilities and for each fire asset, its purpose, usage criteria, and configuration.

This is important because the fire might be expanding rapidly due to chemicals and also be a burning inferno on the 17-floor of a tall building. So we need the firemen with the correct skills in tackling this specific type of fire and also, we need a fire truck that has ladders that can reach a distance high enough for such a building. With lives at stake, wasting time with human interactions desperately trying to find the right vehicle or just sending the nearest but badly equipped truck can have devastating consequences:

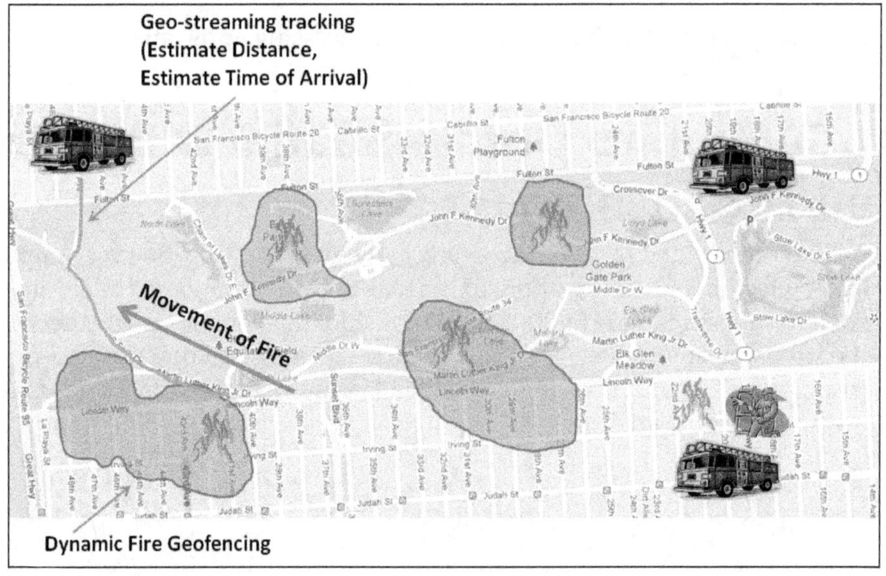

This is a very mission critical Use Case but there are also many less dramatic cases and in this chapter we will discuss the fundamentals of tracking any kind of objects such as on-land and off-shore vehicles and how they can be related to areas of interest, such as bus stops, bus stations, and shipping hazards.

While there are already systems that can provide these types of capabilities, most are generally hand coded industry and company-specific solutions that involve very complicated software that is hard to write and maintain, difficult to dynamically change, and very complex to implement. You will discover that by using Oracle Event Processing, with its combination of a Java-based platform and abstracted continuous query language, creating such applications can be relatively fast and easy to implement.

In this chapter we will only be focusing on the key aspects of using geo-streaming and geo-fencing in the context of Oracle Event Processing. Various vendors do provide varying collections of spatial capabilities and some provide a vast array of materials that discuss related topics. In reality this content could fill another book or even a collection of books, so if you want to learn more details, we recommend that you simply search the Internet for "Oracle Spatial".

Basic geospatial concepts and use cases

We will focus now on some specific terms and their definitions used by Oracle Event Processing relating to its implementation of geospatial techniques during the development of event-driven applications.

Geo-streaming

When studying geo-streaming for Oracle Event Processing, the event-types that are generated by the moving object include a collection of tracking-related context, generally an identifier such as a license plate number, bus route name, or bus number together with the current longitude and latitude position of that vehicle. The latitude and longitude values are the geographic coordinates used to define any location on Earth and are measured in degrees, since the Earth is a sphere.

For example, consider the following values:

```
8,2,-122.473419676926,37.7241533792509
```

The first value in this `.csv` (comma-separated value) file entry is the identification number for a bus, bus number `8`. By having this event-type property Oracle Event Processing can be used to collect comprehensive profiling information about the bus, such as the capacity of this bus, its general route, and previous travel times between bus stops.

The next value, `2`, is simply a sequence number that can indicate an incremental value or the current event time.

The next two values are the longitude and latitude position values that relate to the immediate bus position, `-122.473419676926, 37.7241533792509`. By using one of the many free Internet tools, you can use these values to identify this related point on a map:

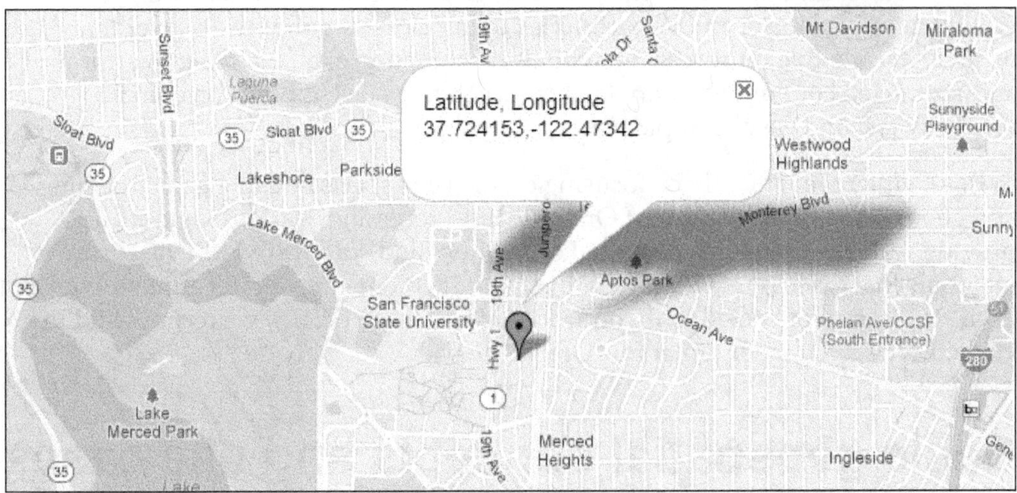

Using these concepts we can create an event stream in a Java application, or have the information read from a `.csv` file using the available load generation testing tool (`RUNLOADGEN`) provided by Oracle Event Processing. This can simulate the event flow from the real-world GPS device or sensor.

For example, the following content is of a `.csv` file of vehicle movement events:

```
8,15,-122.471259972159,37.7088702786799
8,16,-122.47139451801,37.7076677852903
8,17,-122.471550447123,37.706466872009
8,18,-122.471696850204,37.7052652951831
8,19,-122.471770960283,37.7040596480638
8,20,-122.471805885683,37.7028528367994
8,21,-122.47177428746,37.701645791032        < -------- Note this
position
```

Using this technique it is a great way to test new geo-streaming based Oracle Event Processing applications, as you will learn later in this chapter.

Geo-fencing

Once we can effectively track the movement of an object using geo-streaming capabilities, in most use cases we would like to associate that movement position in relation to something else. In the same way as indicated previously, you can use CQL to compare the moving events with a specific point such as a bus stop.

For example:

```
Bus Stop Location --- > 1,1,-122.47177428746,37.701645791032 < ------
Look Familiar?
```

If you study the event-type properties described in the vehicle movement event `.csv` file in the geo-streaming section, you will notice that the last movement's event coordinates match the bus stop event-type properties shown in the preceding example. In the next section on the Oracle Spatial Data Cartridge we will show how easy it is now to define a CQL statement that will enable the determination of when and where a moving bus vehicle reaches a new bus stop.

Before we continue and study the fairly simple capability for a spatial geo-fencing event pattern matching to a single location point, you should be aware that many moving object applications need to be more sophisticated and require a comparison, not to a single point, but to an area or a complex polygon shape. More difficult still is that this area can also be constantly moving, its shape definition potentially frequently changing.

These areas can be stored in a database as complex spatial object definitions and can generate new events by using various programming techniques such as Advanced Queuing. Oracle Advanced Queuing provides a database-integrated message queuing functionality and leverages the functions of the Oracle database so that messages can be stored and propagated between queues on different machines and databases. By using this kind of capability, these object definitions that change can invoke an event message which can be passed to Oracle Event Processing for immediate re-evaluation against the currently monitored associated geo-streaming resources.

Geographical tools, such as Oracle Mapviewer, can be used to relatively easily define these area definitions and store them into a database. Using these tools you can also define buffer zones surrounding the areas, making the computed determination of "near an area" or "in an area" more straightforward.

For example, if you wanted to create geo-fenced areas that represented fire zones in the city of London, you can use the tool to select multiple points around the required area, in any form of complex shape. As the first and last points are joined, the tool will take this area definition and place the required spatial data into the database. This final action could then be used to trigger a spatial area definition event message to be sent dynamically to the Oracle Event Processing application for assessment:

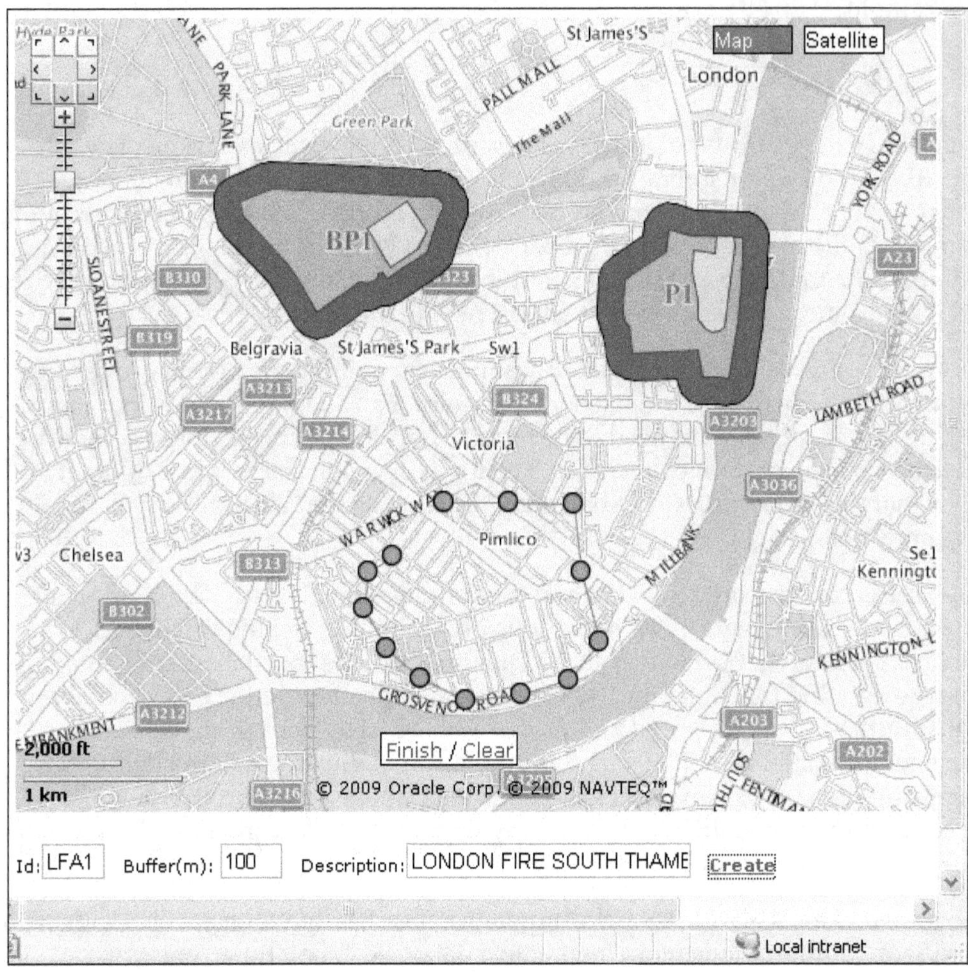

In a mission critical situation room or a control and command center, these areas can be created and removed on demand, but at the same time more elegant Event Processing applications can be written to programmatically manipulate (create/replace/update/delete) these areas, so as to automate much of the needed human interaction requirements.

These areas do not need to be fire outbreaks but could easily be related to traffic congestion, toll charging, or air pollution zones and locations in the oceans which represent hazards such as coral reefs or sand banks:

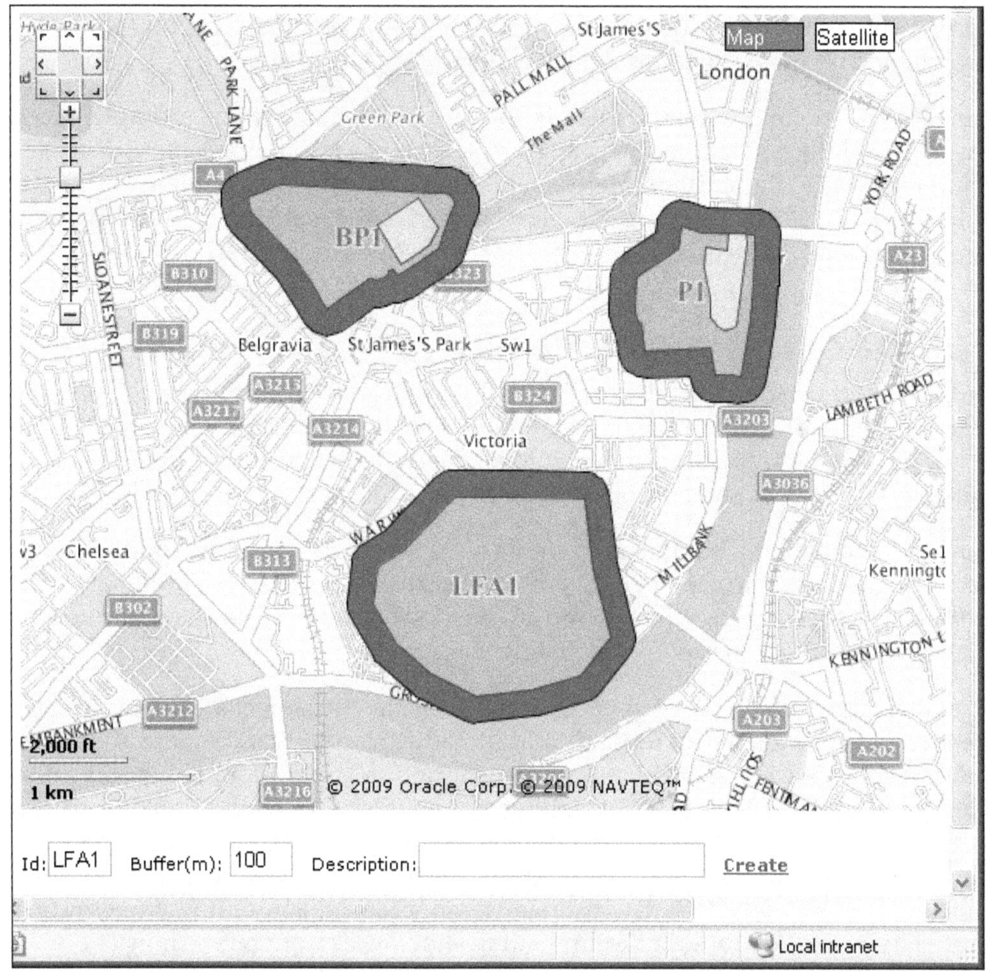

Oracle MapViewer is a JEE service for rendering maps using spatial data managed by Oracle Spatial and Oracle Event Processing. It provides services and tools that hide the complexity of spatial data queries and cartographic rendering, while providing customizable options for more advanced users, such as geo-fencing creation, manipulation, and deletion.

To clarify the relevance of these specific components, Oracle Spatial technology has been integrated with Oracle Event Processing using the Spatial Data Cartridge. Geospatial data geometries, such as geo-fence areas or points, can be stored in a database accessed by both, Oracle Event Processing applications and Oracle MapViewer. Oracle Event Processing applications can generate location events that will update mapping information rendered by MapViewer.

This is described later in this chapter, in the case of the bus location example, where Oracle Event Processing location events are sent out as HTTP publish messages to its integrated HTTP Publish-Subscribe server, so that web applications can subscribe to these HTTP pub-sub events and when they arrive the web application can invoke MapViewer server functions to render updated geo-location data.

Bus tracking movement event patterns

We have described, in general, how Oracle Event Processing applications can be implemented using its geo-streaming and geo-fencing capabilities, so now we will review the real-world use case relating to a government land transportation bus transit service improvement project requirements.

Many bus and light rail public services now have sophisticated sensors and passenger monitoring devices that can not only provide the streaming GPS signals but also personalized pocket cards which introduce methods that can be used to indicate when a person steps onto a bus and when that person departs.

All of these, and other related events, such as real-time weather satellite information, streaming video cameras on the lamp posts, bridges can be consolidated and used in an effective Oracle Event Processing transportation application. This application could provide immediate alerts to waiting passengers as to the location of their bus, time to arrival, and whether its capacity has been reached. It could also dynamically provide insight as to congestion and weather related delays automatically initiating requests for more buses to satisfy the passenger space demands either by rerouting empty buses on other routes or calling out reserve buses from bus terminals.

As you research the many different requirements for a transportation monitoring and management solution, you will discover many obvious and perhaps some more obscure use cases. Some of the common requirements in any bus tracking solution will encompass the following vehicle movement event patterns:

- Detect when a bus deviates from the predefined route and send an alert. The alert event can be visualized on a custom user interface or used to invoke a business process to take specific actions. While this deviation could be due to traffic congestion from an accident, weather, natural disaster, or simply human error, all of these factors can be dynamically assessed by the event processing application and included in the alert text. A prediction methodology could also be invoked to evaluate, based on historical vehicle movement patterns, possible trends in which different routes are or could be taken:

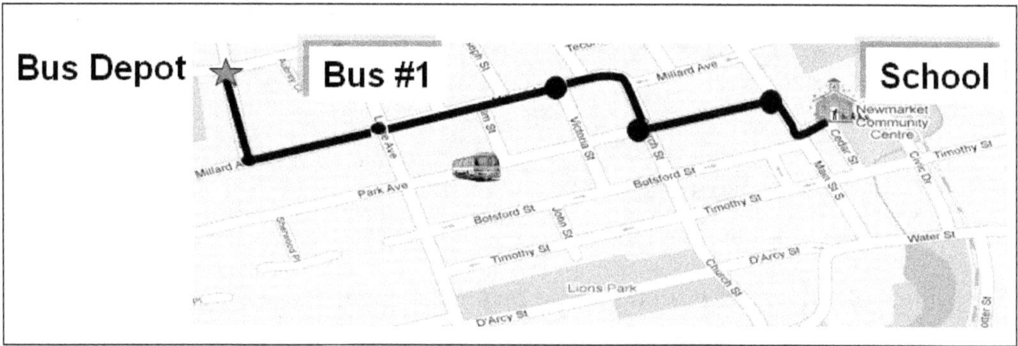

- When on the pre-defined path, detect when the bus is at a bus depot, bus stop, or school. Each static bus depot, bus stop, or place of interest, such as a school, is geo-fenced (or classified as an Event Region) and these areas stored in a relational database. The GPS events are compared to these areas and when the distance between them is less than a certain value, an informational message is generated and processes are invoked to prepare for the arrival of the vehicle.

  When the GPS event is **IN-VOID**, a general term use to describe when the resource is completely inside one of the geo-fenced areas, the system generates an alert message that is visualized on a custom user interface:

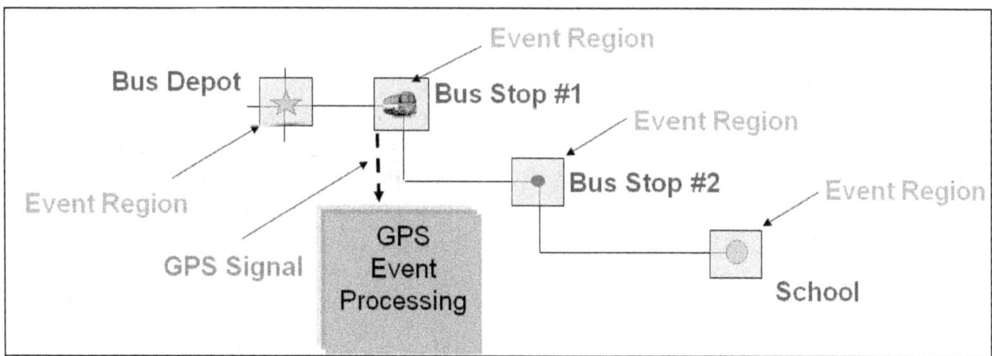

- Provide Event Processing spatial analysis for reassignment and redistribution of all buses in transportation network. When the system detects transportation network "fault" conditions, these can be defined as traffic congestion, road work disruption, vehicle breakdown, or poor weather conditions, the application will invoke processes to optimize available vehicles usage:

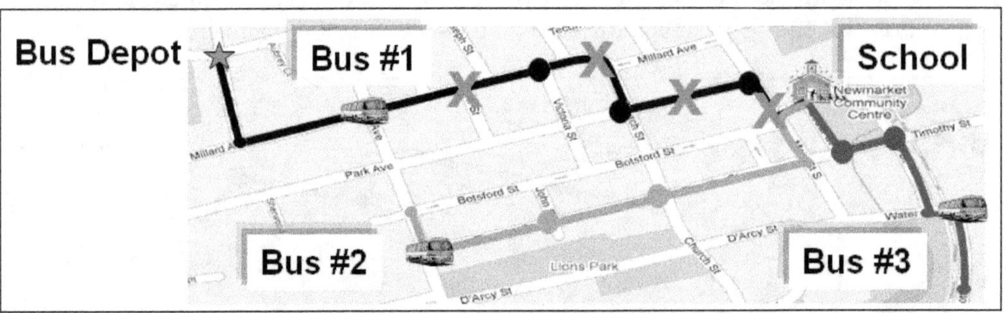

These kinds of innovative systems based on Oracle Event Processing can provide better customer satisfaction and the improved management of passenger flow ensuring all buses are effectively utilized. This, in turn, reduces costs for the government authority in many ways, in fuel costs, staffing levels and even by a reduction in complaint telephone calls from angry disillusioned passengers.

The Oracle Spatial Data Cartridge

So how does all this spatial magic happen? Let us now focus directly on the enabling features provided by the Oracle Event Processing technology, the Oracle Spatial Data Cartridge, and discuss how it can be used in a development context.

In previous chapters we have described the capability to extend the Oracle CQL CEP engine event analysis capabilities in many powerful and rich ways using Data Cartridges. This pluggable architecture also extends to integrate one of the leading industry spatial technology platforms provided with the Oracle Enterprise Edition Database.

The Oracle Spatial Data Cartridge encapsulates the major features of this technology and enables Oracle Event Processing developers to execute these spatial functions directly in the event language and thus can be modified dynamically and reintroduced into the application, changing its logic flow, *without* stopping and restarting the application.

As we have already introduced various bus tracking scenarios we can now review how using the Oracle Event Processing Spatial Data Cartridge can simplify Bus movement event analysis tasks.

Rather than using many complicated lines of software code, you can match the moving bus vehicle positional event properties relative to its known fixed bus stop position by using a Continuous Query Language (CQL) statement which includes an Oracle Spatial Data Cartridge function call. In this statement you can compare the bus stop geometry (its longitude and latitude position, `busstop.geom`) to the moving bus geometry position (`bus.geom`) and ensure that for the correct bus, the spatial points match exactly.

Note the use of the `CONTAIN@spatial` geometric relation operator which directly invokes the use of the Spatial Data Cartridge technology. This operator returns `true` if the defined point values are contained by the geometry and `false` otherwise:

```
<query id="BusArrival">
    ISTREAM(
        select systimestamp() as incidentTime, bus.busId as busId, busstop.seq as stopSeq
        from BusPosGeomStream[NOW] as bus, BusStopRelation as busstop
        where CONTAIN@spatial(busstop.geom, bus.geom, 0.0d) = true and
                bus.busId = busstop.busId
    )
</query>
```

As the Oracle Event Processing architecture is based on OSGi, the Oracle Spatial Data Cartridge itself is defined as part of the application manifest and can be found in the `MANIFEST.MF` file within the application project. The name of this Data Cartridge is `com.oracle.cep.cartridge.spatial`:

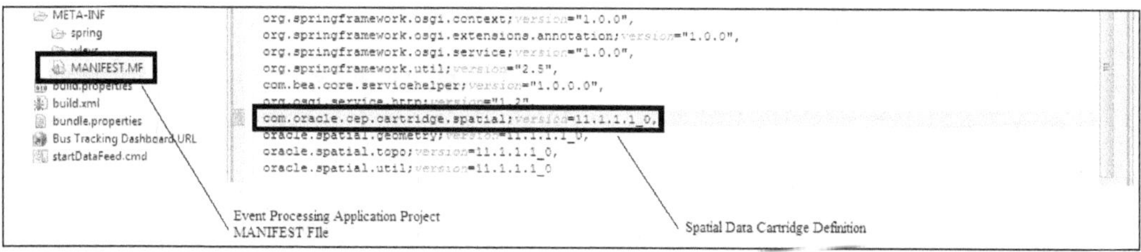

Oracle geospatial features

There are many Oracle Event Processing Spatial features, so you should review the very detailed product documentation on this subject. However, in this section, we will highlight some of the most commonly used Oracle Spatial Data Cartridge statements from various worldwide implemented solutions.

In the previous section we have introduced you to the `CONTAIN` Oracle Spatial geometric relation operator. As this is not a method of the `com.oracle.cep.cartridge.spatial.Geometry` class you invoke this operator without a package prefix simply using `CONTAIN@spatial`:

```
where CONTAIN@spatial(busstop.geom, bus.geom, 0.0d) = true and
      bus.busId = busstop.busId
```

Another useful Oracle Spatial method used in many applications is `DISTANCE`, together with the NN Spatial operator.

`DISTANCE` is a `com.oracle.cep.cartridge.spatial.Geometry` method that calculates the distance between two geometries and returns a double value.

`NN` is a Spatial operator that returns the objects (nearest neighbors) from `geom` that are nearest to the key. In determining how near two geometry objects are, the shortest possible distance between any two points on the surface of each object is used.

For example, you can use these Oracle Spatial capabilities as part of a more complex telecommunication solution to compare the current distance of a customer's smartphone within close proximity to a Wi-Fi base station:

```
select
    dev.deviceId as deviceId,
    dev.moving as moving,
    base.baseLocation as candidateBaseStationId,
    dev.tstamp as tstamp,
    com.oracle.cep.cartridge.spatial.Geometry.distance@spatial(dev.geom, base.geom) as distanceFromBaseStation,
    dev.longitude as devLongitude, dev.latitude as devLatitude,
    base.longitude as baseLongitude, base.latitude as baseLatitude
from DeviceLocationStream[NOW] as dev, BaseStationRelation as base
where (NN@spatial(dev.geom, base.geom, 20.0d) = true)
```

At this point, we have included this rather complex CQL query purely as a reference but we will describe this statement, concepts and its usage aspects in much more detail in a subsequent chapter.

One of the main goals for the Oracle Event Processing Spatial Data cartridge is not only to integrate a comprehensive collection of spatial-related capabilities in the Oracle Event Processing technology but also to provide a simplification and abstraction for the complex methods and operators involved, and enable their use with the CQL CEP processor engine. It should be also noted that in general terms all of these capabilities can be executed without the need for any installed relational database.

Tracking vehicles with an Oracle Event Processing application

We have now introduced the basic features and concepts, and all of the major functions needed for a vehicle tracking solution. So now we will step through the requirements for building and implementing such as solution, using all of these elements.

In the following sections we will show the entire application in the form of its **Event Processing Network** (**EPN**) and then focus on the specific areas related to the use of spatial analysis. Interestingly, most of this application is metadata defined and driven, so in reality there is not a substantial amount of actual Java code required.

Key application elements

The following bus tracking application is a packaged sample that is distributed with the Oracle Event Processing software (in the samples directory/folder) and can provide a useful foundation for more elaborate spatial monitoring and management solutions, which not only applies to vehicle monitoring but also to many other geospatial use cases such as those involving mobile devices. For simplicity, we have packaged this sample as an exported Eclipse project for use with this chapter:

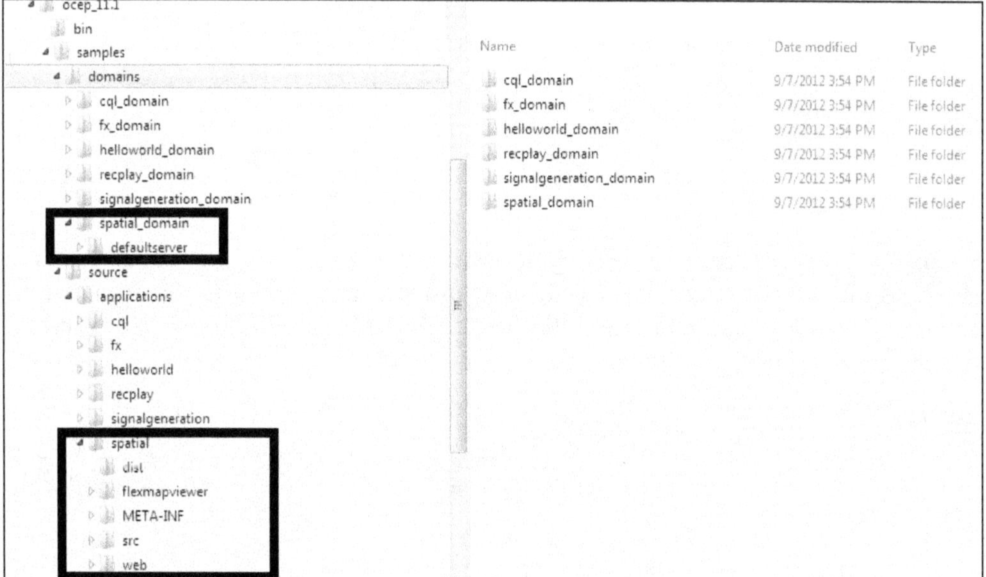

Bus tracking EPN

The bus tracking application Event Processing Network starts with two event adapters:

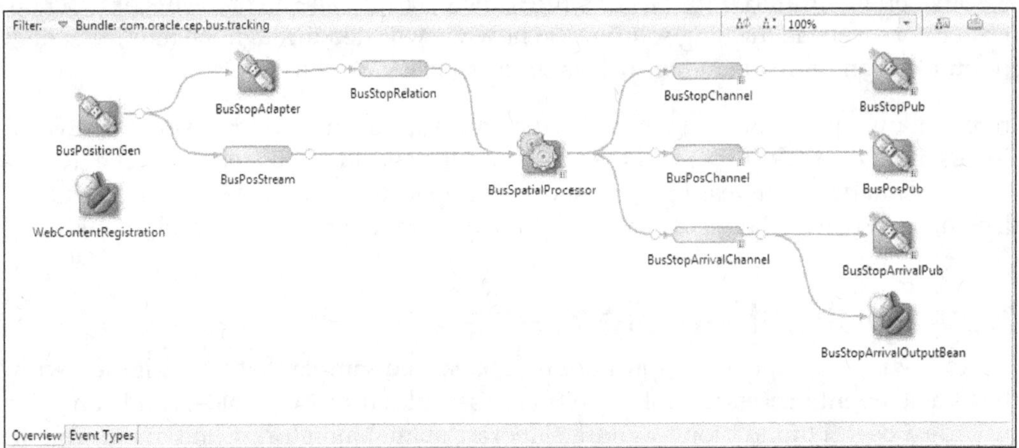

The `BusPositionGen` adapter is an out of the box adapter that listens for events arriving at a specific TCP/IP port which are sent from the `runloadgen` tool:

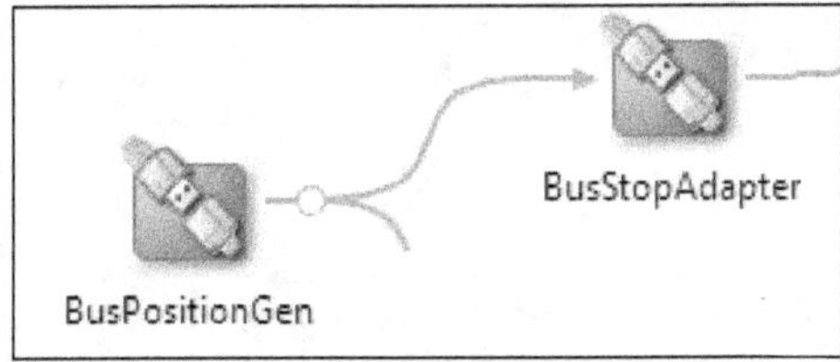

The `runloadgen` tool reads records from a `bus_positions.csv` file that contains the individual movement event data for the bus and streams them into the application. This simulates the actual event data that would come from a GPS device or sensor. The adapter is defined as follows:

```
<wlevs:adapter id="BusPositionGen" provider="csvgen">
    <wlevs:instance-property name="port" value="9020"/>
    <wlevs:instance-property name="eventTypeName" value="BusPos"/>
    <wlevs:instance-property
            name="eventPropertyNames"
            value="busId,seq,longitude,latitude"/>
    <wlevs:listener ref="BusPosStream"/>
    <wlevs:listener ref="BusStopAdapter"/>
</wlevs:adapter>
```

The main processing of the second adapter, `BusStopAdapter`, starts once the application has started to process the individual bus movement position events. It reads from another file called, `bus_stops.csv` and stores the positions of the bus stops in memory for later analysis by the `BusSpatialProcessor` event node, and this adapter is defined as follows:

```
<wlevs:adapter id="BusStopAdapter" class="com.oracle.cep.sample.spatial.BusStopAdapter" >
    <wlevs:instance-property name="path" value="bus_stops.csv"/>
    <wlevs:instance-property name="eventType" value="BusStop"/>
</wlevs:adapter>
```

For reference, the `bus_stops.csv` file read by this second adapter is deployed as an Application artifact from within the `META-INF/wlevs` project folder. The events then flow through the **BusPosStream** and **BusStopRelation** channels using the event-types of **BusPos** and **BusStop** respectively:

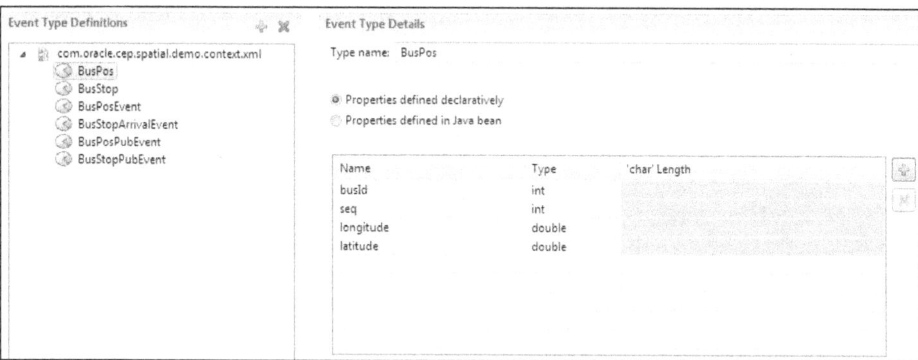

Both of these event-types are defined in the Oracle Event Processing development tooling together with the event-types that are used by the created user interface to visualize the information:

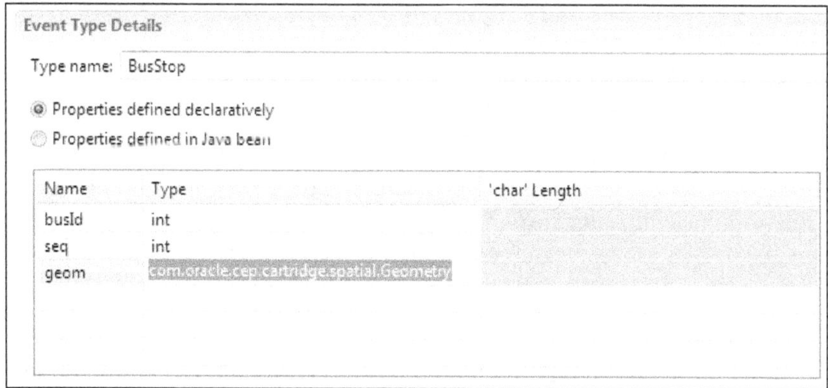

BusSpatialProcessor

Next we have the event processor queries that utilize `CQL VIEWS` and are transient virtual streams or relations. In this case they are used to add geospatial geometry objects to entities in the bus position stream and in bus stop location relation:

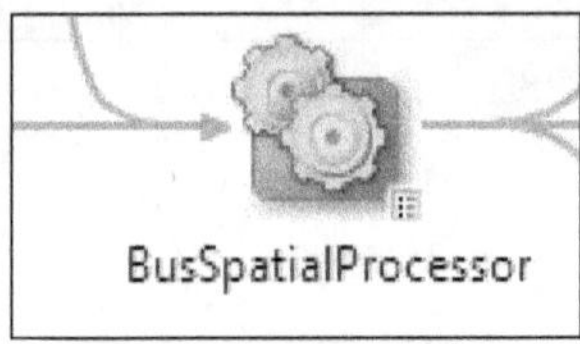

The `BusSpatialProcessor` event node creates a bus view with an ID of `BusPosGeomStream` which uses the Spatial Data Cartridge features to create the geom geometry object which relates to the current position of the moving bus.

The `BusArrival` query then uses the bus view with another Spatial Data Cartridge feature to compare the geometry object value of the moving bus position to the bus stop geometry object values relating to each of the bus stop positions that have been stored in the processors memory. In this example the value `0.0d` is defined so that a match is made if the moving bus position exactly matches the bus stop position.

When the geometries match exactly and the `bus.busId` event-type property of the moving bus is the same as the `busstop.Id` event-type property then this query will send the output event to the BusStopArrivalChannel:

```
<view id="BusPosGeomStream" >
    select bus.busId as busId, bus.seq as seq,
    com.oracle.cep.cartridge.spatial.Geometry.createPoint(8307, bus.longitude, bus.latitude) as geom
    from BusPosStream as bus
</view>

<query id="BusArrival">
    ISTREAM(
        select systimestamp() as incidentTime, bus.busId as busId, busstop.seq as stopSeq
        from BusPosGeomStream[NOW] as bus, BusStopRelation as busstop
        where CONTAIN@spatial(busstop.geom, bus.geom, 0.0d) = true and
              bus.busId = busstop.busId
    )
</query>
```

There is a HTTP publish and subscribe channel adapter that receives the events from the `BusStopArrivalChannel` and the user interface will receive these events and show an bus stop arrival alert message. This application also has a `BusStopArrivalOutputBean` event bean node which is used to show informational messages on the output console.

The remaining two queries in this processor are used to provide information for the user interface with the output events sent to the `BusPosChannel` and `BusStopChannel` channel event nodes. These together with the `BusStopArrivalChannel` channel event node are again used by the HTTP publish and subscribe channel adapter event nodes:

```
    <query id="BusStopOut">
        select busId, seq as id, com.oracle.cep.sample.spatial.OrdsHelper.getOrds(geom) as coords from BusStopRelation
    </query>

    <query id="BusPosOut">
        select systimestamp() as lastTime, busId, longitude, latitude from BusPosStream
    </query>
   </rules>
  </processor>

  <channel>
      <name>BusStopArrivalChannel</name>
      <selector>BusArrival</selector>
  </channel>

  <channel>
      <name>BusPosChannel</name>
      <selector>BusPosOut</selector>
  </channel>

  <channel>
      <name>BusStopChannel</name>
      <selector>BusStopOut</selector>
  </channel>
```

This processor event node definition concludes with three channel definitions that will route the event output as required. Note the usage of the `<selector>` element on the `<channel>` definition. This will ensure that the events are sent to the correct channel.

The remaining section of the Event Processing Network dictates the routing of the events from the channel event nodes to the HTTP publish and subscribe adapter nodes:

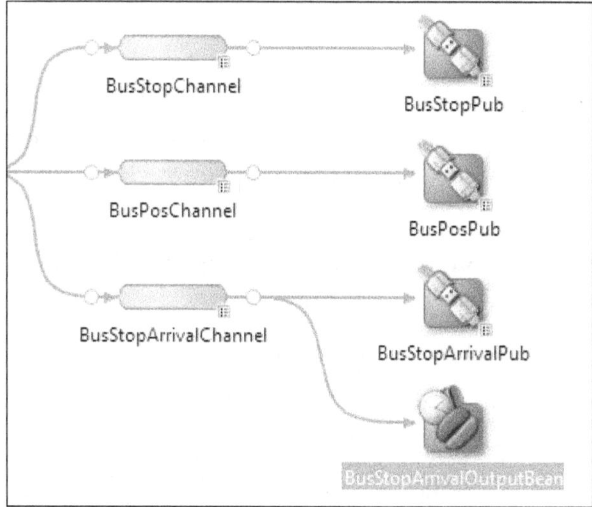

In this sample:

- The `BusStopChannel` channel event node will send related events to the `BusStopPub` HTTP Publish-Subscribe adapter node.
- The `BusPosChannel` channel event node will send related events to the `BusPosPub` HTTP pub-sub adapter node.
- The `BusStopArrivalChannel` channel event node will send related events to the `BusStopArrivalPub` HTTP pub-sub adapter node.

These HTTP pub-sub adapter nodes described in the application using the `<http-pub-sub-adapter>` tags will push the arriving events for any web client user interface that is "listening" for these events and is ready to consume:

```
<http-pub-sub-adapter>
    <name>BusPosPub</name>
    <server-url>http://localhost:9002/pubsub</server-url>
    <channel>/bus/buspos</channel>
    <event-type>BusPosPubEvent</event-type>
</http-pub-sub-adapter>

<http-pub-sub-adapter>
    <name>BusStopPub</name>
    <server-url>http://localhost:9002/pubsub</server-url>
    <channel>/bus/busstop</channel>
    <event-type>BusStopPubEvent</event-type>
</http-pub-sub-adapter>

<http-pub-sub-adapter>
    <name>BusStopArrivalPub</name>
    <server-url>http://localhost:9002/pubsub</server-url>
    <channel>/bus/busstoparrival</channel>
    <event-type>BusStopArrivalEvent</event-type>
</http-pub-sub-adapter>
```

All of the HTTP pub-sub channels used by Oracle Event Processing Applications and managed by the server must each be defined in the Oracle Event Processing domain configuration file.

Each of the required HTTP pub-sub channels are specified using the `<channel-pattern>` tag under the `<http-pubsub>` tag section.

Published HTTP pub-sub events from the Oracle Event Processing application are sent to an HTTP pub-sub server. This HTTP pub-sub server could be accessed directly by using the integrated component of the Oracle Event Processing runtime system or an external HTTP pub-sub server available as part of other application servers, such as the Oracle Weblogic Server:

```
<http-pubsub>
  <name>pubsub</name>
  <path>/pubsub</path>
  <pub-sub-bean>
    <server-config>
      <supported-transport>
        <types>
          <element>long-polling</element>
        </types>
      </supported-transport>
      <publish-without-connect-allowed>true</publish-without-connect-allowed>
    </server-config>
    <channels>


      <element>
        <channel-pattern>/bus/buspos</channel-pattern>
      </element>
      <element>
        <channel-pattern>/bus/busstoparrival</channel-pattern>
      </element>
      <element>
        <channel-pattern>/bus/busstop</channel-pattern>
      </element>

    </channels>
  </pub-sub-bean>
</http-pubsub>
```

As a developer note, HTTP pub-sub adapters can be created and defined, in addition to other event node adapters such as JMS adapters using the available IDE wizard:

To summarize the use of the HTTP pub-sub component of Oracle Event Processing, here are some major advantages:

- It supports transporting events between OEP server and web clients
- Clients don't need to poll for updates (unlike traditional HTTP)
- Clients subscribe to and publish to these special channels, using the Bayeux protocol
- It is a very light weight implementation and the payload is JSON

Bus tracking visual user interface

The user interface for this type of Oracle Event Processing Application can be constructed in many ways using many different types of visualization tools. For this sample application an Adobe™ Flex user interface is provided:

```
<![CDATA[
import org.cometd.*;

import com.adobe.serialization.json.JSON;
import com.adobe.serialization.json.JSONDecoder;

public var h:CometClient;

public static const PUB_SUB_URL_PATH:String = "/pubsub";
public static const DEFAULT_HOST_PORT:String = "localhost:9002";
public var serverHostPort_:String = DEFAULT_HOST_PORT; //default during testing

private function init():void {

        var appUrl:String = Application.application.url;
        var serverHostPort:String = null;
        if(appUrl != null && (appUrl.indexOf("file://") != 0)) {
            serverHostPort = URLUtil.getServerNameWithPort(appUrl);
        }
        if(serverHostPort != null && serverHostPort.length > 0) {
            serverHostPort_ = serverHostPort;
        }
        pubSubUrl_ = "http://" + serverHostPort_ + PUB_SUB_URL_PATH;


    h = new CometClient();
    h.cometURL = "http://localhost:9002/pubsub";
    h.init();

    h.subscribe("/bus/busstop", onMessageReceived, null);
```

As a reference, the provided code snippet shows how an Adobe™ Flex application defines access to the HTTP publish and subscribe channel, then uses the `OnMessageReceived` function to receive each event message:

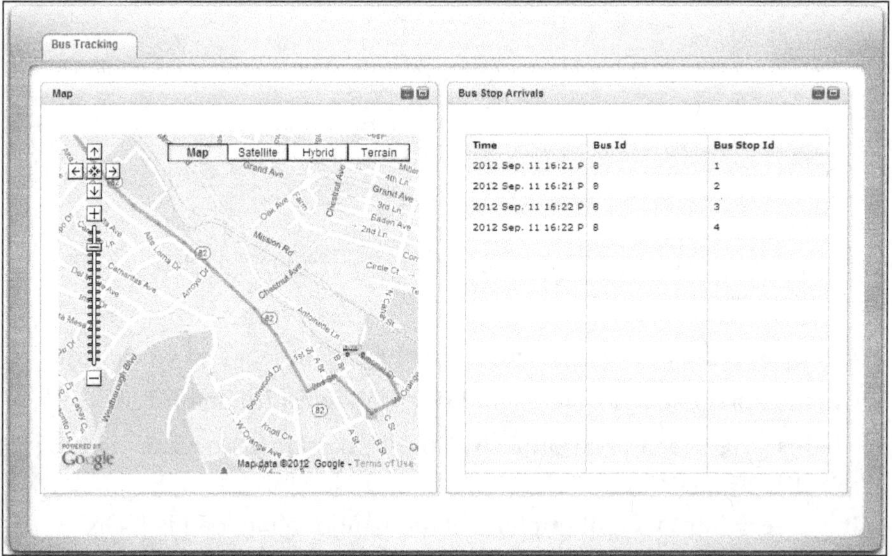

The Adobe™ Flex application then processes each event and displays the moving bus on the defined map, which in the view provided is shown in the left-hand side window and an alert message as the bus passes through each defined bus stop location is shown on the right-hand side window.

How to run this bus tracking sample application

Assuming you have reviewed the `readme.txt` file in the imported project and followed the required configuration and application setup, there are only three steps to successfully evaluate this sample application.

Firstly, using the development tooling, deploy (publish) the Oracle Event Processing Application to an executing server. When you see the messaging in the console indicating a successful loading of the application, you are ready for step two:

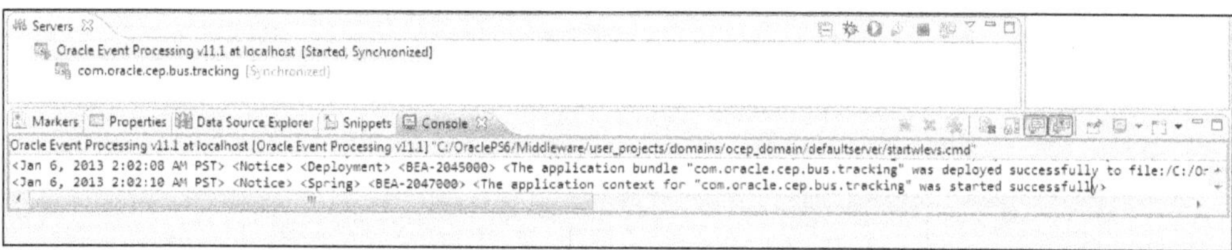

The recommended next step involves starting the user interface, and this can be done with the pre-configured URL. Simply double-click on this project artifact to start a browser and the UI. This is called **Bus Tracking Dashboard.URL**:

The final step is to generate the simulated GPS events using the `runloadgen` tool with the pre-configured windows script file called **startDataFeed.cmd** (on a Windows platform). Again, simply double-click on the project artifact:

Summary

We have described in this chapter the basic concepts for spatial analysis and introduced you to the major related terms and definitions used by the Oracle Event Processing Spatial Data Cartridge and the Oracle Continuous Query Language (CQL).

By stepping you through the bus tracking sample application we have provided you with the information, taken from a real-world example, that can form a solid foundation of knowledge for real-time spatial analysis of moving objects in your own Oracle Event Processing Applications.

11
Extending CQL with Spatial and JDBC

In the previous chapter, you learn how to develop use cases that made use of Oracle Event Processing spatial features. In this chapter, you will learn the details of the Spatial cartridge, which allows you to extend CQL with spatial types and operations. Further, you will also learn how to make arbitrary SQL calls to the database in cases when you need to make use of additional features in the database, for example, that are not yet supported in Oracle Event Processing.

Specifically, you will learn how to:

- Create spatial objects representing points, rectangles, and general polygons
- Determine the spatial relationship between spatial objects
- Understand different coordinate systems, such as the Cartesian and geodetic coordinate system
- Apply table functions that return collections of events
- Make use of SQL statements wrapped in CQL

Creating geometries

In Oracle Event Processing, an event may contain one or more properties that represent a geometry form. These properties are typed as `com.oracle.cep.cartridge.spatial.Geometry`, which is a Java class provided by the Spatial cartridge.

A geometry type may represent the following forms:

- Point
- Rectangle
- Line String
- Polygons

Rectangles and polygons, in general, are also called **closed shapes**, as they are made of lines that link together. The following diagram describes some of these forms:

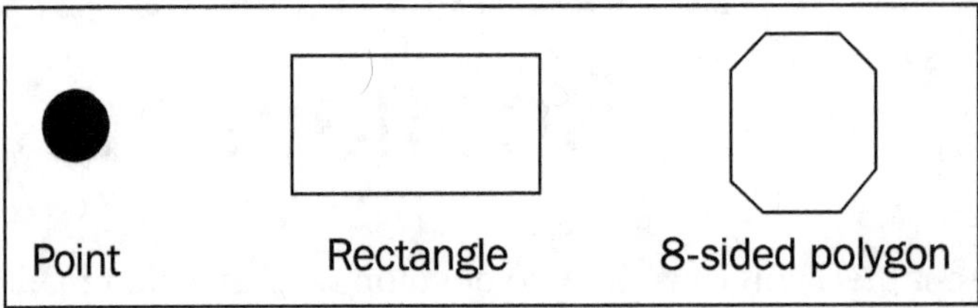

The line (or arc) separating the interior of a polygon from its external is called its **boundary**.

To create an event property containing a point form, you can use the following static Java method on the `Geometry` class:

```
com.oracle.cep.cartridge.spatial.Geometry.createPoint
 @spatial(double x, double y)
```

This method takes two arguments, representing the `x` and `y` coordinate of a two-dimensional point, and returns an object of `Geometry` type.

To avoid having to type the full package name for the `Geometry` class, you can change the application's `MANIFEST.MF` file to import the spatial package, as follows:

```
Import-Package: com.oracle.cep.cartridge.spatial
```

For example, the following query outputs an event containing a geometry point that is created using the properties `x` and `y` from an input event:

```
SELECT
  Geometry.createPoint@spatial(i.x, i.y) as point
FROM
  inputChannel as i
```

Very importantly, note how you need to specify the cartridge link named `spatial`. This is needed as the `Geometry` type is an extended CQL type provided by the Spatial cartridge. The Spatial cartridge is installed out of the box with Oracle Event Processing.

Next, you can use the following method to create a two-dimensional rectangle:

```
Geometry.createRectangle@spatial(
  double minX, double minY,
  double maxX, double maxY)
```

The first two arguments represents the minimum left-most point of the rectangle, and the latter two arguments represents the maximum right-most point of the rectangle. This is shown in the following diagram:

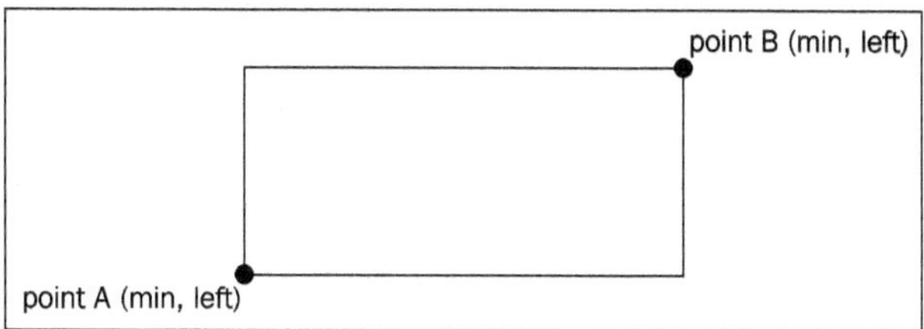

Points and rectangles are by far the most useful forms you will work with when processing events. However, as known, there are other forms of shapes, as the following ones:

- Circles
- Other n-sided polygons, such as pentagons, hexagons, and heptagons
- Line-strings: collection of non-closed lines
- Arc polygons: polygons made of arcs (curves)
- Compound polygons: polygons made of lines and arcs

These shapes are described in the following diagram:

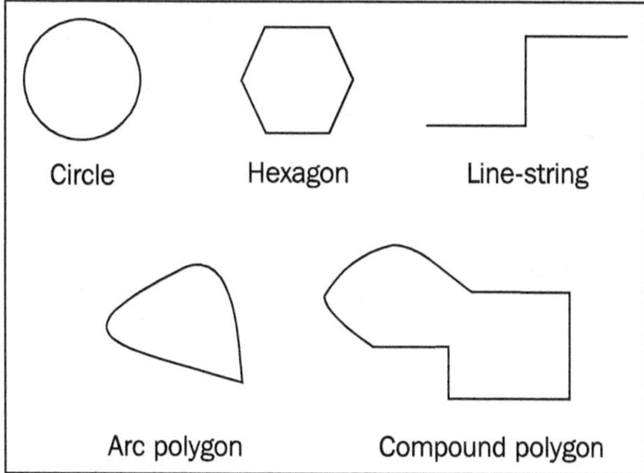

In Oracle Event Processing 11*g*, you need to use a generic `createGeometry()` method to create forms other than points and rectangles. The `createGeometry()` signature is:

```
Geometry.createGeometry(int gtype, int[] elemInfo,
 double[] ordinates)
```

However, understanding all the semantics of the arguments for this method is beyond the scope of this book. For further details, please refer to the Oracle Event Processing Spatial cartridge reference guide at `http://docs.oracle.com/cd/E23943_01/apirefs.1111/e12048/datacartspatial.htm#CHDIBJHI`.

Oracle Event Processing 12*c* will provide convenient methods for creating circles, line-strings, arbitrary (linear) polygons, and general three-dimensional shapes.

How do you interpret the coordinates used as arguments to the `create` methods in the `Geometry` type? For example, are the `x` and `y` coordinates used when creating a point related to the Cartesian plane or do they represent longitude and latitude in Earth's geodetic sphere? This interpretation of the coordinates, that is, how they relate to each other, is determined by its **coordinate system**, also called the **spatial reference system**. This is demonstrated in the following diagram:

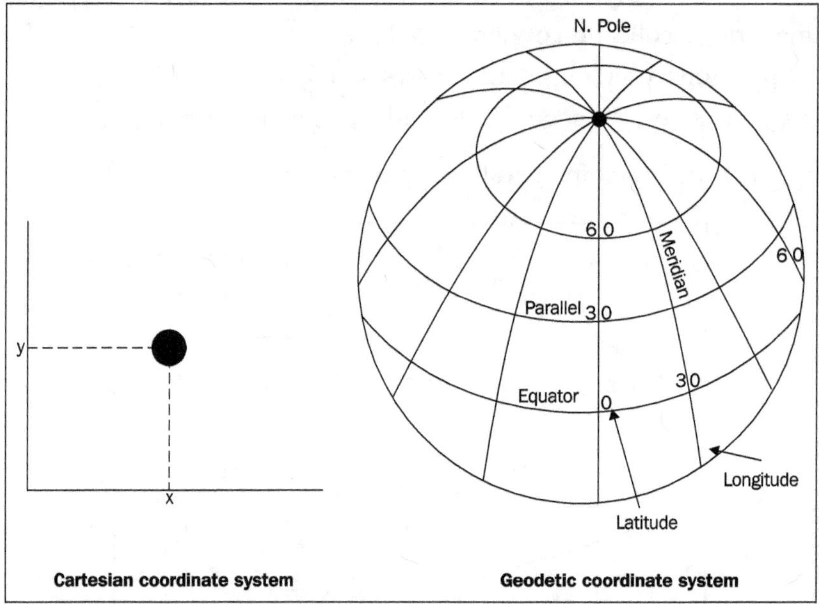

The Spatial cartridge supports two-coordinate systems:

- **Cartesian coordinate system**: These coordinates measure the position of a point from a defined origin along axes that are perpendicular in the represented two-dimensional or three-dimensional space.
- **Geodetic coordinate system**: This is sometimes called geographic coordinates. The coordinates are angular coordinates (longitude and latitude), and are defined relative to a particular Earth geodetic datum. By default, these coordinates are measured in meters.

The Spatial cartridge uses the geodetic coordinate system as its default coordinate system, however you can specify the Cartesian coordinate system by using a **Spatial Reference ID (SRID)** of value `0` in the following overloaded methods for creating polygons:

- `createPoint(int SRID, double x, double y)`
- `createRectangle(int SRID, double x1, double y1, double x2, double y2)`
- `Geometry createGeometry(int gtype, int SRID, int[] elemInfo, double[] ordinates)`

In other words, these are the supported SRID values:

- `Cartesian SRID = 0`
- `Geodetic (latitude/longitude) SRID = 8307 (as defined by the World Geodetic System of 1984 - WGS84)`

Further, you can also change the default coordinate system by defining an application-specific spatial context, a subject we discuss later in this chapter.

In the next section, you will learn how to apply spatial operations in the geometry objects you have created.

Determining if geometries relate to each other

The spatial operations allow you to determine the relationship between two or more geometry objects. Some examples are:

- Geometries are next to each other
- Geometries are contained by one another
- Geometries intersect boundaries

In the last chapter, you used the `contain` operation. Let's start by revisiting it:

```
boolean contain@spatial(
  Geometry containingGeometry,
  Geometry containedGeometry,
  double tolerance)
```

The `contain()` function returns `true` if the `containedGeometry` is contained by the `containingGeometry`, otherwise it returns `false`. A geometry is considered contained by another geometry if all the points that make up the former is completely within the shape of the latter. In particular, a geometry is not considered contained by another geometry if they touch boundaries. This is exemplified in the following diagram:

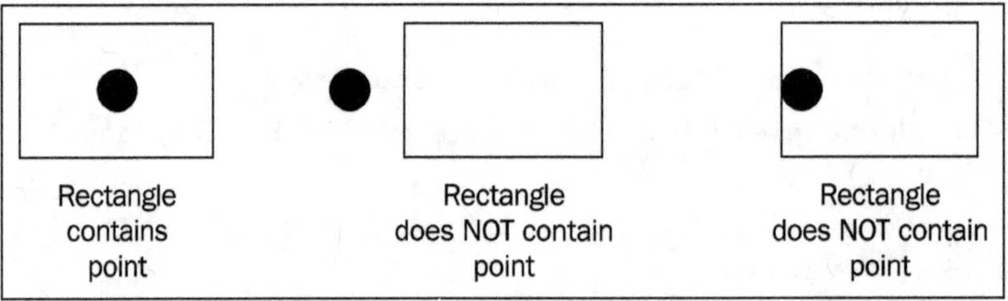

The tolerance argument is used as a measure of accuracy of the data. When you specify a tolerance for the spatial operations, you can think of it as a fuzzy boundary around the geometries. That is, the boundary of a polygon is usually a line with zero thickness. With tolerance, you can imagine a boundary line with a thickness equal to the tolerance.

As the `contain` operation does not consider the boundary of the geometries, the tolerance argument is only applicable for contains when the geometries involved deal with arcs. In this case, the tolerance value is used as a mechanism of densifying the arcs.

> In Oracle Event Processing 11*g*, only two-dimensional points are supported as the second argument (contained geometry) for the contains operation.

As you have seen in the previous chapter, the more interesting use case is not just to check if a geometry contains another geometry, but rather the more general case of checking if any geometry within a collection of geometries contains a determined key geometry. In other words, another way of looking at it is by changing the signature of the `contain` operation to the following pseudo code:

```
boolean contain@spatial(
  /* relation defined with event property of type Geometry */
  Collection<Geometry> anyContainingGeometries,
  Geometry containedGeometry,
  double tolerance)
```

Considering this, here is an example of this usage in a CQL query:

```
SELECT loc.customerId as customerId, shop.name as inShop
FROM locationStream[now] as loc, shopRelation as shop
WHERE contain@spatial(shop.rect, loc.point, 0.0d) = true
```

In this case, there are two input sources. `locationStream` is a stream containing the current location of customers. `ShopRelation` is a relation that contains a rectangle geometry objects representing the physical location of shops in a mall. The query verifies if a point geometry representing the current location of a customer is inside any of the registered shops that are part of the relation, and if it is, outputs the customer ID and the name of the shop that contains the customer location.

The `inside` operation is the exact opposite of the `contain` operation. Its pseudo-code signature is defined as follows:

```
boolean inside@spatial(
  /* relation defined with event property of type Geometry */
  Collection<Geometry> anyContainedGeometries,
  Geometry containingGeometry,
  double tolerance)
```

In this case, the operation is `true` if any geometries in the first argument is contained by the geometry of the second argument. Another way of stating this is that if geometry *A* contains geometry *B*, then geometry *B* is inside geometry *A*.

> In Oracle Event Processing 11*g*, only two-dimensional points are supported as the first argument (contained geometry) to the inside operation.

Next, let's take a look at the most general spatial operation, the `anyinteract` function:

```
boolean anyinteract@spatial(
  /* relation defined with event property of type Geometry */
  Collection<Geometry> geometriesA,
  Geometry geometryB,
  double tolerance)
```

`Anyinteract` returns `true` if `geometryB` has any spatial interaction at all—be it contained, inside, or touching— with any of the geometries in the `geometriesA` collection. In other words, it is a spatial catch all of sorts. This is demonstrated in the following diagram:

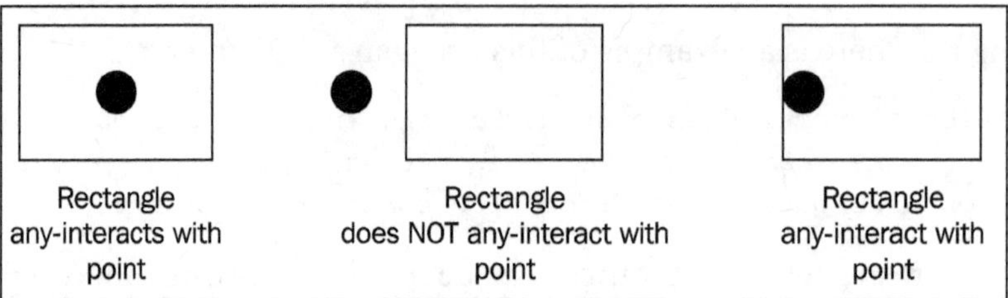

`Anyinteract` is one function where the tolerance value is very useful, as it allows you to effectively increase the boundary of the geometries. For example, consider the following diagram:

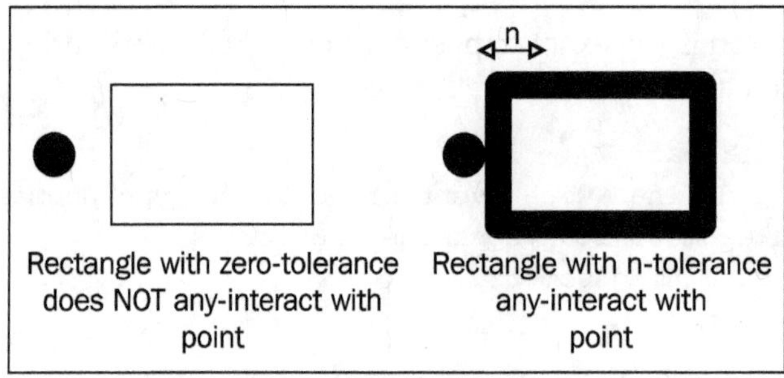

In the first case, a zero tolerance is used, and `anyinteract` returns `false`. In the second case, a tolerance of *n* is used, which effectively increases the boundary of the polygon, resulting in a positive return of `anyinteract`.

In Oracle Event Processing 11*g*, only two-dimensional points are supported as the second argument to the `anyinteract` operation.

The `withindistance` function allows you to determine if a geometry is within a certain distance of another geometry. It is defined as:

```
boolean withindistance@spatial(
   /* relation defined with event property of type Geometry */
  Collection<Geometry> geometries,
  Geometry keyGeometry,
  double distance)
```

The withindistance returns true if there is a point in keyGeometry that is at least the specified distance from a point in geometries. In other words, the withindistance function considers the shortest possible distance between any two points of the geometry objects it uses. For example, you can use withindistance to determine if your car, represented as a point, is within 10 miles of a gas station, the latter represented as a rectangle.

In Oracle Event Processing 11*g*, only two-dimensional points are supported as the second argument (key geometry) in the withindistance operation.

The last remaining spatial operation you will look at in this chapter is the nearest neighbor function, which is defined as:

```
boolean nn@spatial(
  /* relation defined with event property of type Geometry */
  Collection<Geometry> geometries,
  Geometry keyGeometry,
  double tolerance)
```

The nn operation returns true for all geometries in the collection that are the nearest to the key geometry. Let's look at a CQL query as an example:

```
SELECT loc.customerId as customerId, shop.name as nearestShop
FROM locationStream[now] as loc, shopRelation as shop
WHERE nn@spatial(shop.rect, loc.point, 0.0d) = true
```

Next, consider the following diagram as the input to the query:

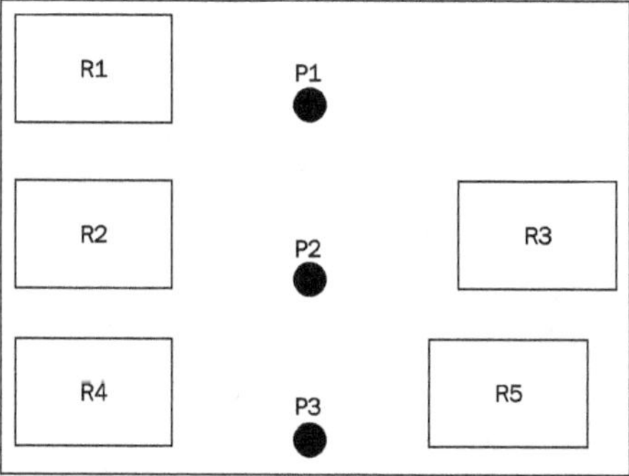

The shopRelation contains rectangles R1, R2, R3, R4, and R5. When point P1 arrives as the first event in locationStream, the nn function is true for rectangle R1. For point P2, the nn function is true only for R2. Finally, when point P3 arrives, the nn function is true for both R4 and R5. This means that in the case of P3, the query outputs two events, one for R4 and another for R5.

The nearest neighbor can be a bit misleading when used in complex queries. For example, let's say you want to find out the nearest shop that sells shoes to your current location. You may mistakenly attempt to do this by authoring a query such as:

```
SELECT loc.customerId as customerId, shop.name as nearestShop
FROM locationStream[now] as loc, shopRelation as shop
WHERE
  nn@spatial(shop.rect, loc.point, 0.0d) = true AND
  shop.type = 'shoes'
```

At a glance, the predicate may look correct, that is, selecting the nearest neighbor that sells shoes. However, what is actually happening is that the query is looking for the nearest neighbor and then makes sure it sells shoes. A better idea would have been to create a view that filters all shops for only those that sells shoes and then apply the `nn` operation.

You may be wondering if finding the nearest neighbor amongst all geometries of a relation for each incoming event is too time consuming. To improve the efficiency of spatial operations, the `geometries` objects need to be indexed. The Spatial cartridge provides its own spatial-optimized indexing implementation for relations containing geometries, which takes care of improving queries that make use of the spatial operations. The spatial index is based upon a R-tree implementation. The R-tree index provides the first level of filtering for the spatial operations. This is done by creating **Minimum Bounding Rectangles** (**MBRs**) for all inserted geometries, and then overlaying these MBRs to improve searching. The following diagram demonstrates the MBR for a (compound) polygon:

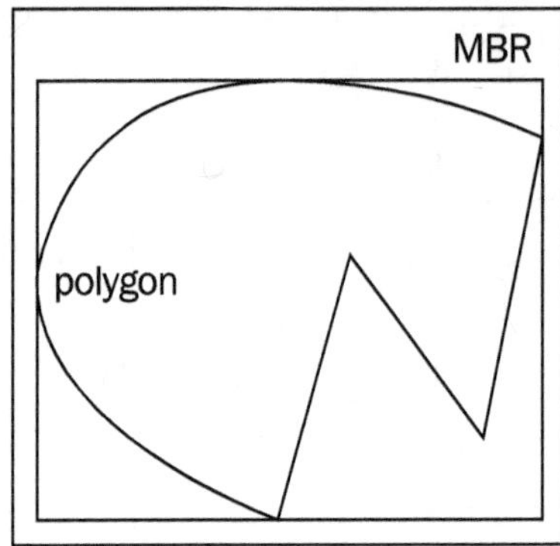

Next, let's take a look at a pictorial representation of how an R-tree would look after being used for indexing the `shopRelation` of the previous example:

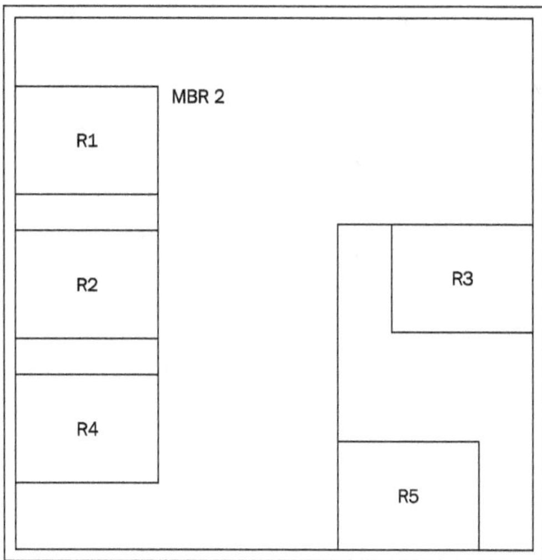

In this section, you learned how to make use of the spatial operations `contain`, `inside`, `anyinteract`, `withindistance`, and `nn` using the geometries you created in the previous section. Next, you will learn how to change the default settings of the spatial cartridge.

Configuring the spatial context

The spatial context provides the configuration needed when creating geometries, and using the spatial operations. You can define a spatial context in the EPN of the Oracle Event Processing application, as demonstrated in the following code snippet:

```
<beans xmlns="http://www.springframework.org/schema/beans"
       xmlns:xsi="http://www.w3.org/2001/XMLSchema-instance"
       xmlns:osgi="http://www.springframework.org/schema/osgi"
       xmlns:wlevs="http://www.bea.com/ns/wlevs/spring"
       xmlns:spatial="http://www.oracle.com/ns/ocep/spatial"
       xsi:schemaLocation="
  http://www.springframework.org/schema/beans
  http://www.springframework.org/schema/beans/spring-beans.xsd
  http://www.springframework.org/schema/osgi
  http://www.springframework.org/schema/osgi/spring-osgi.xsd
```

```
    http://www.bea.com/ns/wlevs/spring
    http://www.bea.com/ns/wlevs/spring/spring-wlevs-v11_1_1_6.xsd"
    http://www.oracle.com/ns/ocep/spatial
    http://www.oracle.com/ns/ocep/spatial/ocep-spatial.xsd">

    <spatial:context
      id="mySpatialContext"
      srid="0"
      tolerance="10"
    />

    <!-- EPN -->
  </beans>
```

Next, you can use this context in CQL, as shown in the following example:

```
SELECT
  Geometry.createPoint@mySpatialContext(i.x, i.y) as point
FROM
  inputChannel as i
```

As you have learned, the default spatial context, which is defined by the link name of `spatial`, uses the geodetic coordinate system. In the previous example, you changed the `createPoint()` and other spatial operations to instead use the Cartesian coordinate system.

The configuration parameters of a spatial context with their defaults are:

- **SMA**: This configuration defines the semi-major axis to be internally by the spatial operations when buffering and applying projections for geodetic geometries. Its default is 6378137.0.
- **ROF**: This configuration defines the reciprocal of flattening that may occur with the SMA parameter. It is likewise used for buffering and projection. Its default is 298.257223563.
- **tolerance**: This is the minimum distance to be ignored in geometric operations. The default is 0.000000001.

By now, you have gone through all the major features of the Spatial cartridge, and should be able to develop very useful and unique applications that make use of both time and space in Oracle Event Processing!

In this section, you learned how to use spatial in CQL. Next, you will learn how to extend CQL to interact directly to a RDBMS through JDBC.

Retrieving external tables using SQL

As you have learned in *Chapter 5, Coding with CQL*, CQL supports the concepts of both streams and relations. Relations are an abstract definition that can represent a database table. So much so that in *Chapter 7, Using Tables and Caches for Contextual Data*, you learned how to populate a relation with data coming from either a RBMS table or a distributed cache. This is done by respectively specifying a table or a cache and linking them to a processor in the EPN.

However, there are cases where you may need additional flexibility when retrieving data from a RDBMS table to be used in CQL. For example, you may need to invoke some PL/SQL function, or you may want to aggregate the data in some particular way before getting the result into CQL for the processing of events.

This fine-grained control can be achieved by using the JDBC cartridge. The JDBC cartridge allows you to define CQL functions whose implementation are done in SQL, and return collections to be treated as relations.

Let's look at the JDBC cartridge by means of a use case. One spatial function that is not supported by the Spatial cartridge in Oracle Event Processing 11*g* is the `touch` function. The `touch` function returns `true` if the boundaries of the geometries intersect. One potential use case for use of `touch` is to determine if a customer is in the entrance of a shop.

We can still use `touch` by going directly to the Oracle database and invoking the database's version of the spatial functions. The following SQL query illustrates this scenario:

```
SELECT shop.name, shop.type
FROM shopTable as shop
WHERE SDO_TOUCH(shop.rect,
  SDO_POINT(:xpos, :ypos)) = 'TRUE'
```

The SQL query has two parameters, which are `xpos` and `ypos`. It uses these parameters to create a point, and then checks if the point touches any of the rectangle geometries that represent the shops and are part of the `shopTable`. If the point touches any of the shops, the query returns the shop name and type (sells shoes).

The SDO package defines all the spatial-related types and functions for the Oracle Enterprise Database.

As it can be noted, this SQL query is making use of the `SDO_TOUCH` and `SDO_POINT` functions, which only exist in the Oracle database and therefore couldn't be invoked directly from CQL or by specifying a table component in the EPN.

To be able to make use of this SQL, you need to wrap it as a CQL table function. This is done by creating a JDBC cartridge context as follows:

```
<jc:jdbc-ctx>
    <name>myJdbcContext</name>
    <data-source>ShopDataSource</data-source>
    <function name="getShopsThatAreTouched">
        <param name="xpos" type="long" />
        <param name="ypos" type="long" />
        <return-component-type>
            packtpub.ioep.ShopInfo
        </return-component-type>
        <sql><![CDATA[
            SELECT shop.name, shop.type
            FROM shopTable as shop
            WHERE SDO_TOUCH(shop.rect,
                SDO_POINT(:xpos, :ypos)) = 'TRUE'
        ]]></sql>
    </function>
</jc:jdbc-ctx>
```

The `getShopsThatAreTouched()` function is a standard user-defined CQL function, however its implementation is done in SQL, rather than in Java. In the definition of this function, you need to specify the input arguments, which in this case are the parameters `xpos` and `ypos`, and the type of the returned component.

The actual execution of the SQL statement occurs in the database through the use of JDBC, therefore be aware of the additional latency. One way of improving this is to batch the processing of events using the API `com.bea.wlevs.ede.api.BatchStreamSender` and `com.bea.wlevs.ede.api.BatchRelationSender`.

It is very important to understand that a SQL query returns a table, that is, a collection of components. In this particular case, the query returns a row per shop that is touched by the point. Even if it is a single row, you have to keep in mind that the row is returned as part of a collection that potentially may have more than a single row. Therefore, in the CQL function's signature you need to specify the type of the row (or component) being returned. As a row generally has more than one column, you will generally specify the return component type as a complex type, that is, a Java-cartridge CQL extended type. Said complex type must support the setting of its component. In Java, this means that the Java Class must provide appropriate setters. In this particular case, it is specified as `ShopInfo`, whose Java class is defined as follows:

```
public class ShopInfo
{
  String name;
  String type;

  public String getName()
  {
    return name;
  }

  public void setName(String name)
  {
    this.name = name;
  }

  public String getType()
  {
    return type;
  }

  public void setType(String type)
  {
    this.type = type;
  }
}
```

The Java class must have both a setter and getter, as the JDBC cartridge uses the setter to populate the returned component, and the CQL query invoking the JDBC cartridge function (`getShopsThatAreTouched`) uses the getter to retrieve the columns' data. Likewise, the type of the JDBC cartridge function arguments can be any CQL type, including the Java-cartridge extended types. In this particular case, the parameters `xpos` and `ypos` are of type `long`.

The JDBC cartridge context has two additional configurations:

- `name`: This is the link ID used in the CQL queries to invoke the JDBC cartridge functions.
- `data-source`: This is the name of the data-source configuration that must exist in the server's global configuration that has access to the Oracle database in question being used.

The JDBC cartridge context must be part of the application's configuration, as in the following example:

```
<ocep:config
  xmlns:ocep="http://www.bea.com/ns/wlevs/config/application"
  xmlns:jc="http://www.oracle.com/ns/ocep/config/jdbc">

  <jc:jdbc-ctx>
    <name>myJdbcContext</name>
    <data-source>ShopDataSource</data-source>
    <function name="getShopsThatAreTouched">
      <param name="xpos" ""type=" long" />
      <param name="ypos" type="long" />
      <return-component-type>packtpub.oep.ShopInfo
      </return-component-type>
      <sql>
        <!-- SQL impl -->
      </sql>
    </function>
  </jc:jdbc-ctx>

  <processor>
    <name>Proc</name>
    <rules>
      <query id="q1">
        <!-- CQL impl -->
      </query>
    </rules>
  </processor>
</ocep:config>
```

The final aspect of this is the actual invocation of the JDBC cartridge functions in CQL. As expected, you need to specify a link name that maps to the JDBC cartridge context that defines the functions being invoked. However, there is one additional step. Remember how the functions are table functions that return collections, rather than a single element? Because of this, you need to make use of a TABLE construct in CQL, informing that the return of the called function represents a relation and therefore can be used in the CQL's FROM clause. This is demonstrated in the following code snippet:

```
SELECT loc.customerId, shopRelation.shopInfo.name
FROM
 locationStream[now] as loc,
 TABLE(
  getShopsThatAreTouched@myJdbcContext(loc.xpos, loc.ypos) AS
   shopInfo) as shopRelation
```

The table construct takes as argument a table function, and two aliases. The inner alias, in this case shopInfo, is associated to the return component (row), and the outer alias, in this case shopRelation, is associated as the name of the relation being created to support the table function.

Interestingly, the TABLE construct can be used not only with JDBC cartridge functions, but also with any function or Java method that returns a Java iterable type. This allows you to create relations on the fly, as shown in the following example:

```
SELECT loc.customerId, addrRelation.addrInfo.tel
FROM
 locationStream[now] as loc,
 TABLE(
  getShopsThatAreTouched@myJdbcContext(loc.xpos, loc.ypos) AS
  shopInfo) as shopRelation,
 TABLE(packtput.oep.Shop.getPhoneNumbers(
  shopRelation.shopInfo.name)
   AS addrInfo OF CHAR) AS addrRelation
```

The Shop.getPhoneNumbers() method is naively implemented in the following code:

```
public static List<String> getPhoneNumbers(String shopName)
{
  // Map<String, List<String>> directory = ...
  return directory.get(shopName);
}
```

When used with Java methods, you need to explicitly define the type of the return component by using the `OF` clause. In this case, as the method returns a list of Strings, the `OF` clause is specified as a `String` (native CQL `CHAR`).

As you can see, the combination of the `TABLE` construct with the JDBC cartridge allows you to leverage advanced features of external databases and systems.

Summary

In this chapter you learned how to create different geometry types in CQL using the Spatial cartridge, such as points, rectangles, and arbitrary polygons. The geometry objects are layered on different coordinate systems. The Cartesian coordinate system and the geodetic coordinate system are supported.

Next, you learned how to use different spatial operations. These operations allow you to determine if a geometry contains, is inside, is within distance, or interacts with another geometry. Further, you can find the nearest neighbor a geometry in relation to another collection of geometries. All of these spatial operations are executed in memory during processing of CQL queries and optimized by being indexed using an R-tree data structure.

A spatial context can be created in the EPN to set spatial-related configuration, such as the default coordinate system to be used.

You also learned how to use the JDBC cartridge to invoke any arbitrary SQL statement. This is done by wrapping the SQL statements as CQL table functions. Table functions are functions that return a collection of components and thus can be materialized as a CQL relation in the `FROM` clause.

In the next and final chapter, you will look into the future of Oracle Event Processing

12

Looking Ahead: The Future of Oracle Event Processing

In this chapter, we will consider the future of Oracle Event Processing and describe some of the many ways this technology may evolve over the coming years. The topics we will cover are as follows:

- Possible technology strategic directions
- Evolving development environments
- Service-oriented architecture integration
- Event intelligence on the computing edge with sensor integration
    - Digital inclusion
    - M2M – enabling the Internet of Things
- Fast data for big data enablement
- Looking around the corner with predictive analytics
- Advancing performance with hardware embedded
- The growing event processing standards

Possible technology strategic directions

The future for Event Processing is bright, filled with innovation and growth. We expect that over the next few years many new businesses will adopt and embrace these next generation platforms that do not force you to conform to the limitations of imposed, rather mechanical, technology implementations but is designed as life is itself, to handle a world full of events that bombard you all the time, from many different sources and in most cases in many unexpected ways.

As you have learnt through the proceeding chapters, Oracle Event Processing has been architected to create and enable boundless numbers of powerful event-driven applications that can provide a self awareness and self discovery approach that some day may let machines manage and control many aspects of a person's lifestyle. Humans are fast, but machines are faster and traditional legacy technologies for business are in many cases just not "equipped" for the demands of the future. Event-driven features may eventually be bonded into the hardware itself, as we discuss later, driving instantaneous response times not in microseconds but nanoseconds and beyond.

While all industries have a place for Oracle Event Processing, the *Internet of Things* as it relates to telecommunications, transportation and energy and in particular, health and life sciences will unleash a new breed of solutions. Entertainment monitoring will spawn another collection of Event Processing solutions, from smart next generation theme parks, to online gaming, with a collection of use cases only limited by ones imagination from improving a guests experience to sample as many rides as possible in the shortest period of time or trapping fraudulent playing event patterns in a game of poker.

Other examples of these next generation solutions for telecommunications will provide dynamic manipulation of everyone's communication smart devices, switching services from standard cellular networking to digital WIFI optimizing and thus reducing critical overloading based on a person's temporal static spatial movement patterns. A new generation of biodata analysis devices will emerge that constantly monitor body event patterns and functions watching for a fluctuation that might be the difference between life and death. In fact, ones entire existence as a citizen of the world can be, and probably will be monitored to improve the quality of life and effectively protect it:

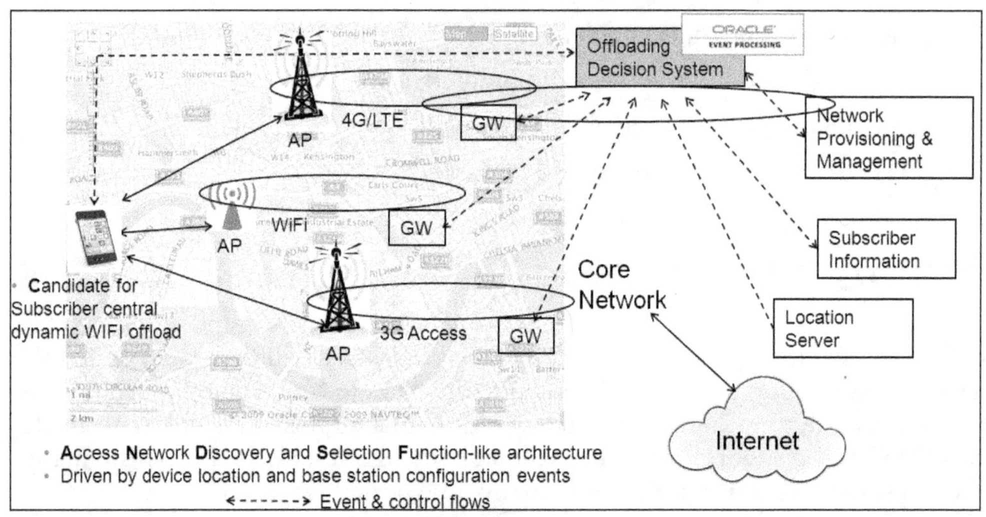

In this chapter we will take a look at just some of the technology advancements where Oracle Event Processing may focus to further enable these business needs and give you an exciting insight to those capabilities.

Evolving developer environments

The ongoing need to create innovative event-driven solutions quickly, efficiently and to comprehend the vast array of emerging features is always a challenge for developers. The fact that Oracle Event Processing is 100 percent Java platform-based does blend itself to enabling a large community of software developers already familiar with this language.

However, continuing to simplify the developer experience of Oracle Event Processing is always a major goal. With the many Oracle products there is a growing demand to integrate and consolidate the development capabilities from the many diverse coding disciplines ranging from WebLogic Server Web application creation to the definition of SOA EDN events using the **Event Definition Language** (**EDL**). All of this functionality provided in a single development environment will enable this collective innovative community to more rapidly create, test, implement, and maintain holistic solutions that encompass not only Oracle Event Processing but also Oracle Service-orientated Architecture and Java Enterprise Edition solutions at the same time.

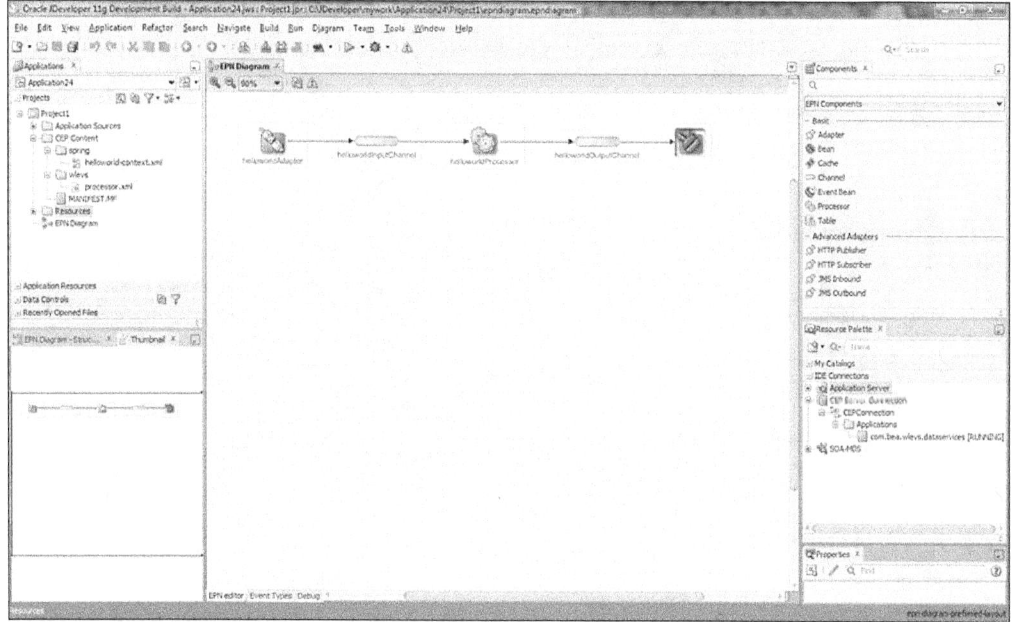

The Oracle JDeveloper **Integrated Development Environment** (**IDE**) would be a logical choice to embrace this initiative and is a free development platform that simplifies the evolution of Java-based SOA and Java EE applications. JDeveloper offers complete end-to-end development for Oracle Fusion Middleware and Oracle Fusion Applications with support for the full development life cycle. Consequently to include a substantially enhanced collection of Oracle Event Processing application development capabilities in JDeveloper that emulate what is currently available in the plugin environment for the Eclipse IDE, would bring together a new and exciting **Event Stream Processing** (**ESP**) dimension.

These capabilities would augment the existing Eclipse Developer capabilities by additionally including a more wizard-based approach to the creation of Event Processing Network artifacts, such as Event Adapters and Event Processors. A new event adapter palette of out of the box event driven items could be available that will immensely simplify the "drag-and-drop" construction of applications, ease of maintenance and a significantly reduced time to production deployments.

Service-oriented Architecture integration

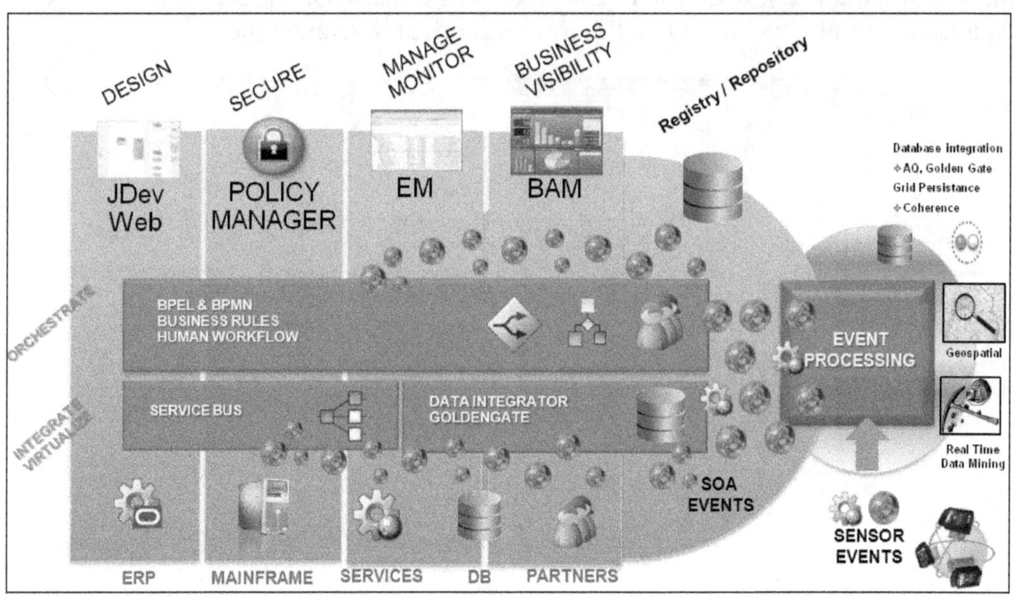

A more productive integration with other SOA technologies could be realized by enabling the definition and integration of familiar SOA frameworks such as the EDN, the Event Delivery Network. This event-driven framework emits and consumes business events from the various components of SOA and Business Process platforms such as when an event message is placed on an Enterprise Service Bus message queue or when a new Business Process starts.

All of the events used by the EDN are stored in a common repository which can be interrogated and used by an Integrated Development Environment so the creation and modification of each event type definition will be significantly simplified. In addition, these persisted event definitions can now be used globally across not only a single application but any application that can connect to the repository.

As with the EDN integration, embedding with the **Oracle WebLogic Server** (**WLS**) **Java Enterprise Edition** (**JEE**) so that the CEP engine itself is directly available, enabling other communities of Java developers to leverage the power of the CQL, with the caveat that this is for a category of applications that may not need the performance and low latencies as in most event-driven solutions, but may still require the analysis of a complex set of SOA business events.

Event intelligence on the computing edge with Sensor integration

A major artifact of the *Internet of Things* is Sensor devices. These types of event-driven equipment can range dramatically from a relatively "dumb" temperature sensor that may transmit an ID followed by an environmental value on a fairly constant basis, to sophisticated analysis sensors that not only detect movement, but combine with the distribution of light sensitivity, accelerometer movement (otherwise known as tilt or gesture analysis) and even radar movement assessment providing an advanced fusion sensor architecture that does not just rely on one integrated sensor but consolidates all of sensors together to make more intelligent assessments.

Over the past few years, we have encountered most of these types of sensors and even a collection of more obscure sensing devices. A common sensor now that is often integrated with Oracle Event Processing is the **Sensor Platform for Oracle Technology** (**SPOT**). This kind of Oracle sensor is popular with the academic communities around the world and the basic device has three layers, the first being a sensor board (intrusion, humidity, temperature, shock), the next layer is the processor board with support for GPS, GPRS, Iridium communication and finally, a battery, which does not have an extended life, but holds enough power for a few hours. The SPOT is connected using wireless communication and supports both Mesh Networking and over the air programming. The user programs executing on this device are entirely in Java and it is estimated that over 25,000 of these SPOT devices being used worldwide.

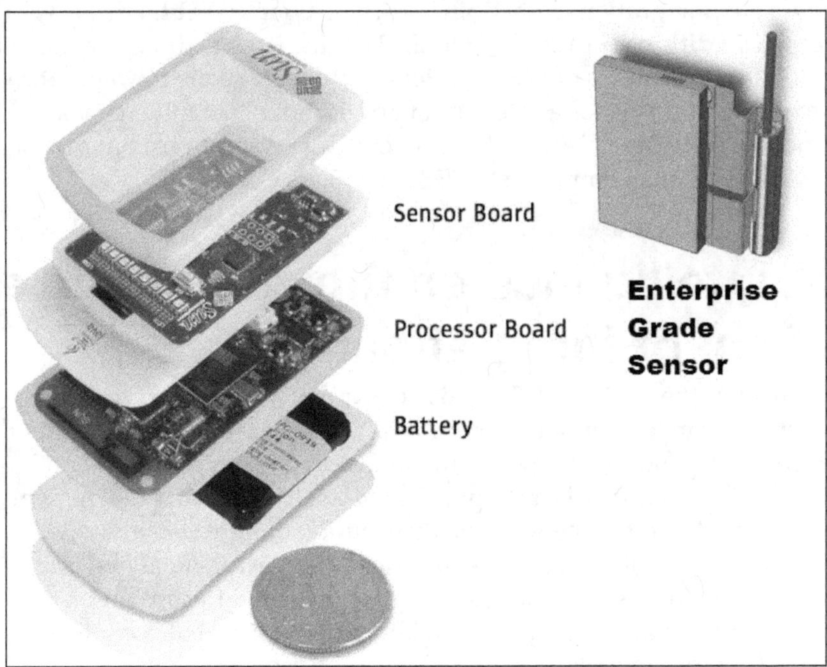

Fairly recently, the SPOT device has evolved into a much more commercially accepted Enterprise grade sensor, which has many applications, such as part of a shipping container tracking solution, where it is a self-contained, self-sufficient unit with a very long, possibly days of, extended battery life which has additional satellite communication and embraces the sensor fusion architecture.

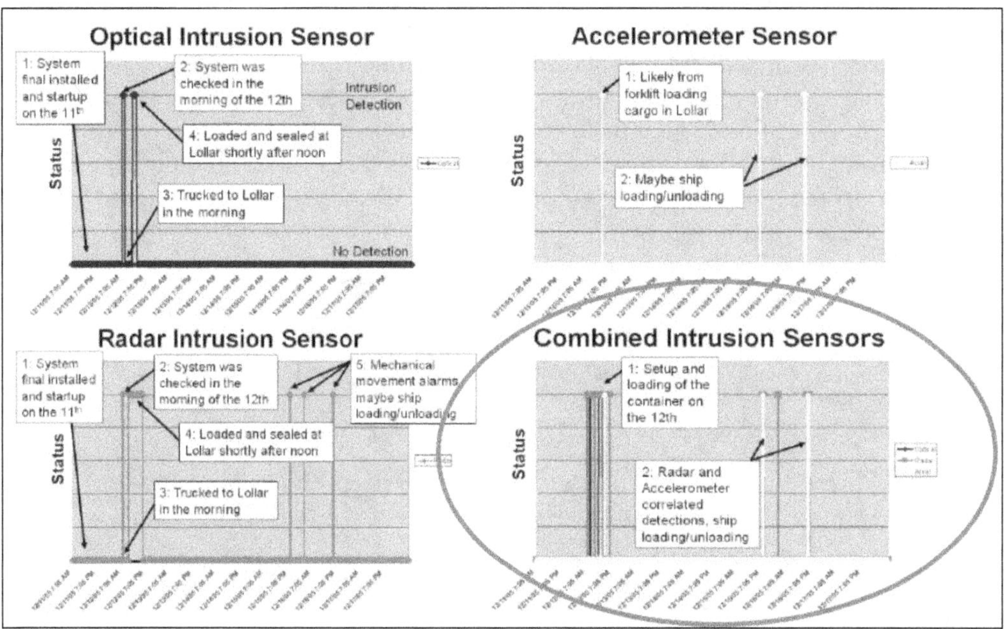

We have already discussed in much detail the use of devices in various geo-spatial and geo-streaming analysis scenarios using GPS signals, which applies not only to transportation, but also to a wide varying collection of possible military applications. As we delve deeper into this topic let's now imagine and focus on a world of Digital Inclusion.

Digital Inclusion is part of another vast array of Event-Driven use cases that we often call Smart Cities, where every aspect of a person's life and their communities are monitored and managed. Just a few of these monitored life elements could include a person's movement patterns around the home, individual and collective vehicle and traffic flow management, surrounding pollution and general environment monitoring and management, personal usage of utilities, water, power, and shopping pattern analysis. This latter use case is a common requirement in the retail industry where immediate, personalized and targeted coupons or offer incentives can be provided to shoppers based on their real-time movement patterns. These are just a few capabilities for Smart City solutions. Digital Inclusion itself is a fascinating topic as it requires a large amount of varied sensing devices and ensures that everyone could benefit from event-driven technologies, even those with medical issues such as those with significant mental disabilities.

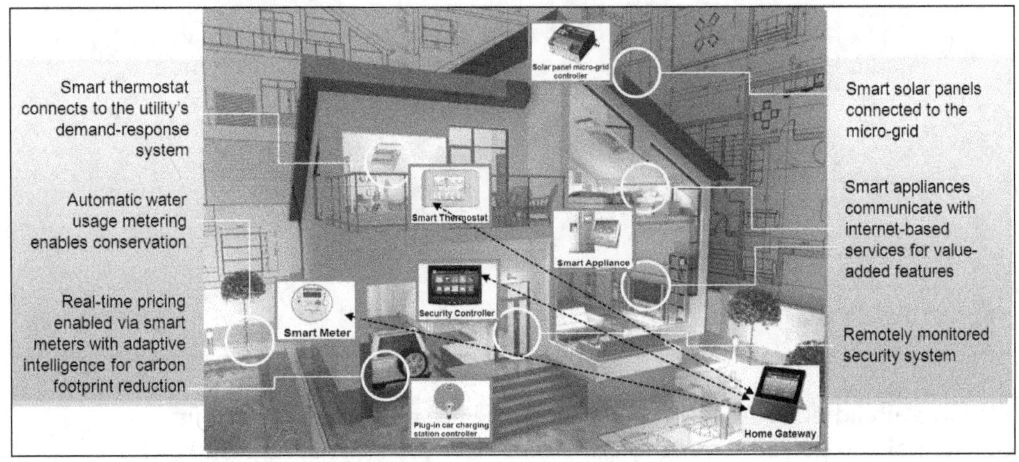

These people suffering with, for example, dementia, could have their daily movement patterns monitored with a connected Smart Home of the future, using floor sensors, their food and beverage consumption and menus monitored with sensor tags on each food or drink item, and an accelerometer sensor as part of each utensil, this so that each unique movement event pattern when stirring a coffee or making a cake can be recorded. A whole collection of individual environmental sensors could be included to monitor the surrounding temperature, humidity, and light sensitivity to help maintain a complete real-time event life pattern analysis of that individual patient. So that repetitive acceptable life patterns are ignored, but on that one occurrence when his or her life pattern is abnormal and indicates a potential danger, then a mission critical event-driven solution can notify nearby emergency services to react and avert a possible life threatening situation.

Before we close this introduction on the Oracle Event Processing Sensor integration strategy, we should also touch on **Machine-to-Machine** (**M2M**) enablement.

M2M is basically a framework that allows devices to communicate with business applications or other automated intelligent devices. M2M has a whole slew of related characteristics, such as dealing with a multitude of different devices with different features, low powered, generally critical in nature, limited functionality, and no human intervention. Most M2M solutions now, such as a remote hardware printer management and monitoring platform, are custom and one-off propriety solutions, and if assembled separately would frequently have issues with latency in response times, data loss, resilience, low agility, no diagnostics, and high support costs.

As we look to the future, we envisage Oracle Event Processing as the core component of a published reference M2M architecture that encompasses the three main domains—the device, the Java platform, and the associated streaming data. This would provide an integrated event processing system to track and analyze data in real time enabling real-time intelligence on the device, which leads us to the powerful embedding capabilities now supported by Oracle Event Processing, enabled with by the OSGi-based architecture discussed later in this chapter.

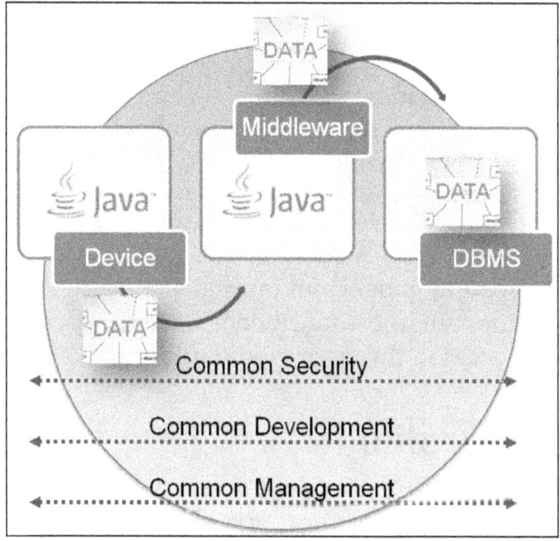

Due to its modular implementation architecture, Oracle Event Processing blends itself to enabling another new world of event-driven intelligence on the "edge", with some businesses already using this technology, discovering that they can "manipulate" the Oracle Event Processing Java Container and unleash its powerful event analysis on a new collection of "smart" devices that had past restrictions because of the available disk and memory footprints. Using the embedded profile it could be possible to not only leverage this technology at the Enterprise tier but at both the department and computing "edge" tiers.

Event container platform manipulation profiles

An embedded profile, and the many other profiles that may arrive in the future is a capability that has its concept history entrenched back in the early days of the products design and evolution, and came from demands that businesses would like to have complete flexibility in configuring an event server Java container technology for any specific type of domain or machine implementation. This would provide the ability to use an event-driven platform in very specific ways, to solve any specific collection of related event-driven business problems in a very distributed and scalable architecture.

This powerful technology implementation capability goes far beyond what most, if not all, other current software vendors can deliver, providing a business methodology to manipulate every functionality module component within the product stack.

Hence a main design goal for Oracle Event Processing was to be built on an Equinox OSGi-based backbone, leveraging existing mature services from the WebLogic Server platform such as the threading model and management, logging and a web container and then "layering" on top with those additional services specific to event-driven requirements, all constructed in this very modular fashion.

The Embedded profile

An Embedded OSGi profile for Oracle Event Processing, when available could be configured to enable functionality appropriate for edge device deployments, where there is limited device or gateway processor power, memory, or disk foot print. For example, to optimize memory usage, GUI management tool capabilities could be removed (command line is supported), clustering, event record/playback, a subset of adapters, spatial and JDBC data cartridges could also be removed. Also the Oracle Coherence bundle could be removed as generally, this in-memory caching data grid capability would be defined and managed at the Enterprise Tier. For more details on the configuration of the embedded profile see the future Oracle Event Processing documentation.

Embedding Oracle Event Processing on edge devices allows initial processing, such as early event filtering and pattern matching, to be pushed to the actual event sources which will improve scalability and responsiveness for the entire solution. This additional level of "intelligence on the edge" also distributes the processing analysis to encourage extremely high performance.

Determining the Oracle Event Processing modules that will be loaded and used is specified during the Server startup and so the required command could be defined as follows, depending of the operating system involved:

```
-./startwlevs.sh -disableregistry -loadFeatureSet com.bea.wlevs.embedded
```

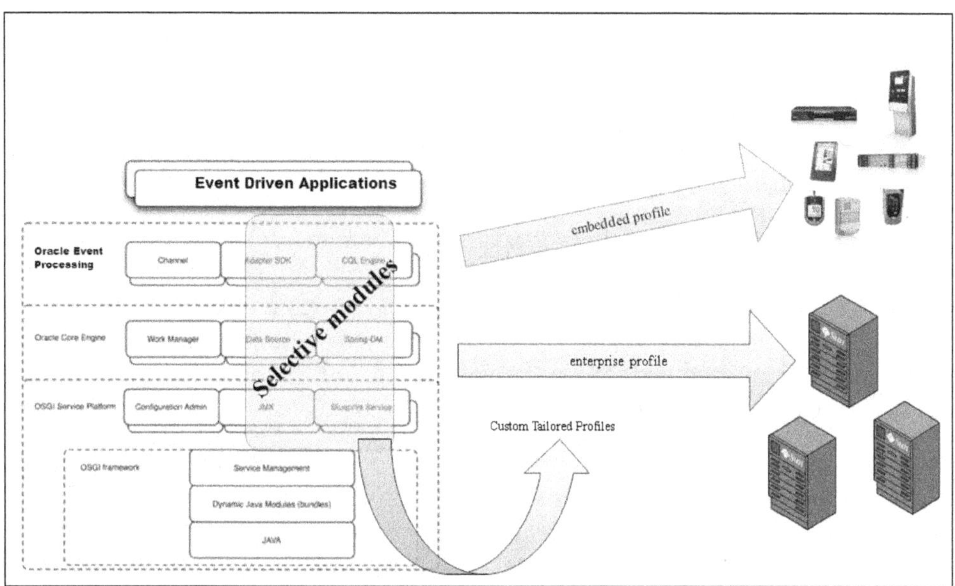

This enablement of intelligent edge event processing will ensure a highly scaleable and distributed event-driven architecture, encourages another endless collection of opportunities which now arise due to this unique functionality, and as these features evolve may need to be the subject of another specialized publication.

Fast Data for Big Data

As we have highlighted many times in this book, the *Internet of Things*, including a vast array of sensor devices, streaming video data, more diverse and complicated business applications and the exploding world of online social media outlets have given rise to a proliferation of not only structured, but now unstructured data that needs to be stored and analyzed efficiently and effectively. This demand has driven a new data persistence domain called Big Data.

Big Data is being defined in many different ways, and in many cases the views and definitions by the various vendors vary and are generally swayed in favor of their particular solutions. However, in general, it is agreed that Big Data is categorized using the three *Vs*. This refers firstly, to the *Volume* of data that now exists and will substantially increase of the coming years, then we have the *Velocity* of the data which can, in many cases stream into a company's computing infrastructure at data rates making it virtually impossible to analyze effectively before most of its time sensitive value has perished. Finally there is the *Variety* of the data, which may be formed of unstructured information that can arrive in many ways, from many diverse event sources such as **Instant Messenger** (**IM**) text messages or comments from social media data feeds, or from video cameras now populating most towns and cities around the globe.

Oracle Event Processing could provide features to interact transparently with Big Data stores such as the **Hadoop Distributed File System** (**HDFS**) and Oracle NoSQL Database, and would subsequently provide a holistic Fast Big Data solution platform that enables businesses to "Get ahead of the Curve".

So Oracle Event Processing, in this context is now being classified as Fast Data, that fills the real-time processing analysis latency gap inherent in many Big Data implementations, to filter out "noise" (stock data ticks with no change), add context (by correlating multiple sources) and increase relevance, identifying certain critical conditions as you insert data into a data warehouse and therefore, move time-critical analysis to the front of the process.

A typical example would be to leverage Big Data for the long-term historical analysis of traffic patterns and congestion for future urban planning—where to build a new road or position new traffic signals, using country wide image traffic cameras. However, at the same time use Fast Data, Oracle Event Processing for the monitoring in real time of the metadata from these cameras to ensure license plates/tags are not used on multiple vehicles in different towns at the same time, immediately alerting law enforcement or security agencies on these suspicious circumstances for response and resolution. In conjunction with facial recognition cameras on bridges and traffic light gantries, this use case could be extended to immediately identify who possibly may be driving the offending vehicle, and whether they have a criminal record or are flagged on some kind of "watch list".

Other Fast Data value in monitoring the streaming metadata from traffic cameras could be for real-time Toll Road charging, so that individual vehicles would be levied an immediate cost based on the current congestion, time of day and perhaps, even weather conditions.

These kinds of solutions would need a comprehensive hardware and software architecture that would not only encompass an Event Processing technology but would also need transparent Big Data integration to quickly profile the vehicles and drivers, perhaps an in-memory prediction/behavioral product to assess possible next location movement patterns, a method to effectively visualize the information and inevitably Engineered Systems/Hardware to handle the massive amounts of stored data and the required processing power.

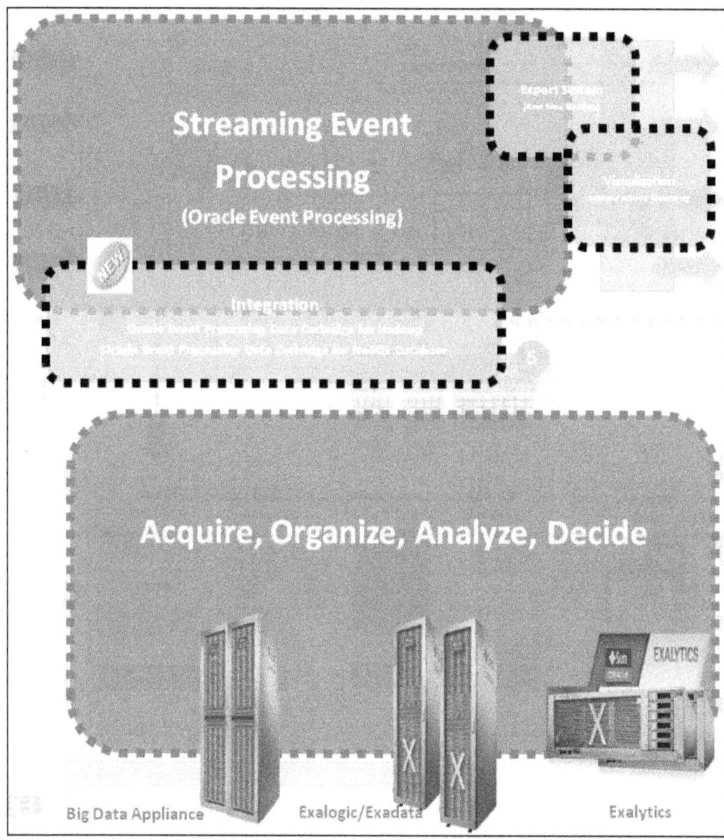

So an additional *V* is for the *Value* that can now be extracted from this data even before it is stored in Big Data using Oracle Event Processing. Understanding the veracity in these Big Data event streams will become an ever increasing challenge for a business and combining Oracle Event Processing together with Big Data offerings, a complete Fast Big Data platform will mature to effectively address these needs.

Fast data sample

If we delve more into the potential use of Oracle Event Processing as the Fast Data solution for Big Data, we can explore the basic principles on how a possible basic event-driven application can be implemented with the required integration to the HDFS. To kick off, assuming Hadoop has been successfully installed on the required operating system (we will assume Linux in the following scenario) the start script for Oracle Event Processing (`startwlevs.sh`) should be slightly modified to add this location:

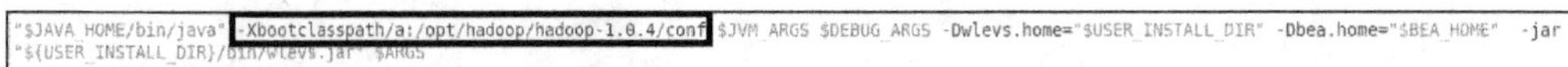

"$JAVA_HOME/bin/java" -Xbootclasspath/a:/opt/hadoop/hadoop-1.0.4/conf $JVM_ARGS $DEBUG_ARGS -Dwlevs.home="$USER_INSTALL_DIR" -Dbea.home="$BEA_HOME" -jar
"${USER_INSTALL_DIR}/bin/wlevs.jar" $ARGS

As the application is constructed, the access to the data in the HDFS could be defined in the associated Projects String context file. In the case of this hypothetical solution, the data that will be referenced in the CQL is using a path called `/events/message.txt`:

```
EPN: com.oracle.fastdataHadoop    hadoopfile-context.xml
            <wlevs:property name="serial" type="bigint"/>
            <wlevs:property name="sender" type="int"/>
            <wlevs:property name="senderName" type="char"/>
            <wlevs:property name="weight" type="float"/>
            <wlevs:property name="message" type="char"/>
        </wlevs:properties>
        </wlevs:event-type>
    </wlevs:event-type-repository>

    <hadoop:file id="messageFile" event-type="Message" path="/events/message.txt" separator=","/>

    <!-- Adapter can be created from a local class, without having to go through a adapter factory -->
    <wlevs:adapter id="helloworldAdapter" class="com.oracle.fastdatahadoop.HelloWorldAdapter" advertise="true" >
        <wlevs:instance-property name="suspended" value="false"/>
    </wlevs:adapter>

    <wlevs:channel id="helloworldInputChannel" event-type="MessageEvent" advertise="true">
        <wlevs:listener ref="helloworldProcessor"/>
        <wlevs:source ref="helloworldAdapter"/>
    </wlevs:channel>

    <!-- The default processor for OCEP 11.0.0.0 is CQL -->
    <wlevs:processor id="helloworldProcessor" >
        <wlevs:table-source ref="messageFile"/>
    </wlevs:processor>

    <wlevs:channel id="helloworldOutputChannel" event-type="SMSEvent" advertise="true">
        <wlevs:listener>
            <bean class="com.oracle.fastdatahadoop.HelloWorldBean"/>
        </wlevs:listener>
        <wlevs:source ref="helloworldProcessor"/>
```

The **Event Processing Network (EPN)** sample application, which in this case could be a simple extension to the standard "hello world" application would have the message file visualized with an event node that is directly connected to the processor node:

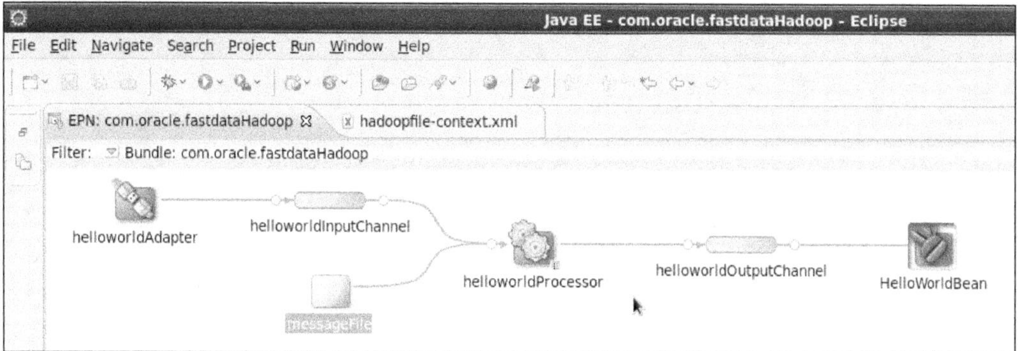

The CQL in this case, held in the **helloworldProcessor** event node, checks if the MessageEvent's "messageNumber" can be found in `message.txt` file's field called `serial`:

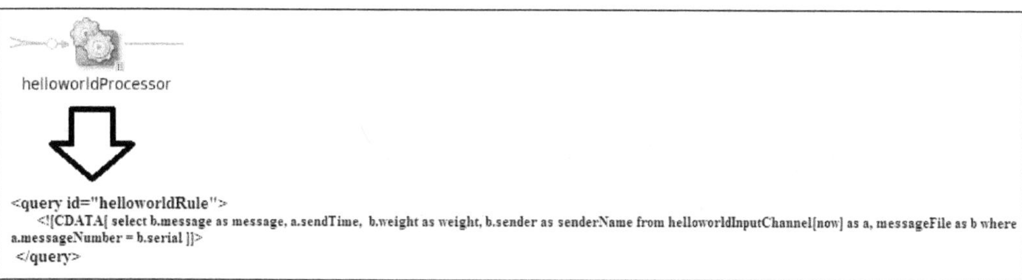

As this sample would be using a new Oracle Event Processing Data Cartridge for Hadoop as one would expect, the application's manifest file would also have a reference to this capability. The specific name of this data cartridge could be `com.oracle.cep.cartridge.hadoop.spring`.

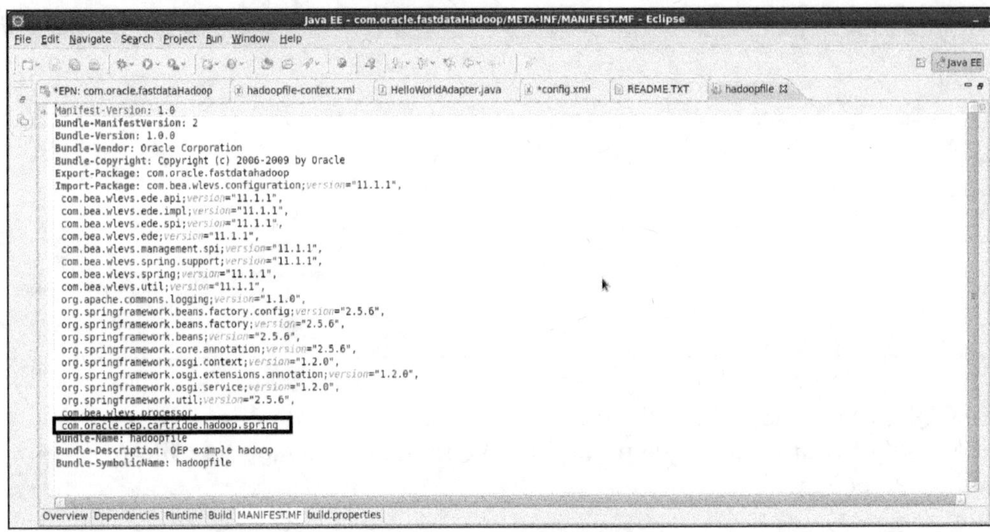

Finally, the possible application output in a console could show the interaction with the Hadoop system and the relevant results. More details on this type of capability may evolve in subsequent versions of Oracle Event Processing. So watch out for emerging samples on **Oracle Technology Network (OTN)** pages.

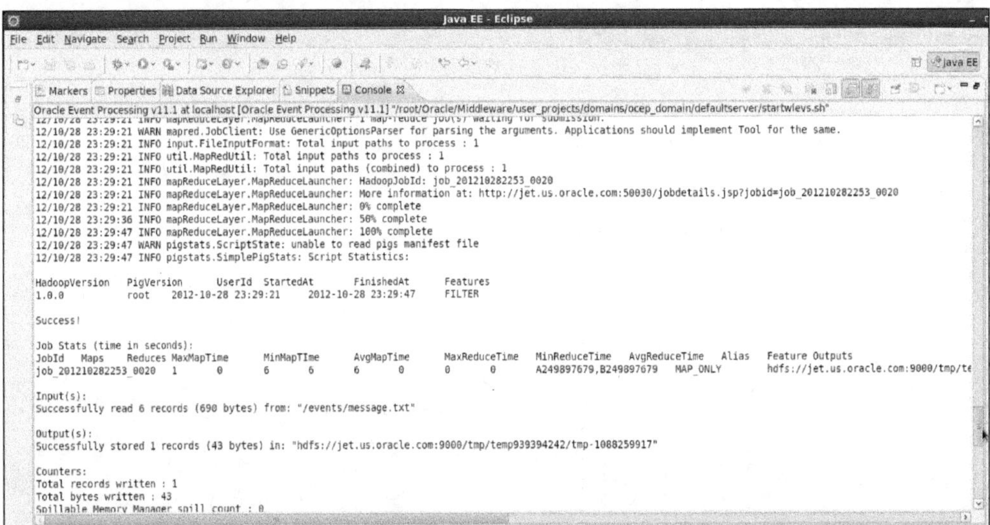

Looking around the corner with predictive analytics

In the same way as we discussed "Getting ahead of the Curve" in relation to Big Data, Oracle Event Processing solutions invariably entail some form of Predictive Event Analysis requirements to anticipate and prepare for longer term situations as a business's solutions become more advanced and they want to "Look around the Corner".

In many cases, Oracle Event Processing facilitates various methods for Predictive Analysis, for example, the identification of a single event, or collection of events in a pattern can indicate with much certainty, that a future event or set of events will also occur. This can be achieved using the standard integral features already available in the technology. However the ability to leverage longer term data, collected over a period of weeks, months, or years and then using a "model" from this data to score against current streaming event data is sometimes also needed. This is a more "fuzzy" prediction and the scoring results are never usually 100 percent certain, but will provide enough accuracy to determine an action in your EPN processing.

More on analytics

Before we study a possible related use case and the concepts of future Oracle Event Processing predictive capabilities, let's broadly touch upon the meaning of analytics.

Analytics is generally the analysis of data, in a batch processing oriented mode, for patterns, trends, insights, and what-if scenarios and encompasses two broad categories

- Precise
- Predictive or probabilistic

The short-term Precise category can relate to the scenario described at the beginning of this section already supported by Oracle Event Processing. The second provides for Frontline Analytics that is the analysis of data "in motion" (Real Time Streaming Predictive Analytics) using Data at Rest, which is from persisted information in a relational database, or data that is accumulated and modeled in memory.

These more "fuzzy" kinds of predictive analytics can be achieved by integrating additional Oracle or other vendors technologies, such as Oracle Real Time Decisions (RTD) an in-memory behavioral and prediction engine or using various techniques available with the **Oracle Data Mining** (**ODM**) solution, which is an option of the Oracle Relational Database Management System Enterprise Edition. This technology contains many data mining and data analysis algorithms such as classification, prediction, regression, associations, anomaly detection, feature extraction, and more specialized analytics.

A Predicting Use Case

Let's review, at a high level, the steps one could use for predicting fraud in an insurance monitoring scenario, where vehicle insurance claims are being constantly "streamed" and visualized using a solution platform, from all over the state of California:

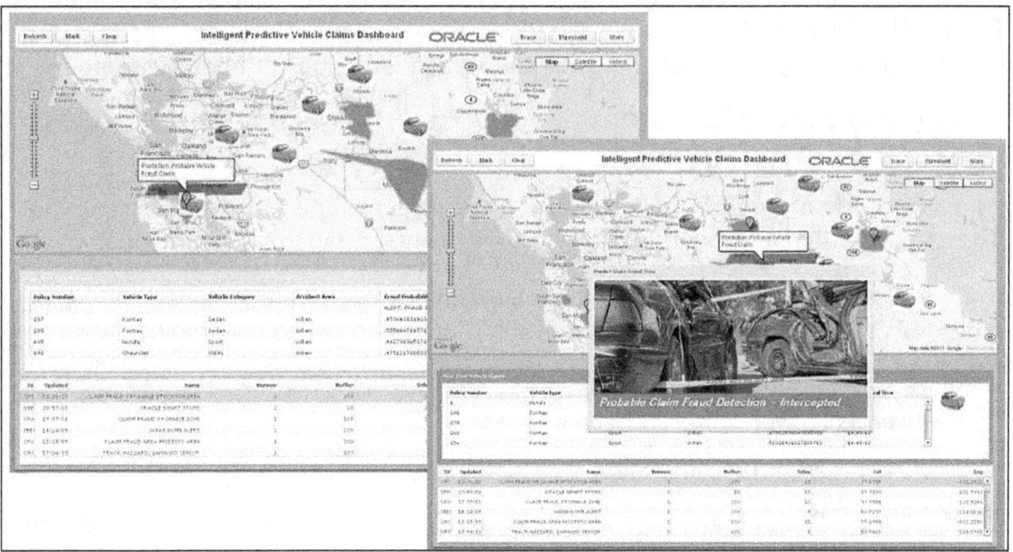

Based on the long history information stored in an Oracle Enterprise Edition database for each insured driver and all of the past claim data, a prediction model can be dynamically created and used by the Oracle Event Processing CQL engine to compare each new insurance claim streaming event with this model resulting in a related "score" that will reflect the likelihood of a fraudulent claim submission. The results of each analysis could then be simply reflected on the output console, sent to another technology for downstream analysis or shown visually on a real time command and control dashboard display that could portray the current vehicle location and owner details who is now submitting the claim.

This kind of solution can be achieved by combining Oracle Event Processing with Oracle Data Mining and leverages the latter's rich set of algorithms and functionality to do predictive analytics on the available historical data with the real time model scoring on the individual streaming insurance claim events performed by Oracle Event Processing.

This introduces another capability to extend the event-driven platform by invoking any arbitrary external computation using RDBMS from within the CQL engine and this extensibility facility is known as the JDBC Data Cartridge.

Understanding the "Fuzzy" results

When executing this type of solution, unlike the precise pattern matching results in other Oracle Event Processing applications, we can see how the returned responses from the scoring processing provides only an **indication** of possible issues with the specific insurance claims. To emphasize the kind of analysis provided, below are two events from an extract of some possible console output: one relatively "normal" and other relatively "abnormal".

A "normal" looking output event could have its probability of being anomalous being less than 60 percent (%).

```
Event is: eventType=DataMiningOutEvent object=q1  time=2904821976256
S.CQLMONTH=Dec, S.WEEKOFMONTH=5, S.DAYOFWEEK=Wednesday, S.MAKE=Honda,
S.ACCIDENTAREA=Urban, S.DAYOFWEEKCLAIMED=Tuesday, S.MONTHCLAIMED=Jan,
S.WEEKOFMONTHCLAIMED=1, S.SEX=Female, S.MARITALSTATUS=Single,
S.AGE=21, S.FAULT=Policy Holder, S.POLICYTYPE=Sport - Liability,
S.VEHICLECATEGORY=Sport, S.VEHICLEPRICE=more than 69000, S.FRAUDFOUND=0,
S.POLICYNUMBER=1, S.REPNUMBER=12, S.DEDUCTIBLE=300, S.DRIVERRATING=1,
S.DAYSPOLICYACCIDENT=more than 30, S.DAYSPOLICYCLAIM=more than 30,
S.PASTNUMOFCLAIMS=none, S.AGEOFVEHICLES=3 years, S.AGEOFPOLICYHOLDER=26
to 30, S.POLICEREPORTFILED=No, S.WITNESSPRESENT=No, S.AGENTTYPE=External,
S.NUMOFSUPP=none, S.ADDRCHGCLAIM=1 year, S.NUMOFCARS=3 to 4,
S.CQLYEAR=1994, S.BASEPOLICY=Liability, probability=.58931702982118561
isTotalOrderGuarantee=true\nAnamoly probability: .58931702982118561
```

An "abnormal" output event that indicates a possible anomaly could have a much higher probability result of 89 percent. The determination of the scoring percentage that indicates either, normal or abnormal is fairly subjective and really depends on the use case and **Service Level Agreement** (**SLA**) thresholds determined by the specific business.

However, in terms of an insurance claim situation, when your event-driven solution application does identify a higher probability result and there is likely to be something wrong with it, this particular request could be passed for human intervention where a close look would reveal that the value of the "deductible" field {10} is not "normal", and has influenced the analysis.

What exactly constitutes normal here? This requires further research but for example, if you run a query on the database to find all distinct values for the "deductible" field and it returned the set `{300, 400, 500, 700}`, as the amounts generally selected by customers, then a value `{10}` would seem suspicious.

```
Event is: eventType=DataMiningOutEvent object=q1  time=2598483773496
S.CQLMONTH=Dec, S.WEEKOFMONTH=5, S.DAYOFWEEK=Wednesday, S.MAKE=Honda,
S.ACCIDENTAREA=Urban, S.DAYOFWEEKCLAIMED=Tuesday, S.MONTHCLAIMED=Jan,
S.WEEKOFMONTHCLAIMED=1, S.SEX=Female, S.MARITALSTATUS=Single,
S.AGE=21, S.FAULT=Policy Holder, S.POLICYTYPE=Sport - Liability,
S.VEHICLECATEGORY=Sport, S.VEHICLEPRICE=more than 69000, S.FRAUDFOUND=0,
S.POLICYNUMBER=1, S.REPNUMBER=12, S.DEDUCTIBLE=10, S.DRIVERRATING=1,
S.DAYSPOLICYACCIDENT=more than 30, S.DAYSPOLICYCLAIM=more than 30,
S.PASTNUMOFCLAIMS=none, S.AGEOFVEHICLES=3 years, S.AGEOFPOLICYHOLDER=26
to 30, S.POLICEREPORTFILED=No, S.WITNESSPRESENT=No, S.AGENTTYPE=External,
S.NUMOFSUPP=none, S.ADDRCHGCLAIM=1 year, S.NUMOFCARS=3 to 4,
S.CQLYEAR=1994, S.BASEPOLICY=Liability, probability=.89171554529576691
isTotalOrderGuarantee=true\nAnamoly probability: .89171554529576691
```

Extending insurance solutions and JDBC data cartridge summary

Other sophisticated solutions by insurance companies could be evolved that would combine more event properties streaming from individual motor vehicles, where each vehicle would have an embedded Oracle Event Processing technology that is immediately and constantly determining the driver's profile in terms of excessive breaking, swerving corners at high speed, not driving on the correct side of the road, performance in bad weather conditions, and so on. Vehicle insurance companies could then use these capabilities for including services such as dynamic variable insurance charging each week or month based on this real-time analysis.

To conclude, the JDBC Data Cartridge is another Oracle Event Processing enabling capability that can be used within the Event processor engine that lets you execute a SQL query against a database, and then use it's returned results in a CQL query. This functionality being achieved by associating, the SQL query with a JDBC cartridge function definition, as we show below in this sample code extract:

```
<?xml version="1.0" encoding="UTF-8"?>
<jdbcctxconfig:config
```

```
    xmlns:jdbcctxconfig="http://www.bea.com/ns/wlevs/config/
application"
    xmlns:jc="http://www.oracle.com/ns/ocep/config/jdbc">
    <jc:jdbc-ctx>
        <name>Oracle11gR2</name>
        <data-source>DataMining</data-source>
        <function name="prediction2">
            <param name="CQLMONTH" type="char"/>
            <param name=". . . . . . . . . . . . .
            <return-component-type>char</return-component-type>

        <sql><![CDATA[
            SELECT to_char(PREDICTION_PROBABILITY(CLAIMSMODEL, '0'
USING *))
                AS probability
            FROM (
                SELECT      :CQLMONTH AS MONTH,
                            :. . . . . . . . . . .
                FROM dual)
             ]]>
        </sql>
        </function>
    </jc:jdbc-ctx>
</jdbcctxconfig:config>
```

Using a CQL query you can subsequently call the JDBC cartridge function, which executes the associated SQL query against the database. In terms of the specific implementation, the function call must be enclosed in the `TABLE` clause, which lets you use the SQL query results as a CQL relation in the CQL query making that function call.

```
<?xml version="1.0" encoding="UTF-8"?>
<wlevs:config xmlns:wlevs="http://www.bea.com/ns/wlevs/config/
application">

    <processor>
        <name>DataMiningProc</name>
        <rules>
            <query id="q1"><![CDATA[
                ISTREAM(
                  SELECT S.CQLMONTH,
                         . . . . . . .,
                         S.BASEPOLICY,
                         C.F AS probability
                  FROM
                         StreamDataChannel [NOW] AS S,
                         TABLE(prediction2@Oracle11gR2(
                             S.CQLMONTH,
                             . . . . . .
```

```
                                      S.BASEPOLICY) AS F of char) AS C)
            ]]></query>
        </rules>
    </processor>
</wlevs:config>
```

This type of sophisticated prediction and probabilistic analysis is a capability that will be constantly enhanced in the event-driven platforms of the future as we strive to a higher "plain" where these technologies and the associated hardware have the ability to be self aware and self determining, and thus making far more intelligent immediate assessment decisions.

Advancing performance with embedded hardware

Another topic to review in this futuristic chapter was discussed somewhat in the *Event intelligence on the computing edge with sensor integration* section. But here we refer to expanding the capabilities by enhancing the latest engineered systems which are a combination of both hardware and software to provide completely integrated advanced Application solution platforms.

Oracle Event Processing, to some extent, already includes hardware assist capabilities, inherited from the integration with Oracle Coherence using Oracle Exalogic InfiniBand and Flash memory on Oracle Exa Series hardware. However, the ability for the event-driven platform to be more tightly "coupled" with the available hardware systems and to directly leverage and interact with specific hardware features that will accelerate logic processing performance and radically minimize application latencies, will be a focus area for the future.

The other interesting direction may involve "imprinting" some or most of the event processing application model directly in the firmware. This would undoubtedly provide phenomenal performance and low latencies for the event driven applications that execute and could enable neural-like processing capabilities that could eventually empower machines to a higher level of intelligent multitasking decision execution.

The growing event processing standards

As at the time of writing this chapter, there are no official major standards for Event Processing languages. As we have discussed in other chapters there are various forms of language implementations depending on the vendor. However, there is a technical body called the **Event Processing Technical Society (EPTS)** that is striving to set some guidelines and taxonomy of terms for this domain.

Oracle Corporation is one of the steering committee members of EPTS and its objective is the development of shared understanding for event processing terminology.

The society believes that through communicating the shared understanding developed within the group it would assist in driving the emergence of effective interoperation standards, would encourage academic research, and the creation of training curriculum. In turn it would lead to the establishment of event processing as a discipline in its own right. The EPTS members hope that through a combination of academic research, vendor experience/participation and customer data they will be able develop a unified glossary, language, and architecture that would homogenize Event Processing.

The EPTS has provided some very useful information on common nomenclature and particularly sharing some of the same terms as used in the Oracle Event Processing Event Processing Network (EPN). For more information on this topic, we recommend that you search the Internet for *Event Processing Glossary*.

However, while a formal standardized language is still pending, as you have observed in this book the CQL statements are extremely close to the semantics of SQL, which as an existing standard, and is generally very familiar to most IT groups. The pattern matching capabilities of the language has been submitted to the ANSI SQL Standards board and this submission has received a positive reception.

For more information on this specific pattern matching standard you can search the Internet for *Information Technology – Database Language SQL – Row Pattern Recognition (SQL/RPR) - INCITS 500-2012 specifies the syntax and semantics of database language facilities that support row pattern matching using regular expressions.*

In any case, adopting CQL as your event processing language of choice should not be a radical or worrying learning curve, as it does already have its roots in familiar "territory", so its users can just leverage their existing **Structured Query Database** (**SQL**) language knowledge, and very quickly implement powerful event-driven applications.

The only new major challenges, which we have covered in significant detail through-out this book, come with the language extensions relating to the temporal or event number window definitions needed in stream processing, event pattern matching and the capabilities of the growing ecosystem of Oracle Event Processing Data Cartridges.

Summary

We have described in this chapter just a few of the expected evolutionary strategy directions for the Oracle Event Processing technology over the coming years, which will simplify the development life cycle for building event-driven applications, extend the event intelligence to the computing edge, combine with Big Data to resolve the processing latency analysis gap, integrate extreme processing event hardware driven performance and how it may eventually form an implementation foundation for evolving event language standards.

While most the content provided was hypothetical and conceptual, there are already ongoing projects and initiatives by academic groups and technology companies that may make some or all of these capabilities a reality very soon.

During your journey through this book we have provided a considerable amount of conceptual and in many chapters, significant detail on the major topic of using Oracle Event Processing. This will provide you will a complete foundation of knowledge on what is, and what may be the future of this fast moving and exciting technology. If you want to learn more, we recommend that you research the Oracle Technology Network (OTN) on the Internet, to augment your now growing skills, with a collection of interesting whitepapers, presentations, and samples.

Good luck to you as you leap into our world of Event Processing.

Index

Symbols

<channel> definition 265
<selector> element 265
<wlevs:event-type> element 91

A

active/active 230
ActiveMQ server 241
active/passive 230
adapter configuration, OEP application 96
Adobe Flex user interface 268
Anyinteract 278
application class-space policy 190
application configuration
  about 96
  adapter configuration 96
  cache configuration 98
  channel configuration 97
  server configuration 99
ApplicationIdentityAware interface 79

B

Big Data 300
Big Data explosion 9
bloombergMarketFeed 141
boundary
  about 272
  requisites 256, 257
bundles 36
BusArrival query 264
bus.busId event-type property 264
BusPosChannel 265
BusPosChannel channel event node 266
BusPositionGen adapter 262
BusSpatialProcessor 264-266
BusSpatialProcessor event node 263
BusStopAdapter 263
BusStopArrivalChannel 264
BusStopArrivalChannel channel event node 265, 266
BusStopArrivalOutputBean event bean node 264
BusStopChannel 265
BusStopChannel channel event node 266
busstop.Id event-type property 264
bus tracking application
  about 261
  key application elements 261
  running 269
bus tracking EPN 262, 263
bus tracking movement event patterns 256-258
bus tracking visual user interface 268, 269

C

cache
  about 174
  used, as event sources abd sinks 177-179
cache configuration, OEP application
  about 98
  elements 98
  eviction-policy element 98
  idle-time 98
  max-size element 98
  time-to-live 98
  work-manager-name 98
caching system
  about 174
  setting up 174, 175

Call Detail Record (CDR) events 14
Capital Markets 32
CardTransactionCache 178
cartesian coordinate system 275
CEP
about 7, 111
used, for solving customer problems 12-16
CEP languages
about 21
event processors 27
example 22
processor event node 23
processor extensibility 26
channel 92
channel configuration, OEP application 97
class loading 189
closed shapes 272
coherence
monitoring, in Visualizer 183
coherence cache configuration 99
command line, Oracle Event Processing
controlling 55-57
Complex Event Processing. *See* **CEP**
component model
implementing 90
component type infrastructure
extending 105
conceptional model 110
concurrency
implementing, with processors 224-227
configuration parameters, spatial context
ROF 282
SMA 282
tolerance 282
constant value range window 129
containedGeometry 276
contain() function 276
CONTAIN@spatial geometric relation operator 259
continuous joins 135
Continuous Query Language. *See* **CQL**
coordinate system 274
Core Engine 36
correlation variable groups
about 207
DEFINE clause 207
MEASURES clause 207
working with 207
correlation variables 199
CQL
about 38, 107, 108
concepts 38, 39
destinations, establishing 109
examples 40, 41
extending, with OEP cartridges 185, 186
external tables, retrieving with SQL 283-287
fundamentals 108
geometric relationship, determining 275-281
geometries, creating 271
models, processing 110, 111
native types 142
numeric data types 143
pattern matching 199
sources, establishing 109
spatial context, configuring 281, 282
SQL 130
timing models 144, 145
XML, processing with 194-196
CQL and Java integration
about 186-188
ambiguities, handling 192
class loading 189-191
JavaBeans conventions, using 193
CQL CEP processor engine 260
CQL join 136
CQL query
about 108
structure 111, 112
syntax 111
createGeometry() method 274
CSV adapter
about 70, 71
eventPropertyNames 70
eventTypeName 70
port 70
csvgen 70
custom adapters
configuring 78
OEP adapter APIs, reviewing 79, 80
OSGi services, leveraging 82, 83
packaging 83-86

customer problems
solving, CEP platforms used 12-16

D

Data Cartridge Domain Specific Extensibility 39
data cartridges 26
Demand Response (DR) solutions 13
destinations 109
Digital Inclusion 296
Directed Flow Graph 19
DisposableBean interface 79
DSTREAM operator 123

E

Eclipse environment
features 54, 55
IDE 54
visualization 55
Elvis 32
Embedded profile 298, 299
Enterprise Java Beans (EJBs) 34
EPN
about 19, 303
event adapters 20
event cache 21
event channels 20
event processors 21
structure 20
EPN extensions
adapters, setting up 91, 92
caching 94, 95
channels, configuring 92
CQL processing, enabling 94
database table, defining 94
event-beans, implementing 93
event type repository, creating 91
exploring 90
Spring bean, defining 90
EPN HA adapter 240
event
about 17
enriching, with cache 176
enriching, with database table 173, 174
predicting 29
event adapters 20
event bean
implementing 179-182
event cache 21
event channels 20
event container platform manipulation profiles 298
event correlation and aggregation 24
Event Definition Language (EDL) 291
Event Delivery Network (EDN) 293
Event Driven Architecture (EDA) 28
Event Driven SOA (ED-SOA)
about 29
diagrammatic representation 28
Event-Driven Solution Platform 7
Event-Driven technology
benefits 9, 11
event filtering 23
event intelligence
extending, to computing edge with Sensor integration 293-298
EventPartitioner example 223
event pattern matching 24
event processing
about 7, 229
example 7, 8
Event Processing Network. *See* **EPN**
Event Processing Technical Society (EPTS) 311
event processors
about 21, 27
concurrency, using with 224
events, Oracle Event Processing
creating 65
event stream 17, 18
event stream processing
elements 16
event type
about 18
example 18
eventTypeNames property 70
event type repository
about 164
used, for browsing metadata 164
event type system, Oracle Event Processing 65-67
evolving developer environments 291, 292
Exalogic node 218

exciting Event Stream Processing (ESP) dimension 292
external tables, CQL
retrieving, SQL used 283-287

F

Fast Data 300
Fast Data capabilities 11
Fast Data sample 302-304
Financial Front Office 32

G

Garbage Collection (GC) 229
geodetic coordinate system 275
geo-fencing 249, 253-255
geometric relationship
determining 275-281
geometries
boundary 272
closed shapes 272
creating 271-275
geospatial event processing 249
geospatial techniques
bus tracking movement event patterns 256
geo-fencing 253
geo-streaming 251
geo-streaming 251, 252
getName() method 193
Global Positioning Systems (GPS) 250
goingUpPrice property 202
greedy match 204
growing event processing standards 311

H

HA adapter 240
HA application
about 240
ActiveMQ server 241
JMS Message Client 241-243
solution sample, running 244-246
Visualizer tooling, reviewing 247
Hadoop Distributed File System (HDFS) 300
HA solution sample
running 244, 245
heat maps 12
HelloWorldAdapterFactory 84
high availability, OEP
about 230
failure scenarios 232, 233
issues 230-232
high availability QoS
about 234
lightweight queue trimming 236-238
precise recovery with JMS 239, 240
simple failover 234, 235
simple failover, with buffering 236
HTTP pub-sub adapter 72-78
HTTP pub-sub adapter nodes 266
HTTP pub-sub component
about 266
advantages 267

I

InitializingBean interface 79
inputChannel 109
InputEventType 109
Integrated Development Environment (IDE) 292
IN-VOID 257
isName() method 193
ISTREAM operator 122

J

Java Boolean native type 187
Java Connector Architecture (JCA) 34
Java Event-Driven Server
about 33, 35, 38
Bundles 36
OSGi 36
Java Language Specification (JLS) 193
Java platform approach 34
Java Script Object Notation (JSON) 72
JDBC data sources
setting up 172
JMS adapter 68, 69, 240
JMS Message Client 241, 242
JMX API framework 37
joins
about 131, 132

external sources 136
streaming sources 136
JRockit JVM 38

K

key application elements, bus tracking application
about 261
BusSpatialProcessor 264
bus tracking EPN 262
bus tracking visual user interface 268
key elements, event stream processing
about 16
EPN 19
event 17
event stream 17, 18
event type 18

L

Last Event window 130
lightweight queue trimming
about 236, 237
advantages 237
implementing 237, 238
like operator 143
loadgen utility 71
locationStream 277

M

M2M (Machine-to-Machine) 297
marketFeed stream 195
MATCH_RECOGNIZE clause 202
MATCH_RECOGNIZE operator 199
memory sizing observations 229
Minimum Bounding Rectangles (MBRs) 280
model of processing 109
myProp property 192

N

native types, CQL
BIGINT 142
BOOLEAN 142
BYTE(size) 142
CHAR(size) 142
DOUBLE 142
FLOAT 142
INTEGER 142
INTERVAL 142
TIMESTAMP 142
XMLTYPE 142
network performance tuning 229
NOW window 130
numeric data types, CQL
XMLTYPE 143

O

OEP adapter APIs
ApplicationIdentityAware 79
DisposableBean 79
InitializingBean 79
ResumableBean 79
RunnableBean 79
StageIdentityAware 79
StreamSource 79
OEP applications
configuration, changing 155-158
logging service, configuring 147-151
progress, monitoring 165-169
provisioning 151-154
server-wide configuration, managing 159
OEP cartridges
CQL, extending with 185, 186
OEP threading model
about 219
threading, optimizing in channels 220-222
OEP Visualizer 72
OnMessageReceived function 268
Open Services Gateway initiative. *See* **OSGi**
Oracle CEP cartridges 185
Oracle Data Mining (ODM) solution 306
Oracle Event Processing
about 31
bus tracking application 261
caches, using as event sources and sinks 177-179
caching systems, setting up 174, 175
coherence, monitoring in Visualizer 183
command line, controlling 55-57
custom adapter, configuring 78

event bean, implementing 179-182
event language 38
events, converting 65
events, creating 65
events, enriching with cache 176
events, enriching with database table 173, 174
event type system 65
geospatial techniques 251
high availability 230
Java platform approach 34
JDBC data sources, setting up 172
performance 217
platform adapters 68
scaling 219
Visualizer 58
Oracle Event Processing applications
creating 43-53
developing 41-43
tips 54
Oracle Event Processing Data Cartridge 304
Oracle Event Processing, future
event intelligence, extending to computing edge with Sensor integration 293-298
evolving developer environments 291, 292
Fast Data for Big Data 299
growing event processing standards 311
performance, advancing with embedded hardware 310
Predictive Analysis 305
Service-oriented Architecture integration 293
technology strategic directions 289, 290
Oracle geospatial features 260
Oracle MapViewer 78, 255
Oracle NoSQL Database 300
Oracle Spatial 249-251
Oracle Spatial Data Cartridge 258, 259
Oracle Technology Network (OTN) 218
Oracle Technology Network (OTN) pages 304
Oracle WebLogic Server JEE 293
ordering-constraint attribute 224
ordered 226
partition ordered 225
unordered 224
OSGi 36
output events 108

P

partitioned parallelism
about 227
versus, pipelined parallelism 227, 228
partitioned windows 119
path 167
pattern matching
about 199, 201
controlling 204, 206
correlation groups, working with 207-210
expiring patterns 211, 212
greedy match 204
partitioning events 202
pattern expressions 203
reluctant match 204
pattern-matching query 200
pattern quantifiers 203
performance
about 217
advancing, with embedded hardware 310, 311
improving, with batching 228
pipelined parallelism 228
Plain Old Java Object (POJOs) 21
platform adapters, Oracle Event Processing
about 68
CSV adapter 70, 71
HTTP pub-sub adapter 72-78
JMS adapter 68, 69
Portable Object Format (POF) 175
precise recovery with JMS 239
Predictive Analysis
abnormal looking output event 307
about 305
analytics 305
fuzzy results 307
insurance solutions, extending 308
JDBC data cartridge summary 308-310
normal looking output event 307
use case, predicting 306, 307
priceAsStringValuethat 187
Processor Event Node 21
processor event node methodologies

about 23
event correlation and aggregation 24
event filtering 23
event pattern matching 24
synthetic or business event 25
processor extensibility 26
proliferation
about 9
issues 9

Q

query
event properties 108

R

Real-Time Situation Awareness 8
relation 110
reluctant match 204
ResumableBean interface 79
reutersMarketFeed 141
Rich Internet Application (RIA) 58
RSTREAM operator 125
runloadgen tool 262
RunnableBean interface 79

S

sample HA Event Processing application 233, 234
scalability
versus, high availability 216
scatter charts 12
sendInsertEvent() method 178
Sensor integration
used, for extending event intelligence to computing edge 293
server class-space policy 190
server configuration, OEP application
resources, defining 99, 101, 103, 105
server-wide configuration, managing
concurrency, controlling with work managers 159, 160
contextual data, accessing with data sources 160-163
metadata, browsing with event type repository 164
work managers 159
Service Orientated Architecture (SOA) 9
setName() method 193
set operations
about 140
EXCEPT 140
IN 140
INTERSECT 140
MINUS 140
NOT IN 140
UNION 140
UNION ALL 140
ShipPositionGen 70
ShopRelation 277
simple failover
about 234
configuring 235
simple failover, with buffering 236
SLIDE subclause 128
SOA EDN events 291
SOA integration 293
sources 109
spatial context
configuration parameters 282
configuring 281, 282
Spatial Reference ID (SRID) 275
spatial reference system 274
SPOT (Sensor Platform for Oracle Technology) 294
Spring development framework 90
SQL
about 130
aggregations 136
external sources 136
joins 131-133
ordering 137-139
set operations 140
views 139
SQL99 commands 130
StageIdentityAware interface 79
startsWith() method 187
stream 110, 113
StreamSource interface 79
structure, CQL query 111

Structured Query Database (SQL) language 312
substring() method 187
symbol event property 186
synthetic or business event 25

T

technology strategic directions 289, 290
Time and Event Driven (TED) team 31
toUpperCase() method 187
trend 218

U

upstream backup 230

V

view 139
Visualizer 58
  application executing, reviewing 60
  Event Processing Network tab 59
  features 59
  parameters, changing 62, 63
  Query Wizard tab 61
  using 59
Visualizer Monitoring and Management tooling 37
Visualizer tooling
  reviewing, for HA implementation 247

W

water events 111
Web Services 34
withindistance 279
window
  constant value range window 129
  Last Event window 130
  NOW window 130
  output 120-125
  output, controlling with slides 126, 127
  partitioned windows 119
  streams, restricting with Windows 112-116
  total ordered time-stamped stream 145
  tuple-based window 116-118
  unbounded window 128
work managers
  used, for controlling concurrency 159, 160
W stock trading pattern 33

X

XML
  processing, with CQL 194-197
xmlattribute functions 196
XML document sources
  handling 197, 198
XML fragments 194
xmltable function 197

Thank you for buying

Getting Started with Oracle Event Processing 11*g*

About Packt Publishing

Packt, pronounced 'packed', published its first book "Mastering phpMyAdmin for Effective MySQL Management" in April 2004 and subsequently continued to specialize in publishing highly focused books on specific technologies and solutions.

Our books and publications share the experiences of your fellow IT professionals in adapting and customizing today's systems, applications, and frameworks. Our solution based books give you the knowledge and power to customize the software and technologies you're using to get the job done. Packt books are more specific and less general than the IT books you have seen in the past. Our unique business model allows us to bring you more focused information, giving you more of what you need to know, and less of what you don't.

Packt is a modern, yet unique publishing company, which focuses on producing quality, cutting-edge books for communities of developers, administrators, and newbies alike. For more information, please visit our website: `www.packtpub.com`.

About Packt Enterprise

In 2010, Packt launched two new brands, Packt Enterprise and Packt Open Source, in order to continue its focus on specialization. This book is part of the Packt Enterprise brand, home to books published on enterprise software - software created by major vendors, including (but not limited to) IBM, Microsoft and Oracle, often for use in other corporations. Its titles will offer information relevant to a range of users of this software, including administrators, developers, architects, and end users.

Writing for Packt

We welcome all inquiries from people who are interested in authoring. Book proposals should be sent to author@packtpub.com. If your book idea is still at an early stage and you would like to discuss it first before writing a formal book proposal, contact us; one of our commissioning editors will get in touch with you.

We're not just looking for published authors; if you have strong technical skills but no writing experience, our experienced editors can help you develop a writing career, or simply get some additional reward for your expertise.

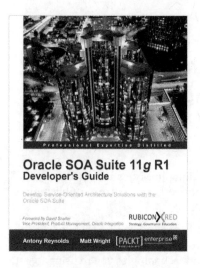

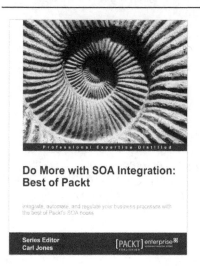

[PACKT] enterprise
PUBLISHING
professional expertise distilled

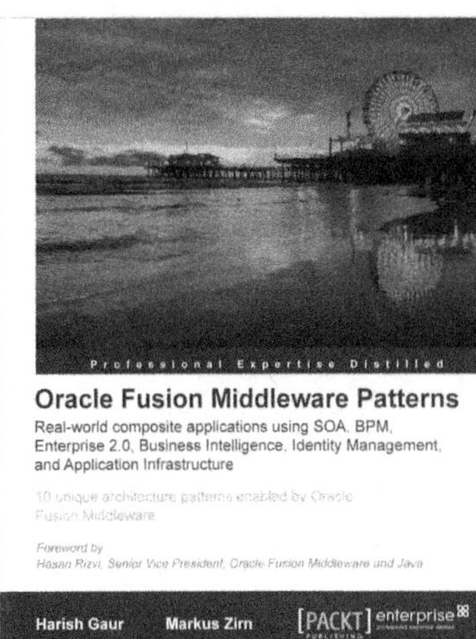

Oracle Fusion Middleware Patterns

ISBN: 978-1-84719-832-7 Paperback: 224 pages

10 unique architecture patterns enabled by Oracle Fusion Middleware

1. First-hand technical solutions utilizing the complete and integrated Oracle Fusion Middleware Suite in hardcopy and ebook formats
2. From-the-trenches experience of leading IT Professionals
3. Learn about application integration and how to combine the integrated tools of the Oracle Fusion Middleware Suite - and do away with thousands of lines of code

---

Oracle SOA Infrastructure Implementation Certification Handbook (1Z0-451)

ISBN: 978-1-84968-340-1 Paperback: 372 pages

Successfully ace the 1Z0-451 Oracle SOA FoundationPractitioner exam with this hands on certifi cation guide

1. Successfully clear the first stepping stone towards becoming an Oracle Service Oriented Architecture Infrastructure Implementation Certified Expert
2. The only book available to guide you through the prescribed syllabus for the 1Z0-451 Oracle SOA Foundation Practitioner exam
3. Learn from a range of self-test questions to fully equip you with the knowledge to pass this exam

Please check **www.PacktPub.com** for information on our titles

www.ingramcontent.com/pod-product-compliance
Lightning Source LLC
LaVergne TN
LVHW062305060326
832902LV00013B/2054

* 9 7 8 1 8 4 9 6 8 4 5 4 5 *